Rhetorical Mode
for Effective Writing

Rhetorical Models for Effective Writing

Third edition

J. Karl Nicholas
Western Carolina University

James R. Nicholl
Western Carolina University

HarperCollinsPublishers

Library of Congress Cataloging in Publication Data

Main entry under title:
Rhetorical models for effective writing.

   Includes index.
   1. College readers. 2. English language — Rhetoric.
I. Nicholas, J. Karl (James Karl), 1939–
II. Nicholl, James R.
PE1417.R49   1985   808'.0427   84-26080
ISBN 0-673-39230-9

**Copyright ©1985 by J. Karl Nicholas and James R. Nicholl
All Rights Reserved.
Printed in the United States of America.**

ISBN 0-673-39230-9

9 8 7 6

KPF

Acknowledgments

   Eudora Welty, excerpted from "A Worn Path," from *A Curtain of Green and Other Stories*. Reprinted by permission of Harcourt Brace Jovanovich, Inc.
   Willa Cather, "Hanover, Nebraska," excerpted from *O Pioneers*. Copyright 1913 by Willa Cather. Reprinted by permission of Houghton Mifflin Company.
   William Paulk, "The White Glove," from *Georgia Review,* 14 (Summer, 1960). Reprinted by permission of the author.
   Gilbert Highet, "Subway Station," excerpted from *Talents and Geniuses*. Copyright © 1957 by Gilbert Highet. Reprinted by permission of Curtis Brown, Ltd.
   Robert B. Parker, "Private Eye Calling," from *God Save the Child*. Copyright © 1974 by Robert B. Parker. Reprinted by permission of Helen Brann Agency.
   Mary McCarthy, "Miss Gowrie," from *Memories of a Catholic Girlhood*. Copyright 1953 by Mary McCarthy. Reprinted by permission of Harcourt Brace Jovanovich, Inc. First published in *The New Yorker*.
   James Agee, "Shady Grove, Alabama, July, 1936," from *Let Us Now Praise Famous Men* by James Agee and Walker Evans. Copyright 1939, 1940 by James Agee. Copyright 1942 by James Agee and Walker Evans. Copyright renewed © 1960 by Walker Evans. Copyright renewed © 1969 by Mia Fritsch Agee. Reprinted by permission of Houghton Mifflin Company.

Richard Wright, "Granny's Fall," from *Black Boy*. Copyright 1937, 1942, 1944, 1945 by Richard Wright. Reprinted by permission of Harper & Row, Publishers, Inc.

Jane Jacobs, "Morning Ballet," from *The Death and Life of Great American Cities*. Copyright © 1961 by Jane Jacobs. Reprinted by permission of Random House, Inc.

N. Scott Momaday, "Mating Flight," excerpted from pp. 17–18 of *House Made of Dawn*. Copyright © 1966, 1967, 1968 by N. Scott Momaday. Reprinted by permission of Harper & Row, Publishers, Inc.

Irwin Shaw, "Eighty-Yard Run," from *Mixed Company*. Copyright 1940, renewed © 1968 by Irwin Shaw. Reprinted by permission of the author.

Mary E. Mebane, "Nonnie's Day," from *Mary: An Autobiography*. Copyright © 1981 by Mary Elizabeth Mebane. Reprinted by permission of Viking Penguin Inc.

Langston Hughes, "Saved from Sin," from *The Big Sea*. Copyright 1940 by Langston Hughes. Copyright renewed © 1968 by Arna Bontemps and George Houston Bass. Reprinted by permission of Hill and Wang, a division of Farrar, Straus and Giroux, Inc.

Virginia Woolf, "The Death of the Moth," from *The Death of the Moth and Other Essays*. Reprinted by permission of Harcourt Brace Jovanovich, Inc. and Chatto & Windus, The Hogarth Press.

Lincoln Barnett, "Relativity," from *The Universe and Dr. Einstein*, Second Revised Edition. Copyright 1948 by Harper & Brothers. Copyright 1950, 1957 by Lincoln Barnett. Reprinted by permission of William Morrow & Co.

James A. Fixx, "Asking the Wrong Questions," from *Saturday Review*, November 7, 1964, p. 26. Copyright © 1964 Saturday Review. Reprinted by permission.

Lewis Thomas, "Clever Animals," and "Alchemy," from *Late Night Thoughts on Listening to Mahler's Ninth Symphony*. Copyright © 1982 by Lewis Thomas. Originally published in *Discover*. Reprinted by permission of Viking Penguin Inc.

William D. Ellis, "Solve That Problem — With Humor," from *Reader's Digest*, May 1973. Condensed from *The Christian Herald*. Copyright © 1973 by the Reader's Digest Assn., Inc. Reprinted by permission.

Edwin Way Teale, "The Legs of Insects," from *The Strange Lives of Familiar Insects*. Copyright © 1962 by Edwin Way Teale. Reprinted by permission of Dodd, Mead & Company.

William Safire, "I Led the Pigeons to the Flag," from *New York Times* Magazine, May 27, 1979. Copyright © 1979 by The New York Times Company. Reprinted by permission.

Mortimer J. Adler, "Three Kinds of Book Owners" and "How to Mark a Book" from "How to Mark a Book," from *Saturday Review of Literature*, July 6, 1940. Copyright 1940 by Mortimer J. Adler, copyright renewed © 1967 by Mortimer J. Adler. Reprinted by permission of the author.

Seymour Martin Lipset, "Intellectuals" from "The Egghead Looks At Himself," from *New York Times*, November 17, 1957. Copyright © 1957 by The New York Times Company. Reprinted by permission.

E. B. White, "The Three New Yorks" and "Democracy" from "Here Is New York," from *The Essays of E. B. White*. Copyright 1949 by E. B. White. Reprinted by permission of Harper & Row, Publishers, Inc.

Rachel Carson, "Types of Whales" and "Formation of the Earth" from *The Sea Around Us*. Copyright © 1950, 1951, 1961 by Rachel L. Carson. Renewal copyright © 1979 by Roger Christie. Reprinted by permission of Oxford University Press.

Gerald Durrell, "The Naturalist's What's What," from *The Amateur Naturalist*. Text copyright © 1982 by Gerald Durrell. Copyright © 1982 by Dorlin Kindersley Ltd., London. Reprinted by permission of Alfred A. Knopf, Inc.

John Holt, "Three Kinds of Discipline," from *Freedom and Beyond*. Copyright © 1972 by John Holt. Reprinted by permission of E. P. Dutton & Co., Inc.

Alvin Toffler, "The Duration of Human Relationships," from *Future Shock*. Copyright © 1970 by Alvin Toffler. Reprinted by permission of Random House, Inc.

Eric Berne, "Can People Be Judged by Their Appearances?" from *A Layman's Guide to Psychiatry and Psychoanalysis*. Copyright © 1947, 1957, 1968 by Eric Berne. Reprinted by permission of Simon & Shuster, Inc.

Charles Kuralt, "Maine Clambake," from *Saturday Review*, June 26, 1976. Copyright © 1976 by Saturday Review. Reprinted by permission.

Irma S. Rombauer and Marion Rombauer Becker, "Carving a Fowl," from *Joy of Cooking*. Copyright © 1931, 1936, 1941, 1942, 1943, 1946, 1951, 1952, 1953, 1962, 1963, 1964, 1975 by the Bobbs-Merrill Company, Inc. Reprinted by permission.

Grace Lichtenstein, "Brewing Coors," in "Rocky Mountain High," from *New York Times Magazine*, December 28, 1975. Copyright © 1975 by The New York Times Company. Reprinted by permission.

Alice Gray, "Mosquito Bite" from "Daughters of Dracula," from *Sports Afield* Magazine, June 1977. Copyright © 1977 The Hearst Corporation. All rights reserved. Reprinted by permission of The Hearst Corporation and Alice Gray.

Dr. Robert Kadesch, text of "Centrifugal Force" and drawings on pp. 14 and 17 from *The Crazy Cantilever and Other Science Experiments*. Copyright © 1961 by Robert Kadesch. Reprinted by permission of Harper & Row, Publishers, Inc.

Staff of *Fortune* Magazine. "Riveting a Skyscraper," from "Skyscrapers: Builders and Their Tools," *Fortune*, October 1930. Copyright © 1930 by Time Inc. Reprinted by permission.

Ellen Willis, "Women and Blacks," from "Whatever Happened to Women?" in *Mademoiselle*, September 1969. Copyright © 1969 by Mademoiselle. Reprinted by permission of the author.

Rachel Carson, "Fable for Tomorrow," from *Silent Spring*. Copyright © 1962 by Rachel L. Carson. Reprinted by permission of Houghton Mifflin Company.

Tom Wolfe, "Columbus and the Moon," from "Op-Ed," *New York Times*, July 20, 1979. Copyright © 1979 The New York Times Company. Reprinted by permission.

W. H. Auden, "Postscript: The Almighty Dollar," from *The Dyer's Hand and Other Essays*. Copyright © 1962 by W. H. Auden. Reprinted by permission of Random House, Inc.

Harry Kemelman, "Education and Training," from *Common Sense in Education*. Copyright © 1970 by Harry Kemelman. Reprinted by permission of Crown Publishers, Inc.

J. Anthony Lukas, "Pinball," from "The Inner Game of Pinball," from *The Atlantic Monthly*, December 1979. Copyright © 1979 by The Atlantic Monthly Company. Reprinted by permission of the author.

Neil Postman and Charles Weingartner, "The Change Revolution," from *Teaching as Subversive Activity*. Copyright © 1969 by Neil Postman and Charles Weingartner. Reprinted by permission of Delacorte Press.

William Humphrey, "The Salmon Instinct," from *Farther Off from Heaven*. Copyright © 1976, 1977 by William Humphrey. Reprinted by permission of the author.

Jonathan Schell, "The Destructive Power of a One-Megaton Bomb on New York City," from *The Fate of the Earth*. Copyright © 1982 by Jonathan Schell. Originally published in *The New Yorker*. Reprinted by permission of Alfred A. Knopf, Inc.

Aldo Leopold, "Thinking Like a Mountain," from *A Sand County Almanac, and Sketches Here and There*. Copyright 1949, 1977 by Oxford University Press.

Loren Eiseley, "How Flowers Changed the World," from *The Immense Journey*. Copyright © 1975 by Loren Eiseley. Reprinted by permission of Random House, Inc.

Anne Nichols, "Slang," from "Don't Sell Slang Short," by Anne Nichols from *Tradition and Dissent: A Rhetoric Reader*, edited by Florence B. Greenberg and Anne P. Heffley. Copyright © 1967 by the Bobbs-Merrill Company, Inc. Reprinted by permission of the publisher.

H. W. Fowler, "Abstractitis," from *A Dictionary of Modern English Usage* by H. W. Fowler, second edition revised by Sir Ernest Gowers. Copyright © 1965 by Oxford University Press. Reprinted by permission of the publisher.

W. Nelson Francis, "Good," from *The English Language, An Introduction*. Copyright © 1963, 1965 by W. W. Norton & Co., Inc. Reprinted by permission.

Edgar Sturtevant, "Language," from *An Introduction to Linguistic Science*. Copyright © 1947 by Yale University Press. Reprinted by permission of Yale University Press.

William Zinsser, "Clutter," from *On Writing Well,* Second Edition. Copyright © 1980 by William K. Zinsser. Reprinted by permission of the author.

Margaret Mead and Rhoda Metraux, "Superstitions," from *A Way of Seeing*. Copyright © 1970 by Margaret Mead and Rhoda Metraux. Reprinted by permission of the Institute for Intellectual Studies.

Robin Roberts, "Strike Out Little League," from "My Turn" in *Newsweek,* July 21, 1975. Copyright © 1975 by Newsweek, Inc. All rights reserved. Reprinted by permission.

Martin Luther King, Jr., excerpted from "Letter from a Birmingham Jail, April 16, 1963" from *Why We Can't Wait*. Copyright © 1963 by Martin Luther King, Jr. Reprinted by permission of Harper & Row, Publishers, Inc.

Christopher Lasch, "The New Illiteracy," from *The Culture of Narcissism*. Copyright © 1979 by W. W. Norton & Co., Inc. Reprinted by permission of the publisher.

Arthur Ashe, "Send Your Children to the Libraries," from *New York Times,* February 6, 1977. Copyright © 1977 by The New York Times Company. Reprinted by permission.

Louise Montague, "Straight Talk about the Living Together Arrangement," from *Reader's Digest,* April 1977. Copyright © 1977 by The Reader's Digest Association, Inc. Reprinted by permission.

Norman Cousins, "How to Make People Smaller Than They Are," from *Saturday Review,* December 1978. Copyright © 1978 Saturday Review Magazine. Reprinted by permission.

Isaac Asimov, "The Case against Man," from *Science Past — Science Future*. Copyright © 1970 by Field Enterprises. Reprinted by permission of Doubleday & Company.

Alleen Pace Nilsen, "Sexism in English: A Feminist View," from *Female Studies 6: Closer to the Ground*. Copyright © 1972 by Nancy Hoffman, Cynthia Secor, and Adrian Tinsley. Reprinted by permission of The Feminist Press, Old Westbury, NY.

Walter Lippmann, "Balance of Power," from *The Atlantic Monthly,* August 1939. Copyright © 1939, 1967 by The Atlantic Monthly Company. Reprinted with permission of the President and Fellows of Harvard College.

George Orwell, "The Tramp-Monster Myth," from *Down and Out in Paris and London*. Reprinted by permission of Harcourt Brace Jovanovich, Inc. and A. M. Heath & Company Ltd.

Peter Drucker, "What Employees Need Most," from "How To Be An Employee" in *Fortune,* May 1952. Copyright © 1952 by Time Inc. Reprinted by permission of the author.

Virginia Hall, "Bad Grammar Seen as Unsafe," from *Kansas City Times*. Copyright © 1979 The Kansas City Star Company. Reprinted by permission of the author and *Kansas City Times*.

Ronald Dworkin, "On Not Prosecuting Civil Disobedience," from *The New York Review of Books*. Copyright © 1968 Nyrev, Inc. Reprinted with permission of The New York Review of Books.

Sydney J. Harris, "Gun Control: Shifting the Blame," from "Handgun Deaths: Firearms Lobby Shifts Blame from Guns to Gunslinger," *Chicago Sun–Times,* January 4, 1984. Copyright © News Group Chicago, Inc. 1984. Reprinted by permission of the Chicago Sun-Times.

Carl Sagan, "Life after Death," from *Broca's Brain*. Copyright © 1979 by Carl Sagan. Reprinted by permission of Random House, Inc.

Judy Syfers, "Why I Want a Wife," from *Ms.,* December 31, 1971. Copyright © 1971 by Judy Syfers. Reprinted by permission of the author.

Grace April Oursler Armstrong, "Let's Keep Christmas Commercial," from *The Saturday Evening Post,* December 18, 1975. Copyright © 1965 The Curtis Publishing Company. Reprinted by permission of the author.

Val Wilson, "Let My Son Play," from *Sports Illustrated,* March 14, 1983. Copyright © 1983 Time Inc. All rights reserved. Reprinted by permission.

Ron Harley, "Unnatural Metamorphosis," from *Farm Quarterly,* May–June 1971. Reprinted by permission of the author.

Marya Mannes, "Wasteland," from *More in Anger.* Copyright © 1958 by Marya Mannes. Reprinted by permission of David J. Blow.

A. M. Rosenthal, "There Is No News from Auschwitz," *New York Times Magazine,* April 16, 1961. Copyright © 1961 by The New York Times Company. Reprinted by permission.

Preface

This edition of *Rhetorical Models for Effective Writing,* like its predecessors, is more than just another collection of essays for use in English composition courses. For over a decade, *Rhetorical Models* has helped thousands of students develop their ability to read moderately difficult prose and to write effectively. When those skills are combined with critical, informed thinking (especially encouraged by this book's extensive argumentation section), students can use their enhanced communications skills to make valuable contributions to society on several levels. At the same time they can derive personal satisfaction from success in business, science, education, or other fields.

Rhetorical Models begins with an essay added for this edition, "Rhetoric and the Writing Process," designed to help students understand (1) rhetoric, (2) the time-honored tradition of using models to teach rhetoric, and (3) the components of the writing process. Then, because one must read well to become well informed (and to understand some of the book's model essays), an essay providing hints for improving students' reading comprehension precedes the main body of the book. An appendix, a glossary of useful terms, and an index of authors are the book's final features.

The book's main body has three parts, based on a writer's main intended purpose: (1) Narrative-Descriptive Writing, (2) Expository Writing (explanatory), and (3) Argumentative Writing (persuasive). A further division results in thirteen major sections, each devoted to an important technique or rhetorical strategy for organizing and presenting written ideas. Each section provides an introductory explanation of the technique plus numerous professionally written models of varying lengths, from short single paragraphs to moderately long essays, chosen to illustrate effective use of the technique. In addition, student-written paragraphs and essays are included in each section, showing that apprentices can master each technique. These samples should boost the morale of fainthearted or previously unsuccessful student writers. The writing models are normally arranged within their respective sections in order of increasing difficulty, and each selection is followed by discussion questions intended to help readers notice both content and form. A separate Instructor's Manual provides suggested answers to these questions, along with additional teaching aids such as suggested writing topics.

The writing models were chosen (1) to demonstrate clearly the appropriate technique or rhetorical strategy; (2) to be in a style worthy of study; and (3) in the case of professional writing, to have subject matter more timeless than timely. The editors, despairing of trying to catch and ride the next brief wave of topicality, decided instead to be eclectic and even sometimes a little old-fashioned in their choices. Nevertheless, the selections should prove interesting, especially to those who can become interested in well-wrought prose that often contains important ideas and provokes critical thought.

Users of previous editions will notice a number of new reading selections; some of the best new student selections were gleaned from student papers nominated for our university's Ashby Wade Award for Excellence in Freshman Composition. Students whose nominated work has been used more than once are Mary Ann Budahl, Tina Desautels, Delisa Ensley, and Vince Gentry.

We again gratefully acknowledge revision suggestions from the book's users, especially these: Joseph Cosenza, St. John's University (New York); Rosanna Grassi and Dalean Henry, Syracuse University; Rebecca Argall, Mary Barth, and Michael Hennessy, Memphis State University; Jean Marie Moisan, Western Kentucky University; Joseph L. Sanders, Lakeland Community College (Ohio); David Roberts, Bluefield State College (West Virginia); Carlanda Green, Edward Hoeffner, Peter Huggins, Joanna Hutt, Tommy Morgan, and Ralph Voss, University of Alabama; Timothy H. Robinson, St. Edward's University (Texas); James E. Fuller, Larry D. Griffin, Pamela R. Howell, and Sylvia Major, Midland College (Texas); Steven Crabill, Indiana/Purdue University; Lawrence Beloof, Asa Fallis, and Michele Hester, West Hills Community College (California); J. David Harrell, Jefferson State Junior College (Alabama); Harry Dean, Larry Longerbeam, and Paul Putt, Cleveland State Community College (Tennessee); Charles Kemnitz and Reginald Martin, University of Tulsa; Rebecca Crump, Louisiana State University; Marie McAllister, Marilyn McCaffrey, and Nancy Yee, Fitchburg State College (Massachusetts); Ely Fuller, Babson College; Gretchen Swanson, Lakewood Community College (Minnesota); Marvin Zuckerman, Los Angeles Valley College; Ralph Eavenson, Sierra College (California); Jon Ford, Alameda College (California); Carlene Walker, University of Texas at El Paso; A. Wayne DeLoach, Winifred Hall Harris, and Charles M. Petko, Troy State University-Montgomery (Alabama); George Bocek, Peggy Bull, Sue Coody, Barbara McGugar, and Brenda Shull, Weatherford College (Texas); Virginia T. Bemis, Patty Mack-Drouhard, and Joan Robertson, North Central Technical College (Ohio); Rose M. Pell, Indiana State University; Barry L. Logan, California State University-Fresno; E. J. Dallas, Community College of Allegheny County (Pennsylvania); Samuel R. Parker, University of Tennessee-Knoxville; Ruth Elizabeth Shore, Fisher Junior College (Massachusetts); Mary L. Tucker, Patrick Henry State Junior College (Alabama).

Our gratitude extends to the Little, Brown staff, especially Carolyn Potts, Barbara Breese, and Adrienne Weiss, and to Cobb/Dunlop Publisher Services for professional aid and support. Further thanks go to our colleague, William Paulk, for use of his published work, to our fine secretary, Mrs. Nancy Norgaard, and to Paul O'Connell, who believed in us all the way. Final thanks must go to our students, especially those whose writing we have included. Some are remembered, too many are forgotten, but most learned to read and write better with the help of earlier editions of this book. Their experiences have made *Rhetorical Models* better than it might have been, though any mistakes in it are still ours.

J. K. N.
J. R. N.

Contents

Topical Contents — xxi

Rhetoric and the Writing Process — 1

Improve Your Reading — 5

Types of Writing — 16

Narrative-Descriptive Writing 19

Section 1: Description — 22

Paragraphs: Description — 25
- Phoenix Jackson   *Eudora Welty*   25
- The Bunk House   *John Steinbeck*   26
- Hanover, Nebraska   *Willa Cather*   27
- The White Glove   *William Paulk*   28
- Subway Station   *Gilbert Highet*   29

Student Work: Description — 30
- Ruth   30
- Evelyn's Drudgery   31
- Thanksgiving Dinner — Before   31
- Thanksgiving Dinner — After   32
- My Dormitory Room   32
- Dude   33

Essays: Description   **35**
    Private Eye Calling   *Robert B. Parker*   35
    Boyhood Memories   *Mark Twain*   38
    Miss Gowrie   *Mary McCarthy*   42
    Shady Grove, Alabama, July, 1936   *James Agee*   46

Section 2: Narration   **51**

Paragraphs: Narration   **54**
    Granny's Fall   *Richard Wright*   54
    Morning Ballet   *Jane Jacobs*   55
    Mating Flight   *N. Scott Momaday*   56
    Eighty-Yard Run   *Irwin Shaw*   57

Student Work: Narration   **60**
    On-the-Job Training   60
    On the Intermediate Slope   61
    The Day's Last Flight   62
    Going for the Gold   63
    The Kiss   64

Essays: Narration   **67**
    Nonnie's Day   *Mary E. Mebane*   67
    Saved from Sin   *Langston Hughes*   69
    The Death of the Moth   *Virginia Woolf*   72
    Look at Your Fish   *Samuel H. Scudder*   75

Expository Writing   **81**

Section 1: Examples   **84**

Paragraphs: Examples   **86**
    American Women in Wartime   *Margaret Truman*   86
    The Actor's Voice   *Stanley Kahan*   87
    Form and Design in Mexico   *Stuart Chase*   87
    Beauty   *Ralph Waldo Emerson*   88
    Relativity   *Lincoln Barnett*   89

Student Work: Examples   **91**
    Fear   91
    A Mother's Feelings   92
    Beyond Words   92

    Art Majors Are Different   93
    Restaurants   94
    Accelerated Incubation   96

Essays: Examples   98
    Asking the Wrong Questions   *James A. Fixx*   98
    Clever Animals   *Lewis Thomas*   101
    Solve That Problem — With Humor
        William D. Ellis   104
    The Legs of Insects   *Edwin Way Teale*   108
    I Led the Pigeons to the Flag   *William Safire*   110

Section 2: Classification   115

Paragraphs: Classification   118
    Three Kinds of Book Owners   *Mortimer J. Adler*   118
    Intellectuals   *Seymour Martin Lipset*   118
    The Three New Yorks   *E. B. White*   119
    Types of Whales   *Rachel Carson*   120

Student Work: Classification   122
    Cat Fanciers   122
    Political Viewpoints   122
    Popular Diets   123
    Waitresses   124
    T-Shirt Inscriptionalia   125

Essays: Classification   128
    The Naturalist's What's What   *Gerald Durrell*   128
    Three Kinds of Discipline   *John Holt*   133
    The Duration of Human Relationships
        Alvin Toffler   137
    Can People Be Judged by Their Appearances?
        Eric Berne   140

Section 3: Process   145

Paragraphs: Process   147
    Maine Clambake   *Charles Kuralt*   147
    Formation of the Earth   *Rachel Carson*   147
    Carving a Fowl   *Irma S. Rombauer*
        and Marion Rombauer Becker   148
    Brewing Coors   *Grace Lichtenstein*   149

Student Work: Process   151
   Registration   151
   Successful Sketching   152
   Tobacco Production   152
   Donating Blood   153
   I Remember, Granner   155

Essays: Process   157
   Mosquito Bite   *Alice Gray*   157
   Centrifugal Force   *Robert Kadesch*   159
   Making Tappa   *Herman Melville*   162
   Riveting a Skyscraper   *Fortune*   164

Section 4: Comparison   168

Paragraphs: Comparison   171
   Boxing and Fencing   *Paul Gallico*   171
   Two Americas   *J. William Fulbright*   171
   Women and Blacks   *Ellen Willis*   172
   The Old Practitioner and the Young
      Oliver Wendell Holmes   173

Student Work: Comparison   174
   Private and Public Bathrooms   174
   Comparing Mechanics   175
   Senior Prom: The Dream and the Reality   176
   The Changing World of Women   177
   Traveling the White Water   178

Essays: Comparison   180
   Fable for Tomorrow   *Rachel Carson*   180
   Columbus and the Moon   *Tom Wolfe*   182
   The Almighty Dollar   *W. H. Auden*   185
   Education and Training   *Harry Kemelman*   187

Section 5: Analogy   191

Paragraphs: Analogy   193
   The Flight of a Sparrow   *Bede*   193
   Renewal from the Roots   *Woodrow Wilson*   194
   A River Pilot's Knowledge   *Mark Twain*   194
   Daedalus and Icarus   *Sir Arthur Eddington*   195

Student Work: Analogy   **197**
    Freshman English   197
    My Friend, the Pen   198
    Fraternal Itch   198
    Sunbathing on Scott Beach   199
    Fishing for the Buyer   200

Essays: Analogy   **202**
    Pinball   *J. Anthony Lukas*   202
    The Change Revolution   *Neil Postman
        and Charles Weingartner*   203
    The Salmon Instinct   *William Humphrey*   205
    Feeding the Mind   *Lewis Carroll*   208

Section 6: Cause and Effect   **213**

Paragraphs: Cause and Effect   **215**
    W-a-t-e-r   *Helen Keller*   215
    Little Lost Appetite   *Andrew Ward*   216
    Habit   *William James*   216
    The Destructive Power of a One-Megaton Bomb
        on New York City   *Jonathan Schell*   217

Student Work: Cause and Effect   **220**
    Why Students Leave College   220
    When a DC-10 Crashes   221
    Study Habit Blues   222
    Robert Redford Moves to Lenoir   223
    The Downfall of Downtown   225

Essays: Cause and Effect   **228**
    Thinking Like a Mountain   *Aldo Leopold*   228
    Causes of the American Spirit of Liberty
        Edmund Burke   231
    How Flowers Changed the World   *Loren Eiseley*   236
    Crime and Criminals   *Clarence Darrow*   245

Section 7: Definition   **256**

Brief Examples: Definition   **259**
    Some Campus Definitions   259
    Eight Definitions of Religion   260

Some Definitions from *The Devil's Dictionary*
    Ambrose Bierce   261

Paragraphs: Definition   264
    Slang   *Anne Nichols*   264
    Abstractitis   *H. W. Fowler*   265
    Good   *W. Nelson Francis*   266
    Democracy   *E. B. White*   267

Student Work: Definition   268
    Women   268
    Jelly Rot   269
    Laughter   269
    Defining Crime   270
    Feminist   271

Essays: Definition   273
    Language   *Edgar H. Sturtevant*   273
    Clutter   *William Zinsser*   275
    Alchemy   *Lewis Thomas*   277
    Superstitions   *Margaret Mead and Rhoda Metraux*   281

Argumentative Writing   287

Section 1: Inductive Proofs   293

Paragraphs: Inductive Proof   296
    Strike Out Little League   *Robin Roberts*   296
    Violence in the Sixties   *Arthur Schlesinger*   297
    Wait?   *Martin Luther King, Jr.*   297
    The New Illiteracy   *Christopher Lasch*   298

Student Work: Inductive Proof   300
    A Simple Complaint   300
    The Zero-Year Jinx   300
    Let Women Fight   301
    Beer on Campus   302
    Let's Drive Fifty-five   303

Essays: Inductive Proof   305
    Send Your Children to the Libraries   *Arthur Ashe*   305
    Straight Talk about the Living-
       Together Arrangement   *Louise Montague*   308

How to Make People Smaller Than
    They Are   *Norman Cousins*   313
The Case against Man   *Isaac Asimov*   316
Sexism in English: A Feminist View
    Alleen Pace Nilsen   322

Section 2: Deductive Proofs   331

Paragraphs: Deductive Proof   336
    If the Slave Is a Man   *Abraham Lincoln*   336
    Balance of Power   *Walter Lippmann*   337
    The Tramp-Monster Myth   *George Orwell*   338
    Laws We Need Not Obey   *Martin Luther King, Jr.*   339

Student Work: Deductive Proof   341
    Let's Eat at Home Instead   341
    The Right to Pray in School   341
    The Plight of the Railroads   342
    CIA Immunity   343
    No Finals for A-Students   344

Essays: Deductive Proof   346
    What Employees Need Most   *Peter Drucker*   346
    Bad Grammar Seen as Unsafe   *Virginia Hall*   350
    The Declaration of Independence
        Thomas Jefferson   353
    A Declaration of Sentiments
        Elizabeth Cady Stanton   357
    The Duty of a Citizen   *Plato*   361

Section 3: Refutation   368

Paragraphs: Refutation   372
    For the Death Penalty   *William F. Buckley, Jr.*   372
    The Right to Die   *Norman Cousins*   372
    On Not Prosecuting Civil Disobedience
        Ronald Dworkin   373
    Are Democracies Obstructive?   *Charles W. Eliot*   374

Student Work: Refutation   376
    Death and Logic   376
    The Pleasures of Dormitory Life   376
    Guns Aren't for Everyone   377

Against Public Prayer in the Schools 378
Why We Should Study Abbreviations
   in English Class 379

Essays: Refutation 382
Gun Control: Shifting the Blame   *Sydney J. Harris*   382
Life after Death   *Carl Sagan*   384
Why I Want a Wife   *Judy Syfers*   387
Let's Keep Christmas Commercial
   Grace April Oursler Armstrong   390
A Modest Proposal   *Jonathan Swift*   395

Section 4: Emotional Appeals   404

Paragraphs: Emotional Appeals 406
Dunkirk   *Winston Churchill*   406
Liberty or Death   *Patrick Henry*   407
Henry V's Speech at Agincourt
   William Shakespeare   408
Shame   *Malcolm X*   409

Student Work: Emotional Appeals 411
Guns for Self-Defense   411
All Reasons but One   412
Preserve Joyner Hall   412
Cafeteria Food   413
Rock Music and Me   414

Essays: Emotional Appeals 416
Let My Son Play   *Val Wilson*   416
Unnatural Metamorphosis   *Ron Harley*   418
Wasteland   *Marya Mannes*   421
Black Hawk's Farewell   *Black Hawk*   423
There Is No News from Auschwitz
   A. M. Rosenthal   425

Appendix 429
How to Mark a Book   *Mortimer J. Adler*   429
A Brief Introduction to Common Logical Fallacies   434
The Method of Scientific Investigation
   Thomas Henry Huxley   445

Glossary 453
Index of Authors 461

Topical Contents

Viewpoints on Economics and Government

Two Americas   *J. William Fulbright*   171
The Almighty Dollar   *W. H. Auden*   185
Renewal from the Roots   *Woodrow Wilson*   194
Fishing for the Buyer   200
The Downfall of Downtown   225
Causes for the American Spirit of Liberty
    Edmund Burke   231
Crime and Criminals   *Clarence Darrow*   245
Democracy   *E. B. White*   267
Defining Crime   270
Violence in the Sixties   *Arthur Schlesinger*   297
Wait?   *Martin Luther King, Jr.*   297
The Zero-Year Jinx   300
Let Women Fight   301
If the Slave Is a Man   *Abraham Lincoln*   336
Balance of Power   *Walter Lippmann*   337
Laws We Need Not Obey   *Martin Luther King, Jr.*   339
The Right to Pray in School   341
CIA Immunity   343
Declaration of Independence   *Thomas Jefferson*   353
Declaration of Sentiments   *Elizabeth Cady Stanton*   357
The Duty of a Citizen   *Plato*   361
For the Death Penalty   *William F. Buckley, Jr.*   372
On Not Prosecuting Civil Disobedience
    Ronald Dworkin   373

Are Democracies Obstructive? *Charles W. Eliot* 374
Death and Logic 376
Unnatural Metamorphosis *Ron Harley* 418

Viewpoints on Language, Literature, and Learning

Look at Your Fish *Samuel H. Scudder* 75
The Actor's Voice *Stanley Kahan* 87
I Led the Pigeons to the Flag *William Safire* 110
Education and Training *Harry Kemelman* 187
Freshman English 197
The Change Revolution *Neil Postman
  and Charles Weingartner* 203
Feeding the Mind *Lewis Carroll* 208
W-a-t-e-r *Helen Keller* 215
Habit *William James* 216
Eight Definitions of Religion 260
Some Definitions from *The Devil's Dictionary*
  Ambrose Bierce 261
Slang *Anne Nichols* 264
Abstractitis *H. W. Fowler* 265
Good *W. Nelson Francis* 266
Language *Edgar H. Sturtevant* 273
Clutter *William Zinsser* 275
The New Illiteracy *Christopher Lasch* 298
How to Make People Smaller Than They Are
  Norman Cousins 313
Sexism in English: A Feminist View
  Alleen Pace Nilsen 322
What Employees Need Most *Peter Drucker* 346
Bad Grammar Seen as Unsafe *Virginia Hall* 350
Why We Should Study Abbreviations in English Class 379
How to Mark a Book *Mortimer J. Adler* 429

Viewpoints on Leisure

Eighty-Yard Run *Irwin Shaw* 57
On the Intermediate Slope 61
The Day's Last Flight 62
Going for the Gold 63
The Kiss 64
Beauty *Ralph Waldo Emerson* 88
Successful Sketching 152

Topical Contents

Boxing and Fencing   *Paul Gallico*   171
Senior Prom: The Dream and the Reality   176
Traveling the White Water   178
Sunbathing on Scott Beach   199
Pinball   *J. Anthony Lukas*   202
Feeding the Mind   *Lewis Carroll*   208
Strike Out Little League   *Robin Roberts*   296
Send Your Children to the Libraries   *Arthur Ashe*   305
Rock Music and Me   414
Let My Son Play   *Val Wilson*   416

Viewpoints on Nature and Ecology

Subway Station   *Gilbert Highet*   29
Private-Eye Calling   *Robert B. Parker*   35
Mating Flight   *N. Scott Momaday*   56
The Day's Last Flight   62
The Death of the Moth   *Virginia Woolf*   72
Fear   91
Accelerated Incubation   96
The Legs of Insects   *Edwin Way Teale*   108
Types of Whales   *Rachel Carson*   120
The Naturalist's What's What   *Gerald Durrell*   128
Formation of the Earth   *Rachel Carson*   147
Mosquito Bite   *Alice Gray*   157
Fable for Tomorrow   *Rachel Carson*   180
The Salmon Instinct   *William Humphrey*   205
Thinking Like a Mountain   *Aldo Leopold*   228
How Flowers Changed the World   *Loren Eiseley*   236
The Case against Man   *Isaac Asimov*   316
Unnatural Metamorphosis   *Ron Harley*   418
Wasteland   *Marya Mannes*   421

Viewpoints on Science and Technology

Look at Your Fish   *Samuel H. Scudder*   75
Relativity   *Lincoln Barnett*   89
Clever Animals   *Lewis Thomas*   101
Brewing Coors   *Grace Lichtenstein*   149
Donating Blood   153
Centrifugal Force   *Robert Kadesch*   159
Making Tappa   *Herman Melville*   162
Riveting a Skyscraper   *Fortune*   164

Topical
Contents

xxiii

Columbus and the Moon   *Tom Wolfe*   182
Daedalus and Icarus   *Sir Arthur Eddington*   195
The Destructive Power of a One-Megaton Bomb
     on New York City   *Jonathan Schell*   217
Alchemy   *Lewis Thomas*   277
The Plight of the Railroads   342
The Method of Scientific Investigation
     Thomas Henry Huxley   445

Viewpoints on Social Existence

Thanksgiving Dinner — Before   31
Thanksgiving Dinner — After   32
Shady Grove, Alabama, July, 1936   *James Agee*   46
Granny's Fall   *Richard Wright*   54
Morning Ballet   *Jane Jacobs*   55
Nonnie's Day   *Mary E. Mebane*   67
American Women in Wartime   *Margaret Truman*   86
Fear   91
Solve That Problem — With Humor   *William D. Ellis*   104
Intellectuals   *Seymour Martin Lipset*   118
The Three New Yorks   *E. B. White*   119
T-Shirt Inscriptionalia   125
The Duration of Human Relationships   *Alvin Toffler*   137
Can People Be Judged by Their Appearances?
     Eric Berne   140
Maine Clambake   *Charles Kuralt*   147
Women and Blacks   *Ellen Willis*   172
Senior Prom: The Dream and the Reality   176
The Changing World of Women   177
The Flight of the Sparrow   *Bede*   193
My Friend, the Pen   198
Fraternal Itch   198
The Change Revolution   *Neil Postman
     and Charles Weingartner*   203
The Salmon Instinct   *William Humphrey*   205
Little Lost Appetite   *Andrew Ward*   216
Robert Redford Moves to Lenoir   223
Crime and Criminals   *Clarence Darrow*   245
Laughter   269
Defining Crime   270
Superstitions   *Margaret Mead
     and Rhoda Metraux*   281

Violence in the Sixties   *Arthur Schlesinger*   297
Wait?   *Martin Luther King, Jr.*   297
Let's Drive Fifty-five   303
Straight Talk about the Living-Together Arrangement
    Louise Montague   308
If the Slave Is a Man   *Abraham Lincoln*   336
The Tramp-Monster Myth   *George Orwell*   338
Laws We Need Not Obey   *Martin Luther King, Jr.*   339
The Right to Pray in School   341
Bad Grammar Seen As Unsafe   *Virginia Hall*   350
For the Death Penalty   *William F. Buckley, Jr.*   372
The Right to Die   *Norman Cousins*   372
On Not Prosecuting Civil Disobedience
    Ronald Dworkin   373
Death and Logic   376
Guns Aren't for Everyone   377
Against Public Prayer in the Schools   378
Gun Control: Shifting the Blame   *Sydney J. Harris*   382
Life after Death   *Carl Sagan*   384
Why I Want a Wife   *Judy Syfers*   387
Let's Keep Christmas Commercial
    Grace April Oursler Armstrong   390
A Modest Proposal   *Jonathan Swift*   395
Shame   *Malcolm X*   409
Guns for Self-Defense   411
All Reasons but One   412
Unnatural Metamorphosis   *Ron Harley*   418
Wasteland   *Marya Mannes*   421
Black Hawk's Farewell   *Black Hawk*   423
There Is No News from Auschwitz   *A. M. Rosenthal*   425

Viewpoints on Other Times, Other Places

The Bunk House   *John Steinbeck*   26
Hanover, Nebraska   *Willa Cather*   27
Boyhood Memories   *Mark Twain*   38
Shady Grove, Alabama, July, 1936   *James Agee*   46
Morning Ballet   *Jane Jacobs*   55
Going for the Gold   63
Form and Design in Mexico   *Stuart Chase*   87
Restaurants   94
Making Tappa   *Herman Melville*   162
The Almighty Dollar   *W. H. Auden*   185

Causes for the American Spirit of Liberty
    Edmund Burke   231
Declaration of Independence   *Thomas Jefferson*   353
Declaration of Sentiments   *Elizabeth Cady Stanton*   357
Dunkirk   *Winston Churchill*   406
Liberty or Death   *Patrick Henry*   407
Henry V's Speech at Agincourt   *William Shakespeare*   408
Black Hawk's Farewell   *Black Hawk*   423

Viewpoints on School and College Life

My Dormitory Room   32
Dude   33
Miss Gowrie   *Mary McCarthy*   42
Art Majors Are Different   93
Asking the Wrong Questions   *James Fixx*   98
Three Kinds of Book Owners   *Mortimer Adler*   118
Registration   151
Private and Public Bathrooms   174
Freshman English   197
Fraternal Itch   198
Why Students Leave College   220
Study Habit Blues   222
Some Campus Definitions   259
A Simple Complaint   300
Beer on Campus   302
No Finals for A-Students   344
Bad Grammar Seen as Unsafe   *Virginia Hall*   350
The Pleasures of Dormitory Life   376
Why We Should Study Abbreviations in English Class   379
Preserve Joyner Hall   412
Cafeteria Food   413

Viewpoints on Women

Phoenix Jackson   *Eudora Welty*   25
The White Glove   *William Paulk*   28
Ruth   30
Evelyn's Drudgery   31
Miss Gowrie   *Mary McCarthy*   42
The Kiss   64
Nonnie's Day   *Mary E. Mebane*   67
American Women in Wartime   *Margaret Truman*   86

A Mother's Feelings   92
Beyond Words   92
I Remember, Granner   155
Women and Blacks   *Ellen Willis*   172
The Changing World of Women   177
Women   268
Feminist   271
Let Women Fight   301
Sexism in English: A Feminist View
   Alleen Pace Nilsen   322
A Declaration of Sentiments   *Elizabeth Cady Stanton*   357
Why I Want a Wife   *Judy Syfers*   387

Viewpoints on Work

The Bunk House   *John Steinbeck*   26
Evelyn's Drudgery   31
Private-Eye Calling   *Robert B. Parker*   35
On-the-Job Training   60
Nonnie's Day   *Mary E. Mebane*   67
The Actor's Voice   *Stanley Kahan*   87
Carving a Fowl   *Irma S. Rombauer
   and Marion Rombauer Becker*   148
Tobacco Production   152
Riveting a Skyscraper   *Fortune*   164
The Old Practitioner and the Young
   Oliver Wendell Holmes   173
Comparing Mechanics   175
The Changing World of Women   177
A River Pilot's Knowledge   *Mark Twain*   194
Send Your Children to the Libraries   *Arthur Ashe*   305
Bad Grammar Seen as Unsafe   *Virginia Hall*   350
What Employees Need Most   *Peter Drucker*   346
Why I Want a Wife   *Judy Syfers*   387

Rhetorical Models
for Effective Writing

Rhetoric and the Writing Process

Few human activities are more important or more complex than the uniquely human form of expression that we call writing. Writing is especially important as the means for all lasting human communication; our beliefs, histories, laws, contracts, deeds, and wills all find permanent form in writing. Indeed, the use of writing distinguishes humans from all other creatures, and civilized humans from uncivilized ones. We use writing to describe, to tell or narrate, to explain, and to persuade.

Because writing is so important, centuries ago people began to ponder its various elements to learn how and why writing works. Consequently, various fields of study developed, each with its own designation. Most of us know, for instance, that grammar is one of those fields and that grammarians study such pieces of writing as words and sentences. The focus of this book, however, is not on any such narrow field; rather, it is on the study of writing in the broadest sense — on what the Greeks and Romans called *rhetoric*.

These two cultures, and most of their European successors over the centuries, valued and honored effective speech and writing. When it became clear that a person's ability as an orator and as a writer could be improved through training, professional teachers of rhetoric (or rhetoricians) began to hold classes. Just as you will do using this book, Greek and Roman pupils studied examples (or models) of writing and speaking, thereby learning the most effective and appropriate techniques of conveying their own ideas to specific reading and listening audiences. We will not concern ourselves with speech in this book, although several of the examples of writing that we include were originally speeches. Rather, we have provided examples of effective written expression — or *rhetorical models*.

You understand, of course, that these models are unique; other people wrote them for purposes and audiences and times that are different from yours. But just as you can learn how to score on the court or field by imitating the successful scoring move of an athlete, you can learn how to write by imitating the successful approaches of other writers. You can also understand that just as success in athletics, music, computer programming, or any other field does not come automatically or without practice and effort, so writing success requires study and hard work. No piece of writing in this book sprang instantly and perfectly into being. If you could see this introductory essay as we first pieced it together — scarred by strike-overs, insertions, and scratched-out sentences — you would readily understand that no writer creates a perfect piece of writing on the first attempt — or even sometimes on the second or third.

That declaration leads to this one: Writing is a process. Sometimes it begins with an assignment from a boss, teacher, or some other authority figure; sometimes it starts from the heart or the mind (maybe as a sympathy note or a letter of complaint). In any case, faced with the task, you begin the process. Inevitably that process involves three steps. First, there will be a prewriting step, during which you summon up all the resources that you have and bring them to bear on your chosen subject. It is during this step that you will consult actual models (like the ones that appear in this book) of the writing you plan to do. If you have to write a movie review or if you want to set down your recipe for your favorite waffles, it's always a good idea to look up a few reviews or to consult a cookbook to see what others have done. You will consider possible strategies you might want to employ, think about how best to reach your probable reading audience, and tinker with organizational schemes. You'll jot down useful illustrations, write yourself notes, or make outlines. In other words, you will immerse yourself in the subject.

Sooner or later you have to select the most likely of the alternatives you have considered and begin to write. This is the second step, the actual writing of the piece. You may be lucky and discover that your initial strategy or organizational plan works smoothly, with all the concrete details you scribbled down earlier falling neatly into place. That seldom happens, however. More often you will have several false starts, plans whose promise evaporates when you put them into execution. Sometimes new and better ideas occur to you as you write. Sometimes you realize you have forgotten to take proper account of what your audience knows — or doesn't know. Sometimes you must reject it all and start again after supper or a good night's sleep. If you keep at it, though, you will eventually reach the third and final step — revision of your completed first draft.

During revision you will need to be conscious of grammar and style. You want to insure that your sentences are formally correct. A standard reference grammar like the *Little, Brown Handbook* will assist you in correcting any usage errors that have crept into your writing during the preceding step, when you were busily transferring ideas from your brain onto the paper. Now is the time to make sure that subjects and verbs agree, to insert commas and semicolons, and to check for spelling faults. Just as important, though more difficult, is the matter of style, for now you are choosing not between the acceptable and the unacceptable but between several alternatives, all of which are acceptable but some of which are more effective than others. So you will have to check your sentences over to make sure they say in the most effective and most emphatic way precisely what you intended. Asking someone else to read and criticize what you have written is an excellent strategy at this point. Reading your words aloud is another useful strategy for many writers.

As you become more proficient, you will be able to juggle numerous grammatical and stylistic considerations as you write your first draft, pausing momentarily to determine the appropriate case of a pronoun, deciding between a semicolon or a period, or recasting a sentence for better effect. But in most cases it is best to avoid too much revision during step two. Under no circumstances should step three be ignored.

It should now be clear to you that the value of this book lies chiefly in the assistance it offers you in the first step of the writing process — prewriting — the activity that gets you ready to write. It provides two very obvious benefits, as well as some other, more subtle ones. Obviously you need to have something to write about, and these readings furnish a kind of launchpad for your prose flights by providing interesting, sometimes controversial, materials for you to think about and respond to. These well-written selections, chosen from the works of students and professional writers, illustrate a variety of writing strategies or organizational plans. The shorter selections and student work best illustrate the most frequently employed organizational plans and may serve as models for your own writing. The longer ones are more useful for furnishing the ideas that will eventually grow into your own themes as you read, assimilate, and debate their subject matter.

More subtly, though, any reading that you do — in this book or in any other — will have a lasting effect on your abilities as a writer. Every sentence that you read has the effect of adding to your subconscious mental reservoir of vocabulary, idioms, organizational devices, and stylistic tricks. The advantage of a book like this over your random reading lies in the careful way that the selections have been made, insuring you the widest possible exposure to effective diction and rhetorical strategies.

Thus, since reading is such an important part of the writing process — especially in the prewriting part — it is crucial that you become as good a reader as you possibly can. To that end you should study the essay on reading that follows.

Improve Your Reading

The selections included in this book have been put here for two reasons. The first is to serve as models for the rhetorical patterns you are expected to understand and imitate. The second is to serve as reading assignments.

The need for the second purpose may not be readily apparent to you. You know how to read. You are reading this sentence. You learned how a long time ago. You went through year after year of classroom reading in grammar school and high school — and it may seem pointless to continue that practice here.

If the reading selections in this book were designed merely to furnish you with another chance to read aloud for your classmates, they would be of little value. But there is more at stake here than polishing an acquired skill — a great deal more, in fact, if the person described in the following episode bears any resemblance to you.

Joe and His Troubles

Joe (or Joan, since sex is not an issue here) is disgruntled. He just got back his history quiz with a score of 67 on it. He is sore at the teacher and at himself — at the teacher because the questions on test were too hard, at himself because although he had read the chapters the night before, he couldn't summon up the required information. Something is wrong somewhere, but Joe can't put his finger on it. Damn it all, *he had studied*. Was the teacher a rascal, or was Joe stupid?

The chances are very good that the teacher is no meaner than most and that Joe is not really stupid. But there are some problems. To understand them better, let's go back to the preceding evening and look in on Joe as he studies for the quiz.

First, Joe checks his assignment sheet to locate the chapters he is to read. "Forty-seven pages! That's a bunch — better get it over with."

Throwing himself across his bed, Joe begins to read. Three minutes pass, and he has shifted position five times. Suddenly he realizes that he has no idea at all what the last paragraph was about. Glancing around to see if there is anyone near enough to be bothered by it, Joe goes back and starts to read aloud. "That's the trick; that'll keep the old brain engaged."

"Who you talkin' to?"

"Nobody, just readin' history; got a pile a mile high."

"Say, you wanna go to The Pub? We could get a beer and then catch the X-rateds at the drive-in."

"Naw, I got a quiz tomorrow."

"O.K., suit yourself."

The idea of a cool beer grows more and more appealing. Joe can see the suds, smell the yeasty tang. The lines begin to run together. He hesitates, counts. Only twenty-two more pages, more than halfway there.

"Hey, wait for me. I only got twenty-two more pages."

One last push and Joe is through; he slams the book shut with an air of accomplishment. Now he can enjoy the beer and the show. He has done his work. He has kept his friends waiting, but now he is prepared; he's ready for the quiz.

But he gets a 67.

There is no justice.

Sound familiar? Unfortunately, it's all too familiar. But it can be corrected.

Some Reading Remedies

Let us examine some of the things that Joe did wrong. First, he made himself comfortable. The bed or an overstuffed chair is not a place for serious reading — a whodunit or the latest *Playboy* perhaps, but not the history text. When Joe's body got comfortable, his mind got comfortable too. It started to wander, to think about Gloria and the date last week and . . . and that was when Joe noticed he had read a paragraph without registering a single word.

Joe's chances of keeping his mind from wandering would have been better if he'd sat at his desk in a straight-backed chair. His body and, more important, his mind would have been uncomfortable and consequently more alert. If he'd had a good reading lamp at his desk, so much the better.

The Moving Finger

Joe's attempt to keep his brain engaged by reading aloud was also unsuccessful, not because he was interrupted but because, curiously enough, he could think of Gloria, last week's date, as well as the anticipated beer, just as easily while reading aloud as while reading silently. Here, too, Joe could have done something helpful. Instead of reading aloud, he could have used a technique that is recommended by a number of reading experts; *he could have used his index finger (or a pencil) as a pacer by running it along the line as he read it.** Yet at first glance this way seems no better than reading aloud. Surely finger movement can become as thoughtless and mechanical as reading aloud. The crucial idea, however, is that the finger is used as a pointer or timer. To understand how this pointing mechanism works, you must remember that when Joe was lying down, his body was comfortable, and his mind soon followed suit. But sitting up straight makes his body less comfortable and his mind a little more alert. Joe can make his mind even more responsive if he will move his finger across the page *at a speed that is just a little too fast for comfort*. The object is not to improve Joe's reading speed, although increased speed will be a by-product; the main goal is to force Joe to concentrate. Just as sitting up in a chair makes Joe less comfortable, so following his rapidly moving finger makes his mind race to keep up, allowing no time to dawdle over Gloria, dates, or beer.

Do Something with It

The moving-finger technique will go a long way toward solving Joe's concentration problem. He may get through fairly long stretches of print in less time and with fewer distractions. But Joe has not yet cured his most serious problem, his inability to recall a sizable portion of what he has read. This problem too may be traced back to Joe's reading habits. Remember that when he had finished his reading assignment, he slammed the cover and dashed off to join his buddies at a taproom. There's nothing wrong with the trip to the taproom, and there's a lot to be said for the camaraderie to be found

---

*This practice, together with the branched outlining technique that follows, owes its inspiration to Evelyn Wood's *Reading Dynamics*.

there. But it's very unlikely that the conversation came anywhere near the reading assignment. The course as a whole may have been mentioned, together with some speculations about the instructor's ancestry, but very little if anything from the assigned chapters was introduced into the conversation.

Now let's rewrite the story. Let's suppose that somewhere between the second and third beer Joe had found a reason to mention Douglas MacArthur, one of the names from the assignment that had stuck in his mind. Perhaps the reason was no more substantial than that he'd heard MacArthur had owned a brewery in Manila. But suppose several other people there had prepared for the same test, and the conversation turned to MacArthur, the Philippines, the defense of Corregidor, and the conquest of the Pacific.

"Why didn't MacArthur go in and bomb hell out of Japan instead of pussy-footin' around all those islands?" Joe asks.

"He had to get those islands so he'd have air bases, you jerk. You can't fly a B-29 from San Francisco to Tokyo and back."

As the discussion goes on, Joe finds himself referring more and more to the material covered in the lesson; events but half-remembered fall into place as the give-and-take becomes more heated. The group misses the first reel of *Dial A Degenerate,* but in this version of the story Joe gets a whopping 89 on his history test.

What accounted for the 22-point difference was the fact that Joe *did something with what he'd read.* The surest way to lose a skill — like tennis, bridge, or pinball — is not to use it. The surest way to forget information is not to use it, to let it slip away without putting it to any purpose. By arguing with the drinking buddies over MacArthur's tactics, Joe was organizing and reorganizing the facts that he'd read about the Pacific campaign, forcing them into the wrinkles of his brain, where they would be handy for use again should the occasion arise. And sure enough, the occasion was there the following morning during the quiz, and Joe seized the opportunity.

The lesson here is not that each major exam should be preceded by a night of sodden revelry during which the materials to be covered are blathered about, although worse things could happen; remember the first Joe episode. The lesson is simply that doing something with one's reading — thinking silently about it, discussing it with a friend, writing to Dear Abby about it — is much better than doing nothing.

Outlining

If you haven't the inclination or the money to discuss your assignments over beers at the nearest tavern, one profitable way to do something with your reading is to *outline* it. This is not so disagreeable as it might seem at first, and the practice of actually working with the reading material, instead of pushing doggedly through it, will do wonders for your powers of recall. (There are, of course, various ways to outline and take notes; the method is less important than the fact that you *write down something organized in reaction to the reading assignment.* Use the method about to be described, or another that your instructor recommends, or still another that you learned elsewhere or even created yourself. But in any case, make some sort of outline.) If you use the outline method below, you will proceed in three steps.

Step One — Look It Over

Confront your reading assignment with pencil and paper at the ready. Let's suppose that your assignment is Eric Berne's "Can People Be Judged by Their Appearance?" which begins on page 140 in this book. In the first step you should try to determine as much as you can about what Dr. Berne has to say *without actually reading the essay.* That sounds impossible, but here's how to do it.

You can tell at a glance the title of the essay and its author. That information was probably mentioned in your class schedule. Write it down near the top of the page. It will serve to identify the page when you thumb through your notes later on.

Study the title. A good title will tell you a great deal about the content of an essay or a book. Clearly, this essay deals with the relationship between a person's appearance and his or her behavior. This fact should be borne out in the essay's *thesis statement,* which will probably be located somewhere in the first few paragraphs. That's the next job. Locate the *thesis.* (See the Glossary if you are unfamiliar with this term.)

In the first paragraph you learn that the human embryo is a three-layered tube, each layer of which grows into a different portion of the human anatomy. Ripe stuff, but not really to the point hinted at in the title. Try one more paragraph.

Paragraph two states that sometimes one layer of the embryo will grow larger than the others. It concludes with the sentence, "When this happens, the individual's activities will often be mostly with the overgrown layer." You needn't search any farther; you're not likely to find a better candidate for a thesis statement.

You've now got a solid idea of what the rest of the essay will be about, even how the thesis will be developed. Surely each of the three layers will be discussed in detail. Try to state the thesis as succinctly as possible. When you have it, write it down — right in the middle of your page — and draw a circle around it. The statement might be "Human behavior and appearances are determined by three layers of embryo," or "Layers of human embryo give clues to behavior and appearance," or maybe just "Egg determines man's actions and looks."

Another good idea at this point is to look at any available discussion questions, such as those provided following each writing model in this book; examining those will prepare you to notice at least some major points or features of the assigned reading.

Now look at the rest of the essay. Are there any illustrations, graphs, charts? Studying these is like guessing the story by looking at the pictures in *National Geographic*. It's a way of getting a feel for the essay. In this case the strategy doesn't work — no pictures. So you look for something else. Are there any lists? Is the list concealed in an enumeration subtly marked *first, second,* and so on? Look closely, for such lists usually contain important points. Are there subheadings? The answer here is positive. Your sharp eye catches the italicized words *endomorph, mesomorph,* and *ectomorph* in the fourth paragraph. Again you spot these same terms, still italicized, as subheadings for paragraphs 7, 10, and 12. Surely these peculiar words must have something to do with the three layers of the embryo that Berne was at such pains to point out in the first paragraph. They also represent major divisions of the essay. So draw three lines outward from your central circle and label them respectively: *endomorph, mesomorph,* and *ectomorph*. By now your outline should look like the one at the top of page 11.

Step Two — Read It

You now know where you're going, so go there. Read the essay; it will be easier now that you have some idea of what to expect. Remember, sit up in a hard chair and run your finger along the line as you read, forcing yourself to read faster.

Now suppose that you get as far as the fifth paragraph and the word *viscera* puzzles you. It's a word you've heard before but never really

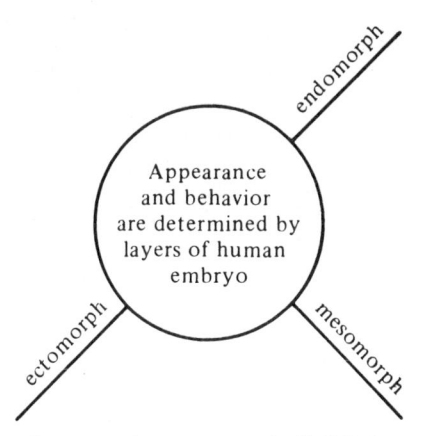

```
                    endomorph
         ╱─────╲
        ╱       ╲
       │ Appearance │
       │ and behavior │
       │ are determined by │
       │ layers of human │
       │   embryo  │
        ╲       ╱
    ectomorph   mesomorph
```

understood. Does it mean the same as *belly*? Is it an organ near the belly? Don't let this momentary distraction slow you down. You've a suspicion of what the word means, so go on — read clear through to the end; don't linger over this word; you'll get back to it.

But how? The trick lies in the finger you are running along the line. Try using your pencil instead. If the word *viscera* bothers you, underscore it or put a check in the margin — but move on. If the whole paragraph made little sense, possibly because you were upset by *viscera,* mark the whole paragraph, but push on. It's marked now, and you can get back to it in step three.

Now you must complete step two. And it is not complete even after you reach the end of the essay. Now that you've read the essay completely and thoroughly, go back to your outline and add more details. For the most part, add them from memory, referring to the text only when you cannot tease a bit of information from your brain. You'll be surprised how good you will get to be at this after a while and how little time it will take. At the end of step two, the outline might look something like the diagram on page 12.

The outline may look messy, but you did it, and it will mean something to you, not just today but, more important, next week during the quiz or next month on the final — and, strangely enough, even ten years from now when you've moved to a new home and found the old outline among the packing boxes. You've made the material a part of you, and you need only the slightest jolt to call it all back. That is why the outline is great to study from; it brings all the essay's ideas — fresh and alive — flooding back to you.

Improve Your
Reading

11

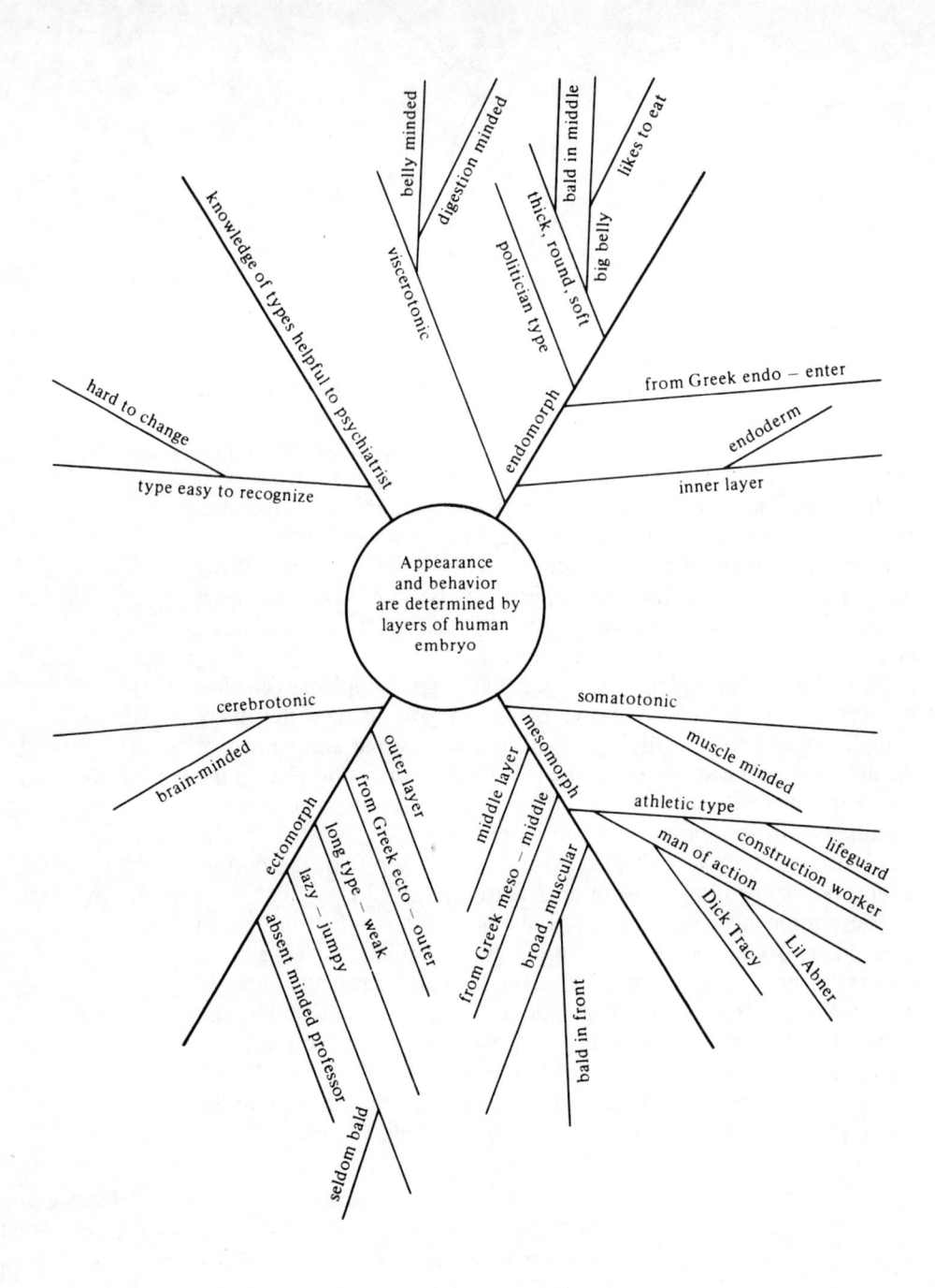

Appearance and behavior are determined by layers of human embryo

endomorph
- from Greek endo — enter
- endoderm
- inner layer
- viscerotonic
  - belly minded
  - digestion minded
- politician type
  - thick, round, soft
  - bald in middle
  - big belly
  - likes to eat

mesomorph
- from Greek meso — middle
- middle layer
- broad, muscular
- bald in front
- somatotonic
  - muscle minded
- athletic type
  - man of action
  - Dick Tracy
  - construction worker
  - lifeguard
  - Lil Abner

ectomorph
- from Greek ecto — outer
- outer layer
- long type — weak
- lazy — jumpy
- absent minded professor
- bald all over
- cerebrotonic
  - brain-minded

General
- knowledge of types helpful to psychiatrist
- hard to change
- type easy to recognize

Step Three — Check the Markings

But there is one more step to complete before you lay your outline page aside. Remember that you marked *viscera* in your text, and perhaps *unrestrained, aggressive,* and *abdomen* also. You rightly left *somatotonic, visceratonic,* and *cerebratonic* alone because you realized that the essay itself was defining those terms, along with *endomorph, mesomorph,* and *ectomorph.* Now is the time to consult the dictionary. Write the words down on your outline page and then look up each word, entering beside it the definition or definitions *in your own words.* Stating the definition in your own words will help to make the word a part of your working vocabulary; you've now done something with it. Next, as a bit more of the same strategy, use the word in a sentence you think up and write down. (It is a good idea to make a single mark in your dictionary beside each word you look up; when you have to look up a word for the third time, go ahead and learn it, since the word clearly is used frequently.)

You were also puzzled by paragraph five. Read it again. The chances are excellent that you'll understand it this time, since you have all the rest of the essay behind you.

Even after you have completed the three steps in the outlining process, there is still one more thing you might wish to do. You might find it useful to mark the text itself so that you can review it more easily should the need arise. (At the same time you will be reinforcing your understanding of what you have read.) As a minimum, underline the thesis statement, plus main ideas and major details, such as names. Write notes and make comments in the margin as you feel the need. (This book has generous margins, inviting your marks, notes, and comments.) Also write down any questions or ideas you feel should be discussed with the instructor. You may also want to number key points and to develop a system of marking to indicate that a point is of primary or of secondary importance, perhaps using double lines for the most important and single lines for the less important. Remember, though, to do such marking only in your books, not in books belonging to a library or another person. (For even more help with careful reading, you should read the first entry in the Appendix, Mortimer Adler's essay, "How to Mark a Book," on p. 429.)

So there you have it. Make your body uncomfortable. Make your brain alert. Do something with your reading. Remember to nudge your brain into alertness by forcing your finger or a pencil along each line, forcing a little more speed and a great deal more attention. Remember also to look over the assignment before you read it, to

How to Read Better

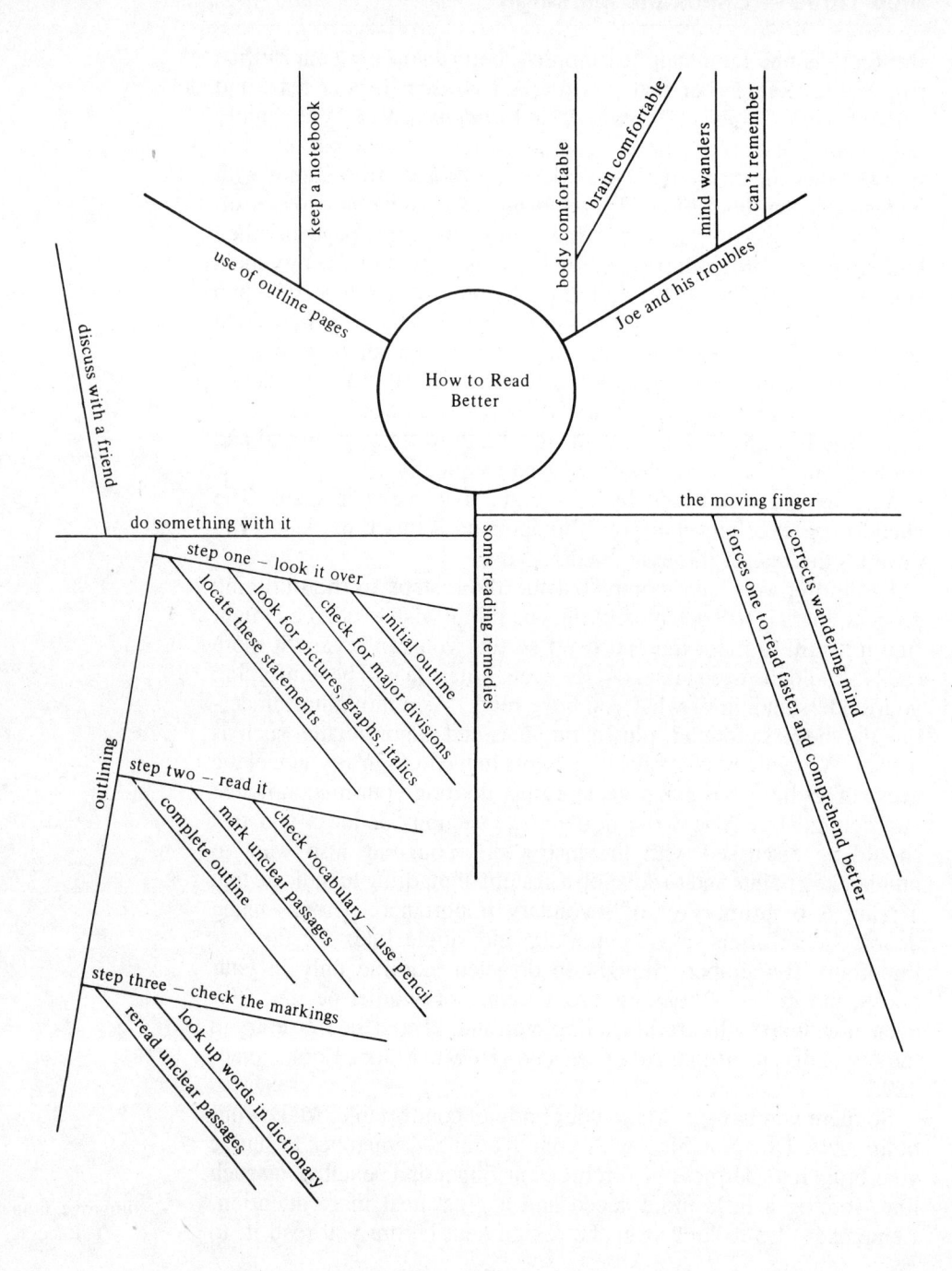

- **use of outline pages**
  - keep a notebook
- **Joe and his troubles**
  - body comfortable
  - brain comfortable
  - mind wanders
  - can't remember
- **some reading remedies**
  - **the moving finger**
    - forces one to read faster and comprehend better
    - corrects wandering mind
  - **do something with it**
    - discuss with a friend
    - **outlining**
      - step one – look it over
        - initial outline
        - check for major divisions
        - look for pictures, graphs, italics
        - locate these statements
      - step two – read it
        - check vocabulary – use pencil
        - mark unclear passages
        - complete outline
      - step three – check the markings
        - look up words in dictionary
        - reread unclear passages

make some sort of outline, to mark puzzling words and sections as well as key portions of the text itself, and then to go back to solve the various puzzles you marked. Finally, when you complete an outline, tear it out and make it a part of your notes for this class. A manila folder would be handy. Every so often your instructor may want to quiz you on your reading, asking questions about (1) the content of certain essays, (2) their rhetorical development, and (3) vocabulary found in these essays. Therefore, a good set of outlines will profit you immediately and in the long run. You'll fare better on any quizzes, and you'll be developing good habits that will help you in all your other college reading — and in all your reading for the rest of your life.

Now for one last point. If you do your job properly on this reading assignment, your outline might look something like the example on the facing page.

Types of Writing

Prose writing may be divided into three types based on the effect the writing is supposed to have on its audience. The first, *narrative-descriptive writing,* strives to make readers see and feel as it presents a scene or series of actions witnessed or imagined by the writer. Travelogues, news accounts, short stories, and novels are examples of narrative-descriptive writing.

The second kind of writing is called *exposition.* In expository writing the writer presumes that readers do not know some piece of information and therefore seeks to explain it. Textbooks, essays and reports, instruction manuals, and legal documents furnish examples of expository writing. It is the most common type of writing in both school and work situations.

The third type of writing is *argumentation,* in which the writer presumes that readers already hold an opinion concerning the subject matter. It is not the purpose of argumentation to add new information (although this is sometimes necessary), but to discuss known information in a way that will persuade readers to change their minds about it, adopting the writer's opinion on the matter. Advertisements, scholarly and scientific treatises, debates, congressional speeches, and editorials offer examples of this kind of writing.

It is important that you understand these divisions, not only because they provide the framework for this book, but because they will help you answer the most important question that will confront you as a writer: What is my purpose in writing? If you want to make your audience see, you will write in a narrative-descriptive mode and use narrative-descriptive techniques. If you want to inform, to educate, to add to the reader's fund of information, then you will write in an expository style, using expository techniques. And if you want to change the minds of your readers, you will write persuasively, using the techniques of argumentation.

You will now begin to examine closely the writing models in this book, studying how both professional and student writers organized and presented their materials, using these three major techniques. Under the guidance of your instructor and this textbook, you will then learn to adapt these techniques to your own writing, in English class as well as in other classes, and at work as well as in school.

Narrative-Descriptive Writing

Narrative-descriptive writing may be essentially either narration or description. Both have as their object an appeal to the senses — so that the reader can see and feel the scenes and actions that the writer is relating. Description concentrates primarily on things (nouns), rather than concerning itself with the actions (verbs) in which the things participate. Writing is purely descriptive when it catches a scene somewhat as a photograph does, frozen into a moment of time but full of things that recommend themselves to us for examination.

Narration, on the other hand, is more than description because it does as much yet goes beyond it. Where description focuses its attention only on nouns, narration focuses on both nouns and verbs. It brings the still photograph to life so that the things described begin to move about and interact.

Here is a strictly descriptive sentence:

1. He was a skinny boy with protruding teeth and enormous freckles.

Notice how the key word *boy*, a noun, is enlarged upon by the other elements in the sentence. The writer is concentrating on description.

Similarly, the writer may concentrate on action:

2. He bounded into the room, throwing off his coat and muffler, tossing his books onto the sofa.

Observe how the phrases introduced by *throwing* and *tossing* enlarge upon the action proposed by the main verb, *bounded,* providing the reader with additional actions occurring simultaneously with the entry into the room.

But writers seldom concentrate on action alone. They usually combine the two techniques and concentrate on both things and actions — nouns and verbs.

3. A skinny boy with protruding teeth and enormous freckles, he bounded into the room, throwing off his coat and muffler, tossing his books onto the sofa.

This combination, then, is what is generally understood to be narration or narrative writing.

So although description may exist apart from narration, narration cannot exist apart from description. To put it another way, we can describe a scene as a still life, as in a portrait or a photograph, without alluding to actions — but we cannot convey *action* without also *describing* the participants involved in those actions.

Since, according to the definitions we have given here, description is the simpler of the two types, that's where we will begin.

Section 1: Description

In learning to write effectively, description is the place to begin because, as was explained on the preceding page, it places the fewest demands on the writer. *In writing a description, a writer, like a painter or sculptor, must render in another medium — in this case, sentences — an accurate copy of what is experienced at one frozen moment in time.* In pure description, *the writer is not concerned with actions.* There are three ways to achieve the writer's goal.

Qualities

Descriptive words usually involve *qualities,* words such as *dull, friendly, awkward,* or even such vague words as *good, bad,* or *nice.* But because these words are vague, they only serve to point a direction in which further development may go. In other words, they merely get things started. If, for example, we write

1. He was a peculiar fellow.

our reader is under no obligation to believe what we say. We have attributed one quality to the noun *fellow*. The reader knows that the fellow is not ordinary, that he's *peculiar*. But beyond that, the reader doesn't know very much. We have only managed to get a description started; we need something more than qualities if we expect a reader to see, feel, and experience the object or scene. We need *details*.

Details

Providing details strengthens the description and makes it vivid. In sentence 1 the reader can see the subject, but dimly; we can improve the image, bring it into sharper focus, by adding details. See what happens when we do:

2. He was a peculiar fellow, wearing a leopard skin over his orange leotard and sporting a yard-long cigarette holder.

Here the added details substantiate the fellow's alleged peculiarity. A more complete description would continue to concentrate on other aspects of the fellow — his hair, his eyes, his teeth, and so on — until sufficient details had been amassed to convey to the reader the writer's intended impression.

Comparisons

The third element of description is not as immediately obvious as the preceding two, yet it leaps most readily to mind when we ask one of the most natural of questions about anything to be described: What does it look like? Suppose we asked this question about the peculiar fellow in sentence 2. We might come up with responses such as the following: "an effete Tarzan," "a gaudy woodland elf," "a seedy imitation of a gladiator," any of which would help to characterize or describe the image proposed by the noun *fellow*.

Comparisons are either *figurative* or *literal*. The ones we've looked at so far are figurative comparisons, because it is only figuratively that we can call the fellow described in 2 a Tarzan, an elf, or a gladiator, for we know he is none of these things. Two figurative comparisons you should be familiar with are the *simile* and the *metaphor*. The simile makes a comparison by asserting that something is *like* something else (he looked *like* a gaudy woodland elf), while a metaphor merely implies the comparison (he *was* a gaudy woodland elf). The literal comparison differs from the figurative in that the comparison could prove to be literally true. (He was dressed ridiculously, as though he were going to a masquerade party.) Literal comparisons usually begin with *as if* or *as though*.

Think as you will, you are not likely to discover any more methods of description, and it is just as well; qualities, details, and comparisons are more than enough in the hands of a capable writer.

Organizing a Description

Each sentence in a description usually focuses on a particular aspect of the thing described. The overall effect is to produce a complete verbal picture. In order to accomplish this aim, the writer must proceed systematically to fill in the space occupied by the scene, so that the reader may see it clearly and completely. For example, if the object described is a landscape, the writer may proceed from left to right, top to bottom, foreground to horizon, or vice versa. If the object is a room or other contained space, the writer may move more systematically around the area, examining each particular in turn — walls, windows, floor, ceiling, furnishings. Each sentence will linger over a certain feature or group of related features before giving way to the next sentence, which will bring into focus an adjoining portion of the scene.

Another technique that provides a description with direction and unity is the statement of a *dominant impression,* usually the *topic sentence* of a paragraph or, in extended descriptions, the *thesis statement*. (See *thesis* in the Glossary.) The writer, for example, may state that the New England farmhouse was bleak, that the room looked a mess, or that the aging lawyer appeared hateful. Each of these dominant impressions must necessarily be confirmed by just those qualities, details, and comparisons that will support the bleakness, the mess, or the hatefulness, while other qualities, details, and comparisons not essential to the dominant impression may be ignored altogether.

Descriptive writing clearly has important practical applications, both in and out of school. Certainly the biology student must describe the laboratory specimen in precise, organized terms, the interviewer's report must draw an accurate word picture of the prospective employee, the criminal investigator's report must systematically portray the scene of the murder, and so on.

Paragraphs:
Description

Phoenix Jackson
Eudora Welty

It was December — a bright frozen day in the early morning. Far out in the country there was an old Negro woman with her head tied in a red rag, coming along a path through the pinewoods. Her name was Phoenix Jackson. She was very old and small and she walked slowly in the dark pine shadows, moving a little from side to side in her steps, with the balanced heaviness and lightness of a pendulum in a grandfather clock. She carried a thin, small cane made from an umbrella, and with this she kept tapping the frozen earth in front of her. This made a grave and persistent noise in the still air, that seemed meditative, like the chirping of a solitary little bird. She wore a dark striped dress reaching down to her shoetops, and an equally long apron of bleached sugar sacks, with a full pocket; all neat and tidy, but every time she took a step she might have fallen over her shoelaces, which dragged from her unlaced shoes. She looked straight ahead. Her eyes were blue with age. Her skin had a pattern all its own of numberless branching wrinkles and as though a whole little tree stood in the middle of her forehead, but a golden color ran underneath, and the two knobs of her cheeks were illuminated by a yellow burning under the dark. Under the red rag her hair came down on her neck in the frailest of ringlets, still black, and with an odor like copper.

Discussion Questions

1. Phoenix Jackson seems to come slowly into focus, as though the author were adjusting the lens of a camera. How does Welty use details to produce this effect? What qualities and comparisons figure in this description?

2. List the major comparisons that Welty uses in this paragraph. Other than sight, what senses are appealed to? Which are particularly effective and why?

The Bunk House
John Steinbeck

The bunk house was a long, rectangular building. Inside, the walls were whitewashed and the floor unpainted. In three walls there were small, square windows, and in the fourth, a solid door with a wooden latch. Against the walls were eight bunks, five of them made up with blankets and the other three showing their burlap ticking. Over each bunk there was nailed an apple box with the opening forward so that it made two shelves for the personal belongings of the occupant of the bunk. And these shelves were loaded with little articles, soap and talcum powder, razors and those Western magazines ranch men love to read and scoff at and secretly believe. And there were medicines on the shelves, and little vials, combs; and from nails on the box sides, a few neckties. Near one wall there was a black cast-iron stove, its stovepipe going straight up through the ceiling. In the middle of the room stood a big square table littered with playing cards, and around it were grouped boxes for the players to sit on.

Discussion Questions

1. Make a sketch of the bunk-house floor plan, showing the arrangement of the features Steinbeck mentions.
2. What details in Steinbeck's description let us know how many hired hands live in the bunk house?
3. What do the contents of the apple-box cabinets tell us about the ranch hands?

Hanover, Nebraska
Willa Cather

One January day, thirty years ago, the little town of Hanover, anchored on a windy Nebraska tableland, was trying not to be blown away. A mist of fine snowflakes was curling and eddying about the cluster of low, drab buildings huddled on the gray prairie, under a gray sky. The dwelling-houses were set about haphazard on the tough prairie sod; some of them looked as if they had been moved in overnight, and others as if they were straying off by themselves, headed straight for the open plain. None of them had any appearance of permanence, and the howling wind blew under them as well as over them. The main street was a deeply rutted road, now frozen hard, which ran from the squat red railway station and the grain "elevator" at the north end of the town to the lumber yard and the horse pond at the south end. On either side of this road straggled two uneven rows of wooden buildings: the general merchandise stores, the two banks, the drug store, the feed store, the saloon, the post-office. The board sidewalks were gray with trampled snow, but at two o'clock in the afternoon the shopkeepers, having come back from dinner, were keeping well behind their frosty windows. The children were all in school, and there was nobody abroad in the streets but a few rough-looking countrymen in coarse overcoats, with their long caps pulled down to their noses. Some of them had brought their wives to town, and now and then a red or a plaid shawl flashed out of one store into the shelter of another. At the hitch-bars along the street a few heavy work-horses, harnessed to farm wagons, shivered under their blankets. About the station everything was quiet, for there would not be another train in until night.

Discussion Questions

1. Willa Cather begins her description of Hanover, Nebraska, with a long shot of the town; she then zooms in to examine the main street, its buildings, people, and animals. Mark the point where a shift is made from a less concrete description to a more concrete one. How many levels of generality do you find?
2. Cather uses the verb *anchored* in a peculiar way, when she describes the way Hanover is situated on the "windy Nebraska tableland." Locate at least two more verbs that are similarly used. What descriptive effect do they have? Are they, strictly speaking, comparisons? Why or why not?

The White Glove
William Paulk

About that time I saw the glove lying there, cool and white and painfully neat. Somebody had left a glove, and a janitor or somebody else had picked it up and left it lying there on the table. It was a small glove, the kind a lady wears. I don't mean the kind of lady who drives a nice late model car; I don't mean the kind who has a chauffeur, either; still, a real lady. It was all flat and the thumb was folded over the palm, and it looked shy and retiring. I could almost imagine a little parlor with a high ceiling and a little marble-topped tea table in front of a Victorian sofa. But the glove wasn't by itself. It lay on a piece of paper, heavy white stationery of the kind elderly ladies prefer for important communications. The paper was sort of propped against the wall behind the table, and I could see that it had writing on it. An entry at the top in an elegant, but spidery hand gave the name of a savings bank, and over to the side, heading a neat column, was written $235.58. Just below that line and indented a little were the words, "U.S. Govm't Bond, Series E, $100.00, cashed 1958," and on a third line, "U.S. Govm't Bond, Series E, $50.00, cashed 1958," with the interest listed just under the bank figure. Almost covered by the glove was a final entry, "Old Age Pension," written in a smaller, almost apologetic hand by the same person, and the amount was covered by the little white glove.

Discussion Questions

1. It is evident that William Paulk is not so much describing a white glove as he is the imagined owner of the glove. What details hint at the character of the glove's owner?
2. What do you think he means by "a real lady"?
3. How does Paulk use comparison? How are the comparisons introduced?

Subway Station
Gilbert Highet

Standing in a subway station, I began to appreciate the place — almost to enjoy it. First of all, I looked at the lighting: a row of meager electric bulbs, unscreened, yellow, and coated with filth, stretched toward the black mouth of the tunnel, as though it were a bolt hole in an abandoned coal mine. Then I lingered, with zest, on the walls and ceiling: lavatory tiles which had been white about fifty years ago, and were now encrusted with soot, coated with the remains of a dirty liquid which might be either atmospheric humidity mingled with smog or the result of a perfunctory attempt to clean them with cold water; and, above them, gloomy vaulting from which dingy paint was peeling off like scabs from an old wound, sick black paint leaving a leprous white undersurface. Beneath my feet, the floor was a nauseating dark brown with black stains upon it which might be stale oil or dry chewing gum or some worse defilement; it looked like the hallway of a condemned slum building. Then my eye traveled to the tracks, where two lines of glittering steel — the only positively clean objects in the whole place — ran out of darkness into darkness above an unspeakable mass of congealed oil, puddles of dubious liquid, and a mishmash of old cigarette packets, mutilated and filthy newspapers, and the débris that filtered down from the street above through a barred grating in the roof. As I looked up toward the sunlight, I could see more débris sifting slowly downward, and making an abominable pattern in the slanting beam of dirt-laden sunlight. I was going on to relish more features of this unique scene: such as the advertisement posters on the walls — here a text from the Bible, there a half-naked girl, here a woman wearing a hat consisting of a hen sitting on a nest full of eggs, and there a pair of girl's legs walking up the keys of a cash register — all scribbled over with unknown names and well-known obscenities in black crayon and red lipstick; but then my train came in at last, I boarded it, and began to read. The experience was over for the time.

Discussion Questions

1. How does Highet organize his description? What parts of the subway station does he focus upon and in what order?
2. How many comparisons do you count in Highet's third sentence, which begins, "Then I lingered . . ."? How are they related?
3. Which descriptive device does Highet use most frequently: qualities, details, or comparisons?

Student Work:
Description

Ruth

Ruth appears to be the typical no-nonsense college student. Her appearance is neat but not meticulous. Her clothing is smart-looking and color-coordinated, with her blue tennis shoes matching her Oxford cloth baby blue shirt, both set off by her white painter pants. No socks indicate she is prepared for a hot day, as does her short-sleeved shirt. Her hair is neatly braided in two sections along the sides and caught in the back by a yellow rubber band, allowing the rest to fall behind her. Although she does not wear much makeup, she is dramatic-looking with her dark brown eyes and hair and her creamy complexion, looking like she should be on an Ivory soap commercial. She doesn't wear fingernail polish, and for jewelry only has on one silver chain with a unique glass charm and, of course, a watch, which every no-nonsense student carries.

Discussion Questions

1. "Ruth" begins with a topic sentence, a general statement that indicates the direction the rest of the paragraph will take. In this case the topic sentence conveys a dominant impression about a girl named Ruth. What is that dominant impression?
2. What details of the description serve to support or reinforce the dominant impression?
3. What, if anything, is gained by repeating the phrase "no-nonsense student" in the first and last sentences of the paragraph?

Evelyn's Drudgery

The smoky air, a grim reminder of Evelyn's drudgery, drifts slowly out of the window. The sewing machines surrounding her, racing and idling, sound like dragsters revving up their motors before a race. Ripping off old binding and sewing on new, Evelyn sits behind her machine toward the end of the second shift. Knuckles gnarled and crooked with arthritis brought on by her years of sewing blankets are another reminder as persistent as the smoke. Sweat rolls down her face like condensed water trickling down a glass. The plastic hairnet she wears to keep her hair out of her eyes only worsens the problem, collecting moisture in huge beads across her forehead and then releasing them to run down behind her frameless glasses. But the highlight of Evelyn's day is approaching, the sounding of the whistle that signals an end to another day at the mill.

Discussion Questions

1. How many senses are appealed to in this description of Evelyn? Which do you find particularly effective? Ineffective? Why?
2. Circle the words that convey qualities. Underscore the portions that provide details, and enclose comparisons in brackets.

Thanksgiving Dinner — Before

The Thanksgiving dinner table was quite a sight. Red and yellow calico placemats adorned the round oak table, with its ten sturdy oak chairs straining under the weight of the happy eaters. All eyes were focused on the center of attention, the golden-brown turkey with stuffing falling out the sides and garnished with lacy green parsley. Spaced evenly around the golden bird were the vegetables, each one in its own special dish that Grandma uses every year: broccoli with creamy cheese sauce, flaming yellow corn on the cob, whipped ivory potatoes, green beans, and fresh garden peas. As one looks at the dishes, with the steam rising up and the aroma filling the room, one feels like a king or queen at a royal banquet. The prayers have been said, the praises sung, and Grandma has given the sign — the feast can begin.

Thanksgiving Dinner — After

The Thanksgiving dinner table was quite a sight. The array of food, originally intended to tease the palate during the prayers, had been reduced to a scene of wreckage. The turkey, once innocent and inviting with its thick, juicy meat and compelling aroma, had become an embarrassingly naked bundle of bones, picked clean by our appetites. Dribblings of cranberry sauce decorated the tablecloth like blood after the carnage. The flowers from the centerpiece had been crumpled by the rapid passing of food from one side to another, leaving a few petals fallen and alone by the empty bowl of what had once been candied yams. Dirty dishes stained brown, red, and yellow surround the table. A few lingering people smile and softly groan as they rub their stomachs in satisfaction, too full to move and too content to try.

Discussion Questions

1. These two paragraphs were written in response to the same assignment, which was to describe a Thanksgiving dinner using qualities, details, and comparisons. The topic sentence was provided. Which paragraph do you consider to be more effective? Why?
2. Each paragraph contains examples of *clichés* (see Glossary, p. 453). Which ones do you notice, and how would you change each to gain freshness and originality?
3. What is the purpose of the colon following "every year" in the first paragraph?
4. Look up *free modifier* in the Glossary. What examples of such modifiers do you find in each of these paragraphs?

My Dormitory Room

When you walk into my room, you are immediately struck by a profusion of colors. The black rug looks very appealing over the bright red mat, which forms a two-foot border all the way around. The brown paneled walls are dull by comparison and tend to subdue the colors on the floor.

The furniture has all the variety of a color wheel you see in department stores. The easy chair, brought from home, is beige, white, and dirty brown, and it presses the black rug snugly against the mat. The desk is the standard college-issue olive green, and it, together with my turquoise bedspread, keeps the black and red from taking charge. 2

Along one wall the makeshift bookcase (Pet Milk and orange crate modern) contains a variegated array of schoolbooks and paperbacks, some standing erect and gathering dust, others stacked on their sides and bristling with white and yellow notepaper. 3

A flick of the light switch brings the crazy ceiling into focus. Some earlier occupant, a crazed student of interior design, painted every other white Celotex square a dark maroon. Perhaps he was a chess fanatic who worked out his problems at night with a flashlight. Whatever its origin, its effect is dazzling — and distracting. 4

The one narrow window with its open venetian blind keeps reality in place. Through it I can see the green lawn stretching down toward the red brick library under a Carolina blue sky — a combination of colors a bit less shocking than those in my room. 5

Discussion Questions

1. The first sentence serves as the thesis statement of "My Dormitory Room." How well does the rest of the essay conform to and support that central idea?
2. What feature of the room is most unusual?
3. What is gained by shifting the viewpoint out of the room in the final paragraph?
4. Assume you are the next inhabitant of this room. Describe the changes you would make and explain why.

Dude

He walks slowly down the hall, with a flowing motion, rising slightly on the balls of his feet with each step. Beneath his white planter's hat, tilted to one side, his carefully groomed Afro flares out, framing a medium-brown face, with a high forehead, a slightly flattened nose, flaring nostrils, and a full, sensuous mouth. A moustache and goatee emphasize his prominent cheekbones, his unblemished skin, the polished glow of his face. 1

Section 1: Description

He wears a long-sleeved silky shirt with the throat open, its vivid colors shimmering as he moves. His high-waisted pants, which match the orange in his shirt, fit tightly, every muscle apparent as he walks. Offwhite shoes with thick brown soles and heels complete his outfit, which is entirely color-coordinated and seems taken from an advertisement in *Ebony*.

Upon reaching his destination, a wall outside a classroom, he leans back against it, his weight shifted off one foot, his pelvis tilted forward. When an attractive girl walks by, he catches her eye and gives her a slow, short nod, measuring her up and down, taking in all her features. When she stops, he talks to her in a deep, quiet voice, gesturing with his hands, the same flowing motions. He smiles once, a small, secret smile, showing large, even teeth. Every few moments he reaches out and lightly touches the girl.

When the bell rings, the crowd comes noisily out of the classroom; then he pushes himself lithely off the wall and strolls in, a brown heel the last thing seen.

Discussion Questions

1. "Dude" is a thorough description of a student — more complete, for instance, than "Phoenix Jackson." Yet the writer has perhaps forgotten something that should have been in the description, something that would be carried. Can you tell what is missing and explain why the omission is important or trivial? Revise the essay somewhere to include the missing thing(s).
2. What kinds of grammatical constructions are "his weight shifted off one foot," "his pelvis tilted forward," "a brown heel the last thing seen"? What effect do they produce?
3. How is this description like the one Eudora Welty did of Phoenix Jackson? How are they different?

Essays:
Description

Private Eye Calling
Robert B. Parker

Robert B. Parker (1932–   ) is a native of Springfield, Massachusetts. Educated at Colby College and Boston University, he has been a technical writer, advertising executive, and college English teacher. In 1974 he began a highly successful series of detective novels featuring a wise-cracking private eye named Spenser. It is Spenser who speaks in the following passage taken from *God Save the Child* (1974). Other Spenser books include *The Godwulf Manuscript* (1974), *Mortal Stakes* (1975), *Promised Land* (1976), *Judas Goat* (1978), *Looking for Rachel Wallace* (1980), *Early Autumn* (1981), *A Savage Place* (1982), *Ceremony* (1982), *The Widening Gyre* (1983), and *Valediction* (1984).

I drove north out of Boston, over the Mystic River Bridge, with the top down on my car. On the right was Old Ironsides at berth in the Navy Yard and to the left of the bridge the Bunker Hill Monument. Between them stretch three-decker tenements alternating with modular urban renewal units. One of the real triumphs of prefab design is to create a sense of nostalgia for slums. At the top of the bridge I paid my toll to a man who took pride in his work. There was a kind of precise flourish to the way he took my quarter and gave me back a dime with the same hand. 1

Out to the right now was the harbor and the harbor islands and the long curving waterfront. The steeple of the Old North Church poked up among the warehouses and lofts. On the East Boston side of the harbor was Logan Airport and beyond, northeast, the contours of the coast. The brick and asphalt and neon were blurred by distance and sunshine and beneath it I got a sense of the land as it once must have been. The silent midsummer buzz of it and copper-colored near-naked men moving along a narrow trail. 2

The bridge dipped down into Chelsea and the Northeast Expressway. Across the other lane, beyond a football field was a Colonel Sanders' fast-food restaurant. The brick and asphalt and neon were no longer blurred and the sense of the land went away. The expressway connects in Saugus to Route One and for the next ten miles is a plastic canyon of sub-sandwich shops, discount houses, gas stations, supermarkets, neocolonial furniture shops (vinyl siding and chintz curtains), fried chicken, big beef sandwiches, hot dogs cooked in beer, quarter-pound hamburgers, pizzas, storm doors, Sear Roebuck, doughnut shops, stockade fencing — preassembled sections — restaurants that looked like log cabins, restaurants that looked like sailing ships, restaurants that looked like Moorish town houses, restaurants that looked like carwashes, carwashes, shopping centers, a fish market, a skimobile shop, an automotive accessory shop, liquor stores, a delicatessen in three clashing colors, a motel with an in-room steam bath, a motel with a relaxing vibrator bed, a car dealer, an indoor skating rink attractively done in brick and corrugated plastic, a trailer park, another motel composed of individual cabins, an automobile dealership attractively done in glass and corrugated plastic, an enormous steak house with life-sized plastic cows grazing out front in the shadow of a six-story neon cactus, a seat cover store, a discount clothing warehouse, an Italian restaurant with a leaning tower attached to it. Overpasses punctuated Route One, tying together the north suburban towns that lined it like culverts over a sewer of commerce. Maybe Squanto had made a mistake. 3

A sign said ENTERING SMITHFIELD, and the land reappeared. There was grass along the highway and maple trees behind it, and glimpses of lake through the trees. I turned off at an exit marked "Smithfield" and drove toward the center of town beneath a tunnel of elm trees that were as old as the town. They bordered the broad street and interlaced thirty feet above it so that the sun shone through in mottled patterns on the street. Bordering the street behind big lawns and flowering shrubs were spacious old houses in shingle or clapboard, often with slate roofs, occasionally with a small barn that had been converted to a garage. Stone walls, rose bushes, red doors with bull's-eye glass windows, a lot of station wagons, most of them with the fake wood on the sides. I was more aware than I had been of the big dent on the side of my car and the tear in the upholstery that I had patched with gray tape. 4

In the center of town was a common with a two-story white clapboard meeting house in the middle. The date on it was 1681. Across the street a white spired church with a big church hall attached, and next to that a new white clapboard library designed in harmony with the meeting house and church. On a stone wall across from the common six teen-age kids, four boys and two girls, sat swinging their bare feet and smoking. They were long-haired and T-shirted and tan. I turned right onto Main Street at the end of the common and then left. A discreet white sign with black printing on it was set in a low curving brick wall. It said Apple Knoll.

It was a development. Flossy and fancy and a hundred thousand a house, but a development. Some of the trees had been left, and the streets curved gently, and the lawns were well landscaped, but all the homes were the same age, and bore the mark of a central intelligence. They were big colonial houses, some garrisoned, some with breezeways, some with peaked and some with gambrel roofs, but basically the same house. Eight or ten rooms, they looked to be, on an acre of land. Behind the houses on my right the land sloped down to a lake that brightened through the trees here and there where the road bent closer.

The Bartletts' home was yellow with dark green shutters and a hip roof. The roof was slate and there were A-shaped dormers protruding from it to suggest a third floor that was more than attic. Doubtless for the servants; they don't mind the heat under the eaves, they're used to it.

A brick walk led up to a wide green front door with sidelights. The brick driveway went parallel to the house and curved right, ending in a turn-around before a small barn, designed like the house and done in the same colors. The blue van was there, and a Ford Country Squire and a red Mustang convertible with a white roof, and a black Chevrolet sedan with a buggy-whip antenna and no markings on the side.

The barn doors were open and swallows flew in and out in sharp graceful sweeps. Behind the house was a square swimming pool surrounded by a brick patio. The blue lining of the pool made the water look artificial. Beyond the pool a young girl was operating a ride-around lawn mower. I parked next to the black Chevy, up against the hydrangea bushes that lined the turn-around and concealed it from the street. Black and yellow bumblebees buzzed frantically at the flowers. As I approached the house a Labrador retriever looked at me without raising his head from his paws, and I had to walk around him to get to the back door. Somewhere out of sight I could hear an air conditioner droning and I was conscious of how my shirt stuck to my back under my coat. I was wearing a white linen sport coat in honor of my trip to the subs and I wished I could take it off. But since I'd made some people in the mob mad at me, I'd taken to wearing a gun everywhere and Smithfield didn't seem like the kind of place where you flashed it around.

Besides the white linen jacket I had on a red checkered sport shirt, dark blue slacks, and white loafers. Me and Betsy Ross. I was neat, clean, alert, and going to the back door. I rang the bell. Ding-dong, private eye calling.   10

Discussion: Content

1. What is Parker's attitude toward the scene he describes in paragraph 3? How can you tell?
2. Who was Squanto? What is meant by the allusion to him at the end of paragraph 3?
3. What do the details in paragraph 4 tell you about that neighborhood? How about the town center in paragraph 5?
4. How does Apple Knoll, described in paragraph 6, contrast with the neighborhood in paragraph 4?
5. What is the significance of the narrator's comment, "Me and Betsy Ross," in paragraph 10?

Discussion: Form

1. We have characterized description as writing that captures a scene without attention to movement. How can such a definition be applied to this piece of writing, which deals with the trip from Boston to Smithfield, a movement over a considerable distance?
2. Are you disturbed by the long catalog of businesses mentioned in paragraph 3? What is its effect?
3. In paragraph 1 Parker makes the comment that the prefab designs typical of urban renewal create a sense of nostalgia for slums. Locate several other instances of his (or his narrator's) interjecting personal observations into the description.

Boyhood Memories
Mark Twain

Samuel Langhorne Clemens (1835–1910), better known as Mark Twain, grew up in and around Hannibal, Missouri, along the banks of the Mississippi River. One of America's greatest writers, especially adept at humorous and descriptive writing, Twain preserved memories of his boyhood for all time in his two best-known novels, *The Adventures of Tom Sawyer* (1876) and *The Adventures of Huckleberry Finn* (1885). In the passage below, Twain displays his almost overwhelming descriptive powers as he recalls youthful experiences on his Uncle John's farm near Florida, Missouri.

I spent some part of every year at the farm until I was twelve or thirteen years old. The life which I led there with my cousins was full of charm, and so is the memory of it yet. I can call back the solemn twilight and mystery of the deep woods, the earthy smells, the faint odors of the wild flowers, the sheen of rain-washed foliage, the rattling clatter of drops when the wind shook the trees, the far-off hammering of woodpeckers and the muffled drumming of wood pheasants in the remoteness of the forest, the snapshot glimpses of disturbed wild creatures scurrying through the grass — I can call it all back and make it as real as it ever was, and as blessed. I can call back the prairie, and its loneliness and peace, and a vast hawk hanging motionless in the sky, with his wings spread wide and the blue of the vault showing through the fringe of their end feathers. I can see the woods in their autumn dress, the oaks purple, the hickories washed with gold, the maples and the sumachs luminous with crimson fires, and I can hear the rustle made by the fallen leaves as we plowed through them. I can see the blue clusters of wild grapes hanging among the foliage of the saplings, and I remember the taste of them and the smell. I know how the wild blackberries looked, and how they tasted; and the same with the pawpaws, the hazelnuts, and the persimmons; and I can feel the thumping rain, upon my head, of hickory nuts and walnuts when we were out in the frosty dawn to scramble for them with the pigs, and the gusts of wind loosed them and sent them down. I know the stain of blackberries, and how pretty it is, and I know the stain of walnut hulls, and how little it minds soap and water, also what grudged experience it had of either of them. I know the taste of maple sap, and when to gather it, and how to arrange the troughs and the delivery tubes, and how to boil down the juice, and how to hook the sugar after it is made; also how much better hooked sugar tastes than any that is honestly come by, let bigots say what they will. I know how a prize watermelon looks when it is sunning its fat rotundity among pumpkin vines and "simblins"; I know how to tell when it is ripe without "plugging" it; I know how inviting it looks when it is cooling itself in a tub of water under the bed, waiting; I know how it looks when it lies on the table in the sheltered great floor space between house and kitchen, and the children gathered for the sacrifice and their mouths watering; I know the crackling sound it makes when the carving knife enters its end, and I can see the split fly along in front of the blade as the knife cleaves its way to the other end; I can see its halves fall apart and display the rich red meat and the black seeds, and the heart standing up, a luxury fit for the elect; I know how a boy looks behind a yard-long slice of that melon, and I know how he feels; for I have been there. I know the taste of the watermelon which has been honestly come by, and I know the taste of the watermelon which has been acquired by art. Both taste good, but the experienced know which tastes best. I know the look of green apples and peaches and pears on the trees, and I know how entertaining they are when they are inside of a person. I know how ripe ones look when they are piled in pyramids under the trees, and how pretty they are and how vivid their colors. I know how a frozen apple looks, in a barrel down cellar in the wintertime, and how hard it is to bite, and how the frost makes the teeth ache, and yet how good it is, notwithstanding. I know the disposition of elderly people to select the specked apples for the children, and I once knew ways to beat the game. I know the look of an apple that is roasting and sizzling on a hearth on a winter's evening, and I know the comfort that comes of eating it hot, along with some sugar and a drench of cream. I know the delicate art and mystery of so cracking hickory nuts and walnuts on a flatiron with a hammer that the kernels will be delivered whole, and I know how the nuts, taken in conjunction with winter apples, cider, and doughnuts, make old people's old tales and old jokes sound fresh and crisp and enchanting, and juggle an evening away before you know what went with the time. I know the look of Uncle Dan'l's kitchen as it was on the privileged nights, when I was a child, and I can see the white and black children grouped on the hearth, with firelight playing on their faces and the shadows flickering upon the walls, clear back toward the cavernous gloom of the rear, and I can hear Uncle Dan'l telling the immortal tales which Uncle Remus Harris was to gather into his book and charm the world with, by and by; and I can feel again the creepy joy which quivered through me when the time for the ghost story was reached — and the sense of regret, too, which came over me, for it was always the last story of the evening and there was nothing between it and the unwelcome bed. 1

    I can remember the bare wooden stairway in my uncle's house, and the turn to the left above the landing, and the rafters and the slanting roof over my bed, and the squares of moonlight on the floor, and the white cold world of snow outside, seen through the curtainless window. I can remember the howling of the wind and the quaking of the house on stormy nights, and how snug and cozy one felt, under the blankets, listening; and how the powdery snow used to sift in, around the sashes, and lie in little ridges on the floor and make the place look chilly in the morning and curb the wild desire to get up — in case there was any. I can remember how very dark that room was, in the dark of the moon, and how packed it was with ghostly stillness when one woke up by accident away in the night, and forgotten sins came flocking out of the secret chambers of the memory and wanted a hearing; and how ill chosen the time seemed for this kind of business; and how dismal was the hoohooing of the owl and the wailing of the wolf, sent mourning by on the night wind.   2

I remember the raging of the rain on that roof, summer nights, and how pleasant it was to lie and listen to it, and enjoy the white splendor of the lightning and the majestic booming and crashing of the thunder. It was a very satisfactory room, and there was a lightning rod which was reachable from the window, an adorable and skittish thing to climb up and down, summer nights, when there were duties on hand of a sort to make privacy desirable.   3

I remember the 'coon and 'possum hunts, nights, . . . and the long marches through the black gloom of the woods, and the excitement which fired everybody when the distant bay of an experienced dog announced that the game was treed; then the wild scrambling and stumblings through briers and bushes and over roots to get to the spot; then the lighting of a fire and the felling of the tree, the joyful frenzy of the dogs . . . and the weird picture it all made in the red glare — I remember it all well, and the delight that everyone got out of it, except the 'coon.   4

I remember the pigeon seasons, when the birds would come in millions and cover the trees and by their weight break down the branches. They were clubbed to death with sticks; guns were not necessary and were not used. I remember the squirrel hunts, and prairie-chicken hunts, and wild-turkey hunts, and all that; and how we turned out, mornings, while it was still dark, to go on these expeditions, and how chilly and dismal it was, and how often I regretted that I was well enough to go. A toot on a tin horn brought twice as many dogs as were needed, and in their happiness they raced and scampered about, and knocked small people down, and made no end of unnecessary noise. At the word, they vanished away toward the woods, and we drifted silently after them in the melancholy gloom. But presently the gray dawn stole over the world, the birds piped up, then the sun rose and poured light and comfort all around, everything was fresh and dewy and fragrant, and life was a boon again. After three hours of tramping we arrived back wholesomely tired, overladen with game, very hungry, and just in time for breakfast.

Discussion: Content

1. What details does Twain use to describe his room? What effect does that selection have or create?
2. How distinctly do you see other places? Uncle Dan'l's kitchen? The locales of hunts? Why?
3. Which of the many things mentioned in the long first paragraph receives the most space? What do you suppose this indicates?

Discussion: Form

1. Paragraph 1 seems intolerably long. Perhaps we are too used to the short paragraphs of newspaper articles. Nonetheless, if you were a modern editor, how would you suggest that Twain divide his paragraph? How would you justify these breaks?
2. Which of Twain's memories cause you to smile? How does Twain evoke this smile?
3. Comment on the overall organization of this description. What plan does Twain follow?

Miss Gowrie
Mary McCarthy

Mary McCarthy (1912–   ) is a native of Washington who went east to attend Vassar College and then began a career writing for the *New Yorker* and other magazines. Her numerous books include *The Groves of Academe* (1952), *Venice Observed* (1956), *The Group* (1963), *Birds of America* (1971), and *The Mask of State* (1974). In 1984 McCarthy was awarded the National Medal for Literature. The essay below, describing one of her teachers at a girls' preparatory school, is from *Memories of a Catholic Girlhood* (1957).

I claimed Miss Gowrie as my discovery. Among the normal Seminary girls, it was thought affected to take Latin unless you "had to" for Eastern college boards or because your parents insisted. You were supposed to groan as you entered her chilly classroom, where the windows were kept open to obviate sleepiness. Miss Gowrie herself wore a maroon cardigan buttoned down over her thin chest winter and fall and spring, and those who sat near the window huddled in their coats during the greater part of the year. If we did our sight poorly, the windows were poked open farther; the long pole with the hook on the end of it came to seem a part of her personality, like Saint Joseph's crook. And her chilblained nature had a queer, raw, stiffened sensitiveness. Like many spinsters in foreign countries, she suffered dreadfully from ideas of reference: any remark delivered in an undertone she took to concern herself and flushed up darkly, like a mulberry. She was touchy about a misdone translation, and the capillaries of her blood system seemed to tell her when you were not primed to recite, even though your hand was waving boldly. And when you knew your lesson, she peremptorily cut you short.

At this time, she must have been about thirty-eight or forty years old. A graduate of Girton and Edinburgh, she had come, probably by way of Canada, to our little church boarding school in the Pacific Northwest. Doubtless she had taught elsewhere, in the outposts of empire; it was her first stay in the States, and she took being Scottish *personally,* just as she took our mistakes in translation. So far as we could determine, she had no private life or history and consisted totally of national attributes (thrift, humorless hard work, porridge-eating, and tea-drinking), like one of those wooden dolls dressed in national costume that they show at fairs and expositions. And her appearance was like an illustration to an anthropologist's textbook. She was extremely dark, with brown skin, brown-black eyes, shiny, straight black hair, and a round skull, on which the hair grew in circular fashion. Her face was round also, with cheekbones like an Eskimo's or a pygmy's. She had a tall frame, stiffly articulated and curiously jerky in its movements. In short, as I now know, she belonged to that ancient Celto-Iberian or possibly Pictish strain that survives in the northern Highlands, and the foreignness we noticed in her may have been proof of the scholar's contention that the British Isles in pre-history were inhabited by non-Aryan aborigines, whose descendants, known to the Roman writers, were the little dark men who worked in tin. Her face, hands, and neck had an almost unnatural cleanness, and her red lips drew back from a set of very white false teeth. This glistening sign of early poverty awed us, as a sign of consecration, like a monk's tonsure.

For the out-of-doors, she wore a very old, but real, sealskin coat, of the same color and texture as her hair; from its unfashionable cut, it

Section 1: Description

seemed to have been inherited from her mother, or even her grandmother, as did her long, flat black shoes. Her diction had an odd distinctness; she spoke with a Cambridge accent, but every syllable was formed concisely and separately, as though English were a prized foreign language she had learned young, by the phonetic method. This effect was heightened when she spoke Latin; her teeth clinked and sometimes the draft from the window seemed to whistle through them.

It was Scotland's pride, she told us, to have been throughout the darker ages a center of classical learning, and her very digestion evoked a dour history of Scottish letters and philosophy; like Carlyle, whom we were studying about in English, and like Carlyle's wife, she was dyspeptic. Her brown skin sometimes paled to a yellow hue, and after the school luncheon she often had gas on her stomach.

Yet Miss Gowrie was not an unpleasant person. The school admitted that she meant well, probably. But she did not understand about the rules. Our principal was a stout executive with the prejudices of an old chatelaine. Fountain pens were forbidden because girls had spotted the walls and floors by shaking the ink down in the pen. No food but fruit was permitted in the rooms, and we were forbidden to eat between meals on our walks or shopping trips, so that we would be sure to do justice to the school table. Each girl came with a list of ten approved correspondents, signed by her family, and she was supposed to get letters from no one else. All packages received through the mail were subject to inspection. None of these rules, however, was enforced, except by Miss Gowrie. There was a tacit understanding, shared even, I think, by the principal, that many of the rules existed for artistic reasons, for form's sake. They gave tone to the school. Candy and cookies and modern novels and love letters from unauthorized individuals poured in through the mails; inspection was cursory; fountain pens were rife. Our first stop on our walks was the corner luncheonette, whose main revenue derived from the Seminary, as everybody knew. The Saturday-morning shopping trip and the Saturday-night movie excursion ended, by immemorial custom, at the downtown Puss 'n Boots or Green Lantern, with the girls treating the chaperones to the latest fancy sundaes. The group of us who rode, on Friday afternoons and Saturday mornings, had our cigarettes tucked in our breeches as we drove out to the riding academy with the chaperone, who usually took advantage of the occasion to have a cigarette herself, privately, with the riding master's wife, and there was a standing order for hamburgers for the whole party at a barbecue place on the highway. When we were taken out Sunday afternoons by "a person designated by the family," many of us went out with undesignated men and came back with liquor on our breath. The vice-principal, who signed us in, was careful not to come too close to us, and in my time no girl was ever reported for drinking, though sometimes we must have reeked of gin. A teacher, meeting us downtown on a Sunday with our "brothers" and "cousins," hurriedly tacked off in another direction. All but Miss Gowrie, who felt it her duty to report.

The young teachers sighed, the girls tapped their heads, the vexed principal wept and took the offender on her lap. Austere and sensible, she hated to impose drastic punishments, because this interfered with the smooth running of the school. In the case of her best students, she was usually satisfied with mere repentance; any clever girl could cry her way out of a jam. Meanwhile, poor Miss Gowrie, rigid and bewildered, pursued her solitary course, deaf to the timid hints of friendly colleagues, who tried to set her on the right course. She was always the last chaperone to be chosen on all-school expeditions, and the ragtail group that got her was looked on with freshened pity: no smoking, no eating, no private jokes would be permitted. At the annual school picnic, hers was the last rowboat to be pushed off from the dock, with a disconsolate trio aboard, while she sat upright, facing the maneuvering oarsman, wearing a bright excursion smile clamped about her teeth. M.C.G. (Make Conversation General), the school rule for table talk, was Miss Gowrie's buoy still as she floated about the waters, never allowing her boat to be guided into one of the charming little shaded coves, out of the principal's sight, where you could catch at the weeping-willow branches and broach the idea of wading. It was sad, for when you got to know her, you found that she was a very simple being, a sort of atrophied girl, fond of an outing and what she considered wholesome fun. But she could not grasp at all our American conception of an outing, which consisted in a sort of mass truancy; on any kind of pleasure party, Miss Gowrie's first concern was to establish an idea of the official. It required character to be a spoilsport on a privileged day, but she rose to the painful occasion with a sort of pathetic, sporting determination, like a trout jumping to the cruel hook.

A cough and a tobacco stain on the second finger of her right hand told us that she was a heavy smoker, but we learned from the riding master's wife that Miss Gowrie steadily refused to take a cigarette anywhere near the Seminary and blinked with disapproval when she heard that other teachers did it. This watchfulness of conscience brooded likewise over her favorites; that is, her better students, for she knew no other measure. You could tell you were in Miss Gowrie's good graces by the bad-conduct marks she set firmly opposite your name in the school record book. In fact, in all her ways she was a stoic of the Roman mold, recalling that matron cited in Pliny, the terrible Arria, who, to encourage her husband to commit suicide, plunged a dagger into her own breast, drew it out, saying, "It doesn't hurt, Paetus," and handed it to him. 7

Discussion: Content

1. What subject did Miss Gowrie teach? Where did she teach? What was her homeland?
2. Miss Gowrie is dark complexioned. How does McCarthy fancifully account for this fact?
3. What was Miss Gowrie's attitude toward rules? What was the attitude of the other teachers and the vice-principal?
4. What details revealed that Miss Gowrie was a heavy smoker?
5. How does McCarthy develop the claim that Miss Gowrie was "a stoic of the Roman mold"?

Discussion: Form

1. What is McCarthy's attitude toward Miss Gowrie? How can you tell?
2. How many paragraphs are devoted to physical description of Miss Gowrie? What do the remaining paragraphs describe?
3. In paragraph 2 McCarthy devotes a couple of sentences to one particular aspect of Miss Gowrie's mouth. She returns to this feature again in paragraph 3. She seems to be setting us up for a particularly well-turned phrase in paragraph 6. Can you spot it?

Shady Grove, Alabama, July, 1936
James Agee

James Agee (1909–1955) was an American journalist, screenwriter, and novelist. His posthumous novel, *A Death in the Family,* won the Pulitzer Prize in 1958. *Agee on Film* (two volumes, 1958, 1960) is a collection of his film criticism and screenplays. The essay below is taken from *Let Us Now Praise Famous Men* (1941), a documentary,

Narrative-
Descriptive
Writing

with photographs by Walker Evans, of the daily life of tenant farmers in Alabama during 1936.

The graveyard is about fifty by a hundred yards inside a wire fence. There are almost no trees in it: a lemon verbena and a small magnolia; it is all red clay and very few weeds. 1

Out at the front of it across the road there is a cornfield and then a field of cotton and then trees. 2

Most of the headboards are pine, and at the far end of the yard from the church the graves are thinned out and there are many slender and low pine stumps about the height of the headboards. The shadows are all struck sharp lengthwise of the graves, toward the cornfield, by the afternoon sun. There is no one anywhere in sight. It is heavily silent and fragrant and all the leaves are breathing slowly without touching each other. 3

Some of the graves have real headstones, a few of them so large they must be the graves of landowners. One is a thick limestone log erected by the Woodmen of the World. One or two of the others, besides a headpiece, have a flat of stone as large as the whole grave. 4

On one of these there is a china dish on whose cover delicate hands lie crossed, cuffs at their wrists, and the nails distinct. 5

On another a large fluted vase stands full of dead flowers, with an inch of rusty water at the bottom. 6

On others of these stones, as many as a dozen of them, there is something I have never seen before: by some kind of porcelain reproduction, a photograph of the person who is buried there; the last or the best likeness that had been made, in a small-town studio, or at home with a snapshot camera. I remember one well of a fifteen-year-old boy in Sunday pants and a plaid pullover sweater, his hair combed, his cap in his hand, sitting against a piece of farm machinery and grinning. His eyes are squinted against the light and his nose makes a deep shadow down one side of his chin. Somebody's arm, with the sleeve rolled up, is against him; somebody who is almost certainly still alive: they could not cut him entirely out of the picture. Another is a studio portrait, close up, in artificial lighting, of a young woman. She is leaned a little forward, smiling vivaciously, one hand at her cheek. She is not very pretty, but she believed she was; her face is free from strain or fear. She is wearing an evidently new dress, with a mail-order look about it, patterns of beads are sewn over it and have caught the light. Her face is soft with powder and at the wings of her nose lines have been deleted. Her dark blonde hair is newly washed and professionally done up in puffs at the ears which in that time, shortly after the first great war of her century, were called cootie

Section 1: Description

garages. This image of her face is split across and the split has begun to turn brown at its edges.

I think these would be graves of small farmers.

There are others about which there can be no mistake: they are the graves of the poorest of the farmers and of the tenants. Mainly they are the graves with the pine headboards; or without them.

When the grave is still young, it is very sharply distinct, and of a peculiar form. The clay is raised in a long and narrow oval with a sharp ridge, the shape exactly of an inverted boat. A fairly broad board is driven at the head; a narrower one, sometimes only a stob, at the feet. A good many of the headboards have been sawed into the flat simulacrum of an hourglass; in some of these, the top has been roughly rounded off, so that the resemblance is more nearly that of a head and shoulders sunken or risen to the waist in the dirt. On some of these boards names and dates have been written or printed in hesitant letterings, in pencil or in crayon, but most of them appear never to have been touched in this way. The boards at some of the graves have fallen slantwise or down; many graves seem never to have been marked except in their own carefully made shape. These graves are of all sizes between those of giants and of newborn children; and there are a great many, so many they seem shoals of minnows, two feet long or less, lying near one another; and of these smallest graves, very few are marked with any wood at all, and many are already so drawn into the earth that they are scarcely distinguishable. Some of the largest, on the other hand, are of heroic size, seven and eight feet long, and of these more are marked, a few, even, with the smallest and plainest blocks of limestone, and initials, once or twice a full name; but many more of them have never been marked, and many, too, are sunken half down and more and almost entirely into the earth. A great many of these graves, perhaps half to two-thirds of those which are still distinct, have been decorated, not only with shrunken flowers in their cracked vases and with bent targets of blasted flowers, but otherwise as well.

Some have a line of white clamshells planted along their ridge; of others, the rim as well is garlanded with these shells. On one large grave, which is otherwise completely plain, a blown-out electric bulb is screwed into the clay at the exact center. On another, on the slope of clay just in front of the headboard, its feet next the board, is a horseshoe; and at its center a blown bulb is stood upright. On two or three others there are insulators of blue-green glass. On several graves, which I presume to be those of women, there is at the center the prettiest or the oldest and most valued piece of china: on one, a blue glass butter dish whose cover is a setting hen; on another, an

Narrative-
Descriptive
Writing

intricate milk-colored glass basket; on others, ten-cent-store candy dishes and iridescent vases; on one, a pattern of white and colored buttons. On other graves there are small and thick white butter dishes of the sort which are used in lunch-rooms, and by the action of rain these stand free of the grave on slender turrets of clay. On still another grave, laid carefully next the headboard, is a corncob pipe.

On the graves of children there are still these pretty pieces of glass and china, but they begin to diminish in size and they verge into the forms of animals and into homuncular symbols of growth; and there are toys: small autos, locomotives and fire engines of red and blue metal; tea sets for dolls, and tin kettles the size of thimbles; little effigies in rubber and glass and china, of cows, lions, bulldogs, squeaking mice, and the characters of comic strips; and of these I knew, when Louise told me how precious her china dogs were to her and her glass lace dish, where they would go if she were soon drawn down, and of many other things in that home, to whom they would likely be consigned; and of the tea set we gave Clair Bell, I knew in the buying in what daintiness it will a little while adorn her remembrance when the heaviness has sufficiently grown upon her and she had done the last of her dancing: for it will only be by a fortune which cannot be even hoped that she will live much longer; and only by great chance that they can do for her what two parents have done here for their little daughter: not only a tea set, and a Coca-Cola bottle, and a milk bottle, ranged on her short grave, but a stone at the head and a stone at the foot, and in the headstone her six month image as she lies sleeping dead in her white dress, the head sunken delicately forward, deeply and delicately gone, the eyes seamed, as that of a dead bird, and on the rear face of this stone the words:

> We can't have all things to please us,
> Our little Daughter, Joe An, has gone to Jesus.

Discussion: Content

1. Based on their size and number, it appears that the greatest number of graves contain the bodies of members of what age group: adults, teenagers, or babies?
2. Name three unusual items or objects decorating the Shady Grove, Alabama, graves. Have you ever seen graves similarly decorated?
3. The three photographs mentioned picture which persons?
4. How do the grave markers of tenant farmers differ from those of landowners?

Section 1: Description

Discussion: Form

1. In "The White Glove," Paulk is able to describe the glove's owner by concentrating on specific details of the glove and its surroundings. In his description Agee seems to be doing the same thing. What are you able to infer about the area's residents, their lives, their hopes, their pleasures, based on the cemetery description? Be specific. What details support your impressions?
2. Examine the last sentence in paragraph 3. Here Agee attributes to inanimate objects, leaves, an ability they lack — breathing. What is the effect of such a tactic? Does he employ similar methods elsewhere?
3. Notice in paragraph 7 of Agee's essay on the graveyard that he doesn't stop after he describes the basic subjects of the porcelainized photographs, but goes further; why do you suppose he does, and is that good or bad?
4. Returning to the imaginary role of motion picture photographer a moment, analyze what Agee has done in his last paragraph, moving from the general to the particular or specific. What is gained by this move?

Section 2: Narration

We mentioned earlier that narration focuses on action or verbs, but that it must also include description. A moment's thought will convince you of the need for including description. You probably will not portray actions or movements very effectively unless you relate to the reader a description of the people or things participating in those actions.

You have also learned that there are but three ways to describe these participants: by assigning qualities, by mentioning details, and by making comparisons. How do you portray the actions in which the participants engage? The answer is simple, because it is exactly the same: qualities, details, and comparisons.

Qualities

When we examined qualities that expanded images proposed by nouns, we came up with words like *funny, dull, friendly* — in other words, adjectives. Now if we want to enlarge on the idea involved in an action (or a verb), we must turn to adverbs. A great many of these adverbs, particularly those that grammarians call adverbs of manner, refer to qualities — characteristics that attach less general, more concrete meaning to the stated action. Take, for example, the following sentence:

1. Roscoe sneezed.

As it is, the sentence delivers a fact to the reader, but not very clearly. Were we to attach to the sentence any of the possible adverbs of manner that appear in 2, we would have a much clearer picture of the event:

2. Roscoe sneezed violently.
repeatedly.
surreptitiously.
noisily.
wetly.

Again, returning to our earlier look at descriptive writing, we recall that *qualities* merely got things started, pointing a direction for further descriptive development. The same is true for qualities assigned to verbs. In order to see vividly the actions involved in a sentence, we need to amplify with details.

Details

Details associated with actions often involve accompanying circumstances or movements occurring at the same time as the action being described. Let us observe the concrete impression that emerges when we add details to sentence 2 above:

3. *Closing his eyes, placing his index finger under his nose,* Roscoe sneezed violently, *his shoulders hunched up and forward, his knees bent.*

The italicized portions of the sentence supply details which enable the reader to visualize more clearly "what happened." Each detail concentrates on circumstances surrounding the sneeze, with the result that the reader may see the event with greater clarity.

Comparisons

Although less valuable than details, *comparisons* are also helpful in creating an impression, particularly a visual one. For example, in the preceding sentence we might further characterize Roscoe's act of sneezing by including the italicized comparison we see below:

4. Closing his eyes and placing his index finger under his nose, Roscoe sneezed violently, his shoulders hunched up and forward, his knees bent, *his lips emitting a fine geyser of spray.*

Here we have used the metaphor *geyser* to describe one effect of the sneeze. In a similar fashion we could have employed other comparisons involving nouns. We could have used a simile to say the sneeze was *like the report of a rifle;* we could have compared it with a *thunderclap* or a *diesel horn,* either of which would have been helpfully suggestive. On the other hand, we may use verbs or verbals to carry off our comparisons. We might have said that Roscoe's sneeze *thundered,* or we might have added such participle phrases as *exploding abruptly, honking noisily,* or *barking ferociously* to call to mind the sounds of dynamite, geese, or dogs.

Organizing a Narrative

Each sentence, each main verb of a narrative passage advances the narrative, step by step, through time. For this reason, a narrative episode is one of the simplest forms of writing to arrange or organize. The writer merely tells a story, arranging the events in chronological order. The only difficulty involved is the need to include enough descriptive material — qualities, details, and comparisons — so that the reader will experience the actions the writer is relating. To achieve this goal the writer must learn to make each sentence count. Short stories and novels often provide examples of narrative writing at its best. However, narration has practical uses too. For instance, the sportswriter must concisely but correctly relate the key plays of a game or match, the folklorist must accurately recount tales told by informants, and the intelligence agent must report all that happened during the course of a surveillance. Clearly narration plays a vital part in the real world.

Paragraphs:
Narration

Granny's Fall
Richard Wright

On one lazy, hot summer night Granny, my mother, and Aunt Addie were sitting on the front porch, arguing some obscure point of religious doctrine. I sat huddled on the steps, my cheeks resting sullenly in my palms, half listening to what the grownups were saying and half lost in a daydream. Suddenly the dispute evoked an idea in me and, forgetting that I had no right to speak without permission, I piped up and had my say. I must have sounded reekingly blasphemous, for Granny said, "Shut up, you!" and leaned forward promptly to chastise me with one of her casual, back-handed slaps on my mouth. But I had by now become adept at dodging blows and I nimbly ducked my head. She missed me; the force of her blow was so strong that she fell down the steps, headlong, her aged body wedged in a narrow space between the fence and the bottom step. I leaped up. Aunt Addie and my mother screamed and rushed down the steps and tried to pull Granny's body out. But they could not move her. Grandpa was called and he had to tear the fence down to rescue Granny. She was barely conscious. They put her to bed and summoned a doctor.

Discussion Questions

1. This paragraph, taken from Wright's autobiography *Black Boy,* is a first-person narrative; that is, the speaker is telling a story in which he himself is a character. What other pieces of writing that you have examined earlier in this text have employed this first-person technique? How is this example different?

2. What is the effect of the short sentence, "I leaped up," which occurs a little past the midpoint of the paragraph?
3. Wright uses a peculiar figurative comparison when he says that his remark must have "sounded reekingly blasphemous." How exactly is this a comparison? Why is it peculiar, and is it effective?

Morning Ballet
Jane Jacobs

The stretch of Hudson Street where I live is each day the scene of an intricate sidewalk ballet. I make my own first entrance into it a little after eight when I put out the garbage can, surely a prosaic occupation, but I enjoy my part, my little clang, as the droves of junior high school students walk by the center of the stage dropping candy wrappers. (How do they eat so much candy so early in the morning?) While I sweep up the wrappers I watch the other rituals of morning: Mr. Halpert unlocking the laundry's handcart from its mooring to a cellar door, Joe Cornacchia's son-in-law stacking out the empty crates from the delicatessen, the barber bringing out his sidewalk folding chair, Mr. Goldstein arranging the coils of wire which proclaim the hardware store is open, the wife of the tenement's superintendent depositing her chunky three-year-old with a toy mandolin on the stoop, the vantage point from which he is learning the English his mother cannot speak. Now the primary children, heading for St. Luke's, dribble through to the south; the children for St. Veronica's cross, heading to the west, and the children for P.S. 41, heading toward the east. Two new entrances are being made from the wings: well-dressed and even elegant women and men with brief cases emerge from doorways and side streets. Most of these are heading for the bus and subways, but some hover on the curbs, stopping taxis which have miraculously appeared at the right moment, for the taxis are part of a wider morning ritual: having dropped passengers from midtown in the downtown financial district, they are now bringing downtowners up to midtown. Simultaneously, numbers of women in housedresses have emerged and as they crisscross with one another they pause for quick conversations that sound with either laughter or joint indignation, never, it seems, anything between. It is time for me to hurry to work too, and I exchange my ritual farewell with Mr. Lofaro, the short, thick-bodied, white-aproned fruit man who stands outside his doorway a little up the street, his arms folded, his feet planted, looking solid as earth itself. We nod; we each glance quickly up and down the street, then look back to each other and smile. We have done this many a morning for more than ten years, and we both know what it means: All is well.

Discussion Questions

1. In this paragraph it is never clearly stated where Hudson Street is located. Yet there are some clues that suggest its location. What are they?
2. What details suggest the ethnic makeup of the neighborhood?
3. In "Private Eye Calling" the narrator moved and observed stationary objects as he passed them; that was descriptive writing. Here the situation is essentially the opposite. How would you characterize this presentation?
4. What technique does Jacobs use to sustain the notion that what she is describing is like a ballet?

Mating Flight
N. Scott Momaday

They were golden eagles, a male and a female, in their mating flight. They were cavorting, spinning and spiraling on the cold, clear columns of air, and they were beautiful. They swooped and hovered, leaning on the air, and swung close together, feinting and screaming with delight. The female was full-grown, and the span of her broad wings was greater than any man's height. There was a fine flourish to her motion; she was deceptively, incredibly fast, and her pivots and wheels were wide and full-blown. But her great weight was streamlined and perfectly controlled. She carried a rattlesnake; it hung shining from her feet, limp and curving out in the trail of her flight. Suddenly her wings and tail fanned, catching full on the wind, and for an instant she was still, widespread and spectral in the blue, while her mate flared past and away, turning around in the distance to look for her. Then she began to beat upward at an angle from the rim until she was small in the sky, and she let go of the snake. It fell slowly, writhing and rolling, floating out like a bit of silver thread against the wide backdrop of the land. She held still above, buoyed up on the cold current, her crop and hackles gleaming like copper in the sun. The male swerved and sailed. He was younger than she and a little more than half as large. He was quicker, tighter in his moves. He let the carrion drift by; then suddenly he gathered himself and stooped, sliding down in a blur of motion to the strike. He hit the snake in the head, with not the slightest deflection of his course or speed, cracking its long body like a whip. Then he rolled and swung upward in a great pendulum arc, riding out his momentum. At the top of his glide he let go of the snake in turn, but the female did not go for it. Instead she soared out over the plain, nearly out of sight, like a mote receding into the haze of the far mountain. The male followed and Abel watched them go, straining to see, saw them veer once, dip and disappear.

Discussion Questions

1. Many of the actions involved in "Mating Flight" occur simultaneously. How does Momaday manage to portray these actions so clearly and without confusion?
2. Contrast these simultaneous actions with the consecutive actions in "Granny's Fall." How are they different?
3. Read this passage aloud when you are alone. Do not hurry your reading and pause very briefly at the commas, a little longer at the semicolons and periods. You should notice that Momaday's prose has qualities we associate more with poetry; what are some of these?

Eighty-Yard Run
Irwin Shaw

The pass was high and wide and he jumped for it, feeling it slap flatly against his hands, as he shook his hips to throw off the halfback who was diving at him. The center floated by, his hands desperately brushing Darling's knee as Darling picked his feet up high and delicately ran over a blocker and an opposing linesman in a jumble on the ground near the scrimmage line. He had ten yards in the clear and picked up speed, breathing easily, feeling his thigh pads rising and falling against his legs, listening to the sound of cleats behind him, pulling away from them, watching the other backs heading him off toward the sideline, the whole picture, the men closing in on him, the blockers fighting for position, the ground he had to cross, all suddenly clear in his head, for the first time in his life not a meaningless confusion of men, sounds, speed. He smiled a little to himself as he ran, holding the ball lightly in front of him with his two hands, his knees pumping high, his hips twisting in the almost girlish run of a back in a broken field. The first halfback came at him and he fed him his leg, then swung at the last moment, took the shock of the man's shoulder without breaking stride, ran right through him, his cleats biting securely into the turf. There was only the safety man now, coming warily at him, his arms crooked, hands spread. Darling tucked the ball in, spurted at him, driving hard, hurling himself along, all two hundred pounds bunched into controlled attack. He was sure he was going to get past the safety man. Without thought, his arms and legs working beautifully together, he headed right for the safety man, stiff-armed him, feeling blood spurt instantaneously from the man's nose onto his hand, seeing his face go awry, head turned, mouth pulled to one side. He pivoted away, keeping the arm locked, dropping the safety man as he ran easily toward the goal line, with the drumming of cleats diminishing behind him.

Discussion

The following is a student paragraph parodying Shaw's use of syntax. Notice how closely the sentences parallel his usage.

The Ten-Predication Run

The chance was ripe and full when he jumped at it, feeling it take shape with his pen, as he racked his brain to find the decorum which would match a football game. The absolute floated by, its subject and verb desperately describing fragmented action, as Shaw put pen to paper deliberately, once and then twice in one sentence after another in the paragraph. He had two predications in the clear and picked up speed, breathing easily, feeling the participial phrases rising and falling down the page, hearing the fervor of the game around him, gathering momentum from them, watching the series of phrases adding speed to his sentence, the whole paragraph, the nouns closing in on him, the verbs fighting for position, the whole page he had to fill, all suddenly clear in his head, for the first time in his story not a meaningless confusion of prepositions, anticipatory *its*, demonstratives. He smiled a little to himself as he wrote, keeping his objective lightly in front of him with its two elements, his syntax pumping hard, his choice of words harmonizing in an almost perfect synthesis of form and content in a short story. There was only the lowly preposition now, coming warily at him, its ears back, head down. Shaw clicked his ball point, compounded his verbs, writing hard, phrasing himself along, all fifteen participial phrases and eleven absolutes bunched in controlled attack. He was sure he was going to get past the preposition. Without thought, his grammar and semantics working perfectly together, he headed right for the preposition, broke its object, feeling the resounding confirmation of the absolute in his structure, seeing the prep go awry, relationship shattered, object pulled to one side. He voiced actively, keeping the absolute locked, dropping the preposition as he easily used an adverb clause, with the preposition never again stealing the absolute behind his back.

In addition to being fun, exercises like this parody can teach you a great deal about style — the variety of available sentence structures and how to select from among them. Now you try it. Change the subject matter but follow Shaw's sentence patterns. You might begin: "The exam was long and frightening, but he began it . . ." or "The dragon was grim and firebreathing, and he advanced toward it. . . ." See what happens.

Student Work:
Narration

On-the-Job Training

Seeing the obvious mistake from across the warehouse, the gray-haired supervisor walked up to the newest of the crew in hopes of enlightening him in the correct way of doing his job. As his pace slowed, the air of hopelessness enveloping him made him resemble the Saturday matinee sheriff ready for the showdown. Scanning the young man's output with a critic's eye, the old man slowly began to nod his head as he silently scrutinized the new boy's work. Finally, like a father having decided on a course of discipline, he reached out his hand to pat the boy's back. Breaking the silence with his patient voice, the knowledgeable elder commended his junior on his work, while making advice about how to remedy an obvious flaw seem like a mere digression. Having diplomatically resolved this problem, old Sharp Eyes took only a moment to glance at his watch before heading toward me.

Discussion Questions

1. Writers of narrative sentences almost always add additional information to their sentences' main clauses. This additional information will appear in any of three positions: (1) before the main clause (*Rustling the pages noisily,* Martha thumbed through the book); (2) after the main clause (Martha thumbed through the book, *rustling the pages noisily*); (3) between the subject and the predicate of the main clause (Martha, *rustling the pages noisily,* thumbed through the book). Which of these three positions does the writer of "On-the-Job Training" seem to prefer?

2. The additional information set off from the main clause, as described in question 1 above, is usually called a *free modifier* (see Glossary). Compare the use of free modifiers in "On-the-Job Training" and in the immediately preceding professionally written paragraph, "Eighty-Yard Run." Determine how many free modifiers are used by each writer and which position(s) each writer tends to use most.

On the Intermediate Slope

I glanced excitedly over to the rolling mountainsides surrounding me, peering through the large flakes of snow that danced downward toward my face. The trees nearby looked cold and lonesome, their bare, brown branches reaching tautly upward and outward, as if seeking warmth and companionship. Farther up, conical evergreens were bunched together, their outer limbs dipping heavily with the weight of the ever-increasing snow, pure in appearance due to its newness and feathered whiteness. The falling snow forced me to lower my face, and I looked down the slope. Like a giant white blanket it stretched in front of me, wide and soft, patterned with brightly colored figures growing constantly smaller, until they disappeared in the haze. Some of the figures moved quickly away, zigzagging efficiently, bent forward slightly, arms akimbo and poles slanting outward in a "V." Others moved more slowly, as if unsure, falling on occasion, only to rise, reclamp their bindings, and proceed on. Haltingly I sidled over to the starting point, my skis sifting the dry powder so that the wind sent it into twisting snake curls. Gathering my mounting courage, and pulling my thick scarf more tightly around my neck, its woolly fibers warming me, I pushed off down the inviting slope, leaving my doubts behind as a fledgling leaves its nest forever.

Discussion Questions

1. "On the Intermediate Slope" lets us play motion picture photographer again, this time through the eyes of the narrator. When does the focus of attention shift? Is the shift necessary? Is it a good idea?

2. Is the ending of the one-paragraph narrative satisfactory? Why or why not?

The Day's Last Flight

With his arm outstretched, the falconer stands in a field of golden flowers, his shadow cast long and narrow by the setting sun. Rolling hills surround him, and his eyes search the cloudless blue sky, while his brown hair waves in the gentle breeze. With an excited leap a rabbit dashes into the open and then disappears under a bush. Silently it lies there, ears flat, exhausted from the few seconds of horror when it was in the open, hoping it has not revealed its hiding place. But the hope is futile. With eyes which can pick up the slightest movement from mile-high altitudes, the falcon makes a bank turn, folds her wings, and goes into an almost vertical dive. With excitement and wonder at the magnificent sight, the man stands and watches, still motionless. Jess bells tinkle as the falcon gains speed and zeroes in on the rabbit's hiding place. The rabbit makes a frantic leap as the predator's shadow enlarges around it, but to no avail. With talons spread the falcon pounces upon her prey, wings now open, head up. Death comes quickly; the rabbit doesn't suffer long. Uttering chirps of excitement, the falcon stands upright on her prize. The falconer, proud of the bird's performance, now walks slowly to her, picks her up, and attaches the leash. Leaving the valley to darkness and night, the sun has set. The day has been long and exhausting for both bird and man, but the last flight has made it worth the time and effort.

Discussion Questions

1. Even though it is clear that the action of "The Day's Last Flight" started well before the one-paragraph narrative begins, we are not faced with a feeling of incompleteness, but with the opposite feeling. How is that managed?
2. Notice that even though the subject of this little story deals with an unfamiliar sport, there is little or no problem understanding the action. Is there, however, any point at which you wished for clarification or explanation?

Going for the Gold

The 14th of April, 1979, was for me a day of joy, victory, and self-realization. The chanting, cheering, and joyous noise that filled the Nigerian evening that day were the result of an event — a track and field meet — that had been properly scheduled and widely advertised, allowing people from many villages and from many walks of life to converge on Arondizuogu Community Stadium after their day's work. Moreover, their hometown hero was going to bring home the gold medal — the most prized trophy in the competition. 1

I was nervous and tense inside, but my body was physically and mentally wide awake, calm on the outside, like a snake enjoying the sun. At the blast of the starting gun, the crowd on the infield started surging toward my position at the far end of the track where the staggered lines marked the starting points for the final leg of the 400 meters. Jogging in place, I tried one last time to focus on the tape marking the finish line, but before I could make it out, there came out of the near corner of my eye five able-bodied boys, running neck and neck like thoroughbreds. In a split second my signal came — "Go!" 2

As soon as I got a feel of the baton in my hand, I was heading for the tape. In my mind's eye was the newsreel of my idol, Carl Lewis, dashing to victory in Helsinki. That borrowed feeling of triumph invigorated my nerves. I was running for joy. Like the sound of an African talking drum, I could hear very clearly the rhythm of my opponents' steps abusing the track alongside me — then behind me. 3

When I hit the tape, my home crowd went wild. Mama said that I performed like her dad the day he won the village wrestling championship. "It is in the family," she said. 4

Discussion Questions

1. The second sentence in the first paragraph is long and complicated. Does it work well or might it be revised to make it work better?
2. The first paragraph sets the stage for the actions that are to be narrated. But the narrator's actual participation in the race does not begin until paragraph 3. What purpose, then, does the second paragraph serve?
3. What clever tactic does the narrator employ to describe the way he pulls ahead of his opponents?

The Kiss

I couldn't believe it. It was like a dream come true. Finally, after drooling over Tom for all my high school years, he had asked me for a date. All my girlfriends looked starry-eyed at Tom whenever he strutted down the halls between classes, though other guys claimed that Tom was not that great. However, they always kept their girlfriends at a distance from him, and they took disco lessons, hoping to become as impressive as Tom was on the dance floor. With his olive skin, jet black hair, and sparkling blue bedroom eyes, Tom was the idol and heart throb of every girl I knew.

The few lucky girls that had the grand opportunity to go out with Tom said that he was the perfect date. Now I had the chance of a lifetime. To go out with Tom would be heaven, and I was sure it would be a night to remember always.

On Monday I had been failing an advanced math test because of goggling at Tom in the next row when he handed me a note that said, "Are you free Saturday night? I would like to take you out." My eyes still fixed on the paper in shock, I automatically nodded a yes, unconscious that he was there and had seen my mouth drop to the floor.

Later that afternoon when I came back down to the ground and the numbness had gone away, I realized I had a lot of preparing to do for my perfect date. A new fifty-dollar dress, a crash diet, a new haircut, exercises, and a new pair of three-inch heels were all part of my plan to win Tom's heart on Saturday night. Insomnia set in as I paced the floor and counted down the hours until the big event. Saturday morning I woke up with an awful surprise. I had large spots all over my face from not eating right. Dark circles under my swollen eyes proved that I had been the victim of sleepless nights. All day I worked on my horrid face, trying to make it look halfway presentable, and succeeding in the end. I had to wash my hair three times to get the new cut to look right. Stiff and sore from the exercises I had begun that week, I soaked in hot bath water for an hour in hopes that I wouldn't groan every time I had to move. My best jewelry and most expensive perfume were used lavishly. By 4:30 I was ready, sitting in the living room looking out the window, though Tom wasn't to arrive until 6:00. Finally he came driving up in his silver Porsche.

With weak knees I ran to the door and flung it open, ready for my night in paradise. There Tom stood, a Greek god, in straight-legged Levis, a flannel shirt, and Adidas tennis shoes. He looked fantastic, but it was totally embarrassing when I remembered that I was very dressed up. As we started out the door I realized that my new shoes

Narrative-
Descriptive
Writing

made me about an inch taller than Tom, an obvious fact I was sure he would notice. I couldn't remember any of the conversations I had practiced in front of the mirror, and it seemed like eternity before we reached the restaurant, even though it was only about five or six miles. He took me to a German-type tavern where he ordered sauerkraut, hot potato salad, and a large German sausage. Since I was near the point of starvation from my diet, the heavy, hot German food made me not only lose my appetite, but become nauseated as well. However, poking bites into my dry mouth and forcing them down my throat gave me a chance to avoid conversation. When the meal was over, the movie theater was our next stop. Inside, the darkness was pleasant, hiding my blemished face and my over-dressy attire. So far the evening just wasn't going the way I had planned. Then Tom casually put his arm around me and took my hand in his, looking over to give me one of his flirtatious grins. I was floating again, and I still don't remember what movie we saw. On the way home I felt more at ease and relaxed with Tom than ever before. Maybe too relaxed, for as I remember back, I chattered the whole time, not letting him get in a word. 5

When we pulled into my driveway, however, I nervously clammed up. It was almost time for the good-night kiss — the grand finale that I had longed to experience since the day I had first seen Tom. He stopped the car and came around the side to open my door. From my seat I looked up at him as he was romantically gazing down into the car at me. It seemed that he was moving downward as if to kiss me through the window. I was eager to meet his kiss and started to lift my face upward to his. I closed my eyes to receive his kiss, and then my lips pressed against the cold, hard glass — the window had not been rolled down. 6

Totally humiliated when I realized what I had done and that Tom was only intending to open my door, I rushed to the house as quickly as my new three-inch heels could carry me, without looking back to see if the Greek god was following me to the door. 7

Discussion Questions

1. This first-person narrative does not actually begin to unfold until paragraph 3. What function do the first two paragraphs serve?
2. Paragraph 4 is devoted to the preparations for the big date. They are listed in great detail. What effect does this listing have on the reader?

3. Paragraph 5, which narrates the events of the evening, is also slanted so that the writer's anxiety is always in the foreground. How many instances of anxiety are added to the narrative?
4. Comment on the effective use of dashes in the crucial sixth paragraph.
5. Could the narrative have ended effectively with paragraph 6? What is the purpose of the last paragraph?

Essays:
Narration

Nonnie's Day
Mary E. Mebane

Mary E. Mebane (1933–   ) was born in Durham, North Carolina. She attended North Carolina College, received her Ph.D. from the University of North Carolina, and now teaches English at the University of South Carolina. Her writing includes a play, *Take a Sad Song* (1975), and her autobiography, *Mary: An Autobiography* (1981), from which this selection is taken.

Nonnie led a structured, orderly existence. Before six o'clock in the morning, she was up, starting her day. First she turned on WPTF and listened to the news and the weather and the music. Later, when WDNC in Durham hired Norfleet Whitted, the first black announcer in the area, she listened first to one station, then to the other. Some mornings it would be "They Traced Her Little Footprints in the Snow," and other mornings it would be black gospel-singing and rhythm-and-blues. Then she would make a fire in the wood stove and start her breakfast. She prepared some meat — fried liver pudding or fatback, or a streak-of-fat streak-of-lean — and made a hoecake of bread on top of the stove, which she ate with either Karo syrup or homemade blackberry preserves, occasionally with store-bought strawberry preserves, or sometimes with homemade watermelon-rind preserves that she had canned in the summer. Then she would drink her coffee, call me to get up, and leave the house in her blue uniform, blue apron, and blue cap — it would still be dark when she left on winter mornings — and go to catch her ride to the tobacco factory (with Mr. Ralph Baldwin at first, and then, when he retired, with Mr. James Yergan). When Miss Delilah still lived in Wildwood, before she and Mr. Leroy separated, she would come by and call from

67

the road and the two of them would walk together to the end of the road near the highway and wait for Mr. Ralph there.

My job after she left was to see that the fire didn't go out in the wood stove, to see that the pots sitting on the back didn't burn — for in them was our supper, often pinto beans or black-eyed peas or collard greens or turnip salad. Occasionally there was kale or mustard greens or cressy salad. The other pot would have the meat, which most often was neck bones or pig feet or pig ears, and sometimes spareribs. These would cook until it was time for me to go to school; then I would let the fire die down, only to relight it when I came home to let the pots finish cooking.

After Nonnie left, I also had the task of getting Ruf Junior up so that he could get to school on time. This presented no problem to me until Ruf Junior was in high school and started playing basketball. Often he would travel with the team to schools in distant towns, sometimes getting home after midnight, and the next morning he would be tired and sleepy and wouldn't want to get up. I sympathized, but I had my job to do. If I let him oversleep, I knew that Nonnie would fuss when she got home. But on the other hand, no matter how often I called to him, he would murmur sleepily, "All right, all right," then go back to sleep. I solved this problem one bitter-cold winter morning. I jerked all the covers off his bed and ran. I knew that the only place he could get warm again would be in the kitchen. (The only fire was in the wood stove.) The fire was already out, so he'd have to make one. After that, I didn't have such a hard time getting him up.

My mother worked as a cutter, clipping the hard ends off each bundle of tobacco before it was shredded to make cigarettes. At noon she ate the lunch she had brought from home in a brown paper bag: a biscuit with meat in it and a sweet potato or a piece of pie or cake. Some of the women ate in the cafeteria, but in her thirty years at the Liggett and Myers factory, she never once did. She always took her lunch. Then she worked on until closing time, caught her ride back to Wildwood, and started on the evening's activities. First she had supper, which I had finished preparing from the morning. After I got older we sometimes had meat other than what had to be prepared in a "pot." It would be my duty to fry chicken or prepare ham bits and gravy.

After supper, she'd read the Durham *Sun* and see to it that we did the chores if we hadn't done them already: slop the hogs, feed the chickens, get in the wood for the next day. Then we were free. She'd get her blue uniform ready for the next day, then listen to the radio. No later than nine o'clock, she would be in bed. In the morning she would get up, turn on the radio, and start frying some fatback. Another day would have started. 5

Discussion: Content

1. What do you learn about Nonnie from the description of her radio listening habits?
2. What may we infer about Nonnie from her breakfast routine?
3. What do you make of the references to the four people mentioned at the end of paragraph 1? Is there any significance to be attached to the fact that the first two have their complete names mentioned along with their titles while the last two are called by title and first name?
4. What further facts about Nonnie's impoverished state are implied by the facts mentioned in paragraphs 2 and 3?
5. What evidence do you find in the final two paragraphs that Nonnie is doing more than surviving, that she is working and planning for a better life for her children?

Discussion: Form

1. Mebane uses free modifiers less often than Irwin Shaw, but when she does use them, in what position does she most frequently place them — before or after the main clause?
2. Examine paragraphs 2–5 and point out the coherence devices that Mebane uses in each paragraph to show the steady passage of time during Nonnie's day.
3. Other than the thesis statement, which begins the selection, what sentences underscore the cyclical, repetitive nature of Nonnie's existence?

Saved from Sin
Langston Hughes

James Langston Hughes (1902–1967) was one of the best known black American writers of his time, active in virtually every type of writing from newspaper columns to plays to poetry to novels. At his death forty-seven books carried his name as either writer or editor. The story below, taken from his autobiography, *The Big Sea* (1940), recalls an experience from his youth in the Midwest.

I was saved from sin when I was going on thirteen. But not really saved. It happened like this. There was a big revival at my Auntie Reed's church. Every night for weeks there had been much preaching, singing, praying, and shouting, and some very hardened sinners had been brought to Christ, and the membership of the church had grown by leaps and bounds. Then just before the revival ended, they held a special meeting for children, "to bring the young lambs to the fold." My aunt spoke of it for days ahead. That night I was escorted to the front row and placed on the mourners' bench with all the other young sinners who had not yet been brought to Jesus. 1

My aunt told me that when you were saved you saw a light, and something happened to you inside! And Jesus came into your life! And God was with you from then on! She said you could see and hear and feel Jesus in your soul. I believed her. I had heard a great many old people say the same thing and it seemed to me they ought to know. So I sat there calmly in the hot, crowded church, waiting for Jesus to come to me. 2

The preacher preached a wonderful rhythmical sermon, all moans and shouts and lonely cries and dire pictures of hell, and then he sang a song about the ninety and nine safe in the fold, but one little lamb was left out in the cold. Then he said: "Won't you come? Won't you come to Jesus? Young lambs, won't you come?" And he held out his arms to all us young sinners there on the mourners' bench. And the little girls cried. And some of them jumped up and went to Jesus right away. But most of us just sat there. 3

A great many old people came and knelt around us and prayed, old women with jet-black faces and braided hair, old men with work-gnarled hands. And the church sang a song about the lower lights are burning, some poor sinners to be saved. And the whole building rocked with prayer and song. 4

Still I kept waiting to *see* Jesus. 5

Finally all the young people had gone to the altar and were saved, but one boy and me. He was a rounder's son named Westley. Westley and I were surrounded by sisters and deacons praying. It was very hot in the church, and getting late now. Finally Westley said to me in a whisper: "God damn! I'm tired o'sitting here. Let's get up and be saved." So he got and was saved. 6

Then I was left all alone on the mourners' bench. My aunt came and knelt at my knees and cried, while prayers and songs swirled all around me in the little church. The whole congregation prayed for me alone, in a mighty wail of moans and voices. And I kept waiting serenely for Jesus, waiting, waiting — but he didn't come. I wanted to see him, but nothing happened to me. Nothing! I wanted something to happen to me, but nothing happened.

I heard the songs and the minister saying: "Why don't you come? My dear child, why don't you come to Jesus? Jesus is waiting for you. He wants you. Why don't you come? Sister Reed, what is this child's name?"

"Langston," my aunt sobbed.

"Langston, why don't you come? Why don't you come and be saved? Oh, Lamb of God! Why don't you come?"

Now it was really getting late. I began to be ashamed of myself, holding everything up so long. I began to wonder what God thought about Westley, who certainly hadn't seen Jesus either, but who was now sitting proudly on the platform, swinging his knickerbockered legs and grinning down at me, surrounded by deacons and old women on their knees praying. God had not struck Westley dead for taking his name in vain or for lying in the temple. So I decided that maybe to save further trouble, I'd better lie, too, and say that Jesus had come, and get up and be saved.

So I got up.

Suddenly the whole room broke into a sea of shouting, as they saw me rise. Waves of rejoicing swept the place. Women leaped in the air. My aunt threw her arms around me. The minister took me by the hand and led me to the platform.

When things quieted down, in a hushed silence, punctuated by a few ecstatic "Amens," all the new young lambs were blessed in the name of God. Then joyous singing filled the room.

That night, for the last time in my life but one — for I was a big boy twelve years old — I cried. I cried, in bed alone, and couldn't stop. I buried my head under the quilts, but my aunt heard me. She woke up and told my uncle I was crying because the Holy Ghost had come into my life, and because I had seen Jesus. But I was really crying because I couldn't bear to tell her that I had lied, that I had deceived everybody in the church, that I hadn't seen Jesus, and that now I didn't believe there was a Jesus anymore, since he didn't come to help me.

Discussion: Content

1. Read the explanation of the term *irony* in this book's Glossary. How is "Saved from Sin" an ironic title? What is ironic about paragraph 6, especially its final sentence?

2. How many times are the children exhorted to be saved? What different people make these requests?
3. How are Westley's and Langston's actions similar? How are they different?
4. Why exactly does Langston lie? Is it merely because the hour is growing late? What general comment about human behavior is made by his action?

Discussion: Form

1. "Saved from Sin," originally entitled "Salvation" in Hughes' autobiography, is a complete anecdote, with a beginning, a middle, and an end. How do the opening paragraphs and the closing paragraph differ from those that deal with the activities at the revival?
2. How is paragraph 11 like the opening and concluding paragraphs?
3. Why does Hughes make paragraphs 5 and 12 one-liners? What is their effect?

The Death of the Moth
Virginia Woolf

Virginia Woolf (1882–1941) was born in London and educated by her father, Sir Leslie Stephen. At the age of thirty she married Leonard Woolf, and together they started a press, collecting about them a group of writers and artists which came to be known as the Bloomsbury Group. Her novels include *Mrs. Dalloway* (1925), *To the Lighthouse* (1927), *Orlando* (1928), and *The Waves* (1931). Her essays appear in *The Common Reader* (1925), *The Common Reader: Second Series* (1932), *Granite and Rainbow* (1958), and the work from which this essay is taken, *The Death of the Moth and Other Essays* (1942).

Moths that fly by day are not properly to be called moths; they do not excite that pleasant sense of dark autumn nights and ivy-blossom which the commonest yellow-underwing asleep in the shadow of the curtain never fails to rouse in us. They are hybrid creatures, neither gay like butterflies nor sombre like their own species. Nevertheless the present specimen, with his narrow hay-coloured wings, fringed with a tassel of the same colour, seemed to be content with life. It was a pleasant morning, mid-September, mild, benignant, yet with a keener breath than that of the summer months. The plough was already scoring the field opposite the window, and where the share had been, the earth was pressed flat and gleamed with moisture. Such vigour came rolling in from the fields and the down beyond that it was difficult to keep the eyes strictly turned upon the book. The rooks too were keeping one of their annual festivities; soaring round the tree tops until it looked as if a vast net with thousands of black knots in it had been cast up into the air; which, after a few moments sank slowly down upon the trees until every twig seemed to have a knot at the end of it. Then, suddenly, the net would be thrown into the air again in a wider circle this time, with the utmost clamour and vociferation, as though to be thrown into the air and settle slowly down upon the tree tops were a tremendously exciting experience. 1

The same energy which inspired the rooks, the ploughmen, the horses, and even, it seemed, the lean bare-backed downs, sent the moth fluttering from side to side of his square of the window-pane. One could not help watching him. One was, indeed, conscious of a queer feeling of pity for him. The possibilities of pleasure seemed that morning so enormous and so various that to have only a moth's part in life, and a day moth's at that, appeared a hard fate, and his zest in enjoying his meagre opportunities to the full, pathetic. He flew vigorously to one corner of his compartment, and, after waiting there a second, flew across to the other. What remained for him but to fly to a third corner and then to a fourth? That was all he could do, in spite of the size of the downs, the width of the sky, the far-off smoke of houses, and the romantic voice, now and then, of a steamer out at sea. What he could do he did. Watching him, it seemed as if a fibre, very thin but pure, of the enormous energy of the world had been thrust into his frail and diminutive body. As often as he crossed the pane, I could fancy that a thread of vital light became visible. He was little or nothing but life. 2

Yet, because he was so small, and so simple a form of the energy that was rolling in at the open window and driving its way through so many narrow and intricate corridors in my own brain and in those of other human beings, there was something marvellous as well as pathetic about him. It was as if someone had taken a tiny bead of pure life and decking it as lightly as possible with down and feathers, had set it dancing and zigzagging to show us the true nature of life. Thus displayed one could not get over the strangeness of it. One is apt to forget all about life, seeing it humped and bossed and garnished and cumbered so that it has to move with the greatest circumspection and

Section 2:
Narration

dignity. Again, the thought of all that life might have been had he been born in any other shape caused one to view his simple activities with a kind of pity.

After a time, tired by his dancing apparently, he settled on the window ledge in the sun, and, the queer spectacle being at an end, I forgot about him. Then, looking up, my eye was caught by him. He was trying to resume his dancing, but seemed either so stiff or so awkward that he could only flutter to the bottom of the window-pane; and when he tried to fly across it he failed. Being intent on other matters I watched these futile attempts for a time without thinking, unconsciously waiting for him to resume his flight, as one waits for a machine, that has stopped momentarily, to start again without considering the reason of its failure. After perhaps a seventh attempt he slipped from the wooden ledge and fell, fluttering his wings, onto his back on the window sill. The helplessness of his attitude roused me. It flashed upon me that he was in difficulties; he could no longer raise himself; his legs struggled vainly. But, as I stretched out a pencil, meaning to help him to right himself, it came over me that the failure and awkwardness were the approach of death. I laid the pencil down again.

The legs agitated themselves once more. I looked as if for the enemy against which he struggled. I looked out of doors. What had happened there? Presumably it was midday, and work in the fields had stopped. Stillness and quiet had replaced the previous animation. The birds had taken themselves off to feed in the brooks. The horses stood still. Yet the power was there all the same, massed outside, indifferent, impersonal, not attending to anything in particular. Somehow it was opposed to the little hay-coloured moth. It was useless to try to do anything. One could only watch the extraordinary efforts made by those tiny legs against an oncoming doom which could, had it chosen, have submerged an entire city, not merely a city, but masses of human beings; nothing, I knew, had any chance against death. Nevertheless after a pause of exhaustion the legs fluttered again. It was superb this last protest, and so frantic that he succeeded at last in righting himself. One's sympathies, of course, were all on the side of life. Also, when there was nobody to care or to know, this gigantic effort on the part of an insignificant little moth, against a power of such magnitude, to retain what no one else valued or desired to keep, moved one strangely. Again, somehow, one saw life, a pure bead. I lifted the pencil again, useless though I knew it to be. But even as I did so, the unmistakable tokens of death showed themselves. The body relaxed, and instantly grew stiff. The struggle was over. The insignificant little creature now knew death. As I

looked at the dead moth, this minute wayside triumph of so great a
force over so mean an antagonist filled me with wonder. Just as life
had been strange a few minutes before, so death was now as strange.
The moth having righted himself now lay most decently and uncom-
plainingly composed. O yes, he seemed to say, death is stronger than
I am. 5

Discussion: Content

1. What kind of moth is it that attracts Woolf's attention?
2. Woolf contrasts the moth's movements with those of what other nearby things?
3. The moth to Woolf seemed pathetic in its brisk movements. Why?
4. As the moth begins to die, what happens to the moving things outside the window?
5. What heroic act does the moth perform before it dies?

Discussion: Form

1. "The Death of the Moth" is surely more than just the narration of the last moments in the life of an insignificant insect. Look up *symbol* in the Glossary. What might the moth stand for?
2. What does Woolf mean to represent by the scene outside the window?
3. As the moth begins to die and the scene outside changes, does the scene's symbolic value change too?

Look at Your Fish
Samuel H. Scudder

Samuel H. Scudder (1837–1911) was an American naturalist, a graduate of Williams College who then attended Lawrence Scientific School at Harvard, where he came under the influence of Professor Jean Louis R. Agassiz, as reported in the essay below. Professor Agassiz (1807–1873) was Swiss-born, an outstanding European scientist, especially in the field of comparative anatomy, who came to America and from 1848 till his death was a great and famous teacher at Harvard. Beyond his influence on future generations of scientists, such as Scudder, Professor Agassiz was also one of the founders of the National Academy of Sciences.

It was more than fifteen years ago that I entered the laboratory of Professor Agassiz, and told him I had enrolled my name in the Scientific School as a student of natural history. He asked me a few questions about my object in coming, my antecedents generally, the mode in which I afterwards proposed to use the knowledge I might acquire, and, finally, whether I wished to study any special branch. To the latter I replied that, while I wished to be well grounded in all departments of zoology, I purposed to devote myself specially to insects.

"When do you wish to begin?" he asked.

"Now," I replied.

This seemed to please him, and with an energetic "Very well!" he reached from a shelf a huge jar of specimens in yellow alcohol. "Take this fish," he said, "and look at it; we call it a haemulon; by and by I will ask what you have seen."

With that he left me, but in a moment returned with explicit instructions as to the care of the object entrusted to me.

"No man is fit to be a naturalist," said he, "who does not know how to take care of specimens."

I was to keep the fish before me in a tin tray, and occasionally moisten the surface with alcohol from the jar, always taking care to replace the stopper tightly. Those were not the days of ground glass stoppers and elegantly shaped exhibition jars; all the old students will recall the huge neckless glass bottles with their leaky, wax-besmeared corks, half eaten by insects, and begrimed with cellar dust. Entomology was a cleaner science than ichthyology, but the example of the Professor, who had unhesitatingly plunged to the bottom of the jar to produce the fish, was infectious, and though this alcohol had a "very ancient and fishlike smell," I really dared not show any aversion within these sacred precincts, and treated the alcohol as though it were pure water. Still I was conscious of a passing feeling of disappointment, for gazing at a fish did not commend itself to an ardent entomologist. My friends at home, too, were annoyed when they discovered that no amount of eau-de-Cologne would drown the perfume which haunted me like a shadow.

In ten minutes I had seen all that could be seen in that fish, and started in search of the Professor — who had, however, left the Museum; and when I returned, after lingering over some of the odd animals stored in the upper apartment, my specimen was dry all over.

I dashed the fluid over the fish as if to resuscitate the beast from a fainting fit, and looked with anxiety for a return of the normal sloppy appearance. This little excitement over, nothing was to be done but to return to a steadfast gaze at my mute companion. Half an hour passed — an hour — another hour; the fish began to look loathsome. I turned it over and around; looked it in the face — ghastly; from behind, beneath, above, sideways, at a three-quarters' view — just as ghastly. I was in despair; at an early hour I concluded that lunch was necessary; so, with infinite relief, the fish was carefully replaced in the jar, and for an hour I was free.

On my return, I learned that Professor Agassiz had been at the Museum, but had gone, and would not return for several hours. My fellow-students were too busy to be disturbed by continued conversation. Slowly I drew forth that hideous fish, and with a feeling of desperation again looked at it. I might not use a magnifying-glass; instruments of all kinds were interdicted. My two hands, my two eyes, and the fish: it seemed a most limited field. I pushed my finger down its throat to feel how sharp the teeth were. I began to count the scales in the different rows, until I was convinced that that was nonsense. At last a happy thought struck me — I would draw the fish; and now with surprise I began to discover new features in the creature. Just then the Professor returned.

"That is right," said he; "a pencil is one of the best of eyes. I am glad to notice, too, that you keep your specimen wet, and your bottle corked."

With these encouraging words, he added:

"Well, what is it like?"

He listened attentively to my brief rehearsal of the structure of parts whose names were still unknown to me; the fringed gill-arches and movable operculum; the pores of the head, fleshy lips and lidless eyes; the lateral line, the spinous fins and forked tail; the compressed and arched body. When I finished, he waited as if expecting more, and then, with an air of disappointment:

"You have not looked very carefully; why," he continued more earnestly, "you haven't even seen one of the most conspicuous features of the animal, which is as plainly before your eyes as the fish itself; look again, look again!" and he left me to my misery.

I was piqued; I was mortified. Still more of that wretched fish! But now I set myself to my task with a will, and discovered one new thing after another, until I saw how just the Professor's criticism had been. The afternoon passed quickly; and when, towards its close, the Professor inquired:

"Do you see it yet?"

Section 2: Narration

"No, I replied, "I am certain I do not, but I see how little I saw before."

"That is next best," said he, earnestly, "but I won't hear you now; put away your fish and go home; perhaps you will be ready with a better answer in the morning. I will examine you before you look at the fish."

This was disconcerting. Not only must I think of my fish all night, studying, without the object before me, what this unknown but most visible feature might be; but also, without reviewing my discoveries, I must give an exact account of them the next day. I had a bad memory; so I walked home by Charles River in a distracted state, with my two perplexities.

The cordial greeting from the Professor the next morning was reassuring; here was a man who seemed to be quite as anxious as I that I should see for myself what he saw.

"Do you perhaps mean," I asked, "that the fish has symmetrical sides with paired organs?"

His thoroughly pleased "Of course! of course!" repaid the wakeful hours of the previous night. After he had discoursed most happily and enthusiastically — as he always did — upon the importance of this point, I ventured to ask what I should do next.

"Oh, look at your fish!" he said, and left me again to my own devices. In a little more than an hour he returned, and heard my new catalogue.

"That is good, that is good" he repeated; "but that is not all; go on"; and so for three long days he placed that fish before my eyes, forbidding me to look at anything else, or to use any artificial aid. "Look, look, look," was his repeated injunction.

This was the best entomological lesson I ever had — a lesson whose influence has extended to the details of every subsequent study; a legacy the Professor had left to me, as he has left it to many others, of inestimable value, which we could not buy, with which we cannot part.

A year afterward, some of us were amusing ourselves with chalking outlandish beasts on the Museum blackboard. We drew prancing starfishes; frogs in mortal combat; hydra-headed worms; stately crawfishes, standing on their tails, bearing aloft umbrellas; and grotesque fishes with gaping mouths and staring eyes. The Professor came in shortly after, and was as amused as any at our experiments. He looked at the fishes.

"Haemulons, every one of them," he said; "Mr. _____ drew them."

True; and to this day, if I attempt a fish, I can draw nothing but haemulons. 28

The fourth day, a second fish of the same group was placed beside the first, and I was bidden to point out the resemblances and differences between the two; another and another followed, until the entire family lay before me, and a whole legion of jars covered the table and surrounding shelves; the odor had become a pleasant perfume; and even now, the sight of an old, six-inch, worm-eaten cork brings fragrant memories. 29

The whole group of haemulons was thus brought in review; and, whether engaged upon the dissection of the internal organs, the preparation and examination of the bony framework, or the description of the various parts, Agassiz's training in the method of observing facts and their orderly arrangement was ever accompanied by the urgent exhortation not to be content with them. 30

"Facts are stupid things," he would say, "until brought into connection with some general law." 31

At the end of eight months, it was almost with reluctance that I left these friends and turned to insects; but what I had gained by this outside experience has been of greater value than years of later investigation in my favorite groups. 32

Discussion: Content

1. Describe Professor Agassiz's teaching method. Do you know or have you had instructors who used a similar method?
2. What did Professor Agassiz say about a pencil?
3. Why was Scudder's lengthy study of a single fish the best *entomological* lesson he ever had?

Discussion: Form

1. This essay is like those that precede it in this section in that it is a narration, relating a series of events. But in actuality it is more than a narrative, and you as reader soon realize this fact. In what paragraph do you begin to suspect that Scudder is telling the story to illustrate some point rather than just to be entertaining? What is his point? Write a single sentence that states Scudder's thesis in general terms.

2. Like the moth in the preceding essay, Scudder's fish takes on a symbolic value. What does it symbolize?
3. What lesson does Professor Agassiz's method of instruction hold for student writers? Could you profit in a similar way if you were told by an instructor to "look at your paragraph"? What sort or sorts of paragraphs might be the most profitable for close study?

Expository Writing

Exposition is the second major type of prose writing. Its purpose is to inform or instruct, to make the reader understand.

In learning how to write good expository prose, you should become familiar with methods of development as old as Aristotle, who first gave them names. (He called these methods *topoi,* or topics.) They may be thought of as convenient ways of thinking — grooves or channels in which the human mind naturally runs.

The first method of development in expository writing is *illustration by example*. It is very closely related to narration. If the writer wants to explain a principle or confirm an observation, a convenient way is to offer an *example,* to tell a story which illustrates the principle. The writer may offer numerous short examples or may choose to develop several, or a single one, more thoroughly.

The second method of expository development is *classification*. Here the writer examines a topic by dividing it into its constituent elements or classes. That is precisely what we are doing right now — dividing expository writing into seven classes.

Process development, the third method, is related to classification in that it classifies events, arranging them in a step-by-step sequence.

The fourth method is *comparison*. Comparison was mentioned earlier in connection with narrative-descriptive writing, but it is also useful in exposition. In applying this method of development, the writer examines two or more objects, persons, or ideas, determining what characteristics they have, or do not have, in common.

Analogy, the fifth method, is like comparison in that it seeks to explain the unfamiliar by comparing it with the familiar.

The sixth method involves *cause* and *effect*. Confronted with a given situation, such as rising fuel prices, the writer may ask, "Why does the situation exist? What will happen if it persists?" In asking these questions and answering them, the writer can establish a causal chain, a series of causes and effects, which will suggest an appropriate arrangement of ideas for writing.

A seventh method of exposition, *definition,* is most useful when the writer wants to introduce to the reader a new and unfamiliar term or concept. This method of development, most often associated with dictionaries, is frequently used along with other methods to furnish brief explanations of terms. But on occasion it may be employed as the chief organizing device in an essay.

Section 1: Examples

Development by examples is one of the most frequently used methods of exposition, especially when the objective is to present new or unfamiliar information.

Once the new or unfamiliar information has been decided upon, the writer must state the case as briefly as possible. A single sentence is best:

1. Differential equations are a terrifying experience.
2. Ellen Brown is clever as well as attractive.
3. Coach Waters can expect a winning season.
4. Neanderthal man practiced a rudimentary form of democracy.

Each of these statements might well serve as the *topic sentence* for an expository paragraph or as the *thesis statement* for an expository essay. The purpose of such sentences is to state a fact or an opinion about which some readers may know little or nothing and, hence, may want or need to know more. Notice that each statement is abstract; a reader, having read it, probably understands the writer's intentions only vaguely. The reader needs something more, and the writer must supply it. That is where examples come in. A student trying to amaze a hometown friend with the rigors of college life might very easily claim that differential equations are difficult to the point of impossibility. If the friend is unimpressed, the novice mathematician might supply evidence by offering several pages of typical homework, bristling with radicals, integrals, summations, and other mysterious symbols. Then there would surely follow a tale of some length and detail, describing the unreadable textbook, cataloging the hours of frustration spent in preparing that assignment, and ending with a terrifying confrontation with the math professor in class. At this point the hometown friend may not be convinced of the intrinsic difficulty of differential equations, but the hardship they pose for the college friend can hardly be questioned. Information has changed hands, and that, after all, is the aim of exposition — to inform.

Notice that the examples used in the situation just described were of two sorts: short examples delivered in quantity — the homework problems — and the single, more fully developed example — the story surrounding the assignment. In using either type of example you will be on familiar ground because both types depend on the techniques you have already observed in your analysis of description and narration. In supplying brief examples, you will be concentrating chiefly on details; in writing a longer example, you will be telling a story — narrating.

The remainder of the thesis statements mentioned above may be handled in a similar fashion. Where one writes that Ellen is clever and attractive, her charms and graces may be listed for examination, or a particularly exemplary chapter in her life may be retold. Similarly, the claim that Coach Waters can expect a good year may be supported by an enumeration of the team's many strong points: the excellent coaching staff, the number of returning lettermen, their speed and tonnage, the moderate to easy schedule . . ., or the writer may elect to elaborate on the monumental successes of the opening game as a sign of things to come. Finally, a series of cultural traits attributed to Neanderthals may prove to be a good way of confirming their practice of democracy; then again, the reconstruction of a day in the life of a Neanderthal community might well be more useful — and more interesting.

And generating interest is important. Examples, because they are concrete, remove the reader from the dull generality of the thesis statement. Examples bring the reader face to face with real events and real people. They make the experience more real and more interesting. Furthermore, in practical terms, learning to use examples effectively is crucial to your own future success, since development by examples is the most common feature of all serious expository and argumentative writing, both in school and at work. Your instructors and your employers will want you to support your ideas with relevant examples — facts, quotations, statistics, and the like. Failure to provide that support will likely mean your own failure, in one way or another, while providing it should result in success — for your ideas and for you.

Of course, examples will seldom be the only method of development in an essay. Very often they will be mingled with comparisons, definitions, causes and effects, and so on, as we shall see in the following sections.

Paragraphs:
Examples

American Women in Wartime
Margaret Truman

Although American women have never been officially involved in combat, a surprising number of them have distinguished themselves in wartime. Deborah Sampson Gannett disguised herself as a man, enlisted in the Continental Army, and fought in several engagements before her true sex was discovered. Bridget Divers, wife of a Civil War private in the First Michigan Cavalry, often rode with the men on scouting and raiding expeditions. Once, traveling with a wagon train that was attacked by Confederate cavalry, she took command of the poorly armed teamsters and fought off the rebel assault. Jacqueline Cochran ferried planes to the U.S. Eighth Air Force in England during World War II.

Discussion Questions

1. The stark simplicity of this paragraph is striking. It contains the barest, yet most essential, elements of expository writing: (a) a statement in general terms about which the reader is not expected to be knowledgeable — a topic sentence, and (b) specific examples which reduce the general statement to a succession of concrete instances. What is the topic sentence, and how many examples does the paragraph contain?
2. Why do you suppose Truman did not mention such women as Molly Pitcher or Clara Barton as examples of women who distinguished themselves in wartime?

The Actor's Voice
Stanley Kahan

It is obvious that the voice can be an important asset to any actor. One of the famous legends of the theater tells of the wonderful vocal expressiveness of the great Polish actress Helena Modjeska. Once at a dinner party, when asked to perform one of her famous scenes for the assembled guests, the actress complied by giving a very brief monologue. Many onlookers were moved to tears by the gripping effect of Modjeska's eloquence, despite the fact that she performed the "scene" in Polish! After she had finished she was asked which great and touching selection she had chosen to move her audience so deeply. It must have been with a sly wink that she confided that in fact she had recited the Polish alphabet. Such effectiveness was made possible not only by her sense of the dramatic but by a supple and expressive voice, delicately tuned to a great versatility and the needs of every occasion.

Discussion Questions

1. How does the way Kahan uses the example technique differ from the way Margaret Truman employed it in "American Women in Wartime"?
2. The last sentence in this paragraph is not a part of the example used to support the topic sentence. What is its purpose?

Form and Design in Mexico
Stuart Chase

It is impossible for Mexicans to produce the humblest thing without form and design. A donkey wears a load of palm leaves arranged on either flank in great green sunbursts. Merchants hang candles by their wicks to make patterns in both line and color. Market coconuts show white new moon strips above the dark, fibrous mass. Serapes are thrown with just the right line over the shoulders of ragged peons, muffling them to the eyes. Merchants in the market will compose their tomatoes, oranges, red seeds and even peanuts into little geometric piles. Bundles of husks will be tied in a manner suitable for suspension in an artist's studio. To the traveler from the north, used to the treatment of cold, dead produce as cold, dead produce, this is a matter of perpetual wonder and delight.

Discussion Questions

1. This paragraph, taken from Chase's book describing life in Mexico in the 1920's, begins with a topic sentence, followed by how many brief supporting examples?
2. What is the function of the last sentence? Why is *this* a key word in that sentence?
3. Notice that Chase tends to describe each example specifically, using qualities, details, and comparisons to create concrete images. Which examples are most concrete? Least concrete?
4. This widespread concern in Mexico with form and design has what effect on "the traveler from the north" — that is, from the United States — such as Chase? Why?

Beauty
Ralph Waldo Emerson

Beauty is the quality which makes to endure. In a house that I know, I have noticed a block of spermaceti lying about closets and mantelpieces, for twenty years together, simply because the tallow-man gave it the form of a rabbit; and, I suppose, it may continue to be lugged about unchanged for a century. Let an artist scrawl a few lines or figures on the back of a letter, and that scrap of paper is rescued from danger, is put in a portfolio, is framed and glazed, and, in proportion to the beauty of the lines drawn, will be kept for centuries. Burns writes a copy of verses, and sends them to a newspaper, and the human race takes charge of them that they shall not perish.

Discussion Questions

1. The topic sentence in this paragraph is fairly hard to decipher when viewed by itself. After reading the rest of the paragraph,

however, the reader is better able to understand Emerson's statement. How might you restate the initial sentence to make it more readily understandable?
2. Is Emerson's use of example similar to the approach of Stanley Kahan or of Margaret Truman?
3. What additional piece of information can you infer from the way Emerson draws and arranges his examples?

Relativity
Lincoln Barnett

Anyone who has ever ridden on a railroad train knows how rapidly another train flashes by when it is traveling in the opposite direction, and conversely how it may look almost motionless when it is moving in the same direction. A variation of this effect can be very deceptive in an enclosed station like Grand Central Terminal in New York. Once in a while a train gets under way so gently that passengers feel no recoil whatever. Then if they happen to look out the window and see another train slide past on the next track, they have no way of knowing which train is in motion and which is at rest; nor can they tell how fast either one is moving or in what direction. The only way they can judge their situation is by looking out the other side of the car for some fixed body of reference like the station platform or a signal light. Sir Isaac Newton was aware of these tricks of motion, only he thought in terms of ships. He knew that on a calm day at sea a sailor can shave himself or drink soup as comfortably as when his ship is lying motionless in harbor. The water in his basin, the soup in his bowl, will remain unruffled whether the ship is making five knots, fifteen knots, or twenty-five knots. So unless he peers out at the sea it will be impossible for him to know how fast his ship is moving or indeed if it is moving at all. Of course if the sea should get rough or the ship change course abruptly, then he will sense his state of motion. But granted the idealized conditions of a glass-calm sea and a silent ship, nothing that happens below decks — no amount of observation or mechanical experiment performed *inside* the ship — will disclose its velocity through the sea. The physical principle suggested by these considerations was formulated by Newton in 1687. "The motions of bodies included in a given space," he wrote, "are the same among themselves, whether that space is at rest or moves uniformly forward in a straight line." This is known as the

Newtonian or Galilean Relativity Principle. It can also be phrased in more general terms: mechanical laws which are valid in one place are equally valid in any other place which moves uniformly relative to the first.

Discussion Questions

1. What general principle is Barnett explaining? Where does he state that principle?
2. How many examples does Barnett use to illustrate the principle?
3. Can you think of any other examples that illustrate this principle?

Student Work:
Examples

Fear

Fear can be used as a powerful tool. I use fear myself when I need to complete assignments for school. By reminding myself of the dreaded F or the embarrassment of being behind, I can frighten myself into completing my work on time. A foreman can use fear as a tool at work to keep production booming. A worker who needs his job to survive will usually work harder when there is fear of losing it. But the most natural kind of fear is that which nature provides. Adrenalin flows quickly when something unexpected happens, allowing fear to be used as a tool by a sudden burst of energy. I once read of a man who lifted the end of a car, freeing a victim wedged beneath. Through fear the man had become a tool — more effective than the jack, which had failed.

Discussion Questions

1. Does the writer use an extended example or a series of brief examples to develop the topic?
2. In the topic sentence the writer states that fear is like a tool. How is this comparison maintained throughout the remainder of the paragraph; that is, how does the writer remind the reader about this crucial similarity?

A Mother's Feelings

A mother's ambivalent feelings about the growth and development of her children were aptly illustrated in a recent episode of the comic strip *Family Circus*. The situation began with the mother scolding her wayward child for writing on the wall. The crisis, innocently precipitated by the mother angrily admonishing the child to "grow up," was climaxed by the child's tearful reply — an eloquent "I will!" This simple, straightforward response evoked a couple of poignant visions for the mother: her son inevitably transformed into manhood, sporting a moustache; his eventual leave-taking, jauntily waving his hand at her. Feeling the pain of her future loss, Mom's scoldings turn to tears as she lovingly picks up the misbehaving child. For her this moment of holding her child — of keeping him small — is simultaneously eternal and impossible. Still holding him close, she begins to clean up the mess that he created, her tears dropping wistfully onto his back.

Discussion Questions

1. The writer uses the word *ambivalent* in the topic sentence — a word that may puzzle some readers. Does the paragraph successfully define this word so that the reader does not have to look it up? If so, how?
2. Is the topic sentence developed by a single extended example or by a series of short examples?
3. Locate sentences in which a *free modifier* (see Glossary)
   a. precedes the main clause
   b. appears between the subject and predicate of the main clause
   c. follows the main clause.

Beyond Words

Perhaps the most striking example of a nonverbal message was not communicated by a professional actor, but by five-year-old Caroline Kennedy. As the world kept vigil at the graveside for John F. Kennedy, Caroline, brave and quiet, stood beside her mother. The child squinted in the blinding flash as cameras tried to record her mute grief, but she stubbornly defended the dignity of her emotions by pulling her black veil over her face. After a long, tense silence, the Kennedy widow knelt solemnly beside the coffin, crossed herself, and bowed her head sadly against the cold, gray box. Now slipping up beside her mother, Caroline also knelt and bowed her head. People were staring and cameras were flashing, when suddenly the child glanced up, straight at the coffin. Slowly, one tiny, white-gloved hand came forward, hesitated, then slipped beneath the flag draping the coffin. And in that gesture, Caroline Kennedy gave us the eloquent image of a child grappling with the enormous, bewildering finality of death. She shed no tears, uttered not a word; she reached out, somberly, poignantly, a child saying good-bye forever in the only way she knew.

Discussion Questions

1. What is meant here by "nonverbal message"? What are some everyday or familiar examples?
2. What familiar nonverbal messages were conveyed by Mrs. Kennedy? How do Caroline's actions differ?
3. Besides being an extended example in support of the topic sentence (in the first sentence), this paragraph also uses what two familiar writing modes, introduced in earlier sections of this book?

Art Majors Are Different

It seems that most of the art majors at this college enjoy being as different as possible from everyone else on campus. The Art Department has a long-standing reputation for attracting a certain type of person: tie-dyed shirts, peasant blouses, black China shoes, and frizzy uncombed hair are typical traits of many art majors. This is not to say that no other department on campus has students that fit this description, but a tour through the Art Building is sure to turn up more such students than can be found elsewhere.

Being an art major myself, it is easy for me to see why people tend to think we are weirded out. We are encouraged to be different, to take things to extremes, to push things to the limit. Our teachers give us assignments that force us to think creatively and differently, assuring us that the more wrapped up in our projects we become, the better and more creative they will be.

Last year Glenda, a girl from Salem, did a series of drawings of mangled and deformed dolls. She worked on the project all semester, and it is no wonder that before the year was over she had begun to look like a zombie herself. Charlene, a printmaker from Florida, was experimenting with methods of portraying hair texture. Each of her efforts featured subjects with increasingly bushy and extravagant hairdos. And sure enough, Charlene's own hair got wilder and wilder. Stranger still was Jock, who became so engrossed in his attempts to capture facial highlights that he started to wear brown eye shadow and a pale blush.

Even I, who consider myself something of a conservative, have been drawn into the madness. I have been doing a lot of work with color this semester, and I just couldn't resist tinting my hair purple — to express what I have learned by working on my project.

It becomes so easy to live what we are trying so hard to learn that we often get laughed at and talked about, but I have yet to meet a business or accounting major with half the guts and character that art majors have.

Discussion Questions

1. What is the thesis of this essay as it is stated in the opening paragraph? How does the second paragraph serve to reinforce the thesis?
2. Why does the writer use a separate paragraph to present the fourth example in the series that started in paragraph 3?
3. The second paragraph contains a couple of improprieties that you might wish to correct — a dangling modifier and a slang expression. Or is it possible to make a case for the effectiveness of either of these constructions?

Restaurants

"You can't judge a book by its cover," an old cliché that has been around for years, applies not only to books, but also to people, cars, homes, and anything else that might be judged by appearance only. The same is also true for restaurants.

Being a man of nationwide traveling experience, I have realized this on several occasions. Although some good restaurants do look nice, and some bad restaurants do look bad, the opposites are also true. Many times I've gone into a nice-looking place and come out disappointed. I've also gone into terrible-looking places and had fine meals.

An example of the former once happened to me while traveling from Kenosha, Wisconsin, to Barrington, Rhode Island. I'd been riding for several hours, and my stomach was beginning to think that my throat had been cut. I pulled off the highway into the parking lot of "Mom's Home Cooking," a restaurant that looked very nice from the outside. Since my mother's food is excellent, I thought I'd found a good place to eat. But after ordering and being served, I found my hamburger was rare, the tomatoes on it were rotten, and the mustard and ketchup so runny that every time I squeezed it to take a bite, I had mustard and ketchup running down my arms. The french fries were so greasy that I could almost drink them, and the milk shake so hot I needed ice to cool it off. I came out with my stomach wishing that my throat *had* been cut.

The other extreme, a terrible-looking place being good, was proven to me late one night as I was en route from Yuba City, California, to Walla Walla, Washington. I was hitchhiking at the time, and again my stomach was empty. There wasn't much traffic, and rides were slow, but I finally caught one that took me to "The Rat's Nest." Maybe that wasn't the name of the place, but it should have been. When I entered, the man behind the bar told me to sit down, but I immediately noticed that there were no chairs — only a bar on which to prop oneself. I was leery about eating there, but didn't have anything to lose except a few dollars and my good health, so what the heck, I thought. I ordered a buffalo burger, potato logs, and cactus juice and must admit that I enjoyed the best restaurant meal I'd ever put my lip over. Not only did it fill me up, but it also reminded me of my mother's cooking that I had been searching for at "Mom's Home Cooking," back somewhere between Barrington, Rhode Island, and Kenosha, Wisconsin.

The old cliché about books and covers certainly applies to restaurants. Just ask anybody who has eaten at "The Rat's Nest."

Discussion Questions

1. How does the notion of descending levels of generality apply to the student essay "Restaurants"? How many distinct levels do you

find? What methods of transition has the writer used between the levels?
2. There are several clichés in this essay; what are they? What might you substitute for them?

Accelerated Incubation

Scientists often experiment with life — its beginning in particular. Some organisms begin development in an egg, and scientists will try to speed up this process by simulated conditions in order to deduce whether or not any abnormalities or impairments will result. 1

But occurrences such as these need not be made in sparkling laboratories to be effective, nor by professionals in white lab coats to be observed. In fact, they may happen quite by accident! 2

A good friend of mine brought to school a small, pungent evergreen bough off her family's Christmas tree. Firmly attached to one side was a white, slightly papery mass of eggs which she recognized as those of a praying mantis. Realizing their valuable quality of devouring crop-eating insects, she resolved to keep them for a professor she knew who would appreciate them in spring. She placed the bough gingerly on her small, high bookshelf, only a few feet above a none-too-cool heater, thinking they would keep until spring. 3

Now, one factor in the early development of organisms is warmth — coolness induces dormancy, warmth induces growth. Insect eggs wait over winter until the warm spring weather mysteriously triggers a mechanism to incubate the offspring to the hatching stage. The papery clump of eggs resting over the heater underwent accelerated incubation. Perfectly formed, slender, green praying mantises with bulging brown eyes, spindly legs, and folded arms emerged in January instead of May. Jumping upon the shelves, walls, down into the window, crawling swiftly over the desk, stereo, and record albums, these tiny creatures had come under bizarre conditions to give us an "experiment." It was quite by nature's accident, and quite to our surprise. 4

Discussion Questions

1. "Accelerated Incubation" furnishes a clear model of the use of extended example. Notice that the example is really created by the

combination of description and narration. What story from your experience could you substitute in order to support the same thesis statement?
2. How well is this student writer applying the lessons of the section on description? Can you spot qualities, details, and comparisons in the essay?

Section 1:
Examples

Essays:
Examples

Asking the Wrong Questions
James A. Fixx

James Fixx (1932–1984) was born in New York and educated at Indiana University and Oberlin College. During his career he worked and wrote for a number of newspapers and magazines. The selection below is taken from *Saturday Review*. Fixx is well known for his books: *Games for the Superintelligent* (1972), *More Games for the Superintelligent* (1976), *The Complete Book of Running* (1976), *James Fixx's Second Book of Running* (1980), and *Jackpot!* (1982).

A society's young people are extremely sensitive seismographs. They frequently register, for those who trouble to read their message, social attitudes that might otherwise be overlooked or only faintly perceived. Yet those attitudes may be as crucial as any that move the society. Consider two cases in point.

The first occurred in a high school class in short-story writing. The class had been meeting for several weeks when one of the students raised his hand to make an observation. "The thing that's been bothering me from the beginning," he said, "is that this whole short-story business doesn't really amount to anything important. Oh, it may be important to the people who write stories and to a handful of people who read them, but it doesn't do anybody any good. It has no real use." The teacher tried to point out that the value of a work of art is seldom precisely measurable in terms of goods produced, or man-hours saved, or an increase in the Gross National Product. But he came off a poor second with a student who persisted in wanting to weigh an art form on some rigidly utilitarian scale.

The second, somewhat different case occurred at one of the nation's best colleges when another student, after two years on campus, simply decided to leave. The problem was not grades or social difficulties or the atmosphere or the college. The student explained it this way: "I wasn't getting anything out of it. I did my work, got good grades, and had some fun. But I couldn't see how it was doing me any good. It all seemed so irrelevant to the things I really care about." 3

De Tocqueville would have had little difficulty in understanding the student's laments. He noticed, nearly a century and a half ago, that in the American character lay a streak of narrow pragmatism — so narrow, in fact, that many Americans would rather have no ideas at all than have ideas that lack an immediate and obvious value. "Their life," he observed, "is so practical, so confused, so excited, so active, that but little time remains to them for thought." And in our own time the longshoreman-philosopher Eric Hoffer has said: "The superficiality of the American is the result of his hustling. . . . People in a hurry cannot think, cannot grow, nor can they decay. They are preserved in a state of perpetual puerility." 4

Hoffer may have put it harshly, but it is probably true that most Americans are inclined, when they think of value, to think primarily of here-and-now utility. We first build a weapon in the form of an automobile, and only later worry about making it safe enough for a sane man to drive. We first devise systems of automation, and only later begin to think about their human consequences. We first create nuclear bombs, and only later wonder how to keep them from destroying us. One cannot, of course, minimize the achievements produced by this pragmatic bent, but neither can one ignore the confusions it has stirred up. And the two students, probably through no fault of their own, were clearly reflecting those confusions. They were troubled and dissatisfied because they were asking for things that it was not in the nature of a high school course or college curriculum to give. 5

Yet the real problem is not all that simple. It is complicated by an opposite impulse — a pragmatism in reverse that creates its own special confusions. This is the impulse that lets a man sit for hours in front of one of the most ingenious communications devices human wit has ever devised while asking from it nothing but an occasional laugh or psychological jolt. It is the impulse that allows a man to be satisfied with a shabbily made product if only it looks right. And it is the impulse that prompts a man to interest himself in art not for its beauty but for the controversies it provokes. The real problem, therefore, is neither the American's pragmatic bent nor its opposite. The problem is his confusion over which trait is relevant at a given time. Too often, in short, we look for the wrong things; we ask the wrong questions. 6

In his *Anti-intellectualism in American Life,* Richard Hofstadter comments on the response of James Clerk Maxwell, the mathematician and theoretical physicist, to the invention of the telephone. Maxwell spoke of "the disappointment arising from its humble appearance"; he found the telephone intellectually boring because its components were so simple even an amateur could build one. Yet, Hofstadter suggests, in looking at the telephone only as a pure scientist rather than as a historian or sociologist or potential user, Maxwell was unnecessarily restricting the range of his imagination. He was asking the telephone to provide values that it did not have to give, while overlooking the simple miracle in it. 7

Maxwell's reaction and those of the two students are useful cautionary tales, clear symbols of the pitfalls of asking the wrong questions. It's all very well to press on to the moon but it might be well, too, to have some notion of what we'll do when we get there. And it's a valuable thing to read a story, so long as we don't expect it to make us richer or healthier or even necessarily happier. Cultivation of the art of making the right distinctions might produce a more creative, more humanly useful strain of pragmatism. At the same time, it might leave more elbow room for the great undertakings that will never be fully measured against any yardstick of usefulness. 8

Discussion: Content

1. According to Fixx, what is there in the character of Americans that the first two examples in this essay illustrate?
2. How does paragraph 3 serve to reinforce the point made by the first two illustrations?
3. Fixx suggests that the overly pragmatic student in the short-story class was asking the wrong question when he challenged the usefulness of the course. What do you suppose would be the right kind of question for such a student to ask?
4. What question does Fixx imply would have been a more suitable one for Maxwell to ask upon examining the telephone?

Discussion: Form

1. Normally a writer presents the thesis of an essay in the opening paragraph, but Fixx does not. Where does he announce it, and why does he put it there?

2. In paragraph 5 Fixx wants to show the truth of Eric Hoffer's claim that Americans are too frequently interested only in here-and-now utility. How does he do this?
3. In paragraph 6 the notion of another shortcoming in the American character is introduced. What is this shortcoming, and how does Fixx explain it?
4. Why does Fixx mention the mathematician-physicist J. C. Maxwell toward the conclusion of the essay?

Clever Animals
Lewis Thomas

Lewis Thomas (1913–   ) is an American physician and medical researcher who has held various important administrative posts at medical schools and medical research centers. A frequent contributor to medical journals and science periodicals, Dr. Thomas has published four books of essays; the essay that appears below is taken from his most recent work, *Late Night Thoughts on Listening to Mahler's Ninth Symphony* (1983). His other books are *The Lives of a Cell* (1974), winner of the National Book Award; *The Medusa and the Snail* (1979); and *The Youngest Science* (1983).

Scientists who work on animal behavior are occupationally obliged to live chancier lives than most of their colleagues, always at risk of being fooled by the animals they are studying or, worse, fooling themselves. Whether their experiments involve domesticated laboratory animals or wild creatures in the field, there is no end to the surprises that an animal can think up in the presence of an investigator. Sometimes it seems as if animals are genetically programmed to puzzle human beings, especially psychologists. 1

The risks are especially high when the scientist is engaged in training the animal to do something or other and must bank his professional reputation on the integrity of his experimental subject. The most famous case in point is that of Clever Hans, the turn-of-the-century German horse now immortalized in the lexicon of behavioral science by the technical term, the "Clever Hans Error." The horse, owned and trained by Herr von Osten, could not only solve complex arithmetical problems, but even read the instructions on a blackboard and tap out infallibly, with one hoof, the right answer. What is more, he could perform the same computations when total strangers posed

Section 1: Examples

questions to him, with his trainer nowhere nearby. For several years Clever Hans was studied intensively by groups of puzzled scientists and taken seriously as a horse with something very like a human brain, quite possibly even better than human. But finally in 1911, it was discovered by Professor O. Pfungst that Hans was not really doing arithmetic at all; he was simply observing the behavior of the human experimenter. Subtle, unconscious gestures — nods of the head, the holding of breath, the cessation of nodding when the correct count was reached — were accurately read by the horse as cues to stop tapping.

Whenever I read about that phenomenon, usually recounted as the exposure of a sort of unconscious fraud on the part of either the experimenter or the horse or both, I wish Clever Hans would be given more credit than he generally gets. To be sure, the horse couldn't really do arithmetic, but the record shows that he was considerably better at observing human beings and interpreting their behavior than humans are at comprehending horses or, for that matter, other humans.

Cats are a standing rebuke to behavioral scientists wanting to know how the minds of animals work. The mind of a cat is an inscrutable mystery, beyond human reach, the least human of all creatures and at the same time, as any cat owner will attest, the most intelligent. In 1979, a paper was published in *Science* by B. R. Moore and S. Stuttard entitled "Dr. Guthrie and Felis domesticus or: tripping over the cat," a wonderful account of the kind of scientific mischief native to this species. Thirty-five years ago, E. R. Guthrie and G. P. Horton described an experiment in which cats were placed in a glass-fronted puzzle box and trained to find their way out by jostling a slender vertical rod at the front of the box, thereby causing a door to open. What interested these investigators was not so much that the cats could learn to bump into the vertical rod, but that before doing so each animal performed a long ritual of highly sterotyped movements, rubbing their heads and backs against the front of the box, turning in circles, and finally touching the rod. The experiment has ranked as something of a classic in experimental psychology, even raising in some minds the notion of a ceremony of superstition on the part of cats: before the rod will open the door, it is necessary to go through a magical sequence of motions.

Moore and Stuttard repeated the Guthrie experiment, observed the same complex "learning" behavior, but then discovered that it occurred only when a human being was visible to the cat. If no one was in the room with the box, the cat did nothing but take naps. The sight of a human being was all that was needed to launch the animal on the series of sinuous movements, rod or no rod, door or no door. It was not a learned pattern of behavior; it was a cat greeting a person. 5

The French investigator R. Chauvin was once engaged in a field study of the boundaries of ant colonies and enlisted the help of some enthusiastic physicists equipped with radioactive compounds and Geiger counters. The ants of one anthill were labeled and then tracked to learn whether they entered the territory of a neighboring hill. In the middle of the work the physicists suddenly began leaping like ballet dancers, terminating the experiment, while hundreds of ants from both colonies swarmed over their shoes and up inside their pants. To Chauvin's ethological eye it looked like purposeful behavior on both sides. 6

Bees are filled with astonishments, confounding anyone who studies them, producing volumes of anecdotes. A lady of our acquaintance visited her sister, who raised honeybees in northern California. They left their car on a side road, suited up in protective gear, and walked across the fields to have a look at the hives. For reasons unknown, the bees were in a furious mood that afternoon, attacking in platoons, settling on them from all sides. Let us walk away slowly, advised the beekeeper sister, they'll give it up sooner or later. They walked until bee-free, then circled the fields and went back to the car, and found the bees there, waiting for them. 7

There is a new bee anecdote for everyone to wonder about. It was reported from Brazil that male bees of the plant-pollinating euglossine species are addicted to DDT. Houses that had been sprayed for mosquito control in the Amazonas region were promptly invaded by thousands of bees that gathered on the walls, collected the DDT in pouches on their hind legs, and flew off with it. Most of the houses were virtually stripped of DDT during the summer months, and the residents in the area complained bitterly of the noise. There is as yet no explanation for this behavior. They are not harmed by the substance; while a honeybee is quickly killed by as little as six micrograms of DDT, these bees can cart away two thousand micrograms without being discommoded. Possibly the euglossine bees like the taste of DDT or its smell, or maybe they are determined to protect other insect cousins. Nothing about bees, or other animals, seems beyond imagining. 8

Discussion: Content

1. How did the horse Clever Hans actually accomplish his amazing computations?

Section 1: Examples

2. Thomas says that Clever Hans receives less credit than he is due. Why?
3. What behavior on the part of the cats they were observing did experimenters Guthrie and Horton mistake for complex learning behavior?
4. What reasons does Thomas suggest for the behavior of the euglossine bees in collecting DDT?

Discussion: Form

1. What is the thesis that Thomas is asserting in this essay. and where is it found?
2. How many examples does Thomas provide to support his thesis?
3. Is there a conclusion to this essay?

Solve That Problem — With Humor
William D. Ellis

William D. Ellis (1918–   ) is an Ohioan who since combat service in World War II has been a writer of best-selling fiction (*The Bounty Lands,* 1952; *Jonathan Blair, Bounty Lands Lawyer,* 1954) and various nonfiction books, such as *The Cuyahoga* ("Rivers of America" series) (1967) and *Clarke of St. Vith: The Sergeant's General* (1974). Ellis is also a frequent contributor of fiction and nonfiction to major American magazines, the essay below being one such example.

A lot of us lose life's tougher confrontations by mounting a frontal attack — when a touch of humor might well enable us to chalk up a win. Consider the case of a young friend of mine, who hit a traffic jam en route to work shortly after receiving an ultimatum about being late on the job. Although there was a good reason for Sam's chronic tardiness — serious illness at home — he decided that this by-now-familiar excuse wouldn't work any longer. His supervisor was probably already pacing up and down with a dismissal speech rehearsed. 1

He was. Sam entered the office at 9:35. The place was as quiet as a loser's locker room; everyone was hard at work. Sam's supervisor approached him. Suddenly, Sam forced a grin and shoved out his hand. "How do you do!" he said. "I'm Sam Maynard. I'm applying for a job I understand became available just 35 minutes ago. Does the early bird get the worm?"

The room exploded in laughter. The supervisor clamped off a smile and walked back to his office. Sam Maynard had saved his job — with the only tool that could win, a laugh.

Humor is a most effective, yet frequently neglected, means of handling the difficult situations in our lives. It can be used for patching up differences, apologizing, saying "no," criticizing, getting the other fellow to do what you want without his losing face. For some jobs, it's the *only* tool that can succeed. It is a way to discuss subjects so sensitive that serious dialogue may start a riot. For example, many believe that comedians on television are doing more today for racial and religious tolerance than are people in any other forum.

Humor is often the best way to keep a small misunderstanding from escalating into a big deal. Recently a neighbor of mine had a squabble with his wife as she drove him to the airport. Airborne, he felt miserable, and he knew she did, too. Two hours after she returned home, she received a long-distance phone call. "Person-to-person for Mrs. I. A. Pologize," intoned the operator. "That's spelled 'P' as in . . ." In a twinkling, the whole day changed from grim to lovely at both ends of the wire.

An English hostess with a quick wit was giving a formal dinner for eight distinguished guests whom she hoped to enlist in a major charity drive. Austerity was *de rigueur* in England at the time, and she had drafted her children to serve the meal. She knew that anything could happen — and it did, just as her son, with the studied concentration of a tightrope walker, brought in a large roast turkey. He successfully elbowed the swinging dining-room door, but the backswing deplattered the bird onto the dining-room floor.

The boy stood rooted: guests stared at their plates. Moving only her head the hostess smiled at her son, "No harm, Daniel," she said. "Just pick him up and take him back to the kitchen" — she enunciated clearly so he would think about what she was saying — "and bring in the *other* one."

A wink and a one-liner instantly changed the dinner from a red-faced embarrassment to a conspiracy of fun.

The power of humor to dissolve a hostile confrontation often lies in its unspoken promise: "You let me off the hook, my friend, and I'll let you off." The trick is to assign friendly motives to your opponent, to smile just a little — but not too much. Canada's Governor-General Roland Michener, master of the technique, was about to inspect a public school when he was faced with a truculent picket line of striking maintenance personnel. If he backed away from the line, he would seriously diminish his office's image; if he crossed it, he might put the government smack into a hot labor issue.

While he pondered the matter, more strikers gathered across his path. Suddenly, the graying pencil-line mustache on Michener's weathered face stretched a little in Cheshirean complicity. "How very nice of you all to turn out to see me!" he boomed. "Thank you. Shall we go in?" The line parted and, by the time the pickets began to chuckle, the governor-general was striding briskly up the school steps.

Next time you find yourself in an ethnically awkward situation, take a lesson from the diplomatic delegates to Europe's Common Market. In the course of history, nearly every member nation has been invaded or betrayed by at least one of the others, and the Market's harmony must be constantly buttressed. One method is the laugh based on national caricatures. Recently, a new arrival at Market headquarters in Brussels introduced himself as a minister for the Swiss navy. Everybody laughed. The Swiss delegate retorted, "Well, why not? Italy has a minister of finance."

Of course, humor is often more than a laughing matter. In its more potent guises, it has a Trojan-horse nature: no one goes on guard against a gag; we let it in because it looks like a little wooden toy. Once inside, however, it can turn a city to reform, to rebellion, to resistance. Some believe, for instance, that, next to the heroic British RAF, British humor did the most to fend off German takeover in World War II. One sample will suffice: that famous story of the woman who was finally extracted from the rubble of her house during the London blitz. Asked, "Where is your husband?" she brushed brick dust off her head and arms and answered, "Fighting in Libya, the bloody coward!"

Similarly, whenever we Americans start taking ourselves a bit too seriously, a grassroots humor seems to rise and strew banana peels in our path. The movement is usually led by professionals: Mark Twain penlancing the boils of pomposity ("Man was made at the end of the week's work, when God was tired."); Will Rogers deflating our lawmakers ("The oldest boy became a Congressman, and the second son turned out no good, too."); Bill Mauldin needling fatuous officers (One 2nd lieutenant to another, on observing a beautiful sunset: "Is there one for enlisted men, too?"). Such masters of comic deflation restore the balance. They bring us back to ourselves.

When life has us in a tight corner, one of the first questions we might ask is, "Can I solve this with a laugh?" Men with giant responsibilities have frequently used this approach to solve giant problems — often with sweeping effect. As Gen. George C. Marshall, U.S. Army Chief of Staff, labored to prepare this then-unready nation to enter World War II, he met stiff opposition from his commander-in-chief regarding the elements that called for the most bolstering. Marshall felt that what we needed most were highly developed ground forces. President Roosevelt was a Navy man who believed that our principal need was for a powerful navy, plus a large air force. In increasingly tense debates with the President, Marshall pushed his argument so hard that he began to foster ever stronger resistance. Finally, during a particularly hot session, the usually stonefaced Marshall forced a grin. "At least, Mr. President," he said, "you might stop referring to the Navy as '*us*' and the Army as '*them*.' "

Roosevelt studied Marshall over his glasses, then unlipped a great show of teeth and laughter. Shortly thereafter, he made a more objective study of Marshall's recommendations and eventually bought the ground-force concept.

Occasionally, humor goes beyond saving arguments, saving face or saving jobs; it can save life itself. Viktor E. Frankl was a psychiatrist imprisoned in a German concentration camp during World War II. As the shrinking number of surviving prisoners descended to new depths of hell, Frankl and his closest prisoner friend sought desperately for ways to keep from dying. Piled on top of malnutrition, exhaustion and disease, suicidal despair was the big killer in these citadels of degradation.

As a psychiatrist, Frankl knew that humor was one of the soul's best survival weapons, since it can create, if only for moments, aloofness from horror. Therefore, Frankl made a rule that once each day he and his friend must invent and tell an amusing anecdote, specifically about something which could happen after their liberation.

Others were caught up in the contagion of defiant laughter. One starving prisoner forecast that in the future he might be at a prestigious formal dinner, and when the soup was being served, he would shatter protocol by imploring the hostess, "Ladle it from the *bottom!*"

Frankl tells of another prisoner, who nodded toward one of the most depised *capos* — favored prisoners who acted as guards and became as arrogant as the SS men. "Imagine!" he quipped. "I knew him when he was only the president of a bank!"

If humor can be used successfully against such odds, what can't you and I do with it in daily life?

Section 1: Examples

Discussion: Content

1. How does the clever young man whose story is told in paragraphs 1–3 use humor to save being fired for tardiness?
2. Where does Ellis explain in nonhumorous terms exactly why humor is such an effective problem-solving device?
3. What is funny about the Swiss delegate's comment in paragraph 11 that the Swiss should have a naval minister if the Italians have a minister of finance?
4. What rule did the Jewish concentration camp prisoners make about the type of anecdotes that they would invent daily?

Discussion: Form

1. What is Ellis' thesis in this essay, and where exactly does he state it?
2. Which illustration receives the most space? Why do you suppose it does?
3. In an earlier edition of this textbook Ellis' essay was placed in the argumentative section. What justification is there for the editors' decision to move it to this section in expository writing?

The Legs of Insects
Edwin Way Teale

Edwin Way Teale (1899–1980) was among the most active American writers on nature and related subjects for over fifty years, his numerous works on nature winning him several national and regional awards. Teale's books include *Byways to Adventure* (1942), *Insect Life* (1944), *North with the Spring* (1951), *Adventures in Nature* (1955), *Audubon's Wildlife* (1964), *The American Seasons* (1976), and *A Walk Through the Year* (1978). The essay below is part of *The Strange Lives of Familiar Insects* (1962).

An insect walks in a manner that is unique among animals. If you possessed six legs and had to use them in walking, how would you move them? That is the problem which instinct has solved for the infinitely varied hosts of the adult insects.

The six legs are usually moved as a series of tripods, three legs at a time. The front and rear legs on one side, and the middle leg on the other, move in unison. Thus, the insect is always securely planted on the ground. It does not have to use a large number of muscles, as we do, just to maintain an erect posture. In walking, the average adult person employs a motor mechanism that weighs about eighty pounds — sixty pounds of muscles and twenty pounds of bones. Each step we take puts about 300 muscles in action. One hundred and forty-four are employed just to balance our spine and keep us upright. 2

Many insects use their legs in specialized ways. The common water-strider employs its forelegs to capture its prey, its oarlike middle legs to propel itself over the water, and its rear legs to guide it in the manner of a rudder. The legs of a dragonfly are held together to form a basket for scooping victims from the air. They are set so far forward on the insect's body that they are almost useless for walking. A dragonfly clings and climbs but hardly ever tries to walk. The monarch is sometimes called "the four-legged butterfly" because of a peculiarity in its use of its legs. This insect holds its forelegs against its body as a general rule and uses only its middle and rear pairs of legs for walking. Male monarchs have short atrophied legs that are virtually useless. 3

For a cow or horse, cat or dog, legs are used almost exclusively as a means of transportation. Among the insects, however, legs have innumerable other uses. Often they are whole tool kits. The rear legs of the bumblebee and the honeybee contain spine-ringed depressions — baskets for carrying pollen home from the fields. The forelegs of the mole cricket and the seventeen-year cicada nymph are enlarged into digging shovels. The swimming legs of the diving beetles are fringed with hairs to increase their effectiveness as oars. 4

Some insects use the claws on their feet to hang themselves up for a night's sleep. The praying mantis employs its spined forelegs as a trap for catching prey. The water-strider has legs with "snowshoes" formed of hairs that keep it from breaking through the surface film. When not in use, these hairs fold up into a slot in the insect's leg. A few moths have similar masses of hairs that open out into white "powder-puffs" just below the knees on the forelegs as a means of attracting their mates. The legs of no other living creatures have as great variety in form and uses as the legs of the insects. 5

Discussion: Content

Section 1: Examples

1. Describe the way insects commonly use their legs to walk.

2. In paragraph 2 of "The Legs of Insects," Teale compares how insects walk with how humans walk. For which creature is walking a more complicated process, and why?
3. Besides for walking, how else, according to Teale, do insects use their legs?

Discussion: Form

1. Locate the topic sentences in each of the five paragraphs of this essay. Which of the five sentences would serve best as the thesis statement for the whole essay?
2. Teale's strategy clearly is to use many examples to support each of the assertions he makes in his topic sentences. How many examples do you find in each of the last three paragraphs?
3. In paragraph 3, why is the monarch butterfly, as described by Teale, a less effective example than the water-strider and the dragonfly?

I Led the Pigeons to the Flag
William Safire

William Safire (1929–   ), an American journalist and author, is a native of New York City who left Syracuse University before graduation to become a reporter for the New York *Herald Tribune*. After launching a successful career as a radio-TV journalist and producer, he was president of his own public relations firm before joining the administration of President Nixon as a speechwriter, 1969–1973. Since 1973 he has been a syndicated columnist for the New York *Times,* where the essay below first appeared. Two books on the Nixon presidency, *Before the Fall* (1975) and *Full Disclosure* (1977), were best-sellers.

The most saluted man in America is Richard Stans. Legions of schoolchildren place their hands over their hearts to pledge allegiance to the flag, "and to the republic for Richard Stans."

With all due patriotic fervor, the same kids salute "one nation, under guard." Some begin with "I pledge a legion to the flag," others with "I led the pigeons to the flag."

This is not a new phenomenon. When they come to "one nation, indivisible," this generation is as likely to say, "One naked individual" as a previous generation was to murmur, "One nation in a dirigible," or "One nation and a vegetable."

"The Stars Bangled Banger" is a great source for these creative mishearings: "the Donzerly light," "oh, the ramrods we washed," "grapefruit through the night" that our flag was still there.

Then there is the good Mrs. Shirley Murphy of the 23d Psalm: "Shirley, good Mrs. Murphy, shall follow me all the days of my life." (Surely, goodness and mercy would not lead us into Penn Station.)

We all hear the same sounds. But until we are directed by the written word to the intended meaning, we may give free rein to our imagination to invent our own meanings. ("Free rein" has to do with letting horses run; some people are changing the metaphor to government, spelling it "free reign.") Children make sounds fit the sense in their own heads. In "God Bless America," the misheard line "Through the night with a light from a bulb" makes more practical sense than "a light from above." Writes David Thomas of Maine: "In Sunday school I used to sing, 'I will follow Henry Joyce,' part of a hymn. Who Henry Joyce was didn't concern me — I was following him at the top of my lungs. When I learned to read, I found the words were 'I will follow and rejoice.'"

Sometimes that awakening never takes place. "To all intents and purposes," a nice old phrase, is sometimes spoken as — and written as — "for all intensive purposes." With the onset of adulthood, correction should not be taken for granted — or "taken for granite." In the song "Lucy in the Sky with Diamonds" (its title subliminally plugging LSD), the phrase "the girl with kaleidoscope eyes" came across to one grandmother as "the girl with colitis goes by."

What is this mistaken hearing called? In a query in this space recently, I remembered that I had called bandleader Guy Lombardo "Guylum Bardo," and asked for other examples of "false homonyms." That was a slight misnomer; homonyms are words pronounced the same, but with different meanings. Along with the other examples sent in — crooner Victor Moan, actress Sophie Aloran, musician "Big Spider" Beck, pro-football back Frank O'Harris, novelist Gorvey Doll — came instruction from linguists too mentionable to numerate. In each category, childlike translation can lead to semantic change.

The Guylum Bardo syndrome — the simple misdivision of words — is called *metanalysis*. Many of the words we use correctly today are mistaken divisions of the past: a "napron" in Middle English became an "apron" — the "n" slid over to the left; an "ekename" of six centuries ago became a "nickname" — the "n" slid to the right.

In a future century, some of today's metanalyses (for "wrong cuttings") may become accepted English. An exorbitant charge is called "a nominal egg," perhaps committed by a "next-store-neighbor"; some runners, poised at the starting line, hear, "On your market — set — go!" Millions of children consider the letter of the alphabet between "k" and "p" to be "ellemeno." Meteorologists on television who speak of "a patchy fog" do not realize that many creative viewers take that to be "Apache fog," which comes in on little cat feet to scalp the unsettled settler. Affiants seeking official witness go to a land called "Notar Republic," and Danny Boy, hero of the "The Londonderry Air," casts a backward glance at what is often thought of as "The London Derrière." Future historians may wonder why chicken-hearted journalists coveted "the Pullet Surprise."

The "José, can you see?" syndrome — the transmutation of words when they pass through different cultures or languages — is known to linguists as the *Law of Hobson-Jobson*. British soldiers in India heard the Mohammedan cry *"Ya-Hasan, ya-Husain!"* and called it "hobson-jobson." Noel Perrin at Dartmouth College reports that American soldiers in Japan transmuted a popular Japanese song, *"Shi-i-na-na Yaru,"* into *"She Ain't Got No Yo-Yo."* Similarly, *"O Tannenbaum"* is sometimes rendered *"Oh, atom bomb."*

Semantic change can come from *malapropisms,* named after Mrs. Malaprop, a character in "The Rivals," a 1775 play by Richard Sheridan. More people than you suspect read and pronounce "misled" as "mizzled," and the verb "to misle" will one day challenge "to mislead." Others hum what they call "the bronze lullaby," though it must spin Brahms in his grave. One fascinating malapropism is "to hold in escarole," which combines the escrow function with the slang metaphor of money as lettuce.

Folk etymology is the term for the creation of new words by mistake or misunderstanding or mispronunciation. "Tawdry," for example, came from Saint Audrey's, a place where cheap merchandise was sold. In today's language, "harebrained" is often giddily and irresponsibly misspelled "hairbrained," perhaps on the notion that the hair is near the brain.

The slurred "and" is one of the prolific changers of phrases. When "hard and fast" is spoken quickly, it becomes "hard 'n' fast," which sometimes gets transformed to "harden-fast rules." In the same way, the old "whole kit 'n' caboodle" is occasionally written as "kitten caboodle," a good name for a satchel in which to carry a cat. ("Up and atom!" is not a member of this group; it belongs with those Christmas carolers singing "Oh, atom bomb.")

Lest you think that such mistakes can never permanently implant themselves in the language, consider "spit 'n' image." One longtime meaning of "spit" is "perfect likeness" — a child can be the very spit of his father. But some writers have mistaken the first two words in the phrase to mean "spitting," or ejection from the mouth, and prissily added the mistaken "g" to the sound of "spitt'n'." Novelist Paul Theroux entitled a chapter of *Picture Palace* "A Spitting Image." From such a respected writer, one expectorates more.

What all-inclusive term can we use to encompass the changes that our brains make in the intended meaning of what we hear? Linguists suggest "homophone," "unwitting paronomasia" and "agnominatio," but those terms sound like fanciful dirty words to me.

I prefer "mondegreen." This is a word coined in a 1954 *Harper's Magazine* article, "The Death of Lady Mondegreen," by Sylvia Wright, which reported on the doings of "Gladly, the cross-eyed bear" (the way many children hear "Gladly the Cross I'd Bear"), and other soundalikes. Miss Wright recalled a Scottish ballad, "The Bonny Earl of Murray" from Thomas Percy's *Reliques of Ancient English Poetry,* which sounded to her like this:

> Ye Highlands and ye Lowlands,
> Oh, where hae ye been?
> They hae slain the Earl Amurray,
> And Lady Mondegreen.

She envisioned the bonny Earl holding the beautiful Lady Mondegreen's hand, both bleeding profusely, but faithful unto death. "By now," Miss Wright wrote, "several of you more alert readers are jumping up and down in your impatience to interrupt and point out that, according to the poem, after they killed the Earl of Murray, they *laid him on the green.* I know about this, but I won't give in to it. Leaving him to die all alone without even anyone to hold his hand — I won't have it."

Thanks to responsive readers, I have a column on sound defects and a whole closetful of mondegreens. But a nuff is a nuff.

Discussion: Content

1. What is the language problem that Safire discusses in this essay? What do linguists call it? What does Safire prefer to call it, and why?

Section 1: Examples

2. What are the four categories of semantic change that Safire describes? Mention an example from each category.
3. What examples of such changed meaning have you heard? Into what category does each go?

Discussion: Form

1. Why does Safire delay announcing his thesis until paragraph 6?
2. Safire uses many examples, but most are short, often presented in a single sentence. Where is the single truly extended example in his essay? Why do you suppose he placed it there?
3. By placing examples of this semantic change into four categories, Safire is using a rhetorical mode or organizational technique that you will study in a later section of this textbook. Look now at the Table of Contents and at the introduction to Expository Writing (pages 82–83) and try to identify that mode.
4. What effect does Safire create by using so many examples?

Section 2: Classification

Where there is no order, human beings attempt to impose it. We look at the welter of stars in the night sky and see bears, dippers, crabs, and scorpions. We look at a classroom full of students and we automatically begin to arrange them into groups. We classify them by sex, into male and female; by race, into whites, blacks, and Orientals; and by size, into big and little or fat and thin. The campus playboy, ignoring his male classmates, will arrange the coeds into an elaborate hierarchy of desirability. And, no doubt, his female counterpart will devise a similar classification for the males in the class. The instructor, in the meantime, is more than likely making still other classifications, according to dress, attentiveness, or mannerisms. One instructor went so far as to classify students into three groups: those who were above distractions, those who were looking for distractions, and those who *were* distractions. Eventually the instructor will make another sort of classification, arranging students into five groups: those who get A's, those who get B's, and so forth.

Some rhetoricians make a distinction between what they call *classification* and *division*. Classification, they say, is an attempt to bring order out of disorder. Division, on the other hand, creates diversity out of unity. Sometimes the distinction is important; sometimes it is trivial. Suppose we view the roomful of students as a unit; then we may *divide* that class into those who are bright, average, or dull. If, however, we view the roomful of students as separate individuals, we may *classify* each one according to his or her membership in the three groups just named.

To use a less trivial example, the Bible may be *classified* as a religious work. But it is *divided* into the Old and New Testaments.

Put simply, an element *within* a hierarchy — i.e., at neither extreme, top or bottom — may be either classified or divided. We classify an element by looking *up* the hierarchy to determine the next highest class to which it belongs. We divide an element by looking *down* the hierarchy to determine its component elements.

There must be a consistent rationale for setting up the divisions within a classification hierarchy. It would make little sense to divide a class into underachievers, overachievers, and athletes. The rationale here seems to be student achievement, but setting up a category for athletes clearly conflicts with the rationale for division. Athletes may belong to either of these groups — or they may belong to neither. And this last possibility points up another shortcoming of this faulty division: the division should be complete, accounting for all the elements in the group. A class may contain underachievers and overachievers, but it will also surely contain members belonging to neither of these extremes, and these average achievers should also figure in the division. Generally speaking then, every classification must have a consistent rationale, and it must be complete.

The rationale may be thought of as a plan for cutting up or dividing an object. The experienced butcher cuts up a steer according to a preconceived plan and furnishes us with steaks, roasts, and other cuts. The backward farmer who does his own butchering sometimes ends up with a great deal of stew meat. A carefully determined rationale will produce the desired results; a haphazard one will produce, at worst, confused or conflicting results and, at best, only ordinary results.

Ordinary or uninteresting results arise from the writer's choosing a too common rationale. Finding an unusual method of classification is the key. We generally cut up apples in the same way, slicing them longitudinally into quarters or eighths, and we come up with very ordinary slices of apple. However, by cutting the apple latitudinally into round slices, we will have, first of all, unusual slices, and we will discover something we may never have noticed: The seeds in the core are arranged in a star-shaped pattern, a fact concealed by the usual method of slicing. Similarly, a well-chosen rationale will often reveal many aspects of the subject that would otherwise have remained hidden.

In each of the following classification paragraphs and essays you should be able to determine fairly early what is being classified or divided and what rationale is being used. Having done that, you should next ascertain whether the rationale is followed consistently and whether the classification is complete. Then later, when using classification in your own writing — for instance, to organize a paper on personality types for a psychology course or a report on advertising strategies for a marketing course — you will want to be sure you follow a rationale consistently and make your classification complete.

Paragraphs:
Classification

Three Kinds of Book Owners
Mortimer J. Adler

There are three kinds of book owners. The first has all the standard sets and best-sellers — unread, untouched. (This deluded individual owns woodpulp and ink, not books.) The second has a great many books — a few of them read through, most of them dipped into, but all of them as clean and shiny as the day they were bought. (This person would probably like to make books his own, but is restrained by a false respect for their physical appearance.) The third has a few books or many — every one of them dog-eared and dilapidated, shaken and loosened by continual use, marked and scribbled in from front to back. (This man owns books.)

Discussion Questions

1. What is the basis or rationale that Adler uses in classifying book owners?
2. Is the classification complete?
3. What effect does Adler achieve by enclosing three of his sentences in parentheses?

Intellectuals
Seymour Martin Lipset

[Intellectuals] are all those who create, distribute and apply culture — the symbolic world of man, including art, science and religion. Within this group, three different levels can be set out.

There is the hard core who are the creators of culture — authors, artists, philosophers, scholars, editors, some journalists. Second, there are those who distribute what others create — performers of various arts, most teachers, most reporters. Third, and the most peripheral group, are those who apply culture as part of their jobs — professionals such as physicians and lawyers.

Discussion Questions

1. Where does Lipset reveal the basis or rationale for his classification of intellectuals?
2. How does Lipset define culture?
3. Whom does Lipset include among the distributors of culture? Among those who apply it?

The Three New Yorks
E. B. White

There are roughly three New Yorks. There is, first, the New York of the man or woman who was born here, who takes the city for granted and accepts its size and its turbulence as natural and inevitable. Second, there is the New York of the commuter — the city that is devoured by locusts each day and spat out each night. Third, there is a New York of the person who was born somewhere else and came to New York in quest of something. Of these three trembling cities the greatest is the last — the city of final destination, the city that is a goal. It is this third city that accounts for New York's high-strung disposition, its poetical deportment, its dedication to the arts, and its incomparable achievements. Commuters give the city its tidal restlessness, natives give it solidity and continuity, but the settlers give it passion. And whether it is a farmer arriving from Italy to set up a small grocery store in a slum, or a young girl arriving from a small town in Mississippi to escape the indignity of being observed by her neighbors, or a boy arriving from the Corn Belt with a manuscript in his suitcase and a pain in his heart, it makes no difference: each embraces New York with the intense excitement of first love, each absorbs New York with the fresh eyes of an adventurer, each generates heat and light to dwarf the Consolidated Edison Company.

Discussion Questions

1. What single nouns used by White in "The Three New Yorks" best describe the three types of persons who perceive New York's "three trembling cities"?
2. Which of the three groups has the most significant vision of and effect on New York, according to White? How does he use the paragraph's form and organization to emphasize that dominance?
3. What is the Consolidated Edison Company and why does White refer to it?
4. White uses a figurative comparison in the third sentence when he refers to the New York of the commuter as a city "devoured by locusts each day and spat out each night." Why is this comparison, perhaps based on Exodus 10: 12–15 in the Bible, particularly appropriate?

Types of Whales
Rachel Carson

Eventually the whales, as though to divide the sea's food resources among them, became separated into three groups: the plankton-eaters, the fish-eaters, and the squid-eaters. The plankton-eating whales can exist only where there are dense masses of small shrimp or copepods to supply their enormous food requirements. This limits them, except for scattered areas, to arctic and antarctic waters and the high temperate latitudes. Fish-eating whales may find food over a somewhat wider range of ocean, but they are restricted to places where there are enormous populations of schooling fish. The blue water of the tropics and of the open ocean basins offers little to either of these groups. But that immense, square-headed, formidably toothed whale known as the cachalot or sperm whale discovered long ago what men have known for only a short time — that hundreds of fathoms below the almost untenanted surface waters of these regions there is an abundant animal life. The sperm whale has taken these deep waters for his hunting grounds; his quarry is the deep-water population of squids, including the giant squid Architeuthis, which lives pelagically at depths of 1500 feet or more. The head of the sperm whale is often marked with long stripes, which consist of a great number of circular scars made by the suckers of the squid. From this evidence we can imagine the battles that go on, in the darkness of the deep water, between these two huge creatures — the sperm whale with its 70-ton bulk, the squid with a body as long as 30 feet, and writhing, grasping arms extending the total length of the animal to perhaps 50 feet.

Discussion Questions

1. What is Carson's rationale for dividing up the whale population?
2. Is her classification complete? Why do you suppose her discussion of squid-eating whales is more extensive than those of the other two classes?
3. Could Carson possibly have used a different rationale — for example, geographical habitat — for her classification? Would the paragraph have been as effective? Why, or why not?

Student Work:
Classification

Cat Fanciers

All who enter my home can be divided into four types based on their reaction to my cats. Obviously terror-struck, some hold an apparent loathing for felines. Others whose reaction is less severe are still extremely reluctant and cautious, somehow feeling very threatened by the common domestic cat. Some people, reacting with complete indifference, carry on as if there weren't a fat calico rubbing against their ankles or a gray shadow darting behind the chairs. My favorite visitors are the enthusiastic, who immediately begin to relate stories of their cats' antics, jabbering away contentedly while one of my cats picks away at their double-knits.

Discussion Questions

1. The student writer of this paragraph states the rationale for division in the topic sentence. What is it?
2. Is the rationale followed consistently?
3. How many classes of cat fanciers does the writer enumerate, and is there any order or method in their arrangement?

Political Viewpoints

There are three types of political viewpoints: conservative, liberal, and moderate. According to Ambrose Bierce, a conservative is a person "in love with all the evils in the world." He has achieved power and wants to keep it. He thinks that he can do this by putting a freeze on the status quo. Bierce also states that a liberal "wants to change all of the existing evils for a whole new set." He doesn't have any power but desperately wants some. A moderate is a person honestly concerned more with his own problems than with society's. He doesn't want power but finds he must pursue it as a defensive measure. He is rational and balanced rather than paranoid and extremist. I have omitted "radical" because that is not a political viewpoint; it is an emotional disturbance.

Discussion Questions

1. Does the student writer ever explicitly state the rationale for classification? What is it?
2. Is the writer concerned about the completeness of his classification? How can you tell?
3. What is the effect of quoting definitions of conservative and liberal taken from Ambrose Bierce's *The Devil's Dictionary* (see p. 261)?

Popular Diets

I'm not sure which of the five most popular diets to try in order to lose ten pounds. My first choice is to take stimulants — speed, diet pills, or caffeine — to decrease my appetite, causing rapid pulse, insomnia, and restlessness in many dieters. Another choice is a liquid diet — water, fruit juices, or high-protein drinks — which results in excessive coldness, sleepiness, and urination. A third choice is a diet high in nutrients, featuring foods rich in protein and carbohydrates. The lack of variety — eating only eggs, nuts, fish, or potatoes — makes this diet hard to maintain. The vegetarian diet, a meatless regimen, has gained favor in the last few years. This diet is designed for a lifetime of health and not for a quick weight loss. The last and most popular diet, the one that everybody tries to stick to, is the avoidance diet, abstaining from various high-calorie foods and beverages. This diet requires a lot of willpower, especially if you have small children, eat out, or attend many social functions. After reviewing the five most popular courses of action, I think I'll save myself the trouble of failure and take up running.

Discussion Questions

1. The writer mentions five types of diets, but is there a clear-cut basis for the division?
2. In addition to naming each type of diet, what extra information does the writer provide?
3. There is a sixth alternative for weight control that the writer introduces obliquely. What is it?

Waitresses

For most of us, eating out is a very special occasion, one that we want to enjoy to the fullest. While there are a number of things that contribute to the success of a restaurant meal — things like comfort, decor, and of course the food itself — most of us would agree that service is an extremely important consideration. In my observations there are three kinds of waitresses.

The first is the waitress who enhances the meal. For instance, she allows an adequate amount of time before taking the order and engages in friendly and pleasant small talk. Her actions are smooth and graceful as she serves the meal and pours the drinks. She does not interfere with the customers' privacy or disturb their conversation.

The second kind of waitress is the one who detracts from the meal. For example, when she comes to pour the drinks, she spills the wine on your favorite outfit. In an effort to apologize, she continually comes by the table to see if everything is all right, disrupting your conversation and privacy.

The last kind is the waitress who neither enhances the meal nor detracts from it. She simply does her job. To label her this way is not really being critical of her. Sometimes this kind of waitress is to be preferred over the first type because some meals, especially the truly elegant ones, really don't need to be enhanced. On such occasions you don't want to recall any particular aspect of the service — either how pleasant or distracting the waitress might have been. You simply want to remember the meal itself.

Discussion Questions

1. The writer divides waitresses into three types according to what quality?
2. Is the classification a satisfactory one?

3. In this essay there is a shift in the way the writer addresses the reader. Where exactly does it occur?
4. Although this student essay lacks a separate conclusion, the reader has a sense of completeness after reading the whole selection. How is that accomplished?

T-Shirt Inscriptionalia

The sight of people wearing T-shirts with slogans, mottoes, phrases, and pictures on their chests and backs has fascinated me for years. The immense variety of T-shirt inscriptionalia and the obvious lack of research about it has led me to begin a taxonomy of this facet of our society. 1

I have labeled the first category *Scholarly Prestige by Identification,* and it includes all references to schools or colleges or institutions of higher learning. This is perhaps the earliest form of the T-shirt message, but it began not with the lowly T-shirt (it was considered underwear in those early days) but with a sweat shirt. In order to gain scholarly prestige by identification, every incoming freshman bought a sweat shirt with the school's crest and colors just as soon as the bookstore was located, and then wore it and washed it and wore it and washed it until it became properly faded and limp. When the elbows gave way, the sleeves were cut off, but it was proudly worn until its emblem of eminence was no longer discernible. 2

These sweat shirts lost their uniqueness when they began to be produced in all sizes — even infant's — and the whole idea of scholarly prestige was covered with Pablum. Then somebody started printing T-shirts, and nowadays a student can own an entire wardrobe of T-shirts bearing the name of the institution with which identification is desired. This can be expressed any number of ways, such as "Western Carolina University," "Western," "The Cats," "WCU," even "Western Carolina is for Lovers." 3

The next category is *Advertising,* containing the most presuming types of T-shirts, those bearing the names of various products. Although these are nothing more than free commercials, the wearer seems to gain an element of status by association with these products. This category includes not only the most blatant form of advertising, which is simply stating the name of the product, such as "Coors," "Levis," or "Adidas"; but it also comprises the sneaky, snooty practice of using a high-class designer's trademark embroidered prominently yet discreetly. It all started with the Izod alligator and now includes Givenchy's, Pierre Cardin's and Geoffrey Beene's initials, as well as Sears' Winnie-the-Pooh.

A related category also involves advertising, but the product seems to be the person wearing the T-shirt. It embraces such mottoes as "Try me," "WOW," "Dangerous Curves," "Bad Company," and (I'm still blushing at this one) "Red Breast."

Another category is based on *Identification with Personalities,* where we find pictures of Shaun Cassidy, Wonder Woman, Holly Hobbie, Charlie's Angels, the Marshall Tucker Band, Darth Vader, etc. Anybody, really, who is somebody can be depicted. This is a relatively new category, for certainly the likenesses of Babe Ruth or Bing Crosby were never displayed upon someone's chest. Now, however, press agents measure success by how well T-shirts with their clients' pictures sell.

The next classification is one I've labeled *Esoterica.* Some examples are the portrait of Beethoven, "Think Snow," "Frodo Lives," "Ecologize," "Jojoba Saves Whales" (by providing a substitute for whale oil), "Chemists have solutions," and my favorite, "Love a Nurse PRN."

However carefully and comprehensively I have tried to categorize this wealth of trivia, I still find that I have some examples of T-shirt designs which I will necessarily have to lump into a *Miscellaneous* class. Included here are a realistic picture of a splattered tomato, a frog with his feet propped on his desk and a sour look on his face saying, "I'm so happy I could just s____!", "Love is lending a helping hand," "Pigs is beautiful," and "Baby ↓."

The printing of T-shirts goes on relentlessly, and as I continue my avocation of researching and categorizing, my knowledge and understanding of the subject broaden. However, a few weeks ago I saw an inscription that still defies classification, because I cannot, for the life of me, figure out what it means. The T-shirt said, simply, "Moss Stuffers."

Discussion Questions

1. Is there such a word as *inscriptionalia?* What does it mean? How do you know?
2. Can you state a consistent rationale for this classification of T-shirt messages?

3. At one point the writer shows obvious concern for the completeness of the classification. How does the writer preclude the possible charge that the classification is incomplete?
4. The writer of this essay is older than the average freshman, a faculty wife who has returned to college to complete a degree. Are there any clues to the writer's age?
5. Discuss the writer's use of parentheses in this essay.

Essays:
Classification

The Naturalist's What's What
Gerald Durrell

Gerald Durrell (1925–   ) is a world-renowned naturalist. Reared with his brother Lawrence (himself a famous author) on the Greek island of Corfu, he developed an enthusiasm for collecting animals that turned into his vocation. After several collecting expeditions for a London zoo, Durrell began organizing his own expeditions and then founded his own animal refuge, the Jersey Wildlife Preservation Trust and Zoological Garden, located on the island of Jersey, where he devotes his time to writing and to caring for the endangered species housed there. Many of his books have been written in order to subsidize his preserve; among them are *My Family and Other Animals* (1956), *Zoo in My Luggage* (1960), *Stationary Ark* (1975), and with his wife, Lee, *The Amateur Naturalist* (1983), from which this selection is taken.

Despite the bewildering and exhilarating diversity of life we see around us, it is still possible to discern some sort of order and organization in nature. Over the centuries, in their exploration of the living world, naturalists such as Linnaeus have assigned organisms to groups so that the members of each group have something in common with one another — just as, for example, in your class at school everyone is about the same age, or in the yellow pages of the telephone directory the stores are classified together according to what they sell. The study of this grouping and classifying of living organisms is called taxonomy.

[On page 129] you can see one general scheme into which we can fit all living things. This particular version is accepted by most naturalists, although there are several other versions, and opinions differ as to which is the best one. But whichever you prefer, all schemes start with main groups; each main group is divided into

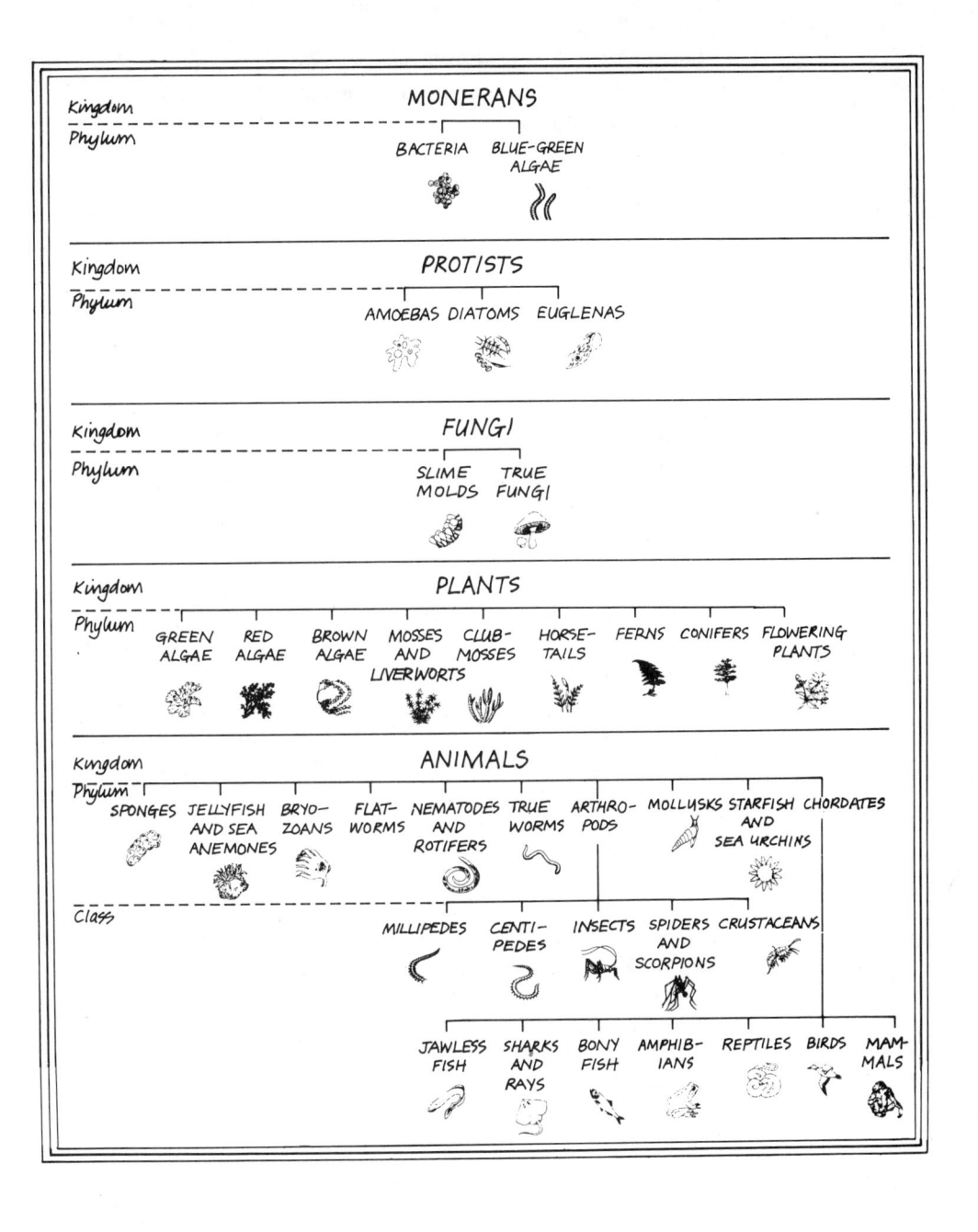

Kingdom	MONERANS								
Phylum	BACTERIA	BLUE-GREEN ALGAE							

Kingdom	PROTISTS								
Phylum	AMOEBAS	DIATOMS	EUGLENAS						

Kingdom	FUNGI								
Phylum	SLIME MOLDS	TRUE FUNGI							

Kingdom	PLANTS								
Phylum	GREEN ALGAE	RED ALGAE	BROWN ALGAE	MOSSES AND LIVERWORTS	CLUB-MOSSES	HORSE-TAILS	FERNS	CONIFERS	FLOWERING PLANTS

Kingdom	ANIMALS								
Phylum	SPONGES	JELLYFISH AND SEA ANEMONES	BRYO-ZOANS	FLAT-WORMS	NEMATODES AND ROTIFERS	TRUE WORMS	ARTHRO-PODS	MOLLUSKS	STARFISH AND SEA URCHINS	CHORDATES
Class							MILLIPEDES, CENTIPEDES, INSECTS, SPIDERS AND SCORPIONS, CRUSTACEANS			JAWLESS FISH, SHARKS AND RAYS, BONY FISH, AMPHIBIANS, REPTILES, BIRDS, MAMMALS

subgroups; each subgroup is broken down still further into smaller subgroups; and so on. You go on doing this until you reach the final group, the species.

Early naturalists used to group organisms as either plants or animals, but the more we know about the natural world the more we see that this old two-kingdom system does not work. The modern system has five kingdoms. Plants are defined as organisms which, by means of *photosynthesis,* trap the energy in sunlight to make their food. To do this they use the green pigment chlorophyll or something very similar. Animals, on the other hand, are things that engulf or ingest (that is, eat) their food. Fungi are regarded as a third kingdom — they "digest" their food externally and then absorb it in liquid form through the body wall. The other two kingdoms both consist of microscopic single-celled creatures. Protists are organisms each of which has a nucleus; they can't be thought of as plants or animals since some can switch from photosynthesis to eating and back again, depending on the conditions. Members of the fifth kingdom, monerans, don't even have a nucleus. They are the simplest organisms and are probably similar to the very early forms of life that evolved on Earth.

The importance of finding out what's what. The grouping and naming of plants and animals is important to a naturalist for two reasons. First, we must remember what Linnaeus was talking about. Classification provides a universal scientific language so that naturalists and biologists all over the world, although perhaps speaking in their own native tongues, can refer to a group or an organism and know that they are all talking about the same one. The second reason is that classification reveals evolution at work and its results. Before the theory of evolution was generally accepted, Linnaeus and other naturalists assigned plants or animals to groups because of structural features they had in common with one another. For example, all the flowering plants were grouped together, as were all the creatures with six legs. But before Darwin, no one had fully realized that the similarity between organisms in a group was due to the fact they were related to each other — that is to say, they were all descended from a common ancestor. It must have been rather like grouping together people called Durrell just because their names were Durrell, and not realizing that they were all related to each other. Darwin's magnificent theory revealed the true reasons for similarities between certain plants or animals — they were related through the process of evolution.

The modern taxonomist continues to classify organisms on the basis of characteristics that they have in common, but he always has to keep in mind that the most important characteristics are those which show how organisms are related to each other. Going back to the analogy with names, it is quite possible that someone else has "invented" the name Durrell quite independently of my family, so that although they have the same name as us they are not related to us. The same thing can happen in nature, and the taxonomist must always be on the lookout for it. Take, for example, bats (which are mammals) and birds. Both have wings, but taxonomists would not consider "having wings" to be a good reason for putting birds and bats in the same group. They know from fossil records that although both bats and birds have a very ancient common ancestor (since mammals and birds descended from the reptiles), their wings developed only *after* the birds and the mammals started their evolution as distinct and separate groups. 5

A good classification scheme helps any naturalist to construct an evolutionary tree, and if you have a book on fossils you can draw one for yourself. The height of the whole tree represents time. Below is a tree that covers the 500 million years since animals with backbones (the vertebrates) first appeared in our fossil records. Each limb and branch coming off the main trunk represents a distinct group evolv-

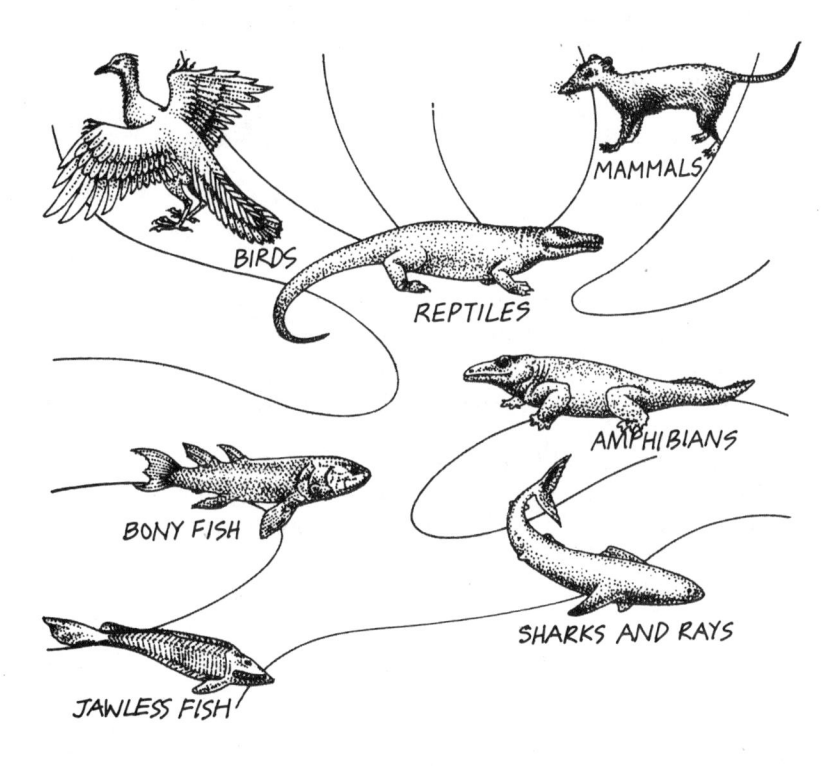

Section 2: Classification

ing, and shows how long ago and from what ancestors it came. You can see for example that the first vertebrate was a strange jawless fish very similar to the lampreys of today. You can also see that the ancestors of today's amphibians (frogs, toads and salamanders) evolved from a fish-like creature about 400 million years ago, and that a primitive amphibian gave rise to the whole range of reptiles about 50 million years later. Reptiles continue today, of course, in the shape of turtles and snakes and lizards. The dinosaurs have long since become extinct. But the reptiles gave rise to the birds and mammals about 180 million years ago. A tree such as this just shows the evolution of the major classes of vertebrates but you can take any branch — let's say the mammals — and study the fine twigs that split off from it. Now one can see the evolution of bats and primates, rodents, carnivores and ungulates. The extreme tips of the twigs on the top of the evolutionary tree represent the species that are living in the world at present. 6

By knowing how to use the system of classification a naturalist can identify the species of a particular organism he is studying; by understanding how the system was set up he can appreciate the organism's place in the evolutionary history of life. For example, some people still think that Darwin said we were descended from chimpanzees. In actual fact, he said nothing of the kind. What he said was that we and the other present-day great apes have a common ape-like ancestor, and from that common ancestor we branched out in different directions — some to become chimpanzees, some to evolve into gorillas, and some to become human beings. 7

Discussion: Content

1. According to Durrell, into how many kingdoms were living organisms originally divided? How many divisions are there today?
2. What name is given to the process of classifying living organisms?
3. Why is this classification process important?
4. How did Darwin account for the similarity of animals or plants that early naturalists placed within a single group?
5. According to Durrell, how long have vertebrates existed?
6. Did Darwin claim that humans were descended from chimpanzees?

Discussion: Form

1. Although Durrell does not state the rationale for the kingdoms into which living organisms are commonly divided, one can readily locate such a basis in paragraph 3. What is it? Does it apply to each of the kingdoms he mentions?
2. In order to illustrate the way pre-Darwinian taxonomists classified organisms, Durrell uses an example. He uses that same example again to show how some similar organisms are not necessarily related. What is that example, and how does it work?
3. Illustrations commonly accompany the written text in magazines, but they may also appear in newspapers and some kinds of books. Durrell uses two visual aids as part of this essay. What features of his subject might have caused him to do so?

Three Kinds of Discipline
John Holt

John Holt (1923–   ), a native of New York, has taught education theory at Harvard University and the University of California at Berkeley. His books include *How Children Fail* (1964), *How Children Learn* (1965), and *Freedom and Beyond* (1972), the work from which this essay is taken.

A child, in growing up, may meet and learn from three different kinds of disciplines. The first and most important is what we might call the Discipline of Nature or of Reality. When he is trying to do something real, if he does the wrong thing or doesn't do the right one, he doesn't get the result he wants. If he doesn't pile one block right on top of another, or tries to build on a slanting surface, his tower falls down. If he hits the wrong key, he hears the wrong note. If he doesn't hit the nail squarely on the head, it bends, and he has to pull it out and start with another. If he doesn't measure properly what he is trying to build, it won't open, close, fit, stand up, fly, float, whistle, or do whatever he wants it to do. If he closes his eyes when he swings, he doesn't hit the ball. A child meets this kind of discipline every time he tries to *do* something, which is why it is so important in school to give children more chances to do things, instead of just reading or listening to someone talk (or pretending to). This discipline is a great teacher. The learner never has to wait long for his answer; it usually comes quickly, often instantly. Also it is clear, and very often points toward the needed correction; from what happened he can not only see that what he did was wrong, but also why, and what he needs to do instead. Finally, and most important, the giver of the answer, call it Nature, is impersonal, impartial, and indifferent. She does not give opinions, or make judgments; she cannot be wheedled, bullied, or fooled; she does not get angry or disappointed; she does not praise or blame; she does not remember past failures or hold grudges; with her one always gets a fresh start, this time is the one that counts.

The next discipline we might call the Discipline of Culture, of Society, of What People Really Do. Man is a social, a cultural animal. Children sense around them this culture, this network of agreements, customs, habits, and rules binding the adults together. They want to understand it and be a part of it. They watch very carefully what people around them are doing and want to do the same. They want to do right, unless they become convinced they can't do right. Thus children rarely misbehave seriously in church, but sit as quietly as they can. The example of all those grownups is contagious. Some mysterious ritual is going on, and children, who like rituals, want to be part of it. In the same way, the little children that I see at concerts or operas, though they may fidget a little, or perhaps take a nap now and then, rarely make any disturbance. With all those grownups sitting there, neither moving nor talking, it is the most natural thing in the world to imitate them. Children who live among adults who are habitually courteous to each other, and to them, will soon learn to be courteous. Children who live surrounded by people who speak a certain way will speak that way, however much we may try to tell them that speaking that way is bad or wrong.

The third discipline is the one most people mean when they speak of discipline — the Discipline of Superior Force, of sergeant to private, of "you do what I tell you or I'll make you wish you had." There is bound to be some of this in a child's life. Living as we do surrounded by things that can hurt children, or that children can hurt, we cannot avoid it. We can't afford to let a small child find out from experience the danger of playing in a busy street, or of fooling with the pots on the top of a stove, or of eating up the pills in the medicine cabinet. So, along with other precautions, we say to him, "Don't play in the street, or touch things on the stove, or go into the medicine cabinet, or I'll punish you." Between him and the danger too great for him to imagine we put a lesser danger, but one he can imagine and maybe therefore want to avoid. He can have no idea of what it would be like to be hit by a car, but he can imagine being shouted at, or spanked, or sent to his room. He avoids these substitutes for the greater danger until he can understand it and avoid it for its own sake. But we ought to use this discipline only when it is necessary to protect the life, health, safety, or well-being of people or other living creatures, or to prevent destruction of things that people care about. We ought not to assume too long, as we usually do, that a child cannot understand the real nature of the danger from which we want to protect him. The sooner he avoids the danger, not to escape our punishment, but as a matter of good sense, the better. He can learn that faster than we think. In Mexico, for example, where people drive their cars with a good deal of spirit, I saw many children no older than five or four walking unattended on the streets. They understood about cars, they knew what to do. A child whose life is full of the threat and fear of punishment is locked into babyhood. There is no way for him to grow up, to learn to take responsibility for his life and acts. Most important of all, we should not assume that having to yield to the threat of our superior force is good for the child's character. It is never good for *anyone's* character. To bow to superior force makes us feel impotent and cowardly for not having had the strength or courage to resist. Worse, it makes us resentful and vengeful. We can hardly wait to make someone pay for our humiliation, yield to us as we were once made to yield. No, if we cannot always avoid using the Discipline of Superior Force, we should at least use it as seldom as we can.   3

There are places where all three disciplines overlap. Any very demanding human activity combines in it the disciplines of Superior Force, of Culture, and of Nature. The novice will be told, "Do it this way, never mind asking why, just do it that way, that is the way we always do it." But it probably *is* just the way they always do it, and usually for the very good reason that it is a way that has been found to work. Think, for example, of ballet training. The student in a class is told to do this exercise, or that; to stand so; to do this or that with his head, arms, shoulders, abdomen, hips, legs, feet. He is constantly corrected. There is no argument. But behind these seemingly autocratic demands by the teacher lie many decades of custom and tradition, and behind that, the necessities of dancing itself. You cannot make the moves of classical ballet unless over many years you have acquired, and renewed every day, the needed strength and suppleness in scores of muscles and joints. Nor can you do the difficult motions, making them look easy, unless you have learned hundreds of easier ones first. Dance teachers may not always agree on all the details of teaching these strengths and skills. But no novice could learn them all by himself. You could not go for a night or two to watch the ballet and then, without any other knowledge at all, teach yourself how to do it. In the same way, you would be unlikely to learn any complicated and difficult human activity without drawing heavily on the experience of those who know it better. But the point is that the authority of these experts or teachers stems from, grows out of their greater competence and experience, the fact that what they do *works,* not the fact that they happen to be the teacher and as such have the power to kick a student out of class. And the further point is that children are always and everywhere attracted to that competence, and ready and eager to submit themselves to a discipline that grows out of it. We hear constantly that children will never do anything unless compelled to by bribes or threats. But in their private lives, or in extracurricular activities in school, in sports, music, drama, art, running a newspaper, and so on, they often submit themselves willingly and wholeheartedly to very intense disciplines, simply because they want to learn to do a given thing well. Our Little-Napoleon football coaches, of whom we have too many and hear far too much, blind us to the fact that millions of children work hard every year getting better at sports and games without coaches barking and yelling at them. 4

Discussion: Content

1. Name the three kinds of discipline that Holt describes, and give an example of each.
2. Why, according to Holt, do most children behave well in church?
3. Which of the three disciplines that Holt discusses most closely resembles the discipline most people think of when they hear the word?
4. Holt asserts that in most situations all three types of discipline are blended together. He offers an example to illustrate that point. What is the example? Show how it provides a blend of the three disciplines.
5. Holt suggests that modern education often fails because teachers do not make sufficient use of which of the disciplines?

Discussion: Form

1. What consistent rationale guides Holt in his division of discipline into three types?

2. Is the classification complete? What about discipline that comes from God or religion? What about self-discipline?
3. After making his classification, how does Holt substantiate it?
4. Holt's essay ends quite abruptly with criticism of Little-Napoleon football coaches. Compose an effective concluding paragraph for the essay.

The Duration of Human Relationships
Alvin Toffler

Alvin Toffler (1928–   ) is an American journalist who has popularized futurology or speculative sociology in such books as *The Futurists* (1972), *Learning for Tomorrow* (1973), *The Third Wave* (1980), and, most notably, *Future Shock* (1970), which has sold over seven million copies in over fifty countries. The essay below, which examines one aspect of the changing pace of modern life, is from that book.

Sociologists like Wirth have referred in passing to the transitory nature of human ties in urban society. But they have made no systematic effort to relate the shorter duration of human ties to shorter durations in other kinds of relationships. Nor have they attempted to document the progressive decline in these durations. Until we analyze the temporal character of human bonds, we will completely misunderstand the move toward super-industrialism.

For one thing, the decline in the *average* duration of human relationships is a likely corollary of the increase in the number of such relationships. The average urban individual today probably comes into contact with more people in a week than the feudal villager did in a year, perhaps even a lifetime. The villager's ties with other people no doubt included some transient relationships, but most of the people he knew were the same throughout his life. The urban man may have a core group of people with whom his interactions are sustained over long periods of time, but he also interacts with hundreds, perhaps thousands of people whom he may see only once or twice and who then vanish into anonymity.

All of us approach human relationships, as we approach other kinds of relationships, with a set of built-in durational expectancies. We expect that certain kinds of relationships will endure longer than others. It is, in fact, possible to classify relationships with other people in terms of their expected duration. These vary, of course, from culture to culture and from person to person. Nevertheless, throughout wide sectors of the population of the advanced technological societies something like the following order is typical:

Long-duration relationships. We expect ties with our immediate family, and to a lesser extent with other kin, to extend throughout the lifetimes of the people involved. This expectation is by no means always fulfilled, as rising divorce rates and family break-ups indicate. Nevertheless, we still theoretically marry "until death do us part" and the social ideal is a lifetime relationship. Whether this is a proper or realistic expectation in a society of high transience is debatable. The fact remains, however, that family links are expected to be long term, if not lifelong, and considerable guilt attaches to the person who breaks off such a relationship.

Medium-duration relationships. Four classes of relationships fall within this category. Roughly in order for descending durational expectancies, these are relationships with friends, neighbors, job associates, and co-members of churches, clubs and other voluntary organizations.

Friendships are traditionally supposed to survive almost, if not quite, as long as family ties. The culture places high value on "old friends" and a certain amount of blame attaches to dropping a friendship. One type of friendship relationship, however, acquaintanceship, is recognized as less durable.

Neighbor relationships are no longer regarded as long-term commitments — the rate of geographical turnover is too high. They are expected to last as long as the individual remains in a single location, an interval that is growing shorter and shorter on average. Breaking off with a neighbor may involve other difficulties, but it carries no great burden of guilt.

On-the-job relationships frequently overlap friendships, and, less often, neighbor relationships. Traditionally, particularly among white-collar, professional and technical people, job relationships were supposed to last a relatively long time. This expectation, however, is also changing rapidly, as we shall see.

Co-membership relationships — links with people in church or civic organizations, political parties and the like — sometimes flower into friendship, but until that happens such individual associations are regarded as more perishable than either friendships, ties with neighbors or fellow workers.

Short-duration relationships. Most, though not all, service relationships fall into this category. These involve sales clerks, delivery people, gas station attendants, milkmen, barbers, hairdressers, etc. The turnover among these is relatively rapid, and little or no shame attaches to the person who terminates such a relationship. Exceptions to the service pattern are professionals such as physicians, lawyers and accountants, with whom relationships are expected to be somewhat more enduring.

This categorization is hardly airtight. Most of us can cite some "service" relationship that has lasted longer than some friendship, job or neighbor relationship. Moreover, most of us can cite a number of quite long-lasting relationships in our own lives — perhaps we have been going to the same doctor for years or have maintained extremely close ties with a college friend. Such cases are hardly unusual, but they are relatively few in number in our lives. They are like long-stemmed flowers towering above a field of grass in which each blade represents a short-term relationship, a transient contact. It is the very durability of these ties that makes them noticeable. Such exceptions do not invalidate the rule. They do not change the key that, across the board, the *average* interpersonal relationship in our life is shorter and shorter in duration.

Discussion: Content

1. What comment does Toffler make about the average length of human relationships?
2. Did the residents of feudal villages have more or fewer human relationships than modern man?
3. What examples does Toffler cite for each of his divisions?
4. Toffler admits that there may be exceptions to his classification, but he likens them to what?

Discussion: Form

1. Alvin Toffler divides human relationships according to their duration, an interesting and fairly unusual rationale, particularly when we consider the ways in which we most frequently think of our relationships with others: professional, romantic, academic, casual, etc. How many ways of classifying human relationships can you think of? How interesting or unusual are they? Do any of them reveal anything about the nature of human relationships that you did not already know?

2. Toffler further subdivides medium-duration relationships. What is his rationale for the subdivision? Could the job of dividing and subdividing have been done differently? What would be the effect of a six-part division based on duration that uses Toffler's division and subdivisions?
3. In making his divisions and subdivisions Toffler clearly uses duration of the relationship as his basis for division, but there is yet another factor that figures in his rationale. He mentions it in each major division. What is it?
4. What is the purpose of paragraphs 2 and 3? What is Toffler doing in the last two sentences of paragraph 3?
5. What is the effect of the concluding paragraph? How does it show Toffler's awareness of the demands imposed by the use of classification as a rhetorical device?
6. What additional rhetorical device does Toffler use in the last paragraph to explain some of the exceptions he mentions?

Can People Be Judged by Their Appearance?
Eric Berne

Eric Berne (1910–1970) was a psychiatrist who practiced in New York and then California. He was also the author of numerous articles and books, including the best-seller *Games People Play* (1964). The essay below is from *A Layman's Guide to Psychiatry and Psychoanalysis* (1968).

Everyone knows that a human being, like a chicken, comes from an egg. At a very early stage, the human embryo forms a three-layered tube, the inside layer of which grows into the stomach and lungs, the middle layer into bones, muscle, joints, and blood vessels, and the outside layer into the skin and nervous system.

Usually these three grow about equally, so that the average human being is a fair mixture of brains, muscles, and inward organs. In some eggs, however, one layer grows more than the others, and when the angels have finished putting the child together, he may have more gut than brain, or more brain than muscle. When this happens, the individual's activities will often be mostly with the overgrown layer.

We can thus say that while the average human being is a mixture, some people are mainly "digestion-minded," some "muscle-minded," and some "brain-minded," correspondingly digestion-bodied, muscle-bodied, or brain-bodied. The digestion-bodied people look thick; the muscle-bodied people look wide; and the brain-bodied people look long. This does not mean the taller a man is the brainier he will be. It means that if a man, even a short man, looks long rather than wide or thick, he will often be more concerned about what goes on in his mind than about what he does or what he eats; but the key factor is slenderness and not height. On the other hand, a man who gives the impression of being thick rather than long or wide will usually be more interested in a good steak than in a good idea or a good long walk.   3

Medical men use Greek words to describe these types of body-build. For the man whose body shape mostly depends on the inside layer of the egg, they use the word *endomorph*. If it depends mostly upon the middle layer, they call him a *mesomorph*. If it depends upon the outside layer they call him an *ectomorph*. We can see the same roots in our English words "enter," "medium," and "exit," which might just as easily have been spelled "ender," "mesium," and "ectit."   4

Since the inside skin of the human egg, or endoderm, forms the inner organs of the belly, the viscera, the endomorph is usually belly-minded; since the middle skin forms the body tissues, or soma, the mesomorph is usually muscle-minded; and since the outside skin forms the brain, or cerebrum, the ectomorph is usually brain-minded. Translating this into Greek, we have the viscerotonic endomorph, the somatotonic mesomorph, and the cerebrotonic ectomorph.   5

Words are beautiful things to a cerebrotonic, but a viscerotonic knows you cannot eat a menu no matter what language it is printed in, and a somatotonic knows you cannot increase your chest expansion by reading a dictionary. So it is advisable to leave these words and see what kinds of people they actually apply to, remembering again that most individuals are fairly equal mixtures and that what we have to say concerns only the extremes. Up to the present, these types have been thoroughly studied only in the male sex.   6

Viscerotonic Endomorph

If a man is definitely a thick type rather than a broad or long type, he is likely to be round and soft, with a big chest but a bigger belly. He would rather eat than breathe comfortably. He is likely to have a wide face, short, thick neck, big thighs and upper arms, and small hands and feet. He has overdeveloped breasts and looks as though he were blown up a little like a balloon. His skin is soft and smooth, and when he gets bald, as he does usually quite early, he loses the hair in the middle of his head first.

The short, jolly, thickset, red-faced politician with a cigar in his mouth, who always looks as though he were about to have a stroke, is the best example of this type. The reason he often makes a good politician is that he likes people, banquets, baths, and sleep; he is easygoing, soothing, and his feelings are easy to understand.

His abdomen is big because he has lots of intestines. He likes to take in things. He likes to take in food, and affection and approval as well. Going to a banquet with people who like him is his idea of a fine time. It is important for a psychiatrist to understand the natures of such men when they come to him for advice.

Somatotonic Mesomorph

If a man is definitely a broad type rather than a thick or long type, he is likely to be rugged and have lots of muscle. He is apt to have big forearms and legs, and his chest and belly are well formed and firm, with the chest bigger than the belly. He would rather breathe than eat. He has a bony head, big shoulders, and a square jaw. His skin is thick, coarse, and elastic, and tans easily. If he gets bald, it usually starts on the front of the head.

Dick Tracy, Li'l Abner, and other men of action belong to this type. Such people make good lifeguards and construction workers. They like to put out energy. They have lots of muscles and they like to use them. They go in for adventure, exercise, fighting, and getting the upper hand. They are bold and unrestrained, and love to master the people and things around them. If the psychiatrist knows the things which give such people satisfaction, he is able to understand why they may be unhappy in certain situations.

Cerebrotonic Ectomorph

The man who is definitely a long type is likely to have thin bones and muscles. His shoulders are apt to sag and he has a flat belly with a dropped stomach, and long, weak legs. His neck and fingers are long, and his face is shaped like a long egg. His skin is thin, dry, and pale, and he rarely gets bald. He looks like an absent-minded professor and often is one.

Though such people are jumpy, they like to keep their energy and don't fancy moving around much. They would rather sit quietly by themselves and keep out of difficulties. Trouble upsets them, and they run away from it. Their friends don't understand them very well. They move jerkily and feel jerkily. The psychiatrist who understands how easily they become anxious is often able to help them get along better in the sociable and aggressive world of endomorphs and mesomorphs. 13

In the special cases where people definitely belong to one type or another, then, one can tell a good deal about their personalities from their appearance. When the human mind is engaged in one of its struggles with itself or with the world outside, the individual's way of handling the struggle will be partly determined by his type. If he is a viscerotonic he will often want to go to a party where he can eat and drink and be in good company at a time when he might be better off attending to business; the somatotonic will want to go out and do something about it, master the situation, even if what he does is foolish and not properly figured out, while the cerebrotonic will go off by himself and think it over, when perhaps he would be better off doing something about it or seeking good company to try to forget it. 14

Since these personality characteristics depend on the growth of the layers of the little egg from which the person developed, they are very difficult to change. Nevertheless, it is important for the individual to know about these types, so that he can have at least an inkling of what to expect from those around him, and can make allowances for the different kinds of human nature, and so that he can become aware of and learn to control his own natural tendencies, which may sometimes guide him into making the same mistakes over and over again in handling his difficulties. 15

Discussion: Content

1. What are the three main types into which Berne divides human appearances?
2. Explain the derivation of each of the terms for the types.
3. Berne furnishes examples of each type. Name one for each type. Supply at least two additional examples of your own for each type.
4. According to Berne, how is this classification of human appearances useful to the psychiatrist? To other persons? What danger is there in classifying people by their appearances? Does Berne warn us about that danger, at least in part?

Discussion: Form

1. What is Berne's basis for classification in this essay?
2. In which paragraph does he define his terms?
3. On what basis are the three major divisions divided further? Is he consistent in his application of these criteria to each class?
4. Which of Berne's examples for each type is most effective? Why?

Section 3: Process

Process analysis is a bit like classification in that it divides a subject into parts. It is a bit like narration in that it orders those parts into a temporal, or step-by-step, sequence. We might say that a process analysis is a classification whose rationale is time.

The purpose of process analysis is a great deal more direct than the telling or narrating of a story or the division of a topic into its classes and subclasses. Process seeks to do one or the other of two things: (1) it seeks to explain to the reader how to do something, or (2) it seeks to inform the reader about how something was done.

Cookbooks provide excellent examples of the first type of process analysis. Recipes are processes described in barest detail — a list of ingredients followed by step-by-step instructions detailing when and how to mix and cook them. The "how-to-do-it" formula confronts us at almost every turn in our daily lives: simple lists of instructions telling how to assemble the thing in the box that you got for Christmas, more complicated directions spelling out how to declare an academic major or apply for graduation, bewildering booklets on how to file state and federal income taxes or to qualify for food stamps, even books purporting to tell you how to enjoy Europe on $25 a day. You will frequently need to use a version of this formula in your own writing, as when you describe the steps in the development of an organism in a biology class or explain how a bill becomes law in Congress for a political science class.

Histories are an example of the second type of process analysis, that is, how things were done. The process described may be as simple as how Ali defeated Foreman to regain his heavyweight crown, or as complicated as how America pursued its manifest destiny from sea to shining sea. Quite often this type of process will involve more than just a simple listing of steps. In retrospect it is easy to see that events often occur simultaneously rather than in sequence. And it is frequently necessary to discuss *why* events occurred as well as how they occurred. You will need to make allowances for such requirements as you organize such process analyses, for writing in history class or elsewhere. Especially if you are planning a technical career you must be able not only to read and understand complicated process analyses fully, but also to write them effectively. The selections and exercises that follow will help you to begin developing those skills.

Paragraphs:
Process

Maine Clambake
Charles Kuralt

The first meal that comes to mind as I ruminate happily through my own recent memories of outdoor eating is a clambake last summer in Maine. Here is the authentic recipe for a clambake: dig a big hole in a beach. If you have a Maine beach to dig your hole in, so much the better, but any beach will do. Line the hole with rocks. Build a big fire on the rocks and take a swim. When the fire is all gone, cover the hot rocks with seaweed. Add some potatoes just as they came from the ground; some corn just as it came from the stalk; then lobsters, then clams, then another layer of seaweed. Cover the whole thing with a tarp and go for another swim. Dinner will be ready in an hour. It will make you very happy. No machine can make a clambake.

Discussion Questions

1. How many steps do you find in this process? Name them.
2. How does Kuralt suggest that the preparers of the clambake spend the required waiting periods?
3. What is the significance of the concluding sentence?

Formation of the Earth
Rachel Carson

The new earth, freshly torn from its parent sun, was a ball of whirling gases, intensely hot, rushing through the black spaces of the universe on a path and at a speed controlled by immense forces. Gradually the ball of flaming gases cooled. The gases began to liquefy, and Earth became a molten mass. The materials of this mass eventually became sorted out in a definite pattern: the heaviest in the center, the less heavy surrounding them, and the least heavy forming the outer rim. This is the pattern which persists today — a central sphere of molten iron, very nearly as hot as it was two billion years ago, an intermediate sphere of semiplastic basalt, and a hard outer shell, relatively quite thin and composed of solid basalt and granite.

Discussion Questions

1. Carson's paragraph discusses important steps in the process of the formation of the earth, but stops short of leaving it ready for habitation by mankind. What additional steps would you list? Be sure to keep them in proper time order.
2. In this short paragraph Carson manages to provide a variety of sentence patterns and lengths; be prepared to discuss those and to comment on their effectiveness.

Carving a Fowl
Irma S. Rombauer
Marion Rombauer Becker

Place the bird, breast side up, on a platter. Insert the fork firmly into the knee joint, pulling the leg away from the body of the bird. Slice the thigh flesh away from the body until the ball-and-socket hip joint is exposed. To sever the thigh joint, make a twisting movement with the knife, and continue to hold the knee joint down firmly with the fork. Cut the joint between the thigh and drumstick. Repeat the above, cutting off the other leg. Arrange pieces attractively on the serving platter. If a large bird is being carved, some slices of meat may be cut from the thigh and the drumstick at this point. Proceed to remove the wings in a similar manner and, if the bird is large, divide the wings at the second joint. To slice the breast, begin at the area nearest the neck and slice thinly across the grain, the entire length of the breast. With a large bird such as a turkey, carve only one side unless more is needed at the first serving.

Discussion Questions

1. This selection does what your instructor will probably not allow you to do; it has no topic sentence but uses the title to announce the thesis. What would be an appropriate introductory sentence?
2. In the best-selling *Joy of Cooking*, these instructions for carving a fowl were accompanied by three illustrations. How, if at all, does this paragraph suffer from the absence of those illustrations? If you were planning the layout for this cookbook, what illustrations would you provide to accompany these instructions?
3. Find instructions for carving a fowl in another cookbook. Which set of instructions is better, and why? Based on that comparison, what suggestions for insuring effective process description can you offer?

Brewing Coors
Grace Lichtenstein

Like other beers, Coors is produced from barley. Most of the big Midwestern brewers use barley grown in North Dakota and Minnesota. Coors is the single American brewer to use a Moravian strain, grown under company supervision on farms in Colorado, Idaho, Wyoming and Montana. At the brewery, the barley is turned into malt by being soaked in water — which must be biologically pure and of a known mineral content — for several days, causing it to sprout and producing a chemical change — breaking down starch into sugar. The malt is toasted, a process that halts the sprouting and determines the color and sweetness (the more the roasting, the darker, more bitter the beer). It is ground into flour and brewed, with more pure water, in huge copper-domed kettles until it is the consistency of oatmeal. Rice and refined starch are added to make mash; solids are strained out, leaving an amber liquid malt extract, which is boiled with hops — the dried cones from the hop vine which add to the bitterness, or tang. The hops are strained, yeast is added, turning the sugar to alcohol, and the beer is aged in huge red vats at near-freezing temperatures for almost two months, during which the second fermentation takes place and the liquid becomes carbonated, or bubbly. (Many breweries chemically age their beer to speed up production; Coors people say only naturally aged brew can be called a true "lager.") Next, the beer is filtered through cellulose filters to remove bacteria, and finally is pumped into cans, bottles or kegs for shipping.

Discussion Questions

1. In the process of brewing Coors (or any beer), just as in many other processes, the materials and equipment involved are just as important as the steps in the process. What are the key ingredients, equipment, and steps in "Brewing Coors"?
2. What extra efforts are taken to make Coors beer special?
3. As is the case with almost any process description, Lichtenstein finds it necessary to briefly explain some elements in further detail for readers unfamiliar with the process. What are a couple of elements receiving such explanations?

Student Work:
To: Process

Registration

Registration on this campus is a classic headache. The lines are long, and you must wait for hours while other people take the cards for the last seats in most of the courses that you intended to sign up for. Next you must get your partially completed schedule approved by the final checker. As you leave the card room, you encounter a bitchy lady requesting that you fill out an address card. After you have filled all these cards out, there will be more forms to be completed, for example, forms to get a parking sticker, forms to get an I.D. made, and forms to get into the card room for Drop-Add so that you can complete your schedule. When you have completed this hectic filling out of forms, there is advisor hunting. The season on advisor hunting begins in late August and continues until Drop-Add is over. Yet it isn't over until you receive the wrong printed schedule back from the computer center with courses meeting at the same hour, or courses that you signed up for not appearing on your schedule at all.

Discussion Questions

1. "Registration" demonstrates that using process as a writing strategy may also often require the use of another expository strategy; what is it?
2. How many problems does this student encounter, as described here? What are other problems, perhaps unique to your own campus?
3. The sentence beginning "After you have filled . . ." uses the word "forms" four different times when the word might have been used just once, with the sentence consequently much shortened. What justification can you provide for keeping the repetition?

Successful Sketching

When beginning a drawing, often putting the first mark down on the empty piece of paper is the hardest part of all. The way I have overcome this problem is to take my pencil and very loosely and lightly make several marks going across the page. This more or less frames my subject, directing my concentration on the view that I wish to capture. Next I start to sketch in the large areas. Working very fast and freely, I concentrate on getting these large areas in the right place with respect to one another. When this is done, I begin putting in the different values that I see. Using the side of my pencil, I quickly color in the largest, darkest areas, being very careful with placement and trying to get the exact shape of the shadows. Next, I take my eraser and begin picking up the highlighted areas. Switching back and forth between putting down the shadows and picking up the highlights, I watch the picture as it emerges. What most people do not realize is that the details of a drawing are the very last thing to be put in; what must come first is the large areas reduced to flat planes of light and dark.

Discussion Questions

1. According to this student, what is often the hardest part of sketching?
2. What is the first step the writer suggests?
3. What comes next?
4. What are the last things to be added to a drawing?
5. Sometimes a description of a process must be converted into instructions. To manage that in this case will require shifting the point of view from first to second person and changing some verbs from passive to active voice and imperative mood (commands). Try that with several sentences of this description so that you will understand how the conversion works.

Tobacco Production

Since I have worked in tobacco, or, as it is sometimes called, "baccer," for eight summers, I consider myself relatively experienced in the production of this crop. There are many steps in the process. These include "pulling plants," which is the removal of the young plants from the plant bed. Next comes "setting out," or transplanting, the tobacco plants in the field. When mature, the plants must be "topped." Topping is removing the blossom from the tops of the plants. Then as the side buds, or suckers, appear, they must be removed in a process that is called "suckering." Most of my time has been spent "priming," the time-consuming job of picking the ripe leaves from the mature plants. After "twining," or tying the leaves on wooden sticks with a string, the tobacco has to be housed. In other words, it must be hung in barns. Then the tobacco must be cured. The green, living tobacco is changed into dry, cured tobacco in this step of the process. After curing, the tobacco must be allowed to "come into order." This means that the dry, crisp tobacco is allowed to absorb a small amount of moisture from the damp night air so it will become more flexible and not crumble when it is being sacked for market, which is the last step in this process.

Discussion Questions

1. How many steps in the process of tobacco production does the writer enumerate? Name them.
2. The writer does not use an enumerating device such as *first, second, third,* . . . to introduce each of the steps in the process. How is each step introduced?
3. The writer is obliged to explain or define a term in each step of the process. In order to insure variety, the writer accomplishes these explanations in a number of different ways. How many? Illustrate them.

Donating Blood

Yesterday my roommate, another friend, and I gave blood to the American Red Cross, each donating a pint of blood in an almost painless process.

Just inside the ground floor entrance to the University Center, volunteers seated at the beginning of a series of tables asked if we were first-time donors and for our identification. From there we were sent with a form bearing our names, addresses, and other personal information to the next table, where a nurse recorded our temperatures and pulse rates, and then directed us on to the Cherokee Room.

Stepping through the double doors, we saw many people in various sections of the large room. The area that caught my eye was where people were actually giving blood; a moment of fear struck me, and butterflies came to life in my stomach.

In the first section of the room blood samples were taken from an earlobe and checked for white cell count, along with our blood pressures, and recorded. A volunteer then proceeded to inquire about our medical histories. Such questions as "Have you had heart trouble, respiratory diseases, epilepsy?" were asked. Each of us was accepted as a donor and given a plastic pint bag. When our names, date, blood type, and donor number were stamped on the bags, we proceeded to the designated area to sit and wait for a vacancy at the tables where the actual donation would take place.

As vacancies occurred each of us went to a different section of tables. Each section contained three tables, a nurse, and a small table where her needed materials were kept. As I sat upon a table, it seemed as if butterflies fluttered wildly in my stomach.

When asking to see the undersides of my arms the nurse tried to start a conversation, as if she knew how scared I was. After I lay down on the table she placed a rubber tube around the upper part of my left arm, and she rubbed red and then yellow antiseptic solutions on the middle underside with cotton balls. Telling me to relax, she placed a needle, connected to the bag by tubing, in a main vein of my left arm. The needle felt like the jab of a knife and continued to sting as the bag filled with blood. I was given a rubber ball to squeeze with my left hand in order to help the blood flow more readily from my vein into the tubing and bag.

About twelve minutes later, when the nurse began to remove the needle, the butterflies in my stomach began to flutter again. But to my surprise I felt no pain; my arm was simply a little numb. I had to hold it up in the air and apply pressure to the vein with a gauze pad for a few minutes, but then the process was finally over and my butterflies died.

After being escorted to the refreshment table, the three of us were given cookies and orange juice. Later, as we walked back to the dorm, a great feeling of warmth and satisfaction beamed inside me.

Discussion Questions

1. "Donating Blood" is more than a process essay. What other writing modes are used?
2. How many major steps in the process are described?

3. How is figurative language used to connect the steps of the process/experience?

I Remember, Granner

My mother's mother probably made the best apple pies I ever tasted. As a tiny girl, I used to watch my Granner make them, and I marveled at her sure, swift movements. Granner needed no recipes, yet her pies always came out delicious, fragrant with love and goodness. I was never too interested in making the crust, but by the time Granner brought out eight plump red apples, she had my full attention. 1

Peeling the apples was my job, and each round, firm apple yielded up its crisp skin in a long spiral. Meanwhile, Granner quartered and cored the apples I had peeled and began slicing them into the crust-lined pans. Often, I pilfered a thick, tangy slice and popped it into my mouth, but she pretended not to notice. 2

When the two pans were heaped full of apples, Granner dusted them generously with cinnamon, then sprinkled a scoopful of sugar over the cinnamon. Next, she dotted each piece with small squares of butter, sprinkled on a pinch or two of ground nutmeg and cloves, then drizzled on the juice of half a lemon. 3

Finally, Granner was ready to place the top crust. She did this by folding the rolled-out dough in half, slipping it over the pie, then flipping the folded half into place. I always felt quite capable and efficient as I then carefully trimmed the excess crust from around each rim and slit six steam holes in each pie-top. When I proudly handed the perfect pies over to Granner, she smiled and slid them into a 375° oven. 4

After twenty minutes, the spicy warmth crept into the living room and enticed us toward the kitchen. My eager taste buds were convinced that the pies were ready, but Granner said it would be twenty minutes more. Finally, it was time to take the steamy prizes from the oven, and I could scarcely wait for them to cool. But with that first bite, I was in a child's heaven, eating in the nippy-sweet warmth of that kitchen, surrounded by an aura of well-being and love. 5

Ten years ago, my Granner died. I grieved over her death for more than a year, until the day my mother called me into the kitchen. On the counter sat two crust-lined pans and eight plump red apples. For a long moment, we just gazed at each other, our eyes glistening. Then we sat down together and made two perfect apple pies, just the way

Granner always did. That day, working out those loving memories, my broken, lonely heart began to heal. But often, especially when I make an apple pie, I remember. Oh, yes, I remember, Granner. 6

Discussion Questions

1. The writer uses verbs and verbals very effectively in this essay. The tensed verbs, coming in a series, show consecutive actions (Granner *dusted* them . . . then *sprinkled* them . . .). On the other hand, tenseless verbs, or verbals, are used to capture simultaneous actions (I was in a child's heaven, *eating* the nippy-sweet . . ., *surrounded* by an aura . . .). Locate at least two additional examples for each of these strategies.
2. To keep the statement of process from becoming too laborious, the writer dismisses part of it in a rather clever way. Can you spot this maneuver?
3. The first five paragraphs of this essay enumerate the steps of a process, but in the sixth paragraph a new objective is introduced. How would you characterize it?
4. The last paragraph is very moving; it appeals to readers' emotions. How exactly is this accomplished?

Essays:
Process

Mosquito Bite
Alice Gray

Alice Gray (1914–   ) majored in entomology and English at Cornell, did a master's in the teaching of natural science at Columbia, and completed the course work for a Ph.D. in entomology at the University of California, Berkeley. From 1937 to 1984 she was associated with the Department of Entomology at the American Museum of Natural History in New York City. Over the years Gray became the department's "Answer Woman," acting as liaison between the staff entomologists and the general public; she talked about insects in the museum and on radio and television shows, and answered a wide range of questions about insects in person and by letter. Gray has contributed numerous articles to natural science publications and also wrote *The Adventure Book of Insects* (1956). Another area of expertise is origami, the Japanese art of paperfolding; that interest led to co-authorship of a second book, *The Magic of Origami* (1977). In the entomological essay below, Gray effectively describes a familiar natural process whose result most of us have felt.

You are now taking a last turn around your yard before going in to dinner. Insect eyes are more sensitive to contrast and motion than to form or color. In your shirt of faded blue denim, you are a moving target no insect could miss. A mosquito zeroes in for a landing. The warmth, moisture and odor of your skin assure her that she has arrived, and the convection currents set up in the cool air by the heat of your body prompt her to cut the motor and let down the landing gear. [1]

On six long legs, she puts down so lightly that you feel nothing. Sensors on her feet detect the carbon dioxide that your skin exhales. Down comes the long proboscis; up go the long back legs, as though to balance it. The little soft lobes at the tip of the proboscis are spread to test the surface. It will do. A sudden contraction of the legs with the weight of the body behind it bends the proboscis backward in an arc while the six sharp blades it has unsheathed are thrust into your skin. Two of the blades are tipped with barbs. These work alternately, shove and hold, shove and hold, pulling the insect's face down and carrying their fellows deeper into your skin.

Once the skin is penetrated, all the blades bend forward and probe as far as they can reach in all directions. (A scientist learned all this by watching through a microscope while a mosquito bit the transparent membrane between the toes of a frog.) With luck, the blades strike a capillary. If they don't, saliva pumped into the wound through a channel in one of the blades stimulates the flow of blood into a pool. And still you feel nothing. Your continued ignorance of attack is probably due, not to any anesthetic effect (although a few mosquitoes do have an anesthetic saliva) but rather to the minute size of the mouthparts, which have simply passed between nerve endings without touching any.

The taste of blood turns on two pumps in the insect's throat. The broadest blade of the mouthparts is rolled lengthwise to form a tube Through it, blood passes upward into the mouth. In a blood meal, volume is what counts — the more blood, the more eggs — and even while the pumping is going on, excess water is passing out at the insect's other end.

In three to five minutes, her body is so swollen that your blood shows pinkly through the taut skin. The stretching of the stomach wall stimulates nerves that turn on a pair of glands in the thorax; the glands, in turn, release a hormone that sets the ovaries to work. Finally, when she has filled herself so full that she can't force in a single additional corpuscle, Madam Mosquito withdraws her mouthparts with a tug and drifts away.

All this time you may have felt nothing, but soon you will begin to itch and later a welt will appear.

Discussion: Content

1. What attracts the mosquito to humans?
2. Why do we seldom feel the bite of the mosquito until after the insect has flown away?
3. How long does it take a mosquito to gorge itself?
4. How did scientists learn of the blade structure of a mosquito's proboscis?

Discussion: Form

1. Which type of process is this — a how-to type or a how-it-was-done type?
2. This essay lacks a thesis statement. Does it suffer for not having one? Write an appropriate thesis statement. Where would you place it?
3. State the purpose of each paragraph in this process; i.e., explain why the author divided up the process in the way she did.

Centrifugal Force
Robert Kadesch

Robert Kadesch (1922–   ), a native of Iowa, received his doctorate in physics from the University of Wisconsin in 1955 and now teaches at the University of Utah. His *Math Menagerie* won the Notable Book of the Year Award from the U.S. Library Association. This selection is taken from Kadesch's first book, *The Crazy Cantilever and Other Science Experiments* (1961).

A potato, a spool, a spoon, and a length of twine can be used to demonstrate what happens when an object — any object — moves in a circular path. 1

Tie one end of a four-foot length of strong twine to a medium-sized potato. Thread the other end of the twine through the hole in the spool and tie it securely to the spoon. Hold the spool so that the potato hangs freely beneath it and the spoon so that it is a short distance from the spool. Now give the spool a quick circular motion so that the spoon will swing around in a small horizontal circle. 2

If you swing the spoon rapidly, the potato will rise all the way up to the bottom of the spool. If the spoon is now swung more slowly, the potato will move downward. You will find that at one particular speed the potato will neither move up nor down. The spoon is now in a circular orbit. 3

This completes the experiment, but from these simple observations much can be learned. 4

"Centrifugal" means "away from the center," literally, "fleeing (that's the "fugal" part of the word) the center" (centri). There is another important word to learn. It is the word "centripetal," which means "moving toward the center." 5

When we observe the action of the potato and the spoon, let us be sure not to confuse centrifugal with centripetal forces. 6

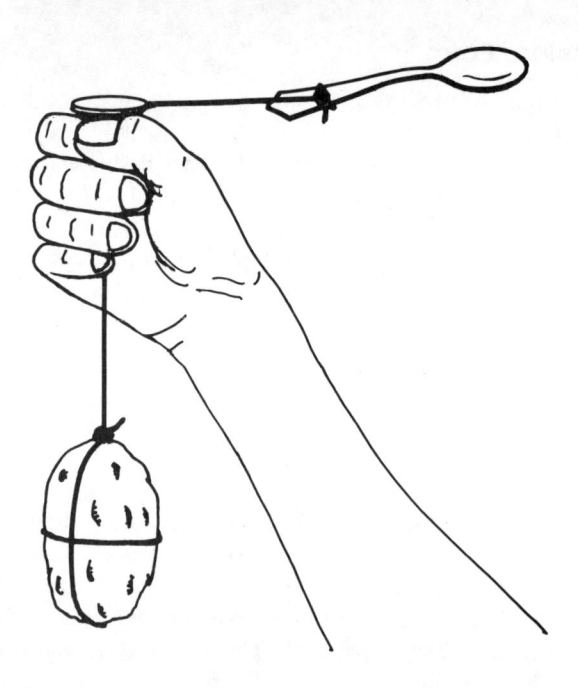

Think about the spoon when it is moving along a circular path and the potato moves neither up nor down. Gravity pulls down on the potato, that is certain. The potato pulls on the twine, and the twine, in turn, exerts an inward force on the spoon. This inward force is a *centripetal* force *on the spoon*. 7

The turning spoon also pulls outward on the twine and the twine pulls upward on the potato. The outward, or *centrifugal,* force acts through the string *on the potato*. There is no centrifugal force acting on the spoon. 8

The twirling spoon is similar to a satellite orbiting the earth. The one and only force acting on the satellite is a centripetal force. This inward force is supplied by the gravitational attraction of the earth. 9

Centrifugal force is exerted *by* the satellite *on* the earth. It is merely the gravitational attraction which the satellite holds for the earth. 10

The gravitational attraction of the earth for the satellite equals the attraction of the satellite for the earth, so that the centripetal and centrifugal forces equal one another. These two forces are oppositely directed: one acts on the earth, the other on the satellite. 11

In our experiment, if the centripetal force on the spoon is too little to keep the spoon in a circular orbit, the potato rises. It falls if the spoon's centripetal force is too great. Without the inward force on the spoon, the spoon would move off along a perfectly straight line.

Expository Writing

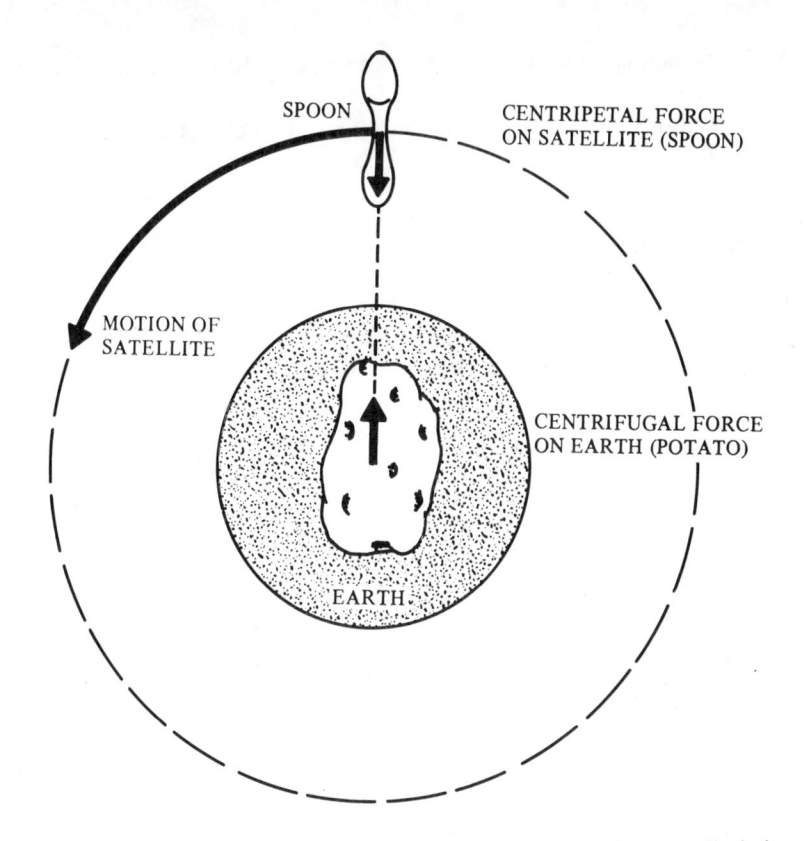

Diagram: Shows Earth (potato) at center with a satellite (spoon) in orbit. Labels: SPOON, CENTRIPETAL FORCE ON SATELLITE (SPOON), MOTION OF SATELLITE, CENTRIFUGAL FORCE ON EARTH (POTATO), EARTH.

When the spoon moves too rapidly, the centripetal force pulls it in, but not enough to bring the spoon into a circular orbit. The potato rises as a result. On the other hand, if the spoon moves slowly, the centripetal force pulls the spoon even farther in than would be required for a circular orbit, and the potato falls. 12

Moons that orbit their planets and planets that orbit the sun behave in a similar fashion. If these move too fast or too slow they no longer move in a perfect circle. Instead, the moons or planets trace out elliptical — or oval — paths. 13

Whether an orbit is elliptical or circular, the only force exerted on the orbiting object is an inward force. A continual inward pull is needed to turn a straight-line path into a circular or an elliptical one. 14

Discussion: Content

1. What is the meaning of centrifugal force? Of centripetal force?
2. Explain how the centrifugal and centripetal forces are exerted in the experiment described in paragraphs 1–3.

3. Does centrifugal force act on the spoon (or on any orbiting object)?
4. What does it mean to say that the spoon (or a planet or moon) is in orbit?

Discussion: Form

1. This essay begins with a description of a process — an experiment with a potato and a spoon. List the steps in that process.
2. What is the author's purpose in paragraph 4?
3. Look up *analogy* in the Glossary or glance ahead at the section devoted to that method of development. The experiment with the potato and the spoon is an analogy that seeks to explain the behavior of satellites. What, for instance, is demonstrated by the rising of the potato? By its falling?

Making Tappa
Herman Melville

Herman Melville (1819–1891) was an American writer who based his early works on his youthful adventures as a sailor. His most famous and greatest work, *Moby Dick* (1851), draws on those experiences. During his lifetime Melville's most popular book was a novel about life among the cannibals of the Marquesan Islands, *Typee* (1846), from which this selection was taken.

Although the whole existence of the inhabitants of the valley seemed to pass away exempt from toil, yet there were some light employments which, although amusing rather than laborious as occupations, contributed to their comfort and luxury. Among these, the most important was the manufacture of the native cloth, — "tappa," — so well known, under various modifications, throughout the whole Polynesian Archipelago. As is generally understood, this useful and sometimes elegant article is fabricated from the bark of different trees. But, as I believe that no description of its manufacture has ever been given, I shall state what I know regarding it. 1

In the manufacture of the beautiful white tappa generally worn on the Marquesan Islands, the preliminary operation consists in gathering a certain quantity of the young branches of the cloth-tree. The exterior green bark being pulled off as worthless, there remains a slender fibrous substance, which is carefully stripped from the stick, to which it closely adheres. When a sufficient quantity of it has been collected, the various strips are enveloped in a covering of large leaves, which the natives use precisely as we do wrapping paper, and which are secured by a few turns of a line passed round them. The package is then laid in the bed of some running stream, with a heavy stone placed over it, to prevent its being swept away. After it has remained for two or three days in this state, it is drawn out, and exposed, for a short time, to the action of the air, every distinct piece being attentively inspected, with a view of ascertaining whether it has yet been sufficiently affected by the operation. This is repeated again and again, until the desired result is obtained.

When the substance is in a proper state for the next process, it betrays evidences of incipient decomposition; the fibers are relaxed and softened, and rendered perfectly malleable. The different strips are now extended, one by one, in successive layers, upon some smooth surface — generally the prostrate trunk of a cocoa-nut tree — and the heap thus formed is subjected, at every new increase, to a moderate beating, with a sort of wooden mallet, leisurely applied. The mallet, made of a hard heavy wood resembling ebony, is about twelve inches in length, and perhaps two in breadth, with a rounded handle at one end, and in shape is the exact counterpart of one of our four-sided razor-strops. The flat surfaces of the implement are marked with shallow parallel indentations, varying in depth on the different sides, so as to be adapted to the several stages of the operation. These marks produce the corduroy sort of stripes discernible in the tappa in its finished state. After being beaten in the manner I have described, the material soon becomes blended in one mass, which, moistened occasionally with water, is at intervals hammered out, by a kind of gold-beating process, to any degree of thinness required. In this way the cloth is easily made to vary in strength and thickness, so as to suit the numerous purposes to which it is applied.

When the operation last described has been concluded, the new-made tappa is spread out on the grass to bleach and dry, and soon becomes of a dazzling whiteness. Sometimes, in the first stages of the manufacture, the substance is impregnated with a vegetable juice, which gives it a permanent color. A rich brown and a bright yellow are occasionally seen, but the simple taste of the Typee people inclines them to prefer the natural tint.

Section 3: Process

Discussion: Content

1. According to Melville, how many and what are the distinct steps in making tappa?
2. What tool is used in making tappa? Has Melville described it fully enough so that you could make a copy? What is the weakness in the description's comparison of the tool to "our four-sided razor-strops"?
3. What is the most common color for finished tappa cloth?

Discussion: Form

1. What is the basis for each of the paragraphs in the selection? Does the paragraph arrangement suggest to you that Melville saw tappa making as consisting of a certain number of processes that contained subprocesses? How would the distinct steps that you enumerated above (in response to the first content question) fit into such an arrangement?
2. Other than by describing the process steps chronologically, how does Melville achieve unity in his essay, especially within individual paragraphs? Mark the words serving transitional functions in paragraphs 2 and 3.

Riveting a Skyscraper
Fortune

Following the success of the newsmagazine *Time* that he had helped found in 1923, Henry R. Luce turned his attention in 1929 to publishing a business magazine called *Fortune*, written for the upper level of American business and financial executives. Luce's timing was bad, with a trial edition appearing about the time of the great stock market crash, but believing that the slump was temporary, he went ahead with his plans. Starting with the first issue in February, 1930, *Fortune* became a publishing miracle, selling for a dollar a copy but gaining in circulation and advertising throughout the Depression. An attractively designed magazine, it became a respected source of information for those in and out of the business world because of its editorial honesty, and it attracted a staff of talented writers, such as James Agee, Susanne K. Langer, Dwight MacDonald, and Archibald MacLeish. The essay printed below, written by *Fortune* staffers, is part of a long article, "Skyscrapers: Builders and Their Tools," published in the October 1930 issue.

The actual process of riveting is simple — in description. Rivets are carried to the job by the rivet boy, a riveter's apprentice whose ambition it is to replace one of the members of the gang — which one, he leaves to luck. The rivets are dumped into a keg beside a small coke furnace. The furnace stands on a platform of loose boards roped to steel girders which may or may not have been riveted. If they have not been riveted there will be a certain amount of play in the temporary bolts. The furnace is tended by the heater or passer. He wears heavy clothes and gloves to protect him from the flying sparks and intense heat of his work, and he holds a pair of tongs about a foot and half long in his right hand. When a rivet is needed, he whirls the furnace blower until the coke is white-hot, picks up a rivet with his tongs, and drives it into the coals. His skill as a heater appears in his knowledge of the exact time necessary to heat the steel. If he overheats it, it will flake, and the flakes will permit the rivet to turn in its hole. And a rivet which gives in its hole is condemned by the inspectors. 1

When the heater judges that his rivet is right, he turns to face the catcher, who may be above or below him or fifty or sixty or eighty feet away on the same floor level with the naked girders between. There is no means of handing the rivet over. It must be thrown. And it must be accurately thrown. And if the floor beams of the floor above have been laid so that a flat trajectory is essential, it must be thrown with considerable force. The catcher is therefore armed with a smallish, battered tin can, called a cup, with which to catch the red-hot steel. Various patented cups have been put upon the market from time to time, but they have made little headway. Catchers prefer the ancient can. 2

The catcher's position is not exactly one which a sportsman catching rivets for pleasure would choose. He stands upon a narrow platform of loose planks laid over needle beams and roped to a girder near the connection upon which the gang is at work. There are live coils of pneumatic tubing for the rivet gun around his feet. If he moves more than a step or two in any direction, he is gone, and if he loses his balance backward he is apt to end up at street level without time to walk. And the object is to catch a red-hot iron rivet weighing anywhere from a quarter of a pound to a pound and a half and capable, if he lets it pass, of drilling an automobile radiator or a man's skull 500 feet below as neatly as a shank of shrapnel. Why more rivets do not fall is the great mystery of skyscraper construction. The only reasonable explanation offered to date is the reply of an erector's foreman who was asked what would happen if a catcher on the Forty Wall Street job let a rivet go by him around lunch hour. "Well," said the foreman, "he's not supposed to."

There is practically no exchange of words among riveters. Not only are they averse to conversation, which would be reasonable enough in view of the effect they have on the conversation of others, but they are averse to speech in any form. The catcher faces the heater. He holds his tin can up. The heater swings his tongs, releasing one handle. The red iron arcs through the air in one of those parabolas so much admired by the stenographers in the neighboring windows. And the tin can clanks.

Meantime the gun-man and the bucker-up have prepared the connection — aligning the two holes, if necessary, with a drift pin driven by a pneumatic hammer — and removed the temporary bolts. They, too, stand on loose-roped boards with the column or the beam between them. When the rivet strikes the catcher's can, he picks it out with a pair of tongs held in his right hand, knocks it sharply against the steel to shake off the glowing flakes, and rams it into the hole, an operation which is responsible for his alternative title of sticker. Once the rivet is in place, the bucker-up braces himself with his dolly bar, a short heavy bar of steel, against the capped end of the rivet. On outside wall work he is sometimes obliged to hold on by one elbow with his weight out over the street and the jar of the riveting shaking his precarious balance. And the gun-man lifts his pneumatic hammer to the rivet's other end.

The gun-man's work is the hardest work, physically, done by the gang. The hammers in use for steel construction work are supposed to weigh around thirty pounds and actually weigh about thirty-five. They must not only be held against the rivet end, but held there with the gun-man's entire strength, and for a period of forty to sixty seconds. (A rivet driven too long will develop a collar inside the new head.) And the concussion to the ears and to the arms during that period is very great. The whole platform shakes and the vibration can be felt down the column thirty stories below. It is common practice for the catcher to push with the gun-man and for the gun-man and the bucker-up to pass the gun back and forth between them when the angle is difficult. Also on a heavy rivet job the catcher and the bucker-up may relieve the gun-man at the gun.

The weight of the guns is one cause, though indirect, of accidents. The rivet set, which is the actual hammer at the point of the gun, is held in place, when the gun leaves the factory, by clips. Since the clips increase the weight of the hammer, it is good riveting practice to knock them off against the nearest column and replace them with a hank of wire. But wire has a way of breaking, and when it breaks there is nothing to keep the rivet set and the pneumatic piston itself from taking the bucker-up or the catcher on the belt and knocking him into the next block. 7

Discussion: Content

1. How many persons are involved in the riveting process? What are their job names? Which job seems to require the most skill? The most strength?
2. What is "the great mystery of skyscraper construction"? Does that distinction seem to be an accurate one? Why or why not?
3. If paragraphs 6 and 7 are read closely, the weight data given for the pneumatic hammer seem contradictory. Do you see the contradiction and can you explain it away?
4. Why do you suppose riveters are "averse to speech in any form"?

Discussion: Form

1. One of the things that makes "Riveting a Skyscraper" interesting reading is the way the author creates for the reader a feeling of danger and of consequent concern for the riveters. How exactly is this accomplished? What words and rhetorical devices create the impression?
2. Notice the final sentence in each paragraph. Comment on any similarities in form and/or effect that you notice. Which of the seven seems least effective, and why?
3. Examine the transitions between paragraphs; what seems to be the writer's preferred transitional technique?

Section 4: Comparison

Comparison, which we have already studied as a narrative-descriptive technique, is equally valuable in expository writing. The similarities that we notice in the world around us may be used to inform as well as to describe. Here is how it is done.

Suppose you wish to inform your reader about the relative merits of two or more people, places, or concepts. There is a procedure that must be followed if the comparison is to be understandable for the reader. First, determine the *topics* to be compared, let us say two baseball teams; then decide what *points* shared by the teams need to be examined. A rough sketch of possible ideas might look like this:

Topic to be compared	*Points of comparison*	*Topic to be compared*
Braves	hitting fielding base-running pitching coaching depth	Cards

To *compare by topics,* begin with the Braves and describe that team's performance with respect to each of the points of comparison. Then repeat the procedure for the Cards. On the other hand, you may choose to *compare by points,* in which case you will start with the first point of comparison, hitting, and discuss the Braves' performance at the plate and then the Cards'. Then you will do the same for fielding, base-running, and so on. As a general rule, if the points of comparison are few, it will be a good idea to compare by topics. If the points of comparison are many, say four or more, or are complex enough to each require detailed discussion that may extend to a paragraph or more, it is wise to compare by points; then your reader will be better able to keep the points of comparison clear and distinct.

Comparison techniques are helpful when you are attempting to inform your reader about familiar things, such as baseball teams, but also when you are trying to introduce and explain unfamiliar things. Comparison enables you to lead your reader into the unfamiliar by way of the familiar. Suppose, for example, you want to explain how the South Sea Islanders you have been studying in Anthropology 201 reckon their standing in their community. You may suppose that your readers know very little about South Sea Islanders, but you can assume that they have some ideas about how their own prestige is determined. Your first step is to enumerate those status markers for Americans — education, wealth, landholdings, lodgings, and means of transportation. These familiar items will make up a partial list of points of comparison. Next, you should add those status markers that apply to that South Seas culture, noting overlaps when they occur. A sketch of the comparison might look like this:

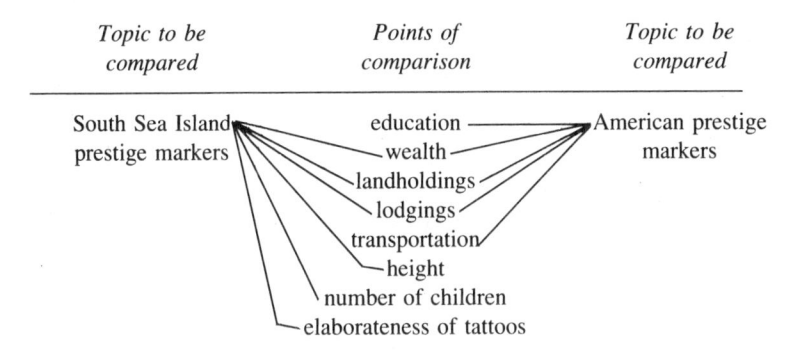

Topic to be compared	Points of comparison	Topic to be compared
South Sea Island prestige markers	education wealth landholdings lodgings transportation height number of children elaborateness of tattoos	American prestige markers

As the arrows show, wealth, landholdings, and lodgings are of equal importance to Islanders and Americans. This much your readers might have suspected. They may be surprised to learn, however, that Islanders do not share the American's reverence for education and transportation. And your readers may be amazed to learn that considerations so unusual as height, number of children, and elaborateness of tattoos become measures of prestige for these distant people.

Examine the following selections, paying attention to the ways that the authors have organized their materials — their use of topics and points. Then you will want to practice applying both means of comparison organization in your own writing, for comparison is of great use. Your English teacher may ask you to compare two characters in a short story, your chemistry teacher may ask you to compare the characteristics of two compounds, your first boss may ask for a report comparing two products or pieces of equipment, and so forth. You'll need to be ready.

Paragraphs:
Comparison

Boxing and Fencing
Paul Gallico

In boxing you feint with foot, head, or hand. You do the same in fencing. In a fight you take the initiative, moving in with leads, or backpedal and wait for a chance to counter. The same holds for a sword fight. With gloves you try to block an opponent's lead or jab. With a weapon this is called a *parry*. And in the ring, having nullified your opponent's lead with a block, you try to knock his head off with a timed counterpunch. Fencers call the same thing a *riposte*. The purpose of both games is to hit without being hit in return.

Discussion Questions

1. Is this comparison organized by points or by topics?
2. What are the topics being compared? What are the points assigned to each topic?
3. What are a *parry* and a *riposte?* Look these terms up in a dictionary. Are they limited to fencing?

Two Americas
J. William Fulbright

There are two Americas. One is the America of Lincoln and Adlai Stevenson; the other is the America of Teddy Roosevelt and the modern super-patriots. One is generous and humane, the other narrowly egotistical; one is self-critical, the other self-righteous; one is sensible, the other romantic; one is good-humored, the other solemn; one is inquiring, the other pontificating; one is moderate, the other filled with passionate intensity; one is judicious and the other arrogant in the use of great power.

Discussion Questions

1. Is this comparison arranged by points or by topics?
2. How many points does Fulbright mention and how does he introduce them?
3. Teddy Roosevelt is associated with the class of superpatriots. What are Stevenson and Lincoln supposed to signify?

Women and Blacks
Ellen Willis

Like the early feminist movement, which grew out of the campaign to end slavery, the present-day women's movement has been inspired and influenced by the black liberation struggle. The situation of women and blacks is similar in many ways. Just as blacks live in a world defined by whites, women live in a world defined by males. (The generic term of human being is "man"; "woman" means "wife of man.") To be female or black is to be peculiar; whiteness and maleness are the norm. Newspapers do not have "men's pages," nor would anyone think of discussing the "man problem." Racial and sexual stereotypes also resemble each other: women, like blacks, are said to be childish, incapable of abstract reasoning, innately submissive, biologically suited for menial tasks, emotional, close to nature.

Discussion Questions

1. Clearly the topics to be compared are revealed in the title. What are the points assigned to each?
2. Willis says, "To be female or black is to be peculiar; whiteness and maleness are the norm." How does she support this idea?
3. Willis claims that both women and blacks are the targets of stereotyped thinking. What are some of the examples of such sterotypes that she mentions?

The Old Practitioner and the Young
Oliver Wendell Holmes

May I venture to contrast youth and experience in medical practice? The young man knows the rules, but the old man knows the exceptions. The young man knows his patient, but the old man knows also his patient's family, dead and alive, up and down for generations. He can tell beforehand what diseases their unborn children will be subject to, what they will die of if they live long enough, and whether they had better live at all, or remain unrealized possibilities, as belonging to a stock not worth being perpetuated. The young man feels uneasy if he is not continually doing something to stir up his patient's internal arrangements. The old man takes things more quietly, and is much more willing to let well enough alone. All these superiorities, if such they are, you must wait for time to bring you. In the meanwhile, the young man's senses are quicker than those of his older rival. His education in all the accessory branches is more recent, and therefore nearer the existing condition of knowledge. He finds it easier than his seniors to accept the improvements which every year is bringing forward. New ideas build their nests in young men's brains. "Revolutions are not made by men in spectacles," as I once heard it remarked, and the first whispers of a new truth are not caught by those who begin to feel the need of an ear-trumpet. Granting all these advantages to the young man, he ought, nevertheless, to go on improving, on the whole, as a medical practitioner, with every year, until he has ripened into a well-mellowed maturity. But, to improve, he must be good for something at the start. If you ship a poor cask of wine to India and back, if you keep it half a century, it only grows thinner and sharper.

Discussion Questions

1. Has Holmes organized his comparison by topics or by points?
2. How many points are enumerated?
3. Near the end of the paragraph he uses the related techinque of analogy; how effective is that use? Do you understand the point he is making?

Student Work:
Comparison

Private and Public Bathrooms

A bathroom is one place where most American girls spend a tremendous amount of time. At home, I have my own bathroom, and it is usually overflowing with various types of makeup, hair dryers, electric curlers, and other items which females use to improve their appearance. Because no one else uses my bathroom, I never have to wait for the shower, and I am able to hop in whenever I feel the need. I am also responsible for the cleanliness of my bathroom, so if I feel like having my personal items scattered in it, I can do so. On the other hand, sharing a community bath in a dorm is strikingly different. For example, there is seldom a moment when I am in the bathroom alone. I have even brushed my teeth as late as 2:30 a.m. and discovered that someone else was taking an early morning shower. In addition, I frequently wait in line for the use of a shower in the mornings. Of course, the only reason waiting in line upsets me is that I begin to run behind in my schedule and miss breakfast. Furthermore, in using a community bath, one has to carry her personal items with her on each trip. I can recall several occasions when I stepped into the shower only to realize that my soap was in my room. Another difference in a community bath is the fact that some people on the hall do not keep it clean. In this case all those involved suffer.

Discussion Questions

1. Is this paragraph organized by topics or by points? How many points are covered? What is gained by this method of organization? What, if anything, is lost by this choice?

2. To help you better understand organization of comparison writing, try creating the appropriate two-level outline, by topics or by points, for this paragraph, filling in the blanks below; then rearrange the topics and points to create an outline for the other form of organization.

Topics	Points
I.	I.
A.	A.
B.	B.
C.	II.
D.	A.
	B.
II. A.	
B.	III.
C.	A.
D.	B.
	IV.
	A.
	B.

3. After completing the outline above based on the student's original organization of her material, what flaws, if any, do you notice in her plan?

Comparing Mechanics

When comparing professional mechanics to the more common variety of backyard shade-tree mechanics, one will certainly notice a number of differences. First, one might look at how each group gains its knowledge. The professional mechanic's knowledge comes from vocational schools and instruction manuals, each emphasizing the latest techniques in sophisticated analysis. The shade-tree mechanic, hanging around service stations and garages, accepts anything he hears as fact until trial and error prove it wrong. Style of dress and general appearance present another contrast. The professional, well groomed and tidy even in his grease spots, wears a uniform of coveralls, the name of his garage stenciled across the back and his own first name above the pencil-filled pocket. His counterpart is more likely to be dressed in nondescript blue jeans, covered with grease from head to toe, his hair slicked back Elvis style, and a cigarette stuck behind his ear. The manner in which the two groups work is also different: the professional going about his work in a quiet and orderly manner, responding politely to the customers' questions, while our friend the shade-tree mechanic will beat and bang, shouting over the noise, "&#%$ this" and "bleep that," as he pounds away. A final point of comparison is the fees charged by each group: the professional working a half hour, taking a break, then working another fifteen minutes and charging $200 for two hours' labor, and the shade-tree mechanic working all day for an honest fee.

Disucssion Questions

1. The writer never defines "backyard shade-tree mechanic." What does the term mean and why is it not defined?
2. How is "Comparing Mechanics" organized, by points or by topics?
3. How many points are covered in the discussion? Why do you suppose the writer used fees charged as the final point?

Senior Prom: The Dream and the Reality

My senior prom was nothing like the way I had expected it to be. I had pictured getting dressed in a blue gown that my aunt would make, one that would cost ninety dollars in any department store. No one else would have a gown as attractive as mine. I imagined my boyfriend coming to the door with a lovely blue corsage, and I would happily inhale its perfume all evening. I also saw us leaving in his brother's burgundy El Dorado. We would make quite a flourish as we went in and out of a series of parties before the prom. After dancing close together into the early morning hours, we would cap the evening with a delicious shrimp dinner.

1

What really happened was somewhat different. My one and only senior prom was held on May 16, 1980, at Burns Senior High. Because of sickness in the family, my aunt had no time to finish my gown. As a result, I had to buy an ugly pink one for twenty dollars at the last minute. As if I didn't have enough problems, my corsage of yellow carnations looked terrible with my pink gown, and it didn't have any memorable scent at all. My boyfriend's brother was out of

Expository Writing

town, so we had to go in a stripped-down Chevy that he used at the speed races on weekends. We went to one party where I drank some red wine that made me very sleepy, and it also upset my stomach. After we finally arrived at the prom, I didn't have much more to eat than a cold roll and some celery sticks. Because my stupid boyfriend and I had had a fight several days before, we ended up leaving early without dancing to my favorite song. We had seen enough of each other that night. 2

Since that night I have become enough of a realist to understand that things never work out quite the way they are planned, but I still doubt that dream and reality will ever be as widely separated as they were that May evening in 1980. 3

Discussion Questions

1. This comparison is clearly accomplished by topics, as the title suggests. What points are associated with the dream, and what corresponding points are elaborated for the reality?
2. This essay contains a concluding paragraph but no introductory one. Do you find that to be a shortcoming?

The Changing World of Women

The life-styles of women have changed drastically in the last thirty years and are still changing today. Basically, there have been four major changes. These have been in sexual attitudes, marriage ideas, marriage roles, and career opportunities. 1

The first major change has been in sexual attitudes. Thirty years ago it was considered taboo for a woman even to say the word "sex" in public. Today women as well as men are able to discuss sex and its problems and joys freely and openly. Additionally, women are now emphasizing their roles as sexual partners and leaders rather than inferiors and followers, and men are accepting that change, too. 2

Another change has been in the idea of marriage. Formerly it was believed that a woman must either marry young or risk becoming a spinster. And a woman who did not marry was thought to be inferior and abnormal. However, today's woman has numerous options open to her besides early marriage. Most important, a single woman is no longer looked down upon by society. 3

A third change has been in the woman's role in marriage. In the past it was generally agreed that a mother's place was in the home and a father's was at work. Today, though, it is perfectly acceptable for a mother to work outside the home. In fact, in some cases the traditional roles have been reversed, so that the homemaker wears a beard with his apron.   4

The last major change has been in career opportunities. Thirty years ago the only jobs available to women were domestic work and, if properly educated, teaching jobs. But today's woman is no longer stereotyped into certain jobs. She has many opportunities open to her, as a business executive, engineer, government leader, and on and on. One notable recent change is that the United States military academies have opened their doors to women, and many are accepting this new challenge.   5

Although the life-styles of women have changed drastically, there are still other changes to come. Yet most women are now accepting the changes and challenges of today's world.   6

Discussion Questions

1. Is "The Changing World of Women" organized clearly? Comment on the use of transitional devices. How many points are covered?
2. Which points are developed most adequately? What examples could be used to clarify or develop the points in each instance? What would be gained by the addition of such examples?
3. A weakness of this student's paper, beyond its lack of specific examples, is the tendency to overgeneralize. Cite one example of this tendency.

Traveling the White Water

There are at least two ways to travel down a river containing white water. One way is in a raft; the other is in a canoe.   1

A raft is made of tear-resistant rubber; therefore, you can hit a lot of rocks and simply bounce off. A river canoe is made of fiber glass or aluminum, so it is necessary to miss as many rocks as possible. A raft is half as wide as it is long, a design that makes it very stable. On the other hand, a canoe is not stable, its length exceeding its width by a factor of five or seven to one. Not surprisingly, careless and unbalanced lateral motion, which is no big deal in a raft, causes a canoe to tip over quite easily.   2

Class I and II rapids — small regular waves with small drops and clear passages that require no maneuvering — can be successfully negotiated in a raft by any beginner. A canoe is altogether different. Class I and II rapids do require the canoeist to be practiced in order to keep the canoe straight on course.   3

Class III and IV rapids — large, numerous, and irregular waves with narrow passages, significant drops, and crosscurrents of fast and powerful water — can be successfully negotiated by the novice rafter without super-precise maneuvering. However, these rapids will quickly damage, if not destroy, a canoe along with its occupants, unless they are skilled and careful.   4

A white-water raft trip is relatively safe. You can even get slightly intoxicated along the way. A white-water canoe trip is a challenge. You can even get slightly killed.   5

Discussion Questions

1. Here is a comparison of raft and canoe travel that is arranged by points. What are these points?
2. The writer has to describe or define items as the comparison is made. What are these items?
3. The conclusion of this essay perhaps strikes you as being quite clever. What makes it so?

Essays:
Comparison

Fable for Tomorrow
Rachel Carson

Rachel Carson (1907–1964) was a scientist and author whose book *Silent Spring* (1962) is generally recognized as having begun the "save our environment" movement in the United States. That book, which made Americans aware of the dangers of pesticides, is the source for the essay below. Carson's writing earned her many honors, including the National Book Award for nonfiction, won by her earlier, best-selling book, *The Sea Around Us* (1951); it is the source of two other, shorter Carson selections in this textbook.

There was once a town in the heart of America where all life seemed to live in harmony with its surroundings. The town lay in the midst of a checkerboard of prosperous farms, with fields of grain and hillsides of orchards where, in spring, white clouds of bloom drifted above the green fields. In autumn, oak and maple and birch set up a blaze of color that flamed and flickered across a backdrop of pines. Then foxes barked in the hills and deer silently crossed the fields, half hidden in the mists of the fall mornings.

Along the roads, laurel, viburnum and alder, great ferns and wildflowers delighted the traveler's eye through much of the year. Even in winter the roadsides were places of beauty, where countless birds came to feed on the berries and on the seed heads of the dried weeds rising above the snow. The countryside was, in fact, famous for the abundance and variety of its bird life, and when the flood of migrants was pouring through in spring and fall people traveled from great distances to observe them. Others came to fish the streams, which flowed clear and cold out of the hills and contained shady pools where trout lay. So it had been from the days many years ago when the first settlers raised their houses, sank their wells, and built their barns.

Then a strange blight crept over the area and everything began to change. Some evil spell had settled on the community: mysterious maladies swept the flocks of chickens; the cattle and sheep sickened and died. Everywhere was a shadow of death. The farmers spoke of much illness among their families. In the town the doctors had become more and more puzzled by new kinds of sickness appearing among their patients. There had been several sudden and unexplained deaths, not only among adults but even among children, who would be stricken suddenly while at play and die within a few hours.

There was a strange stillness. The birds, for example — where had they gone? Many people spoke of them, puzzled and disturbed. The feeding stations in the backyards were deserted. The few birds seen anywhere were moribund; they trembled violently and could not fly. It was a spring without voices. On the mornings that had once throbbed with the dawn chorus of robins, catbirds, doves, jays, wrens, and scores of other bird voices there was now no sound; only silence lay over the fields and woods and marsh.

On the farms the hens brooded, but no chicks hatched. The farmers complained that they were unable to raise any pigs — the litters were small and the young survived only a few days. The apple trees were coming into bloom but no bees droned among the blossoms, so there was no pollination and there would be no fruit.

The roadsides, once so attractive, were now lined with browned and withered vegetation as though swept by fire. These, too, were silent, deserted by all living things. Even the streams were now lifeless. Anglers no longer visited them, for all the fish had died.

In the gutters under the eaves and between the shingles of the roofs, a white granular powder still showed a few patches; some weeks before it had fallen like snow upon the roofs and the lawns, the fields and streams.

No witchcraft, no enemy action had silenced the rebirth of new life in this stricken world. The people had done it themselves.

This town does not actually exist, but it might easily have a thousand counterparts in America or elsewhere in the world. I know of no community that has experienced all the misfortunes I describe. Yet every one of these disasters has actually happened somewhere, and many real communities have already suffered a substantial number of them. A grim specter has crept upon us almost unnoticed, and

Section 4: Comparison

this imagined tragedy may easily become a stark reality we all shall know.

Discussion: Content

1. What animals are affected by the blight described in "Fable for Tomorrow"?
2. Why do the apple trees fail to produce?
3. Is there any clue to the source of blight?
4. What or who is responsible for the blight?
5. What do you suppose has caused the transformation of this town and countryside?

Discussion: Form

1. Is this comparison accomplished by points or by topics?
2. Why is this method particularly suitable?
3. What transitional word serves as a turning point? Where is it?
4. When does the comparison end?
5. Why do you suppose Carson's paragraphs become consistently shorter from 2 through 8? What purpose is served by the longer paragraph, 9?

Columbus and the Moon
Tom Wolfe

Tom Wolfe (1931–   ), a native of Virginia and graduate of Washington and Lee University, began his professional career as a newspaperman, working for the Washington *Post* and the New York *Herald*. Some of his books include *The Kandy-Kolored Tangerine-Flake Streamline Baby* (1965), *The Electric Kool-Aid Acid Test* (1968), *Radical Chic and Mau-Mauing the Flak Catchers* (1970), *The Right Stuff* (1977), and *From Bauhaus to Our House* (1981). The following essay first appeared in the New York *Times* in 1979.

The National Aeronautics and Space Administration's moon landing ten years ago today was a Government project, but then so was Columbus's voyage to America in 1492. The Government, in Columbus's case, was the Spanish Court of Ferdinand and Isabella. Spain was engaged in a sea race with Portugal in much the same way that the United States would be caught up in a space race with the Soviet Union four and a half centuries later.

The race in 1492 was to create the first shipping lane to Asia. The Portuguese expeditions had always sailed east, around the southern tip of Africa. Columbus decided to head due west, across open ocean, a scheme that was feasible only thanks to a recent invention — the magnetic ship's compass. Until then ships had stayed close to the great land masses even for the longest voyages. Likewise, it was only thanks to an invention of the 1940's and early 1950's, the high-speed electronic computer, that NASA would even consider propelling astronauts out of the Earth's orbit and toward the moon.

Both NASA and Columbus made not one but a series of voyages. NASA landed men on six different parts of the moon. Columbus made four voyages to different parts of what he remained convinced was the east coast of Asia. As a result both NASA and Columbus had to keep coming back to the Government with their hands out, pleading for refinancing. In each case the reply of the Government became, after a few years: "This is all very impressive, but what earthly good is it to anyone back home?"

Columbus was reduced to making the most desperate claims. When he first reached land in 1492 at San Salvador, off Cuba, he expected to find gold, or at least spices. The Arawak Indians were awed by the strangers and their ships, which they believed had descended from the sky, and they presented them with their most prized possessions, live parrots and balls of cotton. Columbus soon set them digging for gold, which didn't exist. So he brought back reports of fabulous riches in the form of manpower; which is to say, slaves. He was not speaking of the Arawaks, however. With the exception of criminals and prisoners of war, he was supposed to civilize all natives and convert them to Christianity. He was talking about the Carib Indians, who were cannibals and therefore qualified as criminals. The Caribs would fight down to the last unbroken bone rather than endure captivity, and few ever survived the voyages back to Spain. By the end of Columbus's second voyage, in 1496, the Government was becoming testy. A great deal of wealth was going into voyages to Asia, and very little was coming back. Columbus made his men swear to return to Spain saying that they had not only reached the Asian mainland, they had heard Japanese spoken.

Likewise by the early 1970's, it was clear that the moon was in economic terms pretty much what it looked like from Earth, a gray rock. NASA, in the quest for appropriations, was reduced to publi-

Section 4: Comparison

cizing the "spinoffs" of the space program. These included Teflon-coated frying pans, a ball-point pen that would write in a weightless environment, and a computerized biosensor system that would enable doctors to treat heart patients without making house calls. On the whole, not a giant step for mankind.

In 1493, after his first voyage, Columbus had ridden through Barcelona at the side of King Ferdinand in the position once occupied by Ferdinand's late son, Juan. By 1500, the bad-mouthing of Columbus had reached the point where he was put in chains at the conclusion of his third voyage and returned to Spain in disgrace. NASA suffered no such ignominy, of course, but by July 20, 1974, the fifth anniversary of the landing of Apollo 11, things were grim enough. The public had become gloriously bored by space exploration. The fifth anniversary celebration consisted mainly of about two hundred souls, mostly NASA people, sitting on folding chairs underneath a camp meeting canopy on the marble prairie outside the old Smithsonian Air Museum in Washington listening to speeches by Neil Armstrong, Michael Collins, and Buzz Aldrin and watching the caloric waves ripple.

Extraordinary rumors had begun to circulate about the astronauts. The most lurid said that trips to the moon, and even into Earth orbit, had so traumatized the men, they had fallen victim to religious and spiritualist manias or plain madness. (Of the total seventy-three astronauts chosen, one, Aldrin, is known to have suffered from depression, rooted, as his own memoir makes clear, in matters that had nothing to do with space flight. Two teamed up in an evangelical organization, and one set up a foundation for the scientific study of psychic phenomena — interests the three of them had developed long before they flew in space.) The NASA budget, meanwhile, had been reduced to the light-bill level.

Columbus died in 1509, nearly broke and stripped of most of his honors as Spain's Admiral of the Ocean, a title he preferred. It was only later that history began to look upon him not as an adventurer who had tried and failed to bring home gold — but as a man with a supernatural sense of destiny, whose true glory was his willingness to plunge into the unknown, including the remotest parts of the universe he could hope to reach.

NASA still lives, albeit in reduced circumstances, and whether or not history will treat NASA like the admiral is hard to say.

The idea that the exploration of the rest of the universe is its own reward is not very popular, and NASA is forced to keep talking about things such as bigger communications satellites that will enable live television transmission of European soccer games at a fraction of the current cost. Such notions as "building a bridge to the stars for mankind" do not light up the sky today — but may yet.   10

Discussion: Content

1. From what historical perspective on the moon landing is Wolfe writing? How, if at all, have attitudes toward NASA and space exploration changed since Wolfe wrote this essay?
2. What country was Spain's competitor in the race to win riches in the New World?
3. What invention, perfected in the late 1940's and early 1950's, allowed astronauts to venture out of Earth's orbit?
4. Why has NASA focused increasingly on the importance of the spinoffs from the space exploration rather than on the explorations themselves?
5. Why did Columbus endure such ill fame in his lifetime?

Discussion: Form

1. In this essay we have a strikingly clear example of comparison by points. What are the topics that Wolfe is comparing, and what points do they have in common?
2. The comparison is not quite complete. What point raised in paragraph 8 with respect to Columbus is not countered with a corresponding point for the space program?
3. List some examples Wolfe cites of the "desperate claims" that both Columbus and the space program were forced to make in order to keep their expeditions funded.

The Almighty Dollar
W. H. Auden

W. H. Auden (1907–1973) was born in England and was educated at Oxford University. He emigrated to the United States in 1939 and became a citizen in 1946. He taught and lectured at universities in America and abroad and won numerous honors for his poetry, including the Pulitzer Prize in 1948. Also a master of prose, Auden wrote the brief essay below as part of *The Dyer's Hand and Other Essays* (1962).

Section 4:
Comparison

Political and technological developments are rapidly obliterating all cultural differences and it is possible that, in a not remote future, it will be impossible to distinguish human beings living on one area of the earth's surface from those living on any other, but our different pasts have not yet been completely erased and cultural differences are still perceptible. The most striking difference between an American and a European is the difference in their attitudes towards money. Every European knows, as a matter of historical fact, that in Europe wealth could only be acquired at the expense of other human beings, either by conquering them or by exploiting their labor in factories. Further, even after the Industrial Revolution began, the number of persons who could rise from poverty to wealth was small; the vast majority took it for granted that they would not be much richer nor poorer than their fathers. In consequence, no European associates wealth with personal merit or poverty with personal failure. 1

To a European, money means power, the freedom to do as he likes, which also means that, consciously or unconsciously, he says: "I want to have as much money as possible myself and others to have as little money as possible." 2

In the United States, wealth was also acquired by stealing, but the real exploited victim was not a human being but poor Mother Earth and her creatures who were ruthlessly plundered. It is true that the Indians were expropriated or exterminated, but this was not, as it had always been in Europe, a matter of the conqueror seizing the wealth of the conquered, for the Indian had never realized the potential riches of his country. It is also true that, in the Southern states, men lived on the labor of slaves, but slave labor did not make them fortunes; what made slavery in the South all the more inexcusable was that, in addition to being morally wicked, it didn't even pay off handsomely. 3

Thanks to the natural resources of the country, every American, until quite recently, could reasonably look forward to making more money than his father, so that, if he made less, the fault must be his; he was either lazy or inefficient. What an American values, therefore, is not the possession of money as such, but his power to make it as proof of his manhood; once he has proved himself by making it, it has served its function and can be lost or given away. In no society in history have rich men given away so large a part of their fortunes. A poor American feels guilty at being poor, but less guilty than an American *rentier* who had inherited wealth but is doing nothing to increase it; what can the latter do but take to drink and psychoanalysis? 4

In the Fifth Circle on the Mount of Purgatory, I do not think that many Americans will be found among the Avaricious, but I suspect that the Prodigals may be almost an American colony. The great vice of Americans is not materialism but a lack of respect for matter. 5

Discussion: Content

1. Where in paragraph 1 do you find Auden's thesis statement? Do you agree with it? Why or why not?
2. What is the difference between what money means for a European and what it means for an American?
3. According to Auden, Europeans exploit other people to become wealthy. Whom or what did the Americans exploit?
4. How true is Auden's judgment of the prodigality of Americans in the final paragraph? What, if any, signs of changes in American attitudes toward natural resources have you noticed?

Discussion: Form

1. Is Auden's essay organized by points, topics, or some combination of these? What is gained by his chosen form of organization?
2. Why do you suppose the space devoted to the discussion of the American side of the contrast is lengthier than that for the European side?
3. What is suggested about Auden's intended reading audience by the use of the French term *rentier* and the literary allusion to the Fifth Circle on the Mount of Purgatory in Dante's *Divine Comedy?*

Education and Training
Harry Kemelman

Harry Kemelman (1908–   ) grew up in Boston, receiving his education at Boston University and Harvard. He has worked as both a high school and a college teacher, but he is best known for his detective novels, which feature a crime-solving rabbi. The adventures of Rabbi Small appear in the following: *Friday the Rabbi Slept Late* (1964),

Saturday the Rabbi Went Hungry (1966), *Sunday the Rabbi Stayed Home* (1969), *Monday the Rabbi Took Off* (1972), *Tuesday the Rabbi Saw Red* (1973), *Wednesday the Rabbi Got Wet* (1976), and *Thursday the Rabbi Walked Out* (1978). The selection below is taken from a nonfiction work, *Common Sense in Education* (1970).

To understand the nature of the liberal arts college and its function in our society, it is important to understand the difference between *education* and *training*.

Training is intended primarily for the service of society; education is primarily for the individual. Society needs doctors, lawyers, engineers, teachers to perform specific tasks necessary to its operation, just as it needs carpenters and plumbers and stenographers. Training supplies the immediate and specific needs of society so that the work of the world may continue. And these needs, our training centers — the professional and trade schools — fill. But although education is for the improvement of the individual, it also serves society by providing a leavening of men of understanding, of perception, and wisdom. They are our intellectual leaders, the critics of our culture, the defenders of our free traditions, the instigators of our progress. They serve society by examining its function, appraising its needs, and criticizing its direction. They may be earning their livings by practicing one of the professions, or in pursuing a trade, or by engaging in business enterprise. They may be rich or poor. They may occupy positions of power and prestige, or they may be engaged in some humble employment. Without them, however, society either disintegrates or else becomes an anthill.

The difference between the two types of study is like the difference between the discipline and exercise in a professional baseball training camp and that of a Y gym. In the one, the recruit is training to become a professional baseball player who will make a living and serve society by playing baseball; in the other, he is training only to improve his own body and musculature. The training at the baseball camp is all relevant. The recruit may spend hours practicing how to slide into second base, not because it is a particularly useful form of calisthenics but because it is relevant to the game. The exercise would stop if the rules were changed so that sliding to a base was made illegal. Similarly, the candidate for the pitching staff spends a lot of time throwing a baseball, not because it will improve his physique — it may have quite the opposite effect — but because pitching is to be his principal function on the team. At the Y gym, exercises have no such relevance. The intention is to strengthen the body in general, and when the members sit down on the floor with their legs outstretched and practice touching their fingers to their toes, it is not because they hope to become galley slaves, perhaps the only occupation where that particular exercise would be relevant.

In general, relevancy is a facet of training rather than of education. What is taught at law school is the present law of the land, not the Napoleonic Code or even the archaic laws that have been scratched from the statute books. And at medical school, too, it is modern medical practice that is taught, that which is relevant to conditions today. And the plumber and the carpenter and the electrician and the mason learn only what is relevant to the practice of their respective trades in this day with the tools and materials that are presently available and that conform to the building code.

In the liberal arts college, on the other hand, the student is encouraged to explore new fields and old fields, to wander down the bypaths of knowledge. There the teaching is concerned with major principles, and its purpose is to change the student, to make him something different from what he was before, just as the purpose of the Y gym is to make a fat man into a thin one, or a strong one out of a weak one.

Clearly the two types of learning overlap. Just as the baseball recruit gets rid of excess weight and tightens his muscles at the baseball camp and thereby profits even if he does not make the team, so the law student sharpens his mind and broadens his understanding, even if he subsequently fails the bar exam and goes on to make his living in an entirely different kind of work. His study of law gives him an understanding of the rules under which our society functions and his practice in solving legal problems gives him an understanding of fine distinctions.

On the other hand, the Y member, whose original reason for joining may have been solely to get himself in shape, may get caught up in the institution's basketball program and find that his skill has developed to the point where he can play the game professionally. Similarly, the student who undertakes a course of study merely because it interests him and he wants to know more about it may find that it has commerical value. He has studied a foreign language and literature in order to understand the society that produced it, and then he may find that his special knowledge enables him to get a job as a translator. Or he may find that while his knowledge of chemistry is not of professional caliber, it is still sufficient to give him preference in a particular job over someone who lacks even that modicum of knowledge of the subject. But these are accidental and incidental. In general, certain courses of study are for the service of society and other courses are for self-improvement. In the hierarchy of our educational system, the former are the function of our professional schools and the latter are the function of the colleges of liberal arts.

Discussion: Content

1. According to Kemelman, training serves society, and education serves the individual. What does he mean by that?
2. Are those who do exercises at the Y engaging in an activity that is similar to what Kemelman means by training or by education?
3. Are those who attend baseball camp taking part in training or education?
4. What is the one word that more than any others distinguishes education from training?
5. Are there instances in which training and education overlap?

Discussion: Form

1. This comparison essay is structured according to points. How many points does Kemelman adduce, and where are they treated?
2. In paragraph 3 Kemelman introduces a new pair of topics. What seems to be his purpose in doing so?
3. Paragraphs 6 and 7 do not seem to further the comparison. What is their apparent function?
4. There is no separate concluding paragraph in this essay. Yet toward the end of paragraph 7 there are several sentences that could indeed be set off as a conclusion. Which sentences are these?

Section 5: Analogy

In the last section we examined comparison as an expository or informative tool. There is another type of informative technique that is related closely to comparison. This is *analogy*.

To understand analogy it will be helpful for you to recall another use for comparisons that we discussed much earlier — namely, descriptive comparisons. As a descriptive device comparisons can be *literal*, or possible (He looked as though he had tasted something sour), as opposed to those that are *figurative*, or fantastic (His face resembled a prune).

Literal descriptive comparisons resemble the informative comparisons discussed in the last section. Baseball teams are literally alike. They have certain points in common — personnel, hitting, pitching, fielding, etc. Similarly, human societies can be literally compared with respect to their status symbols — things like wealth, real estate, education, transportation, and the like — even though those societies are as widely separated as those of America and Polynesia. In other words, we think of baseball teams or human societies as things that can be logically compared.

On the other hand, we often are inclined to make comparisons between things that cannot be logically compared. In descriptive writing this is what similes and metaphors are all about. A human face, however withered and wrinkled, will never, literally, look like a prune. The suggestion is that the face you are describing shares with a prune at least one striking characteristic — deep wrinkles. And that comparison is highly descriptive.

Such figurative comparisons can also be highly informative, and when they are, they are called analogies. A very common analogy is the comparison of an echo to bouncing a rubber ball off a wall. Sound waves and bouncing rubber balls have very little in common and cannot logically be compared in the same way that baseball teams or human societies can. Nevertheless, such a figurative comparison is informative simply because the average reader can be expected to envision the movement of a rubber ball more clearly than the movement of sound waves.

A great many difficult or complicated explanations employ the strategy of analogy because it is so helpful in assisting readers to understand the unfamiliar in terms of the familiar. Atomic structures are compared to solar systems with orbiting planets, although planets have nothing in common with the electrons revolving around the atomic nuclei. And human brains are often compared with machines, even though the resemblance is fantastic, to say the least. And electrical current is almost always explained in terms of water flowing through a pipe. Such analogies are successful informative tools because readers, however little they may know about solar systems, machinery, or plumbing, will know more about them than atomic structures, human brains, or electricity.

Remember that Jesus was a successful teacher because he recognized that his listeners knew more about sheep herding, farming, or money lending than they did about the kingdom of heaven. So he used analogies based on such common and familiar activities to explain his vision — and changed the world.

The paragraphs and essays that follow all employ the strategy of analogy, for they compare entities that are essentially dissimilar. But the purpose of each is to lead readers to a better understanding of something unfamiliar by comparing it to something most people already know about. As implied above, you probably have encountered analogies in the reading for physics, chemistry, or other technical and scientific courses; more practice will make you an even better reader of such material. You may also have occasion to use analogy in your own writing, especially as you are called upon to explain concepts learned in your studies: how psychologists view a child's mind as a blank tablet, how biologists view each ecological system as a separate small world, and so forth.

**Paragraphs:
Analogy**

The Flight of a Sparrow
Bede

Another of the king's chief men . . . soon added: "The present life of man, O king, seems to me, in comparison to that time which is unknown to us, like the swift flight of a sparrow through the room wherein you sit at supper in winter, with your commanders and ministers, and a good fire in the midst, whilst the storms of rain and snow prevail abroad; the sparrow, flying in at one door, and immediately out at another, whilst he is within, is safe from the wintry storm; but after a short space of fair weather, he immediately vanishes out of your sight, into the dark winter from which he had emerged. So this life of man appears for a short space, but of what went before, or what is to follow, we are utterly ignorant."

Discussion Questions

1. Analogy is frequently a successful expository tool, for the complex or the unfamiliar may be made understandable by comparison with something simple or familiar. In this regard, the life of man is nothing like the flight of a sparrow, except at the crucial point of resemblance that concerns the king's counselor. This analogy must have been extremely successful, though, because Bede (?673–735), who included this episode in the first history of England, credits it with the conversion of the Northumbrians (in northeast England) to Christianity. How do you suppose this analogy helped convince people to adopt Christianity?
2. What other analogies can you think of that have been used to explain religious principles? What is suggested by the frequent use of analogies to explain religious principles?

Renewal from the Roots
Woodrow Wilson

When I look back on the processes of history, when I survey the genesis of America, I see this written over every page: that the nations are renewed from the bottom, not from the top; that the genius which springs up from the ranks of unknown men is the genius which renews the youth and energy of the people. Everything I know about history, every bit of experience and observation that has contributed to my thought, has confirmed me in the conviction that the real wisdom of human life is compounded out of the experience of ordinary man. The utility, the vitality, the fruitage of life does not come from the top to the bottom. It comes, like the natural growth of a great tree, from the soil, up through the trunk into the branches to the foliage and the fruit. The great struggling unknown masses of the men who are at the base of everything are the dynamic force that is lifting the levels of society. A nation is as great, and only as great, as her rank and file.

Discussion Questions

1. The notion of how a nation renews or rejuvenates itself is one that is fairly foreign to most readers. So Wilson uses an analogy suggesting that this obscure process is really quite like one that even a schoolchild will be familiar with. What is that familiar process that Wilson uses?
2. In the first and second sentences Wilson repeats himself for emphatic effect. What point is he emphasizing, and how do you suppose he might support such a point?

A River Pilot's Knowledge
Mark Twain

First of all, there is one faculty which a pilot must incessantly cultivate until he has brought it to absolute perfection. Nothing short of perfection will do. That faculty is memory. He cannot stop with merely thinking a thing is so and so; he must *know* it; for this is eminently one of the "exact" sciences. With what scorn a pilot was looked upon, in the old times, if he ever ventured to deal in that feeble phrase "I think," instead of the vigorous one "I know!" One cannot easily realize what a tremendous thing it is to know every trivial detail of 1200 miles of river and know it with absolute exactness. If you will take the longest street in New York, and travel up and down it, conning its features patiently until you know every house and window and door and lamp-post and big and little sign by heart, and know them so accurately that you can instantly name the one you are abreast of when you are set down at random in that street in the middle of an inky black night, you will then have a tolerable notion of the amount and the exactness of a pilot's knowledge who carries the Mississippi River in his head. And then if you will go on until you know every street crossing, the character, size, and position of the crossing-stones, and the varying depth of mud in each of those numberless places, you will have some idea of what the pilot must know in order to keep a Mississippi steamer out of trouble. Next, if you will take half of the signs in that long street, and *change their places* once a month, and still manage to know their positions accurately on dark nights, and keep up with these repeated changes without making any mistakes, you will understand what is required of a pilot's peerless memory by the fickle Mississippi.

Discussion Questions

1. Twain seems almost to be groping for a way to make his readers understand how highly a river pilot's memory must be developed, but he finds a way that works. Why, though, do you suppose he chose a street in New York instead of in some other city as the basis for his analogy?
2. Why do you think he insisted on emphasizing the words "change their places" by using italics?
3. Try creating your own analogy between some specialized skill or knowledge and something familiar to all of us.

Daedalus and Icarus
Sir Arthur Eddington

In ancient days two aviators procured for themselves wings. Daedalus flew safely through the middle air and was duly honoured on his landing. Icarus soared upwards to the sun till the wax melted which bound his wings, and his flight ended in fiasco. In weighing their achievements, there is something to be said for Icarus. The classical authorities tell us that he was only "doing a stunt," but I prefer to think of him as the man who brought to light a serious constructional defect in the flying-machines of his day. So, too, in Science. Cautious Daedalus will apply his theories where he feels confident they will safely go; but by his excesses of caution their hidden weaknesses remain undiscovered. Icarus will strain his theories to the breaking-point till the weak joints gape.

Discussion Questions

1. Eddington takes the familiar story of Daedalus and Icarus and uses it to explain a more difficult and poorly understood point about science. What exactly is that point? Who or what do Daedalus and Icarus represent?
2. The pivotal sentence in the paragraph turns out not to be a sentence at all. What is it? Does it upset the paragraph?

Student Work:
Analogy

Freshman English

Freshman English is very much like going to the dentist. The due dates for paragraphs and essays are as ugly on your calendar as dental appointments, and as each one approaches, anxiety increases. You begin each paper with the same feeling of resignation that brings you to the dentist's office, and trying to think of a topic is usually as shallow an activity as the reading of last year's magazines in the waiting room. Anyway, you're too worried about the outcome to think straight. But the most painful part is just getting started, and it's the same at the dentist's: after the painful stab of Novocain, everything settles into dullness. And just as that numbed feeling hangs on while the dentist probes around in your mouth, doing things you can't see, you also have that drugged feeling while you wait to get your paper back, knowing that the teacher is probing around among your sentences. Finally, getting the paper back is like having the Novocain wear off, so that you're now painfully aware of each little probing that has gone on — and even more anxious about the next scheduled appointment.

Discussion Questions

1. In most analogies the points of comparison are few because the subjects to be compared are essentially dissimilar. Here freshman English and a visit to the dentist are certainly dissimilar topics, and yet the student writer has come up with a surprising number of points. How many do you count?
2. One technique that the writer uses effectively is the repetition of key words common to both freshman English and dental visits.

Anxiety is one such word. Can you discover three more such words or expressions?

My Friend, the Pen

This pen, the green and silver one I am using at this moment, is like a friend, having an individual personality that appeals to me. Picking the right color, shape, design, and texture of a pen is as important as choosing a friend because I like my pen to be with me at all times. We spend hours of leisure time together, working puzzles and games, sketching pictures, or creating poetry. Through journals and diaries we share secrets and important thoughts that nobody else knows. My pen looks out for my welfare, keeping me well organized and notified about important dates on my calendar. It is a spokesman for me when I cannot be there personally, writing letters or dashing off notes. Take the time to find a likable pen and befriend it; it will serve you as well as you serve it — like a true friend.

Discussion Questions

1. Like the writer of "Freshman English," this writer has managed to discover a surprising number of points that friends and pens have in common. What are they?
2. In order to be effective, an analogy must lead the reader to a better understanding of an unfamiliar concept by showing how that unfamiliar concept is like something that the reader is familiar with. Does this analogy work this way? What is your estimation of its effectiveness?

Fraternal Itch

Being in a fraternity or sorority is like putting on wool underwear. The benefits do not always compensate for the discomfort. There is the warm, snug feeling of having ready-made friends, but there is always the nagging itch of those two or three that a person simply does not like and cannot get away from. A good brother or sister has to tolerate these itches — to grin and bear them — because to do otherwise would violate established customs. It is not polite to scratch. But after a while, getting rid of the itch becomes a very urgent matter — to get away for the weekend, away for the summer, or out of the organization altogether — a body just has to get out of that underwear.

Discussion Questions

1. List the points that wearing wool underwear and being in a fraternity or sorority have in common.
2. Where does the writer state the thesis of the paragraph?
3. If you are a contented member of a fraternity, sorority, or similar social organization, you may want to challenge this analogy in writing. You may do so by constructing your own analogy whose points of comparison are positive and attractive rather than negative.

Sunbathing on Scott Beach

Sunbathing on Scott Beach is in many respects just like roasting a pig. It is not at all easy for the sunbather or the pig to become well done, but in the event of success, the result in either case is an appetizing delight. To insure success a number of steps must be taken.

First, the sunbather must be properly dressed and spitted — with as much surface area exposed as possible and situated to receive as much direct radiation as possible. Next, the sunbather begins by marinating her body with browning oils and basting it with aromatic spices, both to arouse the appetite of onlookers and to prevent the tender meat from drying out. To achieve an even cooking, continual rotation is necessary.

During the final stages careful observation of the skin must be maintained to determine whether it is ready or not. This is a most difficult step, and only the most trained eye can tell when it is time to remove the carcass from the fire. The sunbather who is reckless in her first roasting will turn out with a skin that is blistered or charred and generally discolored — extremely tender to the touch. And if someone should slap her burnt back, her expression will not be unlike that of a roasted pig with an apple in its mouth.

Discussion Questions

1. One student solved a problem like those posed for you in question 3 at the end of the Twain selection by likening "Sunbathing on Scott Beach" to roasting a pig. Notice how the language used to describe the preparation of the sunbather overlaps the terminology for pig roasting. What effect is thus created?
2. In addition to analogy the writer is making use of another rhetorical method of development already discussed. What is it? What transitional devices clearly point out the writer's concern for this technique?

Fishing for the Buyer

A good salesman in many respects is just like a good fisherman. It is not easy to attract that wary buyer to a lure of merchandise when he does not hunger for the goods offered, yet the good salesman can hook the consumer almost every time.   1

First, like any good fisherman, the salesman entices the buyer with good bait. Some salesmen prefer natural bait, but the majority these days use the much cheaper artificials, with a lot of doubletalk for smell. When he has turned the unlucky customer's head and has his interest, it is then time for the second stage in this delicate process of catching the buyer.   2

The salesman must then make his prey believe the bait is about to escape. There are several ways of doing this. One effective method is to tell the customer that he is not sure he wants to sell this fine object, since it once belonged to his grandmother and perhaps the salesman should keep it in the family and pass it on to his heirs. This shake of the bait seldom fails to make the customer twice as eager to get his jaws around that delightful tidbit that is trying to evade his waiting stomach. Another way to jiggle the bait is to say that the expected new shipment of this item will have to sell for a higher price or will be of inferior quality. In any case, the way is prepared for the final stage.   3

This last stage, perhaps the most difficult, is one that results in a trophy-sized sale if successful. It is easy to get the customer to bite, but hard to get him landed, where he will pay. Many salesmen swear by the "let-'em-run-with-it" method. This enables the customer to take the bait "on time." He is allowed to make monthly payments or to use a charge card. In either case he does not realize what a trap he is getting into until it is too late. One advantage of this method is that in many cases it enables the salesman to use the law as a kind of landing net, not only for gaining the trophy but in somes cases for recovering the bait as well! 4

Yes, a salesman, especially a novice, can learn much from an experienced fisherman, for a buyer is just as eager to take some attractive merchandise bait as a mountain trout is for the right kind of fly. The proof can be found in the thousands of green trophies that fill the wallet-creels of thousands of successful salesmen. 5

Discussion Questions

1. Where does the writer of this essay pause to give concrete *examples?* How does he make clear the steps of the process?
2. Overlapping terminology is also used in "Fishing for the Buyer." Mark the passages that display this "overlapping" language in this model, and then try to incorporate this technique in your own analogy papers.

Essays:
Analogy

Pinball
J. Anthony Lukas

J. Anthony Lukas (1933–   ) is an American journalist who has written for the Baltimore *Sun* and the New York *Times;* he won the Pulitzer Prize for local reporting in 1968. Since 1971 he has been a free-lance writer, his work appearing in such national magazines as *Esquire, Harper's New Republic, Psychology Today,* and *Atlantic Monthly,* from which the following essay has been excerpted. He has written two best-selling books: *Don't Shoot: We Are Your Children!* (1971) and *Nightmare: The Underside of the Nixon Years* (1975).

Pinball is a metaphor for life, pitting man's skill nerve, persistence, and luck against the perverse machinery of human existence. The playfield is rich with rewards: targets that bring huge scores, bright lights, chiming bells, free balls, and extra games. But it is replete with perils, too: culs-de-sac, traps, gutters, and gobble holes down which the ball may disappear forever.   1

Each pull of the plunger launches the ball into a miniature universe of incalculable possibilities. As the steel sphere hurtles into the ellipse at the top of the playfield, it hangs for a moment in exquisite tension between triumph and disaster. Down one lane lies a hole worth thousands, down another a sickening lurch to oblivion. The ball trembles on the lip, seeming to lean first one way, then the other.   2

A player is not powerless to control the ball's wild flight, any more than man is powerless to control his own life. He may nudge the machine with hands, arms, or hips, jogging it just enough to change the angle of the ball's descent. And he is armed with "flippers" which can propel the ball back up the playfield, aiming at the targets with the richest payoffs. But, just as man's boldest strokes and bravest ventures often boomerang, so an ill-timed flip can ricochet the ball straight down "death alley," and a too vigorous nudge will send the machine into "tilt." Winning pinball, like rewarding life, requires delicate touch, fine calibrations, careful discrimination between boldness and folly. 3

Discussion: Content

1. Lukas begins by calling pinball a metaphor for life. What does he mean by that? Is a metaphor the same as an analogy?
2. To what extent does Lukas suggest that man can govern his own destiny in life?

Discussion: Form

1. Aside from the opening sentence, Lukas offers us few overt reminders that there is an analogy at work. How many times and where does Lukas again call the reader's attention to the analogy?
2. If overt reminders are few or absent altogether, as they are in paragraph 2, how is the analogy sustained so that the reader does not forget the ongoing comparison?

The Change Revolution
Neil Postman
Charles Weingartner

Neil Postman and Charles Weingartner both finished doctorates in education at Columbia University in 1958, and not long afterwards they began co-authoring a successful series of books on education. Their titles include *Linguistics: A Revolution of Teaching* (1966), *Language in America* (1970), *The Soft Revolution* (1971), and *The School Book* (1973). Weingartner has been professor of education at the University of South Florida since 1970, while Postman continues as professor of education at New York University, his latest book being *Teaching as a Conserving Activity* (1979). The essay below is excerpted from their best-selling book, *Teaching as a Subversive Activity* (1969).

In order to illustrate what ["Change Revolution"] means, we will use the media . . . and the metaphor of a clock face. Imagine a clock face with sixty minutes on it. Let the clock stand for the time men have had access to writing systems. Our clock would thus represent something like three thousand years, and each minute on our clock fifty years. On this scale, there were no significant media changes until about nine minutes ago. At that time, the printing press came into use in Western culture. About three minutes ago, the telegraph, photograph, and locomotive arrived. Two minutes ago: the telephone, rotary press, motion pictures, automobile, airplane, and radio. One minute ago, the talking picture. Television has appeared in the last ten seconds, the computer in the last five, and communications satellites in the last second. The laser beam — perhaps the most potent medium of communication of all — appeared only a fraction of a second ago. 1

It would be possible to place almost any area of life on our clock face and get roughly the same measurements. For example, in medicine, you would have almost no significant changes until about one minute ago. In fact, until one minute ago, as Jerome Frank has said, almost the whole history of medicine is the history of the placebo effect. About a minute ago, antibiotics arrived. About ten seconds ago, open-heart surgery. In fact, within the past ten seconds there probably have been more changes in medicine than is represented by all the rest of the time on our clock. This is what some people call the "knowledge explosion." It is happening in every field of knowledge susceptible to scientific inquiry. 2

The standard reply to any comment about change (for example, from many educators) is that change isn't new and that it is easy to exaggerate its meaning. To such replies, Norbert Wiener had a useful answer: the difference between a fatal and a therapeutic dose of strychnine is "only a matter of degree." In other words, change isn't new; what is new is the *degree of change*. As our clock-face metaphor was intended to suggest, about three minutes ago there developed a qualitative difference in the character of change. Change changed. 3

This is really quite a new problem. For example, up until the last generation it was possible to be born, grow up, and spend a life in the United States without moving more than 50 miles from home, without ever confronting serious questions about one's basic values, beliefs, and patterns of behavior. Indeed, without ever confronting serious challenges to anything one knew. Stablity and consequent predictability — within "natural cycles" — was the characteristic mode. But now, in just the last minute, we've reached the stage where change occurs so rapidly that each of us in the course of our lives has *continuously* to work out a set of values, beliefs, and patterns of behavior that are viable, or *seem* viable, to each of us personally. And just when we have identified a workable system, it turns out to be irrelevant because so much has changed while we were doing it. 4

Discussion: Content

1. Postman and Weingartner use the analogy of the clock face to illustrate rapid changes in what two areas of human activity?
2. What generalization about change do the authors make after their examination of rapid changes within these two areas?

Discussion: Form

1. How exactly does the clock-face metaphor enable Postman and Weingartner to explain their notion of the increasing degree of change more efficiently?
2. How might you characterize the difference between a metaphor and an analogy?

The Salmon Instinct
William Humphrey

William Humphrey (1924–   ) was born in Texas and attended Southern Methodist University and the University of Texas. His first novel, *Home from the Hill* (1958), brought widespread critical attention. It was followed by *The Ordways* (1965) and *Proud Flesh* (1973). His favorite subject is the American Southwest, and he has chronicled its literature in *Ah Wilderness: The Frontier in American Literature* (1977). The following selection is taken from a book which deals with his boyhood, *Farther Off from Heaven* (1977).

When James I, King of England, was asked why he was going back, after a long absence, to visit his native Scotland, he replied, "The salmon instinct." 1
   The salmon is in his early adolescence when he leaves his native stream, impelled by an irresistible urge for something he has never

known, the salt, salt sea. There he stays for the rest of his life, until he feels another prompting equally irresistible, the urge to reproduce himself. This the salmon can do only in that same stream in which he was born. And so, from distances as great as fifteen hundred miles, the old salmon heads for home.

Many things can, and do, kill the salmon on his long voyage home, but nothing can deter or detour him. Not the diseases and parasites he is prone to, not fishermen, commercial or sporting, not the highest falls. He endures them, he eludes them, he leaps them, impelled by his ardent homesickness. Though long an expatriate, he knows his nationality as a naturalized American knows his, and back to the country of his birth he goes, as though throughout all the years away he has kept his first passport. Through the pathless sea he finds his way unerringly to the river down which he came on his voyage out long ago, and past each of its tributaries, each more temptingly like the one he is seeking the nearer he gets to that special one, as towns in the same county are similar but not the same. When he gets to his, he knows it — as I, for instance, know Clarksville, and would know it even if, like the salmon, I had but one sense to lead me to it. The name given the salmon in Latin is *Salmo salar:* the fish that will leap waterfalls to get back home. Some later Linnaeus of the human orders must have classed me at birth among the Humphreys: in Welsh the name means "One who loves his hearth and home."

But I began to doubt my homing instincts, to think I had wandered too far away, stayed gone too long, when, after crossing the ocean, I went back those thirty-two years later.

I had spent a few days in Dallas first, as the homecoming salmon spends a few days in the estuary to reaccustom himself to sweet water after all his years at sea before ascending to his native stream; for although this is what he now longs for, those uterine waters of his, too sudden a change from the salt is a shock to him. Dallas had always been brackish to me.

The nearer I got to Clarksville the farther from it I seemed to be. This was not where I was spawned. Strange places had usurped the names of towns I used to know. It was like what the British during World War II, fearing an invasion, had done, setting real but wrong place-names and roadsigns around the countryside so that the enemy in, say, Kent would find himself in villages belonging to Lancashire.

Gone were the spreading cottonfields I remembered, though this was the season when they should have been beginning to whiten. The few patches that remained were small and sparse, like the patches of snow lingering on in sunless spots in New England in March and

April. The prairie grass that had been there before the fields were broken for cotton had reclaimed them. The woods were gone . . . grazing land now, nearly all of it. For in a move that reverses Texas history, a move totally opposite to what I knew in my childhood, one which all but turns the world upside down, which makes the sun set in the East, Red River Country has ceased to be Old South and become Far West. I who for years had had to set my Northern friends straight by pointing out that I was a Southerner, not a Westerner, and that I had never seen a cowboy or for that matter a beefcow any more than they had, found myself now in that Texas of legend and the popular image which when I was a child had seemed more romantic to me than to a boy of New England precisely because it was closer to me than to him and yet still worlds away. Gone from the square were the bib overalls of my childhood when the farmers came to town on Saturday. Ranchers now, they came in high-heeled boots and rolled-brim hats, a costume that would have provoked as much surprise, and even more derision, there, in my time, as it would on Manhattan's Madison Avenue. 7

You can never ascend the same river twice, an early philosopher tells us. Its course, its composition are ever changing. Even so, one of its natives knows it, even one, like the salmon, who has spent most of his life away. I had been away from Clarksville since my father's death, and although ever since then I had been surprised each day to find myself alive, I was now an older man than he had lived to be. In that time much had changed in Clarksville; still, it was where I belonged. 8

Just as the salmon must leave home when the time comes, so he must return to round out his life. There where he was born, he dies. 9

Discussion: Content

1. What activity involving Humphrey personally prompted him to contemplate the instinctive behavior of salmon?
2. Following Humphrey, briefly describe the amazing life cycle of the salmon.
3. How do salmon find their way back to their spawning grounds?
4. What surprising changes does Humphrey observe about the land surrounding Clarksville?
5. Why does Humphrey say that the Texas of legend — its cowboys and beef cattle — was more romantic to him as a boy than it was to others?

Section 5: Analogy

Discussion: Form

1. What points do the author's behavior and that of a salmon have in common?
2. What additional similarity does Humphrey contemplate in the last two paragraphs?
3. What expository purpose does the analogy involving the salmon serve in this essay?
4. To make his analogy more successful, Humphrey on occasion personifies salmon, giving them human attributes, and likewise refers to himself using terminology more suitable to salmon. Cite some instances of both uses.

Feeding the Mind
Lewis Carroll

Lewis Carroll was the pseudonym for Charles L. Dodgson (1832–1898), a British mathematician, logician, and teacher at Oxford University. He is best known for nonsense verse, mathematical riddles, fantasies, and children's stories, especially *Alice's Adventures in Wonderland* (1865) and *Through the Looking-Glass* (1872). Carroll's wit and unconventional viewpoint may also be seen in the following essay.

Breakfast, dinner, tea; in extreme cases, breakfast, luncheon, dinner, tea, supper, and a glass of something hot at bedtime. What care we take about feeding the lucky body! Which of us does as much for his mind? And what causes the difference? Is the body so much the more important of the two?

By no means; but life depends on the body being fed, whereas we can continue to exist as animals (scarcely as men) though the mind be utterly starved and neglected. Therefore Nature provides that, in case of serious neglect of the body, such terrible consequences of discomfort and pain shall ensue as will soon bring us back to a sense of our duty; and some of the functions necessary to life she does for us altogether, leaving us no choice in the matter. It would fare but ill with many of us if we were left to superintend our own digestion and circulation. "Bless me!" one would cry, "I forgot to wind up my heart this morning! To think that it has been standing still for the last three hours!" "I can't walk with you this afternoon," a friend would say, "as I have no less than eleven dinners to digest. I had to let them stand over from last week, being so busy — and my doctor says he will not answer for the consequences if I wait any longer!"

Well it is, I say, for us, that the consequences of neglecting the body can be clearly seen and felt; and it might be well for some if the mind were equally visible and tangible — if we could take it, say, to the doctor and have its pulse felt!

"Why, what have you been doing with this mind lately? How have you fed it? It looks pale, and the pulse is very slow."

"Well, doctor, it has not had much regular food lately. I gave it a lot of sugar-plums yesterday."

"Sugar-plums! What kind?"

"Well, they were a parcel of conundrums, sir."

"Ah! I thought so. Now just mind this: if you go on playing tricks like that, you'll spoil all its teeth, and get laid up with mental indigestion. You must have nothing but the plainest reading for the next few days. Take care now! No novels on any account!"

Considering the amount of painful experience many of us have had in feeding and dosing the body, it would, I think, be quite worth our while to try to translate some of the rules into corresponding ones for the mind.

First, then, we should set ourselves to provide for our mind its *proper kind* of food; we very soon learn what will, and what will not, agree with the body, and find little difficulty in refusing a piece of the tempting pudding or pie which is associated in our memory with that terrible attack of indigestion, and whose very name irresistibly recalls rhubarb and magnesia; but it takes a great many lessons to convince us how indigestible some of our favorite lines of reading are, and again and again we make a meal of the unwholesome novel, sure to be followed by its usual train of low spirits, unwillingness to work, weariness of existence — in fact by mental nightmare.

Then we should be careful to provide this wholesome food in *proper amount*. Mental gluttony, or overreading, is a dangerous propensity, tending to weakness of digestive power, and in some cases to loss of appetite; we know that bread is a good and wholesome food, but would like to try the experiment of eating two or three loaves at a sitting?

I have heard of a physician telling his patient — whose complaint was merely gluttony and want of exercise — that "the earliest symptom of hypernutrition is a deposition of adipose tissue," and no doubt the fine long words greatly consoled the poor man under his increasing load of fat.

I wonder if there is such a thing in nature as a *fat mind?* I really think I have met with one or two minds which could not keep up with

Section 5: Analogy

the slowest trot in conversation, could not jump over a logical fence to save their lives, always got stuck fast in a narrow argument, and, in short, were fit for nothing but to waddle helplessly through the world.

Then, again, though the food be wholesome and in proper amount, we know that we must not consume *too many kinds at once*. Take the thirsty haymaker a quart of beer, or a quart of cider, or even a quart of cold tea, and he will probably thank you (though not so heartily in the last case!). But what think you his feelings would be if you offered him a tray containing a little mug of beer, a little mug of cider, another of cold tea, one of hot tea, one of coffee, one of cocoa, and corresponding vessels of milk, water, brandy-and-water, and buttermilk? The sum total might be a quart, but would it be the same thing to the haymaker?

Having settled the proper kind, amount, and variety of our mental food, it remains that we should be careful to allow *proper intervals* between meal and meal, and not swallow the food hastily without mastication, so that it may be thoroughly digested; both of which rules for the body are also applicable at once to the mind.

First as to the intervals: these are as really necessary as they are for the body, with this difference only, that while the body requires three or four hours' rest before it is ready for another meal, the mind will in many cases do with three or four minutes. I believe that the interval required is much shorter than is generally supposed, and from personal experience I would recommend anyone who has to devote several hours together to one subject of thought to try the effect of such a break, say once an hour — leaving off for five minutes only, each time, but taking care to throw the mind absolutely "out of gear" for those five minutes, and to turn it entirely to other subjects. It is astonishing what an amount of impetus and elasticity the mind recovers during those short periods of rest.

And then as to the mastication of the food: the mental process answering to this is simply *thinking over* what we read. This is a very much greater exertion of mind than the mere passive taking in the contents of our author — so much greater an exertion is it, that, as Coleridge says, the mind often "angrily refuses" to put itself to such trouble — so much greater, that we are far too apt to neglect it altogether, and go on pouring in fresh food on the top of the undigested masses already lying there, till the unfortunate mind is fairly swamped under the flood. But the greater the exertion, the more valuable, we may be sure, is the effect; one hour of steady thinking over a subject (a solitary walk is as good an opportunity for the process as any other) is worth two or three of reading only.

And just consider another effect of this thorough digestion of the books we read; I mean the arranging and "ticketing," so to speak, of the subjects in our minds, so that we can readily refer to them when we want them. Sam Slick tells us that he has learned several languages in his life, but somehow "couldn't keep the parcels sorted" in his mind; and many a mind that hurries through book after book, without waiting to digest or arrange anything, gets into that sort of condition, and the unfortunate owner finds himself far from fit really to support the character all his friends give him. 18

"A thoroughly well-read man. Just you try him in any subject, now. You can't puzzle him!" 19

You turn to the thoroughly well-read man, you ask him a question, say, in English history (he is understood to have just finished reading Macaulay); he smiles good-naturedly, tries to look as if he knew all about it, and proceeds to dive into his mind for the answer. Up comes a handful of very promising facts, but on examination they turn out to belong to the wrong century, and are pitched in again; a second haul brings up a fact much more like the real thing, but unfortunately along with it comes a tangle of other things — a fact in political economy, a rule in arithmetic, the ages of his brother's children, and a stanza of Gray's "Elegy"; and among all these the fact he wants has got hopelessly twisted up and entangled. Meanwhile everyone is waiting for his reply, and as the silence is getting more and more awkward, our well-read friend has to stammer out some half-answer at last, not nearly so clear or so satisfactory as an ordinary schoolboy would have given. And all this for want of making up his knowledge into proper bundles and ticketing them! 20

Do you know the unfortunate victim of ill-judged mental feeding when you see him? Can you doubt him? Look at him drearily wandering around a reading-room, tasting dish after dish — we beg his pardon, book after book — keeping to none. First a mouthful of novel — but, no, faugh! he has had nothing but that to eat for the last week, and is quite tired of the taste; then a slice of science, but you know at once what the result of that will be —- ah, of course, much too tough for *his* teeth. And so on through the old weary round, which he tried (and failed in) yesterday, and will probably try, and fail in, tomorrow. 21

Mr. Oliver Wendell Holmes, in his very amusing book *The Professor at the Breakfast-table,* gives the following rule for knowing whether a human being is young or old. "The crucial experiment is this. Offer a bulky bun to the suspected individual just ten minutes before dinner. If this is easily accepted and devoured, the fact of youth is established." He tells us that a human being, "if young, will eat anything at any hour of the day or night." 22

Section 5: Analogy

211

To ascertain the healthiness of the *mental* appetite of a human animal, place in its hands a short, well-written, but not exciting treatise on some popular subject — a mental *bun*, in fact. If it is read with eager interest and perfect attention, *and if the reader can answer questions on the subject afterwards,* the mind is in first-rate working order; if it be politely laid down again, or perhaps lounged over for a few minutes, and then, "I can't read this stupid book! Would you hand me the second volume of *The Mysterious Murder?*" you may be equally sure that there is something wrong in the mental digestion. 23

If this paper has given you any useful hints on the important subject of reading, and made you see that it is one's duty no less than one's interest to "read, mark, learn, and inwardly digest" the good books that fall in your way, its purpose will be fulfilled. 24

Discussion: Content

1. List Carroll's five rules for the proper feeding of the mind.
2. To what process involved in feeding the body does Carroll liken thinking over what we have read?
3. The supposedly well-read person who cannot summon up a piece of needed information is suffering from what failure?
4. How does Oliver Wendell Holmes distinguish a young person from an old one? How does Carroll apply Holmes' rule to the readers he is discussing?

Discussion: Form

1. Although the central analogy here is Carroll's likening reading to eating, he uses at least one other analogical comparison. Locate it.
2. Into how many parts does Carroll *divide* his analogy?
3. Where does he use overlapping language, as the students did in "Sunbathing on Scott Beach" and "Fishing for the Buyer"?
4. What comment would you make about the *tone* of this essay (Carroll's attitude toward his subject and audience)? How does he achieve this stance? What words and phrases reveal this tone?

Section 6: Cause and Effect

Hardly a day goes by that we are not confronted with some perplexing situation, one that evokes in us the question *why?* In asking *why*, we are following a natural line of reasoning, another of those convenient channels in which human thoughts flow — causal analysis.

The answer to any question involving *why* entails a statement of cause. Why did the Japanese attack Pearl Harbor? Why did the cake fail to rise? Why do gentlemen prefer blondes? The answers to these questions will clearly be reasons or causes.

Some of these questions may have but a single answer. The reason for the cake's not rising was the failure of the cook to follow the recipe, which called for baking powder. The reasons for the assault on Pearl Harbor or a gentleman's preference for blondes may be much more complicated. Whatever the causes may be and however complex they may appear, we can make some fairly certain observations about them. They may be divided into *immediate* causes and *remote* causes. For example, we might assert that the attack on Pearl Harbor was precipitated by the abiding commitment of the Japanese nation to sea power — control of the Pacific seaways. If this was true, then the U.S. Pacific fleet posed a threat to control of the Pacific. So it follows that the desire to eliminate a presumed threat was an immediate cause, while the commitment to sea power was a more remote cause. We might go on to claim that the commitment to sea power arose from the geographical isolation Japan as a nation had always enjoyed, an even more remote cause.

You must understand that there can be a number of immediate and remote causes. The threat posed by the U.S. Pacific fleet was not the only immediate cause for the attack on Pearl Harbor; vast petroleum reserves stored at Pearl Harbor could be used by land and air forces to threaten Japan. Likewise, Japan's commitment to nautical supremacy would have been more tolerant of the U.S. Pacific fleet had the Japanese government not entered into an alliance with the Axis bloc, whose implicit aim was world dominion.

The situations we have just analyzed — the fallen cake and the attack on Pearl Harbor — are effects of the causes we have at least partially enumerated. But just as causes may be both immediate and remote, so may effects. More remote effects of the lack of baking powder, beyond the fallen cake, might be the ruination of supper and a loss of esteem for the cook. Less trivially, the attack on Pearl Harbor, while it was the result of Japan's fear of American sea power, was also the cause of a more colossal effect, America's entry into World War II, together with a galvanizing of American sentiments against the Axis powers. So, as you see, effects in turn become causes and lead to other effects, and so on.

When you analyze the following selections, try to determine in each instance whether the writer is informing you of the cause or causes of a particular event or situation, or whether it is the writer's purpose to discuss the effects arising from an event or situation. Or is the writer dealing with both causes and effects?

Bear in mind also just how useful the techniques of cause and effect can be in your own writing. You may be called upon to list the causes for a particular chemical reaction or the reasons why at some point in history a certain political institution failed. You may also be obliged to explain the effects of behavioral psychology on American education or the effects of increased protein consumption in a family's diet. Clearly, the section that follows is an important one. Study it carefully.

**Paragraphs:
Cause and Effect**

W-a-t-e-r
Helen Keller

We walked down the path to the wellhouse, attracted by the fragrance of the honeysuckle with which it was covered. Someone was drawing water and my teacher placed my hand under the spout. As the cool stream gushed over one hand, she spelled into the other the word *water,* first slowly, then rapidly. I stood still, my whole attention fixed upon the motions of her fingers. Suddenly I felt a misty consciousness as of something forgotten — a thrill of returning thought; and somehow the mystery of language was revealed to me. I knew then that "w-a-t-e-r" meant the wonderful cool something that was flowing over my hand. That living word awakened my soul, gave it light, hope, joy, set it free! There were barriers still, it is true, but barriers that could in time be swept away.

Discussion Questions

1. This paragraph is probably the most important one in Helen Keller's autobiography, *The Story of My Life.* If you have read that book, or know something of Miss Keller's life, perhaps from the play or the movie *(The Miracle Worker)* based on it, you understand the importance of this episode. Yet even in the single paragraph there are suggestions, through word choice and figurative language, about the crucial nature of this experience. Identify those key words and figures of speech.
2. The place of this paragraph in a life story also recalls something else: the connection between process, cause and effect, and narration. What event in your life could you relate that integrates these three modes?

Little Lost Appetite
Andrew Ward

I was sitting at an inn with Kelly Susan, my ten-year-old niece, when she was handed the children's menu. It was printed in gay pastels on construction paper and gave her a choice of a Ferdinand Burger, a Freddie the Fish Stick, or a Porky Pig Sandwich. Like most children's menus, it first anthropomorphized the ingredients and then killed them off. As Kelly read it her eyes grew large, and in them I could see gentle Ferdinand being led away to the stockyard, Freddie gasping at the end of a hook, Porky stuttering his entreaties as the ax descended. Kelly Susan, alone in her family, is a resolute vegetarian and has already faced up to the dread that whispers to us as we slice our steaks. She wound up ordering a cheese sandwich, but the children's menu had ruined her appetite, and she spent the meal picking at her food.

Discussion Questions

1. What is the exact cause of Kelly Susan's lost appetite?
2. Although the movement of this paragraph is from cause to effect, the paragraph itself is illustrative of other methods of development you have studied earlier. What methods are those?
3. Look up *personification* in the Glossary. Besides pointing out the anthropomorphizing of the three animals on the menu, Ward uses a more subtle personification. Where is it?

Habit
William James

Habit alone keeps us all within the bounds of ordinance, and saves the children of fortune from the envious uprisings of the poor. It alone prevents the hardest and most repulsive walks of life from being deserted by those brought up to tread therein. It keeps the fisherman and the dock-hand at sea through the winter; it holds the miner in his darkness, and nails the countryman to his log cabin and his lonely farm through all the months of snow; it protects us from invasion by the natives of the desert and the frozen zones. It dooms us all to fight out the battle of life upon the lines of our nurture or our early choice, and to make the best of a pursuit that disagrees, because there is no other for which we are fitted, and it is too late to begin again. It keeps different social strata from mixing. Already at the age of twenty-five you see the professional mannerisms settling down on the young [salesman], on the young doctor, on the young minister, on the young [lawyer]. You see the little lines of cleavage running through the character, the tricks of thought, the prejudices, the ways of the "shop," in a word, from which the man can by and by no more escape than his coat-sleeve can suddenly fall into a new set of folds. On the whole, it is best he should not escape. It is well for the world that in most of us, by the age of thirty, the character has set like plaster, and will never soften again.

Discussion Questions

1. What is gained by the series of brief examples that James furnishes in the third sentence of his paragraph? What more modern ones would you use in revising the paragraph today?
2. Are there any present-day factors that make habit a less important cause of stable human activity than it was at the beginning of this century?

The Destructive Power of a One-Megaton Bomb on New York City
Jonathan Schell

One way to begin to grasp the destructive power of present-day nuclear weapons is to describe the consequences of the detonation of a one-megaton bomb, which possesses eighty times the explosive power of the Hiroshima bomb, on a large city, such as New York. Burst some eighty-five hundred feet above the Empire State Building, a one-megaton bomb would gut or flatten almost every building between Battery Park and 125th Street, or within a radius of four and four-tenths miles, or in an area of sixty-one square miles, and would heavily damage buildings between the northern tip of Staten Island and the George Washington Bridge, or within a radius of about eight miles, or in an area of about two hundred square miles. A conventional explosive delivers a swift shock, like a slap, to whatever it hits, but the blast wave of a sizable nuclear weapon endures for several seconds and can surround and destroy whole buildings. People, of course, would be picked up and hurled away from the blast along with the rest of the debris. Within the sixty-one square miles, the walls, roofs, and floors of any buildings that had not been flattened would be collapsed, and the people and furniture inside would be swept down onto the street. (Technically, this zone would be hit by various overpressures of at least five pounds per square inch. Overpressure is defined as the pressure in excess of normal atmospheric pressure.) As far away as ten miles from ground zero, pieces of glass and other sharp objects would be hurled about by the blast wave at lethal velocities. In Hiroshima, where buildings were low and, outside the center of the city, were often constructed of light materials, injuries from falling buildings were often minor. But in New York, where the buildings are tall and are constructed of heavy materials, the physical collapse of the city would certainly kill millions of people. The streets of New York are narrow ravines running between the high walls of the city's buildings. In a nuclear attack, the walls would fall and the ravines would fill up. The people in the buildings would fall to the street with the debris of the buildings, and the people in the street would be crushed by this avalanche of people and buildings. At a distance of two miles or so from ground zero, winds would reach four hundred miles an hour, and another two miles away they would reach a hundred and eighty miles an hour. Meanwhile, the fireball would be growing, until it was more than a mile wide, and rocketing upward, to a height of over six miles. For ten seconds, it would broil the city below. Anyone caught in the open within nine miles of ground zero would receive third-degree burns and would probably be killed; closer to the explosion, people would be charred and killed instantly. From Greenwich Village up to Central Park, the heat would be great enough to melt metal and glass. Readily inflammable materials, such as newspaper and dry leaves, would ignite in all five boroughs (though in only a small part of Staten Island) and west to the Passaic River, in New Jersey, within a radius of about nine and a half miles from ground zero, thereby creating an area of more than two hundred and eighty square miles in which mass fires were likely to break out.

Discussion Questions

1. Devastation from a one-megaton bomb would result from four immediate effects of the explosion. What are they?

2. Why do you suppose Schell chose to locate the explosion over the Empire State Building?
3. What is gained by comparing the theoretical effects of a one-megaton bomb on New York with the real effects of a much smaller bomb on Hiroshima?
4. If necessary, look up *connotation* and *denotation* in the Glossary. Although Schell tends to use denotative words for his description, now and then he steps out of his objective, scientific pose to use connotative words that electrify his readers' emotions. What ones do you notice?

Student Work:
Cause and Effect

Why Students Leave College

There seem to be five basic reasons why some of our classmates will not be with us when graduation day arrives in four years. The first to leave are the dissatisfied, such as my high school friend who could not adjust to being away from home and among so many strangers. Next to leave are those who get sick or have bad accidents. This happened to a girl down the hall in my dormitory, but she plans to be back after Christmas. Another reason to leave is marriage, either "shotgun" style or being unable to wait until summer or graduation. Also, after the first year or two, some students transfer, either for the reasons that might also make them drop out (get closer to home, marry, money problems) or to earn a degree only offered elsewhere. I, for instance, have been thinking about changing to an engineering major, and I would have to transfer to N.C. State after my sophomore year to finish up. There are two final reasons that cause dropouts: money problems and bad grades. College students everywhere are always short on funds, as seen by such signs as "Dad, Send $. Chip" held up on televised college games; there always seems to be something else to buy — and not just snacks and beer, either. (I know my checkbook balance stays sick, and I've had one emergency loan from home already.) Sometimes even with a part-time job the financial drain cannot be plugged, and students must drop out to work full-time for a while. Finally, some students cannot handle the academic part of college life. For many reasons, from too much partying to weak high school preparation, they flunk out of school. In fact, after looking back over this list, it will be surprising if anyone sitting in this class will be left to graduate in four years.

Expository Writing

Discussion Questions

1. What transitional phrases does the writer use to list the five reasons for leaving school mentioned in the topic sentence?
2. What is the purpose of the sentence that begins, "Also, after the first year or two . . ."? Does this sentence provide a new reason for leaving school? If so, what? If not, why is it in the paragraph?
3. What other expository strategy is abundantly evident in this paragraph?

When a DC-10 Crashes

On the afternoon of May 25, 1979, American Airlines Flight 191, bound for Los Angeles, crashed after its take-off from Chicago's O'Hare Field. There were no survivors, and this immediately led to severe effects on the airlines as well as the traveling public. Many lawsuits were brought against the airline by relatives of the ill-fated passengers. Not only were there lawsuits that would bite deeply into the corporate pocketbook, but the loss of a jet would as well, as did the grounding of all DC-10's — the type of plane that crashed. Because of the Federal Aviation Administration's directive to ground the DC-10, the American traveling public for weeks would lose twelve percent of all passenger seats available on the United States' registered airlines. Not only were there financial problems and problems of overcrowding, but there was the question of the airworthiness of this type of aircraft. After many weeks of careful studies, the jet was found to be airworthy and returned to service, but it had lost the prestige and respect it once had commanded. Even today, people ask before they board a large jet, "Is this a DC-10?"

Discussion Questions

1. The writer of "When a DC-10 Crashes" describes several effects of that crash, dividing the effects into two principal groups. What are they, and what are the effects on each group?
2. This student writer has a favorite transitional phrase, used to emphasize contrasts as well as to add coherence to the paragraph. What is the phrase and where is it found?

3. A common weakness in student writing is the failure to include the sorts of specific facts that clearly relate the writing to the real world outside the classroom. Is that weakness found in this paragraph? Where, if at all, could the paragraph use more facts?

Study Habit Blues

"Just one more cookie and then I *will* start studying." How many times has a student caught herself saying that as the homework piles up and the hours tick by? I myself am a chronic homework procrastinator. I simply will do anything rather than sit down and do homework assignments. But sometimes it is not my fault. It seems that whenever I get serious about sitting down to study, I get distracted.   1

One of the reasons why I get distracted is food, or simply wanting to eat. The minute I sit down to read *The Little, Brown Handbook,* the thought suddenly pops into my head, "Wouldn't a piece of Mom's apple pie be great to eat before I start reading this?" Or if I happen to make the mistake of passing through the kitchen on the way to the den to begin studying and even glance at the refrigerator, I take a detour and concentrate on satisfying my taste buds. Food is my greatest distraction when trying to study.   2

Another thing that I have found distracting when trying to study is the incessant ringing of the telephone. More times than I care to remember, I will be in the middle of studying for a vocabulary test, and the telephone rings. "Hey, it's for you." Naturally, one cannot be rude and decline to speak to the person, and so thirty minutes or more of studying time are used up. This can be very frustrating when I receive four or more phone calls a day.   3

A third reason why I get distracted when attempting to study is the allure of radio and television. Before sitting down to study, I will out of habit turn on the television set or radio, depending on whichever I am closer to at the time. If the "Richard Simmons Show" is on or "Days of Our Lives," I simply cannot move until I learn that new exercise for the hips or find out what is happening between Jessica and Don Craig. The same principle can be applied to the radio. All of the Top Forty rock-and-roll hits are my favorites, and chances are that if I turn the radio on, one of these songs will be playing. So naturally I must hear it in its entirety, and perhaps the one after that, and the one after that, and so on, until an hour or more has passed with no studying done.   4

The above are the main distractions that I encounter when trying to study. But just these few are enough to detain me for hours. So after I have "pigged out" on food, chatted to my friends, and listened to my favorite songs, I must get serious about studying. Unless I just happen to peek into the cookie jar and think, "Just *one* more cookie and then I *will* start studying." 5

Discussion Questions

1. What clever device does the writer use to create an overall sense of unity and completeness in this essay?
2. What device does the writer use to link the discussions of her three main distractions together?
3. What is the effect of mentioning the names of particular television programs, together with the names of characters from one of them, rather than simply mentioning exercise shows and soap operas?

Robert Redford Moves to Lenoir

Lenoir is a small town where almost everyone knows everyone else, or at least who their parents were and who they married. Life is very calm and peaceful, with people enjoying their homes, families, and friends. Nothing of national importance or deserving national attention happens there; a few politicians have campaigned and caused a tremendous momentary stir in the community, but life soon returned to normal. Yet I sometimes wonder what would happen if a movie star like Robert Redford moved to Lenoir. 1

First, the moving van would appear, and neighbors, especially the women, would start looking out their windows, inspecting the furniture and speculating about the newcomer's bank account, life-style, and job. Women all over town would know within twenty-four hours about the new residents. 2

After a week of minor excitement the neighborhood would get back to normal. The movers, painters, carpet servicemen, and various other people will have finished their work, and the only thing lacking will be the arrival of the new neighbors. Then one afternoon a car pulls up in front of the house, and simultaneously women peek out between sheer curtains in bedrooms and living rooms. A tall, beautiful blonde woman steps out of the car, and children pile out behind her, running for the house, excited at the prospect of moving into a new home. Now all spying eyes center on the next person getting out of the car. A tall, rugged blond man with sunglasses on steps out and looks around. As he begins strolling easily toward the house, it is easy to imagine the resulting telephone conversations of the neighborhood women. They are struck nearly dumb by the realization that the man of their dreams is moving into their neighborhood. Robert Redford! It is simply too good to be true!

By nightfall, every woman and teen-aged girl in Lenoir knows of the luck which has befallen them. Some nonbelievers actually ride by the home, hoping for a glimpse of their idol. The men, though, scoff at this excitement and at the way women are acting over this "ordinary" man. Secretly, they are half-jealous and half-curious; so during the following week in the houses near the Redfords' the grass gets cut more often, or the garbage is carried out promptly, or fathers decide that their sons need extra softball practice in the backyard, or friends — even mere acquaintances — drop by for a variety of reasons, mostly contrived. Everyone in town finds something to do in that special neighborhood. In some cases, even old grudges are buried in order to get closer to the house and, for a lucky few, to see its inhabitants.

It is impossible, of course, for small-town people, such as those in Lenoir, to try to act normally when Mrs. Redford walks into a store to buy a dress. Salespeople all but run over one another to wait on her, anticipating a large sale, and also to see if their hero has a wife worthy of him. In the end she smiles graciously and asks to see something a little less expensive, saying the dress is nice, but costs a bit more than she wants to spend. By nightfall the news is out — Mrs. Redford is a sale nut, a bargain hunter!

Meanwhile, the neighborhood is buzzing with still another news item — Robert Redford carries out his own garbage! And his wife was actually overheard asking him to please cut the grass that day. That afternoon when the usual crowd of high-school girls takes the new route home through the Redford neighborhood, they nearly swoon when they spot *him* cutting grass, wearing shorts and no shirt. After that the traffic is terrible in the afternoons.

Men and boys laugh at the women for the crazy way they are acting. But motorcycle sales have nearly tripled since Robert Redford was seen riding one. And after a teen-aged boy discovered that Robert Redford sends his wife a single red rose every day, the sale of roses has also skyrocketed. Jogging has also become the chic exercise since the glamorous couple were seen jogging after dinner in matching sweat suits. 7

Certainly if Robert Redford ever did move to Lenoir, it would be by far the biggest thing ever to happen, and it would be discussed by generations to come. 8

Discussion Questions

1. Perhaps Robert Redford will never move to Lenoir, or to your hometown, but if he did, how would the effects differ from those described in the student essay?
2. How many effects are listed? Are they in the best order?
3. What different results might occur if the new resident were a female movie star?

The Downfall of Downtown

Almost every average-sized American town or city has seen its downtown business decrease considerably since the early 1970's. This drop in business is the result of the construction of huge, modern shopping malls. Until these new creations became popular, most downtown stores were not experiencing any serious financial difficulties. 1

Then, as the 1970's began, the idea of constructing shopping malls just outside the city limits spread like wildfire. Plans were made; convenient sites were selected; contracts were signed; and then construction began. The idea of a mall being located in their hometown always excited the local residents, and they anxiously awaited the grand opening. 2

The location of the mall is in itself a great contributing factor to its success. The shopper is not confronted with countless stoplights and parking meters as he is on Main Street. Instead, his trip to the mall on a freeway or bypass is quick and convenient, and parking in the vast lots is free. 3

The new mall is also always a sight to behold. In the new, spacious stores, the customer is swept away by the pleasing surroundings, which include tasteful displays, modern furnishings, modish young salespersons, and other agreeable features that lure buyers. Not only

Section 6:
Cause and Effect

are the stores themselves pleasing to the customer, but the enclosed areas connecting them are an important element that always brings him back to the mall. Unlike the downtown stores where one must go outside on the street and expose himself to all kinds of inclement weather in order to go from one store to another, the hallways in shopping malls are always kept at a desirable temperature and humidity. There are no passing cars to splash water on shoppers' clothes, no icy winds to blow away hats and chill cheeks and ears, no hills to climb. Instead, there is a pleasant, restful atmosphere, with a variety of plants, a multitude of bubbling fountains, a scattering of comfortable benches, plus several effort-saving escalators. Is it any wonder that consumers abandoned the downtown stores and their inconveniences?

Shortly after the malls are completed, the finer stores move from their old buildings on Main Street to the new mall. Only the small shops, owned by those who cannot afford to lease a space in the mall, are left in the downtown section. Of course, fewer and fewer customers will venture onto Main Street to shop in small, dark, seemingly ancient buildings run by old men and women who crouch in tiny back rooms, sipping coffee between spells of coughing. FOR SALE OR LEASE signs appear on increasing numbers of vacant downtown buildings, so that soon a walk down Main Street is much like a walk down a street in a ghost town.

Thus, because of the success of the malls, downtown business across the nation has been reduced terribly, leading city governments to attempt a variety of rescue efforts, intended to revive that business and bring customers back (and, incidentally, to preserve an important part of the tax base). Such promotions as sidewalk sales and downtown festivals have been tried, mostly vain attempts to boost slow sales. Officials have even tried removing parking meters in order to regain customers.

Generally, however, all such attempts are failures. The malls become increasingly successful, while downtown conditions become even worse. Soon there is nothing left but a few privately owned shops and stores, the chain operations having long since fled to the mall. Many of these remaining stores have no place in a mall even if the owners could afford the rent. For example, one does not expect to see a used clothing store or a paperback book shop in a modern shopping mall, not to speak of a pawn shop or an adult book and novelty store. Other downtown businesses include department stores, often dilapidated. Their operators are usually elderly persons who do not remodel their premises because they question whether or not they will live to see the completion of the project, or else are so set in their ways that they stubbornly refuse to modernize.

It is therefore clear that the downtown areas of most American cities will deteriorate more and more, just as city apartments and homes are also becoming decrepit and unsightly as residents flee to suburban housing developments, often to be nearer the new shopping malls.

Discussion Questions

1. In this essay does the writer concentrate on the causes for the downfall of downtown or upon the effects, or both?
2. What is the purpose of paragraphs 1–5? Of paragraphs 6–8? How do you account for the natural break that occurs between paragraphs 5 and 6?
3. What technique that you studied earlier does the writer use with particular effectiveness in paragraphs 4 and 7?

Essays:
Cause and Effect

Thinking Like a Mountain
Aldo Leopold

Aldo Leopold (1886–1948) was one of America's first ecologists. Educated at Yale, he joined the U.S. Forest Service in 1909 and worked in Arizona and New Mexico. There he developed his "land ethic," which ran counter to the thinking of his day. Rejecting the notion that the environment was something that belonged to mankind, Leopold believed that it was instead a community to which mankind belonged. In a series of essays during the 1920's, '30's, and '40's, Leopold expounded his "ecological consciousness." His philosophy is best summarized in *Sand County Almanac* (1949), from which this essay is taken.

A deep chesty bawl echoes from rimrock to rimrock, rolls down the mountain, and fades into the far blackness of the night. It is an outburst of wild defiant sorrow, and of contempt for all the adversities of the world. 1

Every living thing (and perhaps many a dead one as well) pays heed to that call. To the deer it is a reminder of the way of all flesh, to the pine a forecast of midnight scuffles and of blood upon the snow, to the coyote a promise of gleanings to come, to the cowman a threat of red ink at the bank, to the hunter a challenge of fang against bullet. Yet behind these obvious and immediate hopes and fears there lies a deeper meaning, known only to the mountain itself. Only the mountain has lived long enough to listen objectively to the howl of a wolf. 2

Those unable to decipher the hidden meaning know nevertheless that it is there, for it is felt in all wolf country, and distinguishes that country from all other land. It tingles in the spine of all who hear wolves by night, or who scan their tracks by day. Even without sight or sound of wolf, it is implicit in a hundred small events: the midnight whinny of a pack horse, the rattle of rolling rocks, the bound of a fleeing deer, the way shadows lie under the spruces. Only the ineducable tyro can fail to sense the presence or absence of wolves, or the fact that mountains have a secret opinion about them.

My own conviction on this score dates from the day I saw a wolf die. We were eating lunch on a high rimrock, at the foot of which a turbulent river elbowed its way. We saw what we thought was a doe fording the torrent, her breast awash in white water. When she climbed the bank toward us and shook out her tail, we realized our error: it was a wolf. A half-dozen others, evidently grown pups, sprang from the willows and all joined in a welcoming mêlée of wagging tails and playful maulings. What was literally a pile of wolves writhed and tumbled in the center of an open flat at the foot of our rimrock.

In those days we had never heard of passing up a chance to kill a wolf. In a second we were pumping lead into the pack, but with more excitement than accuracy: how to aim a steep downhill shot is always confusing. When our rifles were empty, the old wolf was down, and a pup was dragging a leg into impassable slide-rocks.

We reached the old wolf in time to watch a fierce green fire dying in her eyes. I realized then, and have known ever since, that there was something new to me in those eyes — something known only to her and to the mountain. I was young then, and full of trigger-itch; I thought that because fewer wolves meant more deer, that no wolves would mean hunters' paradise. But after seeing the green fire die, I sensed that neither the wolf nor the mountain agreed with such a view.

* * *

Since then I have lived to see state after state extirpate its wolves. I have watched the face of many a newly wolfless mountain, and seen the south-facing slopes wrinkle with a maze of new deer trails. I have seen every edible bush and seedling browsed, first to anaemic desuetude, and then to death. I have seen every edible tree defoliated to the height of a saddlehorn. Such a mountain looks as if someone had given God a new pruning shears, and forbidden Him all other exercise. In the end the starved bones of the hoped-for deer herd, dead of its own too-much, bleach with the bones of the dead sage, or molder under the high-lined junipers.

I now suspect that just as a deer herd lives in mortal fear of its wolves, so does a mountain live in mortal fear of its deer. And perhaps with better cause, for while a buck pulled down by wolves

Section 6:
Cause and Effect

can be replaced in two or three years, a range pulled down by too many deer may fail of replacement in as many decades. 8

So also with cows. The cowman who cleans his range of wolves does not realize that he is taking over the wolf's job of trimming the herd to fit the range. He has not learned to think like a mountain. Hence we have dustbowls, and rivers washing the future into the sea. 9

* * *

We all strive for safety, prosperity, comfort, long life, and dullness. The deer strives with his supple legs, the cowman with trap and poison, the statesman with pen, the most of us with machines, votes, and dollars, but it all comes to the same thing: peace in our time. A measure of success in this is all well enough, and perhaps is a requisite to objective thinking, but too much safety seems to yield only danger in the long run. Perhaps this is behind Thoreau's dictum: In wildness is the salvation of the world. Perhaps this is the hidden meaning in the howl of the wolf, long known among mountains, but seldom perceived among men. 10

Discussion: Content

1. What particular problem concerns Leopold in this essay? Where does he state the problem in its clearest terms?
2. Does the particular problem dealt with here have any broader ramifications? Does Leopold allude to them?
3. What does it mean to think like a mountain? What use is Leopold making of this notion?

Discussion: Form

1. Compare the introduction and conclusion of this essay with the student essay "Study Habit Blues." How are they similar?
2. What is the purpose of the narrative in paragraphs 4–6 describing the killing of a wolf?
3. In how many places in the essay does Leopold repeat the idea of thinking like a mountain? Why does he do this?
4. In paragraphs 7–9 Leopold concentrates on immediate and remote effects, even setting this section off with special textual marks. What other methods of development does he use to make his case in these three paragraphs?

Causes for the American Spirit of Liberty
Edmund Burke

Edmund Burke (1729–1797), born in Ireland, was a British journalist, longtime member of Parliament, and political commentator and theorist. The excerpt below is from one of his speeches to Parliament during the stormy days before the American Revolution began. This speech, "Moving Resolutions for Conciliation with the Colonies," was delivered on March 22, 1775 — one day before Patrick Henry made his even more famous "Give me liberty, or give me death!" speech in America.

In this character of the Americans, a love of freedom is the predominating feature which marks and distinguishes the whole; and as an ardent is always a jealous affection, your Colonies become suspicious, restive, and untractable whenever they see the least attempt to wrest from them by force, or shuffle from them by chicane, what they think the only advantage worth living for. This fierce spirit of liberty is stronger in the English Colonies probably than in any other people of the earth, and this from a great variety of powerful causes; which, to understand the true temper of their minds and the direction which this spirit takes, it will not be amiss to lay open somewhat more largely.

First, the people of the Colonies are descendants of Englishmen. England, Sir, is a nation which still, I hope, respects, and formerly adored, her freedom. The Colonists emigrated from you when this part of your character was most predominant; and they took this bias and direction the moment they parted from your hands. They are therefore not only devoted to liberty, but to liberty according to English ideas, and on English principles. Abstract liberty, like other mere abstractions, is not to be found. Liberty inheres in some sensible object; and every nation has formed to itself some favorite point, which by way of eminence becomes the criterion of their happiness. It happened, you know, Sir, that the great contests for freedom in this country were from the earliest times chiefly upon the question of taxing. Most of the contests in the ancient commonwealths turned primarily on the right of election of magistrates; or on the balance among the several orders of the state. The question of money was not with them so immediate. But in England it was otherwise. On this point of taxes the ablest pens, and most eloquent tongues, have been exercised; the greatest spirits have acted and suffered. In order to give the fullest satisfaction concerning the importance of this point, it was

1

not only necessary for those who in argument defended the excellence of the English Constitution to insist on this privilege of granting money as a dry point of fact, and to prove that the right had been acknowledged in ancient parchments and blind usages to reside in a certain body called a House of Commons. They went much farther; they attempted to prove, and they succeeded, that in theory it ought to be so, from the particular nature of a House of Commons as an immediate representative of the people, whether the old records had delivered this oracle or not. They took infinite pains to inculcate, as a fundamental principle, that in all monarchies the people must in effect themselves, mediately or immediately, possess the power of granting their own money, or no shadow of liberty can subsist. The Colonies draw from you, as with their life-blood, these ideas and principles. Their love of liberty, as with you, fixed and attached on this specific point of taxing. Liberty might be safe, or might be endangered, in twenty other particulars, without their being much pleased or alarmed. Here they felt its pulse; and as they found that beat, they thought themselves sick or sound. I do not say whether they were right or wrong in applying your general arguments to their own case. It is not easy, indeed, to make a monopoly of theorems and corollaries. The fact is, that they did thus apply those general arguments; and your mode of governing them, whether through lenity or indolence, through wisdom or mistake, confirmed them in the imagination that they, as well as you, had an interest in these common principles.

They were further confirmed in this pleasing error by the form of their provincial legislative assemblies. Their governments are popular in an high degree; some are merely popular; in all, the popular representative is the most weighty; and this share of the people in their ordinary government never fails to inspire them with lofty sentiments, and with a strong aversion from whatever tends to deprive them of their chief importance.

If anything were wanting to this necessary operation of the form of government, religion would have given it a complete effect. Religion, always a principle of energy, in this new people is no way worn out or impaired; and their mode of professing it is also one main cause of this free spirit. The people are Protestants; and of that kind which is the most adverse to all implicit submission of mind and opinion. This is a persuasion not only favorable to liberty, but built upon it. I do not think, Sir, that the reason of this averseness in the dissenting churches from all that looks like absolute government is so much to be sought in their religious tenets, as in their history. Every one knows that the Roman Catholic religion is at least coeval with most of the governments where it prevails; that it has generally gone hand in hand with them, and received great favor and every kind of support from authority. The Church of England too was formed from her cradle under the nursing care of regular government. But the dissenting interests have sprung up in direct opposition to all the ordinary powers of the world, and could justify that opposition only on a strong claim to natural liberty. Their very existence depended on the powerful and unremitted assertion of that claim. All Protestantism, even the most cold and passive, is a sort of dissent. But the religion most prevalent in our Northern Colonies is a refinement on the principle of resistance; it is the dissidence of dissent, and the protestantism of the Protestant religion. This religion, under a variety of denominations agreeing in nothing but in the communion of the spirit of liberty, is predominant in most of the Northern Provinces, where the Church of England, notwithstanding its legal rights, is in reality no more than a sort of private sect, not composing most probably the tenth of the people. The Colonists left England when this spirit was high, and in the emigrants was the highest of all; and even that stream of foreigners which has been constantly flowing into these Colonies has, for the greatest part, been composed of dissenters from the establishments of their several countries, who have brought with them a temper and character far from alien to that of the people with whom they mixed. 4

Sir, I can perceive by their manner that some gentlemen object to the latitude of this description, because in the Southern Colonies the Church of England forms a large body, and has a regular establishment. It is certainly true. There is, however, a circumstance attending these Colonies which, in my opinion, fully counterbalances this difference, and makes the spirit of liberty still more high and haughty than in those to the northward. It is that in Virginia and the Carolinas they have a vast multitude of slaves. Where this is the case in any part of the world, those who are free are by far the most proud and jealous of their freedom. Freedom is to them, not only an enjoyment, but a kind of rank and privilege. Not seeing there, that freedom, as in countries where it is a common blessing and as broad and general as the air, may be united with much abject toil, with great misery, with all the exterior of servitude; liberty looks, amongst them, like something that is more noble and liberal. I do not mean, Sir, to commend the superior morality of this sentiment, which has at least as much pride as virtue in it; but I cannot alter the nature of man. The fact is so; and these people of the Southern Colonies are much more strongly, and with an higher and more stubborn spirit, attached to liberty than those to the northward. Such were all the ancient commonwealths;

Section 6: Cause and Effect

such were our Gothic ancestors; such in our days were the Poles; and such will be all masters of slaves, who are not slaves themselves. In such a people the haughtiness of domination combines with the spirit of freedom, fortifies it, and renders it invincible.

Permit me, Sir, to add another circumstance in our Colonies which contributes no mean part towards the growth and effect of this untractable spirit. I mean their education. In no country perhaps in the world is the law so general a study. The profession itself is numerous and powerful; and in most provinces it takes the lead. The greater number of the deputies sent to the Congress were lawyers. But all who read, and most do read, endeavor to obtain some smattering in that science. I have been told by an eminent bookseller, that in no branch of his business, after tracts of popular devotion, were so many books as those on the law exported to the Plantations. The Colonists have now fallen into the way of printing them for their own use. I hear that they have sold nearly as many of Blackstone's *Commentaries* in America as in England. General Gage marks out this disposition very particularly in a letter on your table. He states that all the people in his government are lawyers, or smatterers in law; and that in Boston they have been enabled, by successful chicane, wholly to evade many parts of one of your capital penal constitutions. The smartness of debate will say that this knowledge ought to teach them more clearly the rights of legislature, their obligations to obedience, and the penalties of rebellion. All this is mighty well. But my honorable and learned friend on the floor, who condescends to mark what I say for animadversion, will disdain that ground. He has heard, as well as I, that when great honors and great emoluments do not win over this knowledge to the service of the state, it is a formidable adversary to government. If the spirit be not tamed and broken by these happy methods, it is stubborn and litigious. This study renders men acute, inquisitive, dexterous, prompt in attack, ready in defence, full of resources. In other countries, the people, more simple, and of a less mercurial cast, judge of an ill principle in government only by an actual grievance; here they anticipate the evil, and judge of the pressure of the grievance by the badness of the principle. They augur misgovernment at a distance, and snuff the approach of tyranny in every tainted breeze.

The last cause of this disobedient spirit in the Colonies is hardly less powerful than the rest, as it is not merely moral, but laid deep in the natural constitution of things. Three thousand miles of ocean lie between you and them. No contrivance can prevent the effect of this distance in weakening government. Seas roll, and months pass, between the order and the execution; and the want of a speedy explanation of a single point is enough to defeat a whole system. You have, indeed, winged ministers of vengeance, who carry your bolts in their pouches to the remotest verge of the sea. But there a power steps in that limits the arrogance of raging passions and furious elements, and says, *So far shalt thou go, and no farther*. Who are you, that you should fret and rage, and bite the chains of nature? Nothing worse happens to you than does to all nations who have extensive empire; and it happens in all the forms into which empire can be thrown. In large bodies the circulation of power must be less vigorous at the extremities. Nature has said it. The Turk cannot govern Egypt and Arabia and Kurdistan as he governs Thrace; nor has he the same dominion in Crimea and Algiers which he has at Brusa and Smyrna. Despotism itself is obliged to truck and huckster. The Sultan gets such obedience as he can. He governs with a loose rein, that he may govern at all; and the whole of the force and vigor of his authority in his centre is derived from a prudent relaxation in all his borders. Spain, in her provinces, is, perhaps, not so well obeyed as you are in yours. She complies, too; she submits; she watches times. This is the immutable condition, the eternal law of extensive and detached empire. 7

Then, Sir, from these six capital sources — of descent, of form of government, of religion in the Northern Provinces, of manners in the Southern, of education, of the remoteness of situation from the first mover of government — from all these causes a fierce spirit of liberty has grown up. It has grown with the growth of the people in your Colonies, and increased with the increase of their wealth; a spirit that unhappily meeting with an exercise of power in England which, however lawful, is not reconcilable to any ideas of liberty, much less with theirs, has kindled this flame that is ready to consume us. 8

Discussion: Content

1. How many causes for the American spirit of liberty does Burke list? What are they? What ones would you modify or delete? What ones would you add, if any?
2. In what region of the American colonies was the spirit of liberty the strongest? What was the cause of that?
3. What specific subject of study did the colonists prefer? What were some of the results of this common interest?
4. The last cause Burke names affects all empires, as history has shown. Cite instances since Burke's time (1775).

5. Burke discusses the American spirit of liberty as an effect, but it soon became the cause of what? Where in Burke's essay does he make a reference to that future effect of the spirit of liberty?

Discussion: Form

1. What rhetorical method does Burke use to develop each of the causes for the American spirit of liberty?
2. How does Burke's audience apparently affect his tone? How are you aware of the respect that he has for his audience?
3. How is implied analogy used in paragraph 7? Is the comparison effective?
4. Burke's essay, complex in content and discussion, is organized very simply. Outline that organization.
5. What is the purpose of paragraph 8? Why is it particularly effective in fulfilling that function? What image is begun in the first sentence and developed in the second? How appropriate is that image?

How Flowers Changed the World
Loren Eiseley

Loren Eiseley (1907–1977) was one of America's foremost anthropologists and writers. A teacher and administrator at the University of Pennsylvania, he achieved worldwide acclaim with the publication of his *Immense Journey* (1957), a book which traces mankind's passage up the evolutionary scale. It is from this book that the following essay is taken. Other works include *Darwin's Century* (1958), winner of the National Phi Beta Kappa Science Award; *The Firmament of Time* (1960), winner of the John Burroughs Association Medal; *The Invisible Pyramid* (1970); *The Night Country* (1971), winner of the Athenaeum of Philadelphia Literary Award; and his autobiography, *All the Strange Hours* (1975).

A little while ago — about one hundred million years, as the geologist estimates time in the history of our four-billion-year-old planet — flowers were not to be found anywhere on the five continents. Wherever one might have looked, from the poles to the equator, one would have seen only the cold dark monotonous green of a world whose plant life possessed no other color.

Somewhere, just a short time before the close of the Age of Reptiles, there occurred a soundless, violent explosion. It lasted millions of years, but it was an explosion, nevertheless. It marked the emergence of the angiosperms — the flowering plants. Even the great evolutionist, Charles Darwin, called them "an abominable mystery," because they appeared so suddenly and spread so fast.

Flowers changed the face of the planet. Without them, the world we know — even man himself — would never have existed. Francis Thompson, the English poet, once wrote that one could not pluck a flower without troubling a star. Intuitively he had sensed like a naturalist the enormous interlinked complexity of life. Today we know that the appearance of the flowers contained also the equally mystifying emergence of man.

If we were to go back into the Age of Reptiles, its drowned swamps and birdless forests would reveal to us a warmer but, on the whole, a sleepier world than that of today. Here and there, it is true, the serpent heads of bottom-feeding dinosaurs might be upreared in suspicion of their huge flesh-eating compatriots. Tyrannosaurs, enormous bipedal caricatures of men, would stalk mindlessly across the sites of future cities and go their slow way down into the dark of geologic time.

In all that world of living things nothing saw save with the intense concentration of the hunt, nothing moved except with the grave sleepwalking intentness of the instinct-driven brain. Judged by modern standards, it was a world in slow motion, a cold-blooded world whose occupants were most active at noonday but torpid on chill nights, their brains damped by a slower metabolism than any known to even the most primitive of warm-blooded animals today.

A high metabolic rate and the maintenance of a constant body temperature are supreme achievements in the evolution of life. They enable an animal to escape, within broad limits, from the overheating or the chilling of its immediate surroundings, and at the same time to maintain a peak mental efficiency. Creatures without a high metabolic rate are slaves to weather. Insects in the first frosts of autumn all run down like little clocks. Yet if you pick one up and breathe warmly upon it, it will begin to move about once more.

In a sheltered spot such creatures may sleep away the winter, but they are hopelessly immobilized. Though a few warm-blooded mammals, such as the woodchuck of our day, have evolved a way of reducing their metabolic rate in order to undergo winter hibernation, it is a survival mechanism with drawbacks, for it leaves the animal helplessly exposed if enemies discover him during his period of suspended animation. Thus bear or woodchuck, big animal or small, must seek, in this time of descending sleep, a safe refuge in some hidden den or burrow. Hibernation is, therefore, primarily a winter refuge of small, easily concealed animals rather than of large ones.

A high metabolic rate, however, means a heavy intake of energy in order to sustain body warmth and efficiency. It is for this reason that even some of these later warm-blooded mammals existing in our day have learned to descend into a slower, unconscious rate of living during the winter months when food may be difficult to obtain. On a slightly higher plane they are following the procedure of the cold-blooded frog sleeping in the mud at the bottom of a frozen pond.

The agile brain of the warm-blooded birds and mammals demands a high oxygen consumption and food in concentrated forms, or the creatures cannot long sustain themselves. It was the rise of the flowering plants that provided that energy and changed the nature of the living world. Their appearance parallels in a quite surprising manner the rise of the birds and mammals.

Slowly, toward the dawn of the Age of Reptiles, something over two hundred and fifty million years ago, the little naked sperm cells wriggling their way through dew and raindrops had given way to a kind of pollen carried by the wind. Our present-day pine forests represent plants of a pollen-disseminating variety. Once fertilization was no longer dependent on exterior water, the march over drier regions could be extended. Instead of spores simple primitive seeds carrying some nourishment for the young plant had developed, but true flowers were still scores of millions of years away. After a long period of hesitant evolutionary groping, they exploded upon the world with truly revolutionary violence.

The event occurred in Cretaceous times in the close of the Age of Reptiles. Before the coming of the flowering plants our own ancestral stock, the warm-blooded mammals, consisted of a few mousy little creatures hidden in trees and underbrush. A few lizard-like birds with carnivorous teeth flapped awkwardly on ill-aimed flights among archaic shrubbery. None of these insignificant creatures gave evidence of any remarkable talents. The mammals in particular had been around for some millions of years, but had remained well lost in the shadow of the mighty reptiles. Truth to tell, man was still, like the genie in the bottle, encased in the body of a creature about the size of a rat.

As for the birds, their reptilian cousins the Pterodactyls, flew farther and better. There was just one thing about the birds that paralleled the physiology of the mammals. They, too, had evolved warm blood and its accompanying temperature control. Nevertheless, if one had been seen stripped of his feathers, he would still have seemed a slightly uncanny and unsightly lizard.

Neither the birds nor the mammals, however, were quite what they seemed. They were waiting for the Age of Flowers. They were waiting for what flowers, and with them the true encased seed, would bring. Fish-eating, gigantic leather-winged reptiles, twenty-eight feet from wing tip to wing tip, hovered over the coasts that one day would be swarming with gulls. 13

Inland the monotonous green of the pine and spruce forests with their primitive wooden cone flowers stretched everywhere. No grass hindered the fall of the naked seeds to earth. Great sequoias towered to the skies. The world of that time has a certain appeal but it is a giant's world, a world moving slowly like the reptiles who stalked magnificently among the boles of its trees. 14

The trees themselves are ancient, slow-growing and immense, like the redwood groves that have survived to our day on the California coast. All is stiff, formal, upright and green, monotonously green. There is no grass as yet; there are no wide plains rolling in the sun, no tiny daisies dotting the meadows underfoot. There is little versatility about this scene; it is, in truth, a giant's world. 15

A few nights ago it was brought home vividly to me that the world has changed since that far epoch. I was awakened out of sleep by an unknown sound in my living room. Not a small sound — not a creaking timber or a mouse's scurry — but a sharp, rending explosion as though an unwary foot had been put down upon a wine glass. I had come instantly out of sleep and lay tense, unbreathing. I listened for another step. There was none. 16

Unable to stand the suspense any longer, I turned on the light and passed from room to room glancing uneasily behind chairs and into closets. Nothing seemed disturbed, and I stood puzzled in the center of the living room floor. Then a small button-shaped object upon the rug caught my eye. It was hard and polished and glistening. Scattered over the length of the room were several more shining up at me like wary little eyes. A pine cone that had been lying in a dish had been blown the length of the coffee table. The dish itself could hardly have been the source of the explosion. Beside it I found two ribbon-like strips of a velvety-green. I tried to place the two strips together to make a pod. They twisted resolutely away from each other and would no longer fit. 17

I relaxed in a chair, then, for I had reached a solution of the midnight disturbance. The twisted strips were wistaria pods that I had brought in a day or two previously and placed in the dish. They had chosen midnight to explode and distribute their multiplying fund of life down the length of the room. A plant, a fixed, rooted thing, immobilized in a single spot, had devised a way of propelling its

Section 6:
Cause and Effect

239

offspring across open space. Immediately there passed before my eyes the million airy troopers of the milkweed pod and the clutching hooks of the sandburs. Seeds on the coyote's tail, seeds on the hunter's coat, thistledown mounting on the winds — all were somehow triumphing over life's limitations. Yet the ability to do this had not been with them at the beginning. It was the product of endless effort and experiment.

The seeds on my carpet were not going to lie stiffly where they had dropped like their antiquated cousins, the naked seeds on the pine-cone scales. They were travelers. Struck by the thought, I went out next day and collected several other varieties. I line them up now in a row on my desk — so many little capsules of life, winged, hooked or spiked. Every one is an angiosperm, a product of the true flowering plants. Contained in these little boxes is the secret of that far-off Cretaceous explosion of a hundred million years ago that changed the face of the planet. And somewhere in here, I think, as I poke seriously at one particularly resistant seedcase of a wild grass, was once man himself.

When the first simple flower bloomed on some raw upland late in the Dinosaur Age, it was wind pollinated, just like its early pine-cone relatives. It was a very inconspicuous flower because it had not yet evolved the idea of using the surer attraction of birds and insects to achieve the transportation of pollen. It sowed its own pollen and received the pollen of other flowers by the simple vagaries of the wind. Many plants in regions where insect life is scant still follow this principle today. Nevertheless, the true flower — and the seed that it produced — was a profound innovation in the world of life.

In a way, this event parallels, in the plant world, what happened among animals. Consider the relative chance for survival of the exteriorly deposited egg of a fish in contrast with the fertilized egg of a mammal, carefully retained for months in the mother's body until the young animal (or human being) is developed to a point where it may survive. The biological wastage is less — and so it is with the flowering plants. The primitive spore, a single cell fertilized in the beginning by a swimming sperm, did not promote rapid distribution, and the young plant, moreover, had to struggle up from nothing. No one had left it any food except what it could get by its own unaided efforts.

By contrast, the true flowering plants (angiosperm itself means "encased seed") grew a seed in the heart of a flower, a seed whose development was initiated by a fertilizing pollen grain independent of outside moisture. But the seed, unlike the developing spore, is already a fully equipped *embryonic plant* packed in a little enclosed box stuffed full of nutritious food. Moreover, by featherdown attachments, as in dandelion or milkweed seed, it can be wafted upward on gusts and ride the wind for miles; or with hooks it can cling to a bear's or a rabbit's hide; or like some of the berries, it can be covered with a juicy, attractive fruit to lure birds, pass undigested through their intestinal tracts and be voided miles away. 22

The ramifications of this biological invention were endless. Plants traveled as they had never traveled before. They got into strange environments heretofore never entered by the old spore plants or stiff pine-cone-seed plants. The well-fed, carefully cherished little embryos raised their heads everywhere. Many of the older plants with more primitive reproductive mechanisms began to fade away under this unequal contest. They contracted their range into secluded environments. Some, like the giant redwoods, lingered on as relics; many vanished entirely. 23

The world of the giants was a dying world. These fantastic little seeds skipping and hopping and flying about the woods and valleys brought with them an amazing adaptability. If our whole lives had not been spent in the midst of it, it would astound us. The old, stiff, sky-reaching wooden world had changed into something that glowed here and there with strange colors, put out queer, unheard-of fruits and little intricately carved seedcases, and, most important of all, produced concentrated foods in a way that the land had never seen before, or dreamed of back in the fish-eating, leaf-crunching days of the dinosaurs. 24

That food came from three sources, all produced by the reproductive system of the flowering plants. There were the tantalizing nectars and pollens intended to draw insects for pollenizing purposes, and which are responsible also for that wonderful jeweled creation, the hummingbird. There were the juicy and enticing fruits to attract larger animals, and in which tough-coated seeds were concealed, as in the tomato, for example. Then, as if this were not enough, there was the food in the actual seed itself, the food intended to nourish the embryo. All over the world, like hot corn in a popper, these incredible elaborations of the flowering plants kept exploding. In a movement that was almost instantaneous, geologically speaking, the angiosperms had taken over the world. Grass was beginning to cover the bare earth until, today, there are over six thousand species. All kinds of vines and bushes squirmed and writhed under new trees with flying seeds. 25

The explosion was having its effect on animal life also. Specialized groups of insects were arising to feed on the new sources of food and,

Section 6:
Cause and Effect

incidentally and unknowingly, to pollinate the plant. The flowers bloomed and bloomed in ever larger and more spectacular varieties. Some were pale unearthly night flowers intended to lure moths in the evening twilight, some among the orchids even took the shape of female spiders in order to attract wandering males, some flamed redly in the light of noon or twinkled modestly in the meadow grasses. Intricate mechanisms splashed pollen on the breasts of hummingbirds, or stamped it on the bellies of black, grumbling bees droning assiduously from blossom to blossom. Honey ran, insects multiplied, and even the descendants of that toothed and ancient lizard-bird had become strangely altered. Equipped with prodding beaks instead of biting teeth they pecked the seeds and gobbled the insects that were really converted nectar. 26

Across the planet grasslands were now spreading. A slow continental upthrust which had been a part of the early Age of Flowers had cooled the world's climates. The stalking reptiles and the leather-winged black imps of the seashore cliffs had vanished. Only birds roamed the air now, hot-blooded and high-speed metabolic machines. 27

The mammals, too, had survived and were venturing into new domains, staring about perhaps a bit bewildered at their sudden eminence now that the thunder lizards were gone. Many of them, beginning as small browsers upon leaves in the forest, began to venture out upon this new sunlit world of the grass. Grass has a high silica content and demands a new type of very tough and resistant tooth enamel, but the seeds taken incidentally in the cropping of the grass are highly nutritious. A new world had opened out for the warm-blooded mammals. Great herbivores like the mammoths, horses and bisons appeared. Skulking about them had arisen savage flesh-feeding carnivores like the now extinct dire wolves and the saber-toothed tiger. 28

Flesh eaters though these creatures were, they were being sustained on nutritious grasses one step removed. Their fierce energy was being maintained on a high, effective level, through hot days and frosty nights, by the concentrated energy of the angiosperms. That energy, thirty percent or more of the weight of the entire plant among some of the cereal grasses, was being accumulated and concentrated in the rich proteins and fats of the enormous game herds of the grasslands. 29

On the edge of the forest, a strange, old-fashioned animal still hesitated. His body was the body of a tree dweller, and though tough and knotty by human standards, he was, in terms of that world into which he gazed, a weakling. His teeth, though strong for chewing on the tough fruits of the forest, or for crunching an occasional unwary bird caught with his prehensile hands, were not the tearing sabers of the great cats. He had a passion for lifting himself up to see about, in his restless, roving curiosity. He would run a little stiffly and uncertainly, perhaps, on his hind legs, but only in those rare moments when he ventured out upon the ground. All this was the legacy of his climbing days; he had a hand with flexible fingers and no fine specialized hoofs upon which to gallop like the wind. 30

If he had any idea of competing in that new world, he had better forget it; teeth or hooves, he was much too late for either. He was a ne'er-do-well, an in-betweener. Nature had not done well by him. It was as if she had hesitated and never quite made up her mind. Perhaps as a consequence he had a malicious gleam in his eye, the gleam of an outcast who has been left nothing and knows he is going to have to take what he gets. One day a little band of these odd apes — for apes they were — shambled out upon the grass; the human story had begun. 31

Apes were to become men, in the inscrutable wisdom of nature, because flowers had produced seeds and fruits in such tremendous quantities that a new and totally different store of energy had become available in concentrated form. Impressive as the slow-moving, dim-brained dinosaurs had been, it is doubtful if their age had supported anything like the diversity of life that now rioted across the planet or flashed in and out among the trees. Down on the grass by a streamside, one of those apes with inquisitive fingers turned over a stone and hefted it vaguely. The group clucked together in a throaty tongue and moved off through the tall grass foraging for seeds and insects. The one still held, sniffed, and hefted the stone he had found. He liked the feel of it in his fingers. The attack on the animal world was about to begin. 32

If one could run the story of that first human group like a speeded-up motion picture through a million years of time, one might see the stone in the hand change to the flint ax and the torch. All that swarming grassland world with its giant bison and trumpeting mammoths would go down in ruin to feed the insatiable and growing numbers of a carnivore who, like the great cats before him, was taking his energy indirectly from the grass. Later he found fire and it altered the tough meats and drained their energy even faster into a stomach ill adapted for the ferocious turn man's habits had taken. 33

His limbs grew longer, he strode more purposefully over the grass. The stolen energy that would take man across the continents would fail him at last. The great Ice Age herds were destined to vanish. When they did so, another hand like the hand that grasped the stone

Section 6:
Cause and Effect

243

by the river long ago would pluck a handful of grass seed and hold it contemplatively.

In that moment, the golden towers of man, his swarming millions, his turning wheels, the vast learning of his packed libraries, would glimmer dimly there in the ancestor of wheat, a few seeds held in a muddy hand. Without the gift of flowers and the infinite diversity of their fruits, man and bird, if they had continued to exist at all, would be today unrecognizable. Archaeopteryx, the lizard-bird, might still be snapping at beetles on a sequoia limb; man might still be a nocturnal insectivore gnawing a roach in the dark. The weight of a petal has changed the face of the world and made it ours.

Discussion: Content

1. In paragraph 3 Eiseley asserts that flowers changed the face of the planet, that their appearance "contained also the equally mystifying emergence of man." Why exactly is the emergence of man linked to the emergence of flowers?
2. Birds also thrived as a result of the flowers. What affinity do birds have for flowers?
3. Eiseley mentions a disturbing explosion in his living room, one involving a wistaria pod. What does that personal narrative serve to illustrate?
4. Among the mammals, which animals still are throwbacks to earlier times in that they adjust their bodies to the prevailing temperatures rather than keeping a steady body temperature?
5. Which paragraphs describe the human being's emergence as a hunter? As a farmer?

Discussion: Form

1. Where does Eiseley state his thesis?
2. What rhetorical technique is Eiseley employing in paragraphs 16–18?
3. Eiseley draws an analogy in paragraphs 21–22 between animal reproduction and that of plants. How does that analogy work?
4. In paragraph 25 Eiseley classifies the types of food provided by the flowering plant. What are these foods, and what is the basis for the classification?

5. One way to divide Eiseley's essay to see how he has handled the various cause-effect relationships might be the following: paragraphs 1–2, 3–15, 16–19, 20–25, 26–29, 30–33, and 34–35. With what cause or effect does each of these portions deal?

Crime and Criminals
Clarence Darrow

Clarence Darrow (1857–1938) was the most famous criminal lawyer of his time, his two most notable trials being the defense of the child-murderers Leopold and Loeb (he won them life sentences instead of the death penalty) and of John Scopes in the so-called Monkey Trial (Scopes was convicted and fined for teaching the doctrine of evolution in a public school, though impartial observers considered Darrow to have bested his equally famous legal opponent, William Jennings Bryan). Among Darrow's publications are two books, *Crime: Its Cause and Treatment* (1922) and *The Story of My Life* (1932). The selection below, though, was originally a speech made in 1902 to prisoners in the Cook County (Chicago), Illinois, jail.

If I looked at jails and crimes and prisoners in the way the ordinary person does, I should not speak on this subject to you. The reason I talk to you on the question of crime, its cause and cure, is because I really do not in the least believe in crime. There is no such thing as a crime as the word is generally understood. I do not believe there is any sort of distinction between the real moral condition of the people in and out of jail. One is just as good as the other. The people here can no more help being here than the people outside can avoid being outside. I do not believe that people are in jail because they deserve to be. They are in jail simply because they can not avoid it on account of circumstances which are entirely beyond their control and for which they are in no way responsible. 1

I suppose a great many people on the outside would say I was doing you harm if they should hear what I say to you this afternoon, but you can not be hurt a great deal anyway, so it will not matter. Good people outside would say that I was really teaching you things that were calculated to injure society, but it's worthwhile now and then to hear something different from what you ordinarily get from preachers and the like. These will tell you that you should be good and then you get rich and be happy. Of course we know that people do not get rich by being good, and that is the reason why so many of you people try to get rich some other way, only you do not understand how to do it quite as well as the fellow outside.

There are people who think that everything in this world is an accident. But really there is no such thing as an accident. A great many folk admit that many of the people in jail ought not to be there, and many who are outside ought to be in. I think none of them ought to be here. There ought to be no jails, and if it were not for the fact that the people on the outside are so grasping and heartless in their dealings with the people on the inside, there would be no such institution as jails.

I do not want you to believe that I think all you people here are angels. I do not think that. You are people of all kinds, all of you doing the best you can, and that is evidently not very well — you are people of all kinds and conditions and under all circumstances. In one sense everybody is equally good and equally bad. We all do the best we can under the circumstances. But as to the exact things for which you are sent here, some of you are guilty and did the particular act because you needed the money. Some of you did it because you are in the habit of doing it, and some of you because you are born to it, and it comes as natural as it does, for instance, for me to be good.

Most of you probably have nothing against me, and most of you would treat me the same as any other person would; probably better than some of the people on the outside would treat me, because you think I believe in you and they know I do not believe in them. While you would not have the least thing against me in the world you might pick my pockets. I do not think all of you would, but I think some of you would. You would not have anything against me, but that's your profession, a few of you. Some of the rest of you, if my doors were unlocked, might come in if you saw anything you wanted — not out of any malice to me, but because that is your trade. There is no doubt there are quite a number of people in this jail who would pick my pockets. And still I know this, that when I get outside pretty nearly everybody picks my pocket. There may be some of you who would hold up a man on the street, if you did not happen to have something else to do, and needed the money; but when I want to light my house or my office the gas company holds me up. They charge me one dollar for something that is worth twenty-five cents, and still all these people are good people; they are pillars of society and support the churches, and they are respectable.

When I ride on the streetcars, I am held up — I pay five cents for a ride that is worth two-and-a-half cents, simply because a body of men have bribed the city council and legislature, so that all the rest of us have to pay tribute to them.

If I do not want to fall into the clutches of the gas trust and choose to burn oil instead of gas, then good Mr. Rockefeller holds me up, and he uses a certain portion of his money to build universities and support churches which are engaged in telling us how to be good.

Some of you are here for obtaining property under false pretenses — yet I pick up a great Sunday paper and read the advertisements of a merchant prince — "Shirtwaists for 39¢, marked down from $3."

When I read the advertisements in the paper I see they are all lies. When I want to get out and find a place to stand anywhere on the face of the earth, I find that it has all been taken up long ago before I came here, and before you came here, and somebody says, "Get off, swim into the lake, fly into the air; go anywhere, but get off." That is because these people have the police and they have the jails and the judges and the lawyers and the soldiers and all the rest of them to take care of the earth and drive everybody off that comes in their way.

A great many people will tell you that all this is true, but that it does not excuse you. These facts do not excuse some fellow who reaches into my pocket and takes out a five-dollar bill; the fact that the gas company bribes the members of the legislature from year to year, and fixes the law, so that all you people are compelled to be "fleeced" whenever you deal with them; the fact that the streetcar companies and the gas companies have control of the streets and the fact that the landlords own all the earth, they say, has nothing to do with you.

Let us see whether there is any connection between the crimes of the respectable classes and your presence in jail. Many of you people are in jail because you have really committed burglary. Many of you, because you have stolen something: in the meaning of the law, you have taken some other person's property. Some of you have entered a store and carried off a pair of shoes because you did not have the price. Possibly some of you have committed murder. I can not tell what all of you did. There are a great many people here who have done some of these things who really do not know themselves why they did them. I think I know why you did them — every one of you; you did these things because you were bound to do them. It looked to you at the time as if you had a chance to do them or not, as you saw fit, but still after all you had no choice. There may be people here who had some money in their pockets and who still went out and got some more money in a way society forbids. Now you may not yourselves see exactly why it was you did this thing, but if you look at the question deeply enough and carefully enough you would see that there were circumstances that drove you to do exactly the thing which you did. You could not help it any more than we outside can help taking the positions that we take. The reformers who tell you to be good and you will be happy, and the people on the outside who have property to protect — they think that the only way to do it is by building jails and locking you up in cells on weekdays and praying for you Sundays.

I think that all of this has nothing whatever to do with right conduct. I think it is very easily seen what has to do with right conduct. Some so-called criminals — and I will use this word because it is handy, it means nothing to me — I speak of the criminals who get caught as distinguished from the criminals who catch them — some of these so-called criminals are in jail for first offenses, but nine-tenths of you are in jail because you did not have a good lawyer and of course you did not have a good lawyer because you did not have enough money to pay a good lawyer. There is no very great danger of a rich man going to jail.

Some of you may be here for the first time. If we would open the doors and let you out, and leave the laws as they are today, some of you would be back tomorrow. This is about as good a place as you can get anyway. There are many people here who are so in the habit of coming that they would not know where else to go. There are people who are born with the tendency to break into jail every chance they get, and they can not avoid it. You can not figure out your life and see why it was, but still there is a reason for it, and if we were all wise and knew all the facts we could figure it out.

In the first place, there are a good many more people who go to jail in the winter time than in the summer. Why is this? Is it because people are more wicked in winter? No, it is because the coal trust begins to get in its grip in the winter. A few gentlemen take possession of the coal, and unless the people will pay $7 or $8 a ton for something that is worth $3, they will have to freeze. Then there is nothing to do but to break into jail, and so there are many more in jail in the winter than in summer. It costs more for gas in the winter because the nights are longer, and people go to jail to save gas bills. The jails are electric-lighted. You may not know it, but these economic laws are working all the time, whether we know it or do not know it.

There are more people who go to jail in hard times than in good times — few people comparatively go to jail except when they are hard up. They go to jail because they have no other place to go. They may not know why, but it is true all the same. People are not more wicked in hard times. That is not the reason. The fact is true all over the world that in hard times more people go to jail than in good times, and in winter more people go to jail than in summer. Of course it is pretty hard times for people who go to jail at any time. The people who go to jail are almost always poor people — people who have no other place to live first and last. When times are hard then you find large numbers of people who go to jail who would not otherwise be in jail.

Long ago, Mr. Buckle, who was a great philosopher and historian, collected facts and he showed that the number of people who are arrested increased just as the price of food increased. When they put up the price of gas ten cents a thousand I do not know who will go to jail, but I do know that a certain number of people will go. When the meat combine raises the price of beef I do not know who is going to jail, but I know that a large number of people are bound to go. Whenever the Standard Oil Company raises the price of oil, I know that a certain number of girls who are seamstresses, and who work night after night long hours for somebody else, will be compelled to go out on the streets and ply another trade, and I know that Mr. Rockefeller and his associates are responsible and not the poor girls in the jails.

First and last, people are sent to jail because they are poor. Sometimes, as I say, you may not need money at the particular time, but you wish to have thrifty forehanded habits, and do not always wait until you are in absolute want. Some of you people are perhaps plying the trade, the profession, which is called burglary. No man in his right senses will go into a strange house in the dead of night and prowl around with a dark lantern through unfamiliar rooms and take chances of his life if he has plenty of good things of the world in his own home. You would not take any such chances as that. If a man had clothes in his clothes-press and beefsteak in his pantry, and money in the bank, he would not navigate around nights in houses where he knows nothing about the premises whatever. It always requires experience and education for this profession, and people who fit themselves for it are no more to blame than I am for being a lawyer. A man would not hold up another man on the street if he had plenty of money in his own pocket. He might do it if he had one dollar or two dollars, but he wouldn't if he had as much money as Mr. Rockefeller has. Mr. Rockefeller has a great deal better holdup game than that.

The more that is taken from the poor by the rich, who have the chance to take it, the more poor people there are who are compelled to resort to these means for a livelihood. They may not understand it, they may not think so at once, but after all they are driven into that line of employment.

There is a bill before the Legislature of this State to punish kidnaping children with death. We have wise members of the Legislature. They know the gas trust when they see it and they always see it — they can furnish light enough to be seen, and this Legislature thinks it is going to stop kidnaping children by making a law punishing kidnapers of children with death. I don't believe in kidnaping children, but the Legislature is all wrong. Kidnaping children is not a crime, it is a profession. It has been developed with the times. It has been developed with our modern industrial conditions. There are many ways of making money — many new ways that our ancestors knew nothing about. Our ancestors knew nothing about a billion-dollar trust; and here comes some poor fellow who has no other trade and he discovers the profession of kidnaping children. 19

This crime is born, not because people are bad; people don't kidnap other people's children because they want the children or because they are devilish, but because they see a chance to get some money out of it. You cannot cure this crime by passing a law punishing by death kidnapers of children. There is only one way to cure it. There is one way to cure all the offenses, and that is to give the people a chance to live. There is no other way, and there never was any other way since the world began, and the world is so blind and stupid that it will not see. If every man and woman and child in the world had a chance to make a decent, fair, honest living, there would be no jails, and no lawyers and no courts. There might be some persons here or there with some peculiar formation of their brain, like Rockefeller, who would do these things simply to be doing them; but they would be very, very few, and those should be sent to a hospital and treated, and not sent to jail; and they would entirely disappear in the second generation, or at least in the third generation. 20

I am not talking pure theory. I will just give you two or three illustrations. 21

The English people once punished criminals by sending them away. They would load them on a ship and export them to Australia. England was owned by lords and nobles and rich people. They owned the whole earth over there, and the other people had to stay in the streets. They could not get a decent living. They used to take their criminals and send them to Australia — I mean the class of criminals who got caught. When these criminals got over there, and nobody else had come, they had the whole continent to run over, and so they could raise sheep and furnish their own meat, which is easier than stealing it; these criminals then became decent, respectable people because they had a chance to live. They did not commit any crimes. They were just like the English people who sent them there, only better. And in the second generation the descendants of those criminals were as good and respectable a class of people as there were on the face of the earth, and then they began building churches and jails themselves.

A portion of this country was settled in the same way, landing prisoners down on the southern coast; but when they got here and had a whole continent to run over and plenty of chances to make a living, they became respectable citizens, making their own living just like any other citizen in the world; but finally these descendants of the English aristocracy, who sent the people over to Australia, found out they were getting rich, and so they went over to get possession of the earth as they always do, and they organized land syndicates and got control of the land and ores, and then they had just as many criminals in Australia as they did in England. It was not because the world had grown bad; it was because the earth had been taken away from the people.

Some of you people have lived in the country. It's prettier than it is here. And if you have ever lived on a farm you understand that if you put a lot of cattle in a field, when the pasture is short they will jump over the fence; but put them in a good field where there is plenty of pasture, and they will be law-abiding cattle to the end of time. The human animal is just like the rest of the animals, only a little more so. The same thing that governs in the one governs in the other.

Everybody makes his living along the lines of least resistance. A wise man who comes into a country early sees a great undeveloped land. For instance, our rich men twenty-five years ago saw that Chicago was small and knew a lot of people would come here and settle, and they readily saw that if they had all the land around here it would be worth a good deal, so they grabbed the land. You cannot be a landlord because somebody has got it all. You must find some other calling. In England and Ireland and Scotland less than 5 percent own all the land there is, and the people are bound to stay there on any kind of terms the landlords give. They must live the best they can, so they develop all these various professions — burglary, picking pockets and the like.

Again, people find all sorts of ways of getting rich. These are diseases like everything else. You look at people getting rich, organizing trusts, and making a million dollars, and somebody gets the disease and he starts out. He catches it just as a man catches the mumps or the measles; he is not to blame, it is in the air. You will find men speculating beyond their means, because the mania of money-getting is taking possession of them. It is simply a disease; nothing more, nothing less. You can not avoid catching it; but the fellows who have control of the earth have the advantage of you. See what the law is; when these men get control of things, they make the laws. They do not make the laws to protect anybody; courts are not instruments of justice; when your case gets into court it will make little difference whether you are guilty or innocent; but it's better if you have a smart lawyer. And you can not have a smart lawyer unless you have money. First and last it's a question of money. Those men who own the earth make the laws to protect what they have. They fix up a sort of fence or pen around what they have, and they fix the law so the fellow on the outside can not get in. The laws are really organized for the protection of the men who rule the world. They were never organized or enforced to do justice. We have no system for doing justice, not the slightest in the world.

Let me illustrate: Take the poorest person in this room. If the community had provided a system of doing justice the poorest person in this room would have as good a lawyer as the richest, would he not? When you went into court you would have just as long a trial, and just as fair a trial as the richest person in Chicago. Your case would not be tried in fifteen or twenty minutes, whereas it would take fifteen days to get through with a rich man's case.

Then if you were rich and were beaten, your case would be taken to the Appellate Court. A poor man can not take his case to the Appellate Court; he has not the price; and then to the Supreme Court, and if he were beaten there he might perhaps go to the United States Supreme Court. And he might die of old age before he got into jail. If you are poor, it's a quick job. You are almost known to be guilty, else you would not be there. Why would any one be in the criminal court if he were not guilty? He would not be there if he could be anywhere else. The officials have no time to look after all these cases. The people who are on the outside, who are running banks and building churches and making jails, they have no time to examine six hundred or seven hundred prisoners each year to see whether they are guilty or innocent. If the courts were organized to promote justice the people would elect somebody to defend all these criminals, somebody as smart as the prosecutor — and give him as many detectives and as many assistants to help, and pay as much money to defend you as to prosecute you. We have a very able man for State's Attorney, and he has many assistants, detectives and policemen without end, and judges to hear the cases — everything handy.

Most of all our criminal code consists in offenses against property. People are sent to jail because they have committed a crime against property. It is of very little consequence whether one hundred people more or less go to jail who ought not to go — you must protect property, because in this world property is of more importance than anything else.

How is it done? These people who have property fix it so they can protect what they have. When somebody commits a crime it does not follow that he has done something that is morally wrong. The man on the outside who has committed no crime may have done something. For instance: to take all the coal in the United States and raise the price two dollars or three dollars when there is no need of it, and thus kill thousands of babies and send thousands of people to the poorhouse and tens of thousands to jail, as is done every year in the United States — this is a greater crime than all the people in our jails ever committed, but the law does not punish it. Why? Because the fellows who control the earth make the laws. If you and I had the making of the laws, the first thing we would do would be to punish the fellow who gets control of the earth. Nature put this coal in the ground for me as well as for them, and nature made the prairies up here to raise wheat for me as well as for them, and then the great railroad companies came along and fenced it up.

Most of all, the crimes for which we are punished are property crimes. There are a few personal crimes, like murder — but they are very few. The crimes committed are mostly those against property. If this punishment is right the criminals must have a lot of property. How much money is there in this crowd? And yet you are all here for crimes against property. The people up and down the Lake Shore have not committed crimes, still they have so much property they don't know what to do with it. It is perfectly plain why those people have not committed crimes against property; they make the laws and therefore do not need to break them. And in order for you to get some property you are obliged to break the rules of the game. I don't know but what some of you may have had a very nice chance to get rich by carrying the hod for one dollar a day, twelve hours. Instead of taking that nice, easy profession, you are a burglar. If you had been given a chance to be a banker you would rather follow that. Some of you may have had a chance to work as a switchman on a railroad where you know, according to statistics, that you can not live and keep all your limbs more than seven years, and you can get fifty dollars or seventy-five dollars a month for taking your lives in your hands, and instead of taking that lucrative position you choose to be a sneak thief, or something like that. Some of you made that sort of choice. I don't know which I would take if I was reduced to this choice. I have an easier choice.

I will guarantee to take from this jail, or any jail in the world, five hundred men who have been the worst criminals and lawbreakers who ever got into jail, and I will go down to our lowest streets and take five hundred of the most abandoned prostitutes, and go out somewhere where there is plenty of land, and will give them a chance to make a living, and they will be as good as the average in the community.

There is a remedy for the sort of condition we see here. The world never finds it out, or when it does find out it does not enforce it. You may pass a law punishing every person with death for burglary, and it will make no difference. Men will commit it just the same. In England there was a time when one hundred offenses were punishable with death, and it made no difference. The English people strangely found out that so fast as they repealed the severe penalties and so fast as they did away with punishing men by death, crime decreased instead of increased; that the smaller the penalty the fewer the crimes.

Hanging men in our county jails does not prevent murder. It makes murderers.

And this has been the history of the world. It's easy to see how to do away with what we call crime. It is not so easy to do it. I will tell you how to do it. It can be done by giving the people a chance to live — by destroying special privileges. So long as big criminals can get the coal fields, so long as the big criminals have control of the city council and get the public streets for streetcars and gas rights, this is bound to send thousands of poor people to jail. So long as men are allowed to monopolize all the earth, and compel others to live on such terms as these men see fit to make, then you are bound to get into jail.

The only way in the world to abolish crime and criminals is to abolish the big ones and the little ones together. Make fair conditions of life. Give men a chance to live. Abolish the right of private ownership of land, abolish monopoly, make the world partners in production, partners in the good things of life. Nobody would steal if he could get something of his own some easier way. Nobody will commit burglary when he has a house full. No girl will go out on the streets when she has a comfortable place at home. The man who owns a sweatshop or a department store may not be to blame himself for the condition of his girls, but when he pays them five dollars, three dollars, and two dollars a week, I wonder where he thinks they will get the rest of their money to live. The only way to cure these conditions is by equality. There should be no jails. They do not accomplish what they pretend to accomplish. If you would wipe them out there would be no more criminals than now. They terrorize nobody. They are a blot upon any civilization, and a jail is an evidence of the lack of charity of the people on the outside who make the jails and fill them with the victims of their greed.

Discussion: Content

1. What is Darrow's thesis? State it as briefly as possible.
2. What, according to Darrow, is the basic reason for the existence of prisons and prisoners?
3. In what season of the year does Darrow believe more people go to jail? Why? Do you agree, or not?
4. Some of Darrow's examples are outdated, or at least show their age. Which ones are? What would you put in their places? Which examples are still appropriate, indicating that the problem Darrow sees is a continuing one?
5. How is the history of the settlement and development of Australia important in Darrow's discussion?
6. How feasible is Darrow's solution for the problem or effect that he discusses?

Discussion: Form

1. We have learned that exposition seeks to inform, while argumentation seeks to change minds. Darrow's thesis is contrary to run-of-the-mill opinion. Yet we have placed it with exposition rather than argumentation. Can you determine why?
2. In addition to cause and effect, Darrow uses comparison; what are some of the important comparisons that he makes?
3. He also uses examples or illustrations to support his assertions. Locate at least six of these, including one extended example. Comment on their effectiveness.
4. What is Darrow's *tone?* How does he achieve it? Why does he adopt it?
5. Where does Darrow announce his solution to the problem or effect that he discusses? Was it wise to put it there? Why, or why not?

Section 7: Definition

Definition is a fundamental expository device. Because no two people share exactly the same vocabulary, sooner or later you will use a word or expression unknown to your reader. And unless you pause to define the unknown term, your reader will fail to understand you.

Most definitions are very brief and unpretentious; we seldom notice them at all. Look at the following sentence:

Chaucer wrote a treatise on *the astrolabe, a medieval invention that enabled navigators to steer by the stars*.

Tucked away in a paragraph, such a sentence would not call undue attention to itself; nevertheless, it contains an excellent example of a definition, one that contains every element that is essential to a satisfactory definition; one that, in short, follows a simple formula: *x is a y that is z*.

Let us look more closely. The *x* in our formula is simply the thing to be defined, here an astrolabe. The *y* is a larger, more general class to which *x* belongs: the astrolabe belongs to the more general class of *medieval inventions*. The *z* is that information which serves to differentiate *x* from all other members of *y*. In our definition *z* is the information that restricts the domain of medieval inventions to just the one that enabled navigators to steer by the stars, effectively ruling out such medieval inventions as arquebuses, culverins, chastity belts, and plenary indulgences. Here are some more definitions with the essential elements marked for you:

      x   y   z

Pornography is *an attempt to insult sex*. (D. H. Lawrence)

       x   y   z

A *noun* is the *name of a person, place, or thing.*

       x   y   z

A *touchdown* is *a score in football.*

    In most cases the statement of elements x and y is fairly simple. But the formulation of z may be more difficult. Generally speaking, there are two ways to differentiate a member from a larger class: one is to tell what it is not, and the other is to tell what it is — i.e., what makes it unique. The majority of definitions will be of phrase or clause length, as were the examples above. Some particularly troublesome ones may be expanded to a paragraph. Occasionally a writer will use the technique of definition as the controlling pattern for an entire essay. When this happens, the writer is usually trying to define an abstract term, such as love or patriotism, or an unfamiliar or elusive one, such as quasar. Most of the space will be devoted to the z element of the definition formula, and very often the writer will be obliged to use several modes of development to differentiate x from y. The writer may give examples, classify, describe, show causes, even tell a story, all in an attempt to establish the uniqueness of the object or concept being defined. Such longer explanations of a word or expression are known as *extended definitions.*

    Stipulative definitions are another type of explanation of a word or an expression, for another reason. In this case the writer wants to use a word, often a common or familiar one, but in a special or unexpected sense, and consequently must make clear that special use to readers. A brief look at pages of a dictionary will remind you that many English words have several meanings, making stipulative definition an occasional necessity. For instance, if you were going to use the word *gig,* and the word's context did not make clear which of five very different meanings you were using, you would have to explain, perhaps simply in parentheses, perhaps at more length, that you meant a pronged spear for fishing, rather than a boat or a two-wheeled carriage or a military demerit or a musician's job.

    In the following pages you will find model definitions of all three sorts for you to study and learn to use — the typical short ones as well as extended and stipulative definitions. As the foregoing discussion suggests, it is important that you notice and understand definitions in your reading, and that you use them effectively in your writing. Particularly on examinations you will be asked to define special terms for a field of study — you will want to do so accurately and efficiently, following the *x is a y that is z* formula. Likewise, in research papers and reports, especially in your major field, you will often need to define key terms. So what follows is of real value to you as a reader and as a writer.

Brief Examples:
Definition

Some Campus Definitions

PRE-REGISTRATION is a formality which students must endure in order to find out what courses they can't get next term.

A CAMPUS ROCK CONCERT is a social event where the normal behavior is antisocial; the featured group, which had its hit record three years ago, starts playing at least two hours late, if at all.

ROCK CONCERT FOG is a grayish mist that when inhaled causes a general feeling of warmth and an overpowering desire to fly.

A CAMPUS COP is a man, usually retired from a real job, who puts parking tickets on student cars when not drinking coffee or misdirecting traffic.

A PANTY RAID is a congregation of two or three hundred males outside a girls' dorm, chanting in unison, "We want panties!"

A JOCK RAID is a similar occurrence involving approximately a hundred brave girls who gather outside a men's dorm to scream, "We want jocks!"

THE UNIVERSITY CENTER is a place to watch TV, play pool and pinball, Foosball and cards, and flunk out of school.

THE CAFETERIA is a center for gastronomical torture built to test the intestinal fortitude of students.

THE GYMNASIUM is a haven for aspiring athletes and a good place to pick up new towels.

A CAMPUS SNOB is a person who makes you keenly aware that he is not paying any attention to you.

Discussion Questions

1. Do each of these student definitions conform rigidly to the definition formula?

2. How is humor achieved in these definitions? What part of the formula is the chief source of the humor?
3. You will probably find it an interesting exercise to create some definitions for objects or phenomena peculiar to your own campus. Assume your audience to be persons unfamiliar with your surroundings; then prepare a list of ten definitions that will introduce them to your campus.

Eight Definitions of Religion

Religion, after trying to see as best I could what various religions and religious people had in common, I felt impelled to define as the reaction of the personality as a whole to its experience of the Universe as a whole. (Sir Julian Huxley)

Religion is that voice of the deepest human experience. (Matthew Arnold)

Religion is the belief in spiritual things. (E. B. Taylor)

Religion is a daughter of Hope and Fear, explaining to Ignorance the nature of the Unknowable. (Ambrose Bierce)

Religion is the opium of the people. (Karl Marx)

Religion is the propitiation or conciliation of powers superior to man which are believed to direct or control the course of nature and of human life. (Sir James Frazer)

Being religious means asking passionately the question of the meaning of our existence and being willing to receive answers, even if the answers hurt. (Paul Tillich)

Pure religion and undefiled before God is this, to visit the fatherless and widows in their affliction, and to keep oneself unspotted from the world. (Saint James)

Discussion Questions

1. Demonstrate how each of these definitions of religion employs the formula x is a y that is z.

2. How might you adjust those definitions that do not rigidly conform to the formula?

Some Definitions from *The Devil's Dictionary*
Ambrose Bierce

Ambrose Bierce (1842–1914?) was an American journalist, humorist, and satirist, most famous for *The Cynic's Word Book* (now known as *The Devil's Dictionary,* 1906, 1911). A Civil War hero, a self-educated and itinerant journalist, and a constant traveler, Bierce disappeared for good at the age of 72 when he crossed into Mexico during the revolution, perhaps joining the rebel forces of Pancho Villa.

[Editor's note: One of the definition's numerous functions is to amuse.]

ACQUAINTANCE, *n.* A person whom we know well enough to borrow from, but not well enough to lend to. A degree of friendship called slight when its object is poor or obscure, and intimate when he is rich or famous.

BAROMETER, *n.* A ingenious instrument which indicates what kind of weather we are having.

BRAIN, *n.* An apparatus with which we think that we think. That which distinguishes the man who is content to *be* something from the man who wishes to *do* something. A man of great wealth, or one who has been pitchforked into high station, has commonly such a headful of brain that his neighbors cannot keep their hats on. In our civilization, and under our republican form of government, brain is so highly honored that it is rewarded by exemption from the cares of office.

CONNOISSEUR, *n.* A specialist who knows everything about something and nothing about anything else. An old wine-bibber having been smashed in a railway collision, some wine was poured upon his lips to revive him. "Pauillac, 1873," he murmured and died.

FIDDLE, *n.* An instrument to tickle human ears by friction of a horse's tail on the entrails of a cat.

HAPPINESS, *n.* An agreeable sensation arising from contemplating the misery of another.

HASH, *x.* There is no definition for this word — nobody knows what hash is.

HISTORY, *n.* An account mostly false, of events mostly unimportant, which are brought about by rulers mostly knaves, and soldiers mostly fools.

IDIOT, *n.* A member of a large and powerful tribe whose influence in human affairs has always been dominant and controlling. The Idiot's activity is not confined to any special field of thought or action, but "pervades and regulates the whole." He has the last word in everything; his decision is unappealable. He sets the fashions of opinion and taste, dictates the limitations of speech, and circumscribes conduct with a deadline.

LAUGHTER, *n.* An interior convulsion, producing a distortion of the features and accompanied by inarticulate noises. It is infectious and, though intermittent, incurable. Liability to attacks of laughter is one of the characteristics distinguishing man from the animals — these being not only inaccessible to the provocation of his example, but impregnable to the microbes having original jurisdiction in bestowal of the disease. Whether laughter could be imparted to animals by inoculation from the human patient is a question that has not been answered by experimentation.

LEAD, *n.* A heavy blue-gray metal much used in giving stability to light lovers — particularly to those who love not wisely but other men's wives. Lead is also of great service as a counterpoise to an argument of such weight that it turns the scale of debate the wrong way. An interesting fact in the chemistry of international controversy is that at the point of contact of two patriotisms lead is precipitated in great quantities.

MIRACLE, *n.* An act or event out of the order of nature and unaccountable, as beating a normal hand of four kings and an ace with four aces and a king.

OPTIMISM, *n.* The doctrine, or belief, that everything is beautiful, including what is ugly, everything good, especially the bad, and everything right that is wrong. It is held with greatest tenacity by those most accustomed to the mischance of falling into adversity, and is most acceptably expounded with the grin that apes a smile. Being a blind faith, it is inaccessible to the light of disproof — an intellectual disorder, yielding to no treatment but death. It is hereditary, but fortunately not contagious.

REVOLUTION, *n.* In politics, an abrupt change in the form of misgovernment. Specifically, in American history, the substitution of the rule of an Administration for that of a Ministry, whereby the welfare and happiness of the people were advanced a full half-inch. Revolutions are usually accompanied by a considerable effusion of blood, but are accounted worth it — this appraisement being made by beneficiaries whose blood had not the mischance to be shed.

TURKEY, *n.* A large bird whose flesh when eaten on certain religious anniversaries has the peculiar property of attesting piety and gratitude. Incidentally, it is pretty good eating.

WHEAT, *n.* A cereal from which a tolerably good whiskey can with some difficulty be made, and which is used also for bread. The French are said to eat more bread *per capita* of population than any other people, which is natural, for only they know how to make the stuff palatable.

ZENITH, *n.* A point in the heavens directly overhead to a standing man or a growing cabbage. A man in bed or a cabbage in the pot is not considered as having a zenith, though from this view of the matter there was once a considerable dissent among the learned, some holding that the posture of the body was immaterial. These were called Horizontalists; their opponents, Verticalists. The Horizontalist heresy was finally extinguished by Xanobus, the philosopher-king of Abara, a zealous Verticalist. Entering an assembly of philosophers who were debating the matter, he cast a severed human head at the feet of his opponents and asked them to determine its zenith, explaining that its body was hanging by the heels outside. Observing that it was the head of their leader, the Horizontalists hastened to profess themselves converted to whatever opinion the Crown might be pleased to hold, and Horizontalism took its place among *fides defuncti.*

Discussion Questions

1. Bierce adheres strictly to the formula for definitions, but occasionally he embellishes his initial statements with additional comments. What rhetorical mode do these comments usually represent? What is their purpose?
2. How exactly does Bierce inject humor into his definitions? What parts of the definition formula does he take liberties with most frequently?

Paragraphs:
Definition

Slang
Anne Nichols

The definition of slang is vague. The 1957 edition of *The Standard College Dictionary* defines slang in part as "Language, words, or phrases of a vigorous, colorful, facetious, or taboo nature, invented for specific occasions or uses, or derived from the unconventional use of the standard vocabulary." A good deal of modern poetry can be described by the same terms. *The Standard College Dictionary* adds a second definition: "The special vocabulary of a certain class, group, or profession: college *slang*." "The special vocabulary of certain professions" can obviously include the jargon that accompanies most politicians, sociologists, and educators. The lack of preciseness in the dictionary definition does not indicate a weakness in either the dictionary or in slang. Rather, the definition suggests the breadth of slang, a breadth not always acknowledged or understood. A comprehensive definition of slang is further made difficult by the fact that often what used to be slang no longer is. Many people think they know instinctively when they encounter slang, and their response is usually negative. These same people may be surprised, however, to discover what slang *has* been. *Nice* started out as a slang word, and it now occupies a front position in a long and respected list of *nice* but meaningless words. A number of other words, as H. L. Mencken points out in his famous discussion of slang, start out as slang and end up filling vacuums in our existing vocabulary. Among others, Mencken mentions *rodeo, racketeer, to hold up*.

Discussion Questions

1. Nichols initially states that the definition of slang is vague. How does she substantiate this claim?

2. What examples does she supply to illustrate her contention that most of us do not know what slang really is?

Abstractitis
H. W. Fowler

abstractitis. The effect of this disease, now endemic on both sides of the Atlantic, is to make the patient write such sentences as *Participation by the men in the control of the industry is non-existent* instead of *The men have no part in the control of the industry; Early expectation of a vacancy is indicated by the firm* instead of *The firm say they expect to have a vacancy soon; The availability of this material is diminishing* instead of *This material is getting scarcer; A cessation of dredging has taken place* instead of *Dredging has stopped; Was this the realization of an anticipated liability?* instead of *Did you expect you would have to do this?* And so on, with an abstract word always in command as the subject of the sentence. Persons and what they do, things and what is done to them, are put in the background, and we can only peer at them through a glass darkly. It may no doubt be said that in these examples the meaning is clear enough; but the danger is that, once the disease gets a hold, it sets up a chain reaction. A writer uses abstract words because his thoughts are cloudy; the habit of using them clouds his thoughts still further; he may end by concealing his meaning not only from his readers but also from himself, and writing such sentences as *The actualization of the motivation of the forces must to a great extent be a matter of personal angularity.*

Discussion Questions

1. Because Fowler's classic book, *Modern English Usage,* follows a dictionary format, his definitions do not necessarily follow the pattern that we have described. Can you recast the first sentence of this paragraph into the *x* is a *y* that is *z* pattern?
2. Can you restate the definition in less concrete terms?
3. What, according to Fowler, is the danger of abstractitis?

Good
W. Nelson Francis

Applied to language, the adjective *good* can have two meanings: (1) "effective, adequate for the purpose to which it is put" and (2) "acceptable, conforming to approved usage." The first of these is truly a value judgment of the language itself. In this sense the language of Shakespeare, for example, is "good English" because it serves as a highly effective vehicle for his material. On the other hand, the language of a poorer writer, which does not meet adequately the demands put upon it, might be called "bad English." The second meaning of good is not really a judgment of the language itself but a social appraisal of the persons who use it. An expression like *I ain't got time for youse* may be most effective in the situation in which it is used, and hence "good English" in the first sense. But most people, including those who naturally speak this way, will call it "bad English" because grammatical features like *ain't, youse,* and the double negative construction belong to a variety of English commonly used by people with little education and low social and economic status.

Discussion Questions

1. To insure that readers of his book, *The English Language: An Introduction,* will understand the meaning of the common adjective *good* when it is put to special uses — to describe language — the linguist W. Nelson Francis states precisely what he means by the word. How is this one-paragraph definition organized?
2. Francis makes clear that *good* may be used to judge the language itself; what is the other language-related use of *good* that he names?
3. Is it possible for an expression to be *good* in one sense and not in the other?
4. How is it possible for grammatically correct English ever to be wrong, as Francis implies?

Democracy
E. B. White

We received a letter from the Writers' War Board the other day, asking for a statement on "The Meaning of Democracy." It presumably is our duty to comply with such a request, and it is certainly our pleasure. Surely the Board knows what democracy is. It is the line that forms on the right. It is the don't in don't shove. It is the hole in the stuffed shirt through which the sawdust slowly trickles; it is the dent in the high hat. Democracy is the recurrent suspicion that more than half of the people are right more than half of the time. It is the feeling of privacy in the voting booths, the feeling of communion in the libraries, the feeling of vitality everywhere. Democracy is a letter to the editor. Democracy is the score at the beginning of the ninth. It is an idea which hasn't been disproved yet, a song the words of which have not gone bad. It's the mustard on the hot dog and the cream in the rationed coffee. Democracy is a request from a War Board, in the middle of a morning in the middle of a war, wanting to know what democracy is.

Discussion Questions

1. In this paragraph from the World War II era, White defines this abstract term, so important to us all, by using a sentence pattern that seems to follow the x is a y that is z formula. Yet it is not the same. What has gone wrong here?
2. Despite the fact that he plays verbal games with the standard definition formula, many of us will still feel that White has managed to define *democracy* by the end of the paragraph. Why is that?
3. How might a less creative — or playful — writer define *democracy* for the Writers' War Board?

Student Work:
Definition

Women

Women are a source of vitality upon which men draw for a meaningful life. They are suppliers of man's spiritual needs: comfort, inspiration, and charm. Women comfort frustrated husbands by giving receptive ears to their grumblings when they are misunderstood by good friends or discouraged by not getting deserved promotions. Women provide such profound inspiration that many of the greatest works of literature, painting, sculpture, and music have been inspired by their smiles, tears, raptures, and agonies. So irresistible is their charm that men have fought for and given up kingdoms and empires to win their favors. Any man, be he commoner or king, who has been exposed to these unique characteristics will find his life more worth living.

Discussion Questions

1. This student's definition of "Women" is clearly not the sort one will find in a dictionary. How does it differ and what might be a reason for its differing?
2. What role does sentence 2 play in the organization of the rest of the paragraph?
3. As we said in the introduction to this section on definition, the writer of an extended definition may rely on various writing strategies to clarify a term. What two expository techniques are important to this definition?

Jelly Rot

Of all the bad types of leaves to find when sacking tobacco, the worst type is that called the "jelly rot." This plant disease results from a fungus in the soil that is spread over the plants' leaves by rain splashing dirt on them. There is not much a farmer can do about jelly rot but abandon the affected field and destroy the infected plants as soon as possible. Farmers must be specially alert to keep jelly rot leaves out of the tobacco that is sacked for market because they will make all of the tobacco rot, and, of course, no buyer wants a pile of rotten tobacco. In jelly rot leaves the stem, mid-rib, and the area surrounding the mid-rib have rotted. The rot turns the leaf black, gives the stem a texture similar to jelly (hence the name), and gives the entire leaf a sickeningly sweet smell.

Discussion Questions

1. Express the definition of jelly rot in terms of the formula x is a y that is z. The first two sentences of the paragraph will supply you with sufficient material to formulate your definition.
2. If a complete definition for jelly rot can be fashioned from the first two sentences of this paragraph, what is the purpose of the remaining sentences?

Laughter

What is laughter? A bizarre action that is solely a trait of the human race — I think. If you take a closer look, you will realize that people laugh at unconscious, painful situations concerning themselves, friends, or world events. We laugh at cartoons full of violence, such as *Tom and Jerry*, where the mice beat up the cat. We giggle at jokes that portray the weaker side of people. We chuckle at the monkeys in the zoo when the big one picks on the little one. We laugh at our friends or even at strangers when they say something stupid or have a minor accident, such as dropping a lunch tray in the middle of the cafeteria. All of these associations between pain and laughter are too numerous to be overlooked, yet they are mysterious. The only unraveling clue that has shed some light on this strange association is the occurrence of a substance called endomorphine — a natural pain killer that is released in small quantities by our brains every time we laugh. This means that laughter is in reality one of our body's mechanisms for coping with pain — perhaps even its most important one.

Discussion Questions

1. Does the student apply the formulaic statement in composing this definition?
2. What rhetorical devices does the student use to support the definition?

Defining Crime

Oversimplifying, one might say that crime is "the act of breaking the law." However, the meanings of the words "crime" and "law" are so intermeshed that one must consider both to ascertain the meaning of either. Thus, the first definition alone does not yield any real understanding of the term "crime." To understand the concept of crime one must first consider the concept of law.

The law, written or unwritten, is a statement of consensus: what a group of people and/or the governing body of that group agree is appropriate or inappropriate behavior. A crime is any human behavior which is in conflict with that consensus.

One could also define law as the "collective conscience" of a society. One must recognize, however, that some matters of conscience are not public and are therefore not enforceable. Only those matters that can be verbalized, recognized, and regulated can be included in the concept of the public conscience. Before this conscience can be regulated, there must be a recognized authority to translate the morals of a society into a viable pattern of conduct for that society. Under this definition, crime would be a transgression of the public conscience.

One could also argue that the law is an enumeration of cultural norms. In other words, the law is a reflection of how a society expects its members to behave and is more informative than constraining. In keeping with this theory, the definition of "crime" becomes a variation of human behavior which conflicts with the cultural patterns of that society.   4

It has been said that the law is a contract among citizens, or between a citizen and the government. In return for protection of his rights, an individual agrees to behave according to the will of the majority. Upon committing a crime, and thus violating the will of the majority, the individual breaks the contract and consequently loses certain rights as a citizen.   5

We have contemplated the law as a consensus, a collective conscience, an enumeration of norms, or a contract. Regardless of which of these views one takes of the law, it is only through consideration of them all that the definition of crime as "the act of breaking the law" can take on any real meaning.   6

Discussion Questions

1. How many distinct definitions appear in this essay?
2. Although its definitions are clearly stated, one weakness of this essay is the absence of examples to illustrate each of the definitions supplied — examples similar to those provided by Bierce. What examples might you recommend to illustrate the four definitions of the law?
3. "Defining Crime" is an example of a serious definition by a student. However, the approach may at first seem too roundabout. What other choices did the student have? What would you do if you were assigned the same term to define?

Feminist

The best definition of a feminist that I know of is a woman who has gotten fed up. What has she gotten fed up with? There are a number of things.   1

She is fed up with education as it is usually practiced. The girls are made to believe that they can't do math and are taught to make biscuits instead. They are encouraged to become nurses instead of doctors, secretaries instead of engineers, and wives and mothers before everything else. And even in high school sports it's more prestigious to be head cheerleader for the football team or homecoming queen than to be the leading scorer on the girls' basketball team.   2

A feminist is fed up with organized religion — not with religion, but with the way that it's usually organized. Girls are encouraged to become nuns but never priests. They don't lead Sunday school lessons; they prepare the pot-luck buffets and decorate the altars.   3

A feminist is fed up with politics and politicians. The general sentiment is that this game is too rough and too sordid for women, who are too naive to know what is going on, even though the League of Women Voters is still the only source of unbiased information on the candidates and the issues at election time.   4

A feminist is fed up with American society. She likes to have doors opened for her and chairs pulled back, but not at the expense of a couple of thousand dollars less a year in her paychecks. She is sickened by reports of Mrs. X being the *only* woman electrician, board member, representative, judge, etc. She is incensed at the feeling of inadequacy which makes a woman on a quiz program admit that she is "just a housewife." (Whoever heard a man admit that he was "just a lawyer"?) She is fed up with ladies' auxiliaries, where there are no men's auxiliaries. She is fed up with being a second-class citizen in the land of the free and the home of male hypocrites.   5

And now that they are suggesting that she register for the draft, she just may be angry enough to refuse — until they pass the Equal Rights Amendment for her.   6

Discussion Questions

1. The writer of "Feminist" takes the x is a y that is z formula quite seriously and introduces the definition in its barest terms. What is it?
2. What sort of transitional device does the writer use to signal that paragraphs 2 through 5 have a similar purpose, i.e., to support or expand the z portion of the definition?
3. How does the writer support the contentions made in each of the paragraphs 2 through 5?

Essays:
Definition

Language
Edgar H. Sturtevant

Edgar H. Sturtevant (1875–1952) was a professor of linguistics at Yale University, 1923–1943, and earlier taught classics at Columbia University. A former president of the Linguistics Society of America, he authored numerous scholarly articles and books. The definition below comes from one of his last works, *Introduction to Linguistic Science* (1947).

A language is a system of arbitrary vocal symbols by which members of a social group cooperate and interact. 1

The word *system* marks a language off from mere sets of nonsense syllables like a *ta-ra-ra-boom-de-ay* or *a-heigh-and-a-ho-and-a-heigh-nonny-no.* With the proper rhythm and intonation, these or any other groups of syllables can carry a highly emotional message, but they do not form a part of the systematic structure of the English language. In contrast, the sentence *the dog bites the man* is thoroughly systematic; we can transpose the words *dog* and *man* and still be understood by all English-speaking hearers, although the meaning of the sentence *the man bites the dog* is absurd. By means of an entirely different mechanism, the two Latin sentences, *canis hominem mordet* and *homo canem mordet,* stand in a similar relative position; it is only the system of the Latin language that compels us to take the second sentence in a sense that defies all experience. 2

The key word of the phrase *arbitrary vocal symbols* is the noun *symbols.* A symbol necessarily involves a dualism: there must be something that stands for or represents something else, a form combined with a meaning. An *arbitrary symbol* is one whose form has no necessary or natural connection with its meaning. English *dog* has roughly the same meaning as German *Hund,* French *chien,* Latin

273

canis, and hundreds of other words in as many other languages. The only reason why *dog* carries this meaning is that the speakers of English use it with this meaning. The word *vocal* stands in the definition to exclude the human activities denoted by the phrases *gesture language, sign language, written language,* etc. All of these are important activities and proper subjects for investigation, and besides they have obvious connections with audible speech. The only reason for excluding them from our definition is convenience: they are found not to behave in the same way as audible language, and so they cannot conveniently be treated scientifically at the same time.

3

The final clause of the definition, *by which the members of a social group cooperate and interact,* designates the chief function of language in society. There are, of course, other means of cooperation between living beings, as witness the wolf pack, the swarm of bees, etc. Even men may cooperate not only by writing or by gesture but by actual physical compulsion or by a smile or by the raising of an eyebrow. All we mean to say is that among men language is by far the commonest and most important means of cooperation. Society as now constituted could not long continue without the use of language. We must not forget, however, that language may also be used to interfere with the action of a group or to oppose one group to another; we cannot end our definition with the word *cooperate.* A corollary of the final clause of the definition is that a language cannot function normally unless there are at least two speakers of it. When only one speaker remains, the language may be said to be dead.

4

Discussion Questions

1. How does Sturtevant illustrate that languages are systematic?
2. Does the sound of the word *dog,* according to Sturtevant's definition, have any bearing on the word's meaning?
3. Why does Sturtevant distinguish vocal symbols from written symbols, signs, or gestures in his definition?
4. What happens to a language when there is only one speaker of it remaining?

Discussion: Form

1. When does Sturtevant state his definition? What is it?
2. How does he expand this definition?

Clutter
William Zinsser

William Zinsser (1922–   ), a New York native, was educated at Princeton. Formerly a writer, editor, and critic with the New York *Herald Tribune*, he taught from 1970 to 1979 at Yale University, and now serves as Executive Editor of the Book-of-the-Month Club. Among his ten books are *Pop Goes America* (1966), *The Lunacy Boom* (1970), *Writing With a Word Processor* (1983), and the critically acclaimed *On Writing Well* (second edition, 1980), the source for this selection.

Clutter is the laborious phrase which has pushed out the short word that means the same thing. These locutions are a drag on energy and momentum. Even before John Dean gave us "at this point in time," people had stopped saying "now." They were saying "at the present time," or "currently," or "presently" (which means "soon"). Yet the idea can always be expressed by "now" to mean the immediate moment ("Now I can see him"), or by "today" to mean the historical present ("Today prices are high"), or simply by the verb "to be" ("It is raining"). There is no need to say, "At the present time we are experiencing precipitation."

Speaking of which, we are experiencing considerable difficulty getting *that* word out of the language now that it has lumbered in. Even your dentist will ask if you are experiencing any pain. If he were asking one of his own children he would say, "Does it hurt?" He would, in short, be himself. By using a more pompous phrase in his professional role he not only sounds more important; he blunts the painful edge of truth. It is the language of the airline stewardess demonstrating the oxygen mask that will drop down if the plane should somehow run out of air. "In the extremely unlikely possibility that the aircraft should experience such an eventuality," she begins — a phrase so oxygen-depriving in itself that we are prepared for any disaster, and even gasping death shall lose its sting. As for those "smoking materials" that she asks us to "kindly extinguish," I often wonder what materials are smoking. Maybe she thinks my coat and tie are on fire.

Clutter is the ponderous euphemism that turns a slum into a depressed socioeconomic area, a salesman into a marketing representative, a dumb kid into an underachiever, and garbage collectors into waste disposal personnel. In New Canaan, Conn., the incinerator is now the "volume reduction plant." I hate to think what they call the town dump.

Clutter is the official language used by the American corporation — in the news release and the annual report — to hide its mistakes. When a big company recently announced that it was "decentralizing its organizational structure into major profit-centered businesses" and that "corporate staff services will be aligned under two senior vice-presidents" it meant that it had had a lousy year.

Clutter is the language of the interoffice memo ("The trend to mosaic communication is reducing the meaningfulness of concern about whether or not demographic segments differ in their tolerance of periodicity") and the language of computers ("We are offering functional digital programming options that have built-in parallel reciprocal capabilities with compatible third-generation contingencies and hardware").

Clutter is the language of the Pentagon throwing dust in the eyes of the populace by calling an invasion a "reinforced protective reaction strike" and by justifying its vast budgets on the need for "credible second-strike capability" and "counterforce deterrence." How can we grasp such vaporous double-talk? As George Orwell pointed out in "Politics and the English Language," an essay written in 1946 but cited frequently during the Vietnam years of Johnson and Nixon, "In our time, political speech and writing are largely the defense of the indefensible. . . . Thus political language has to consist largely of euphemism, question-begging, and sheer cloudy vagueness." Orwell's warning that clutter is not just a nuisance but a deadly tool did not turn out to be inoperative. By the 1960's his words had come true in America.

I could go on quoting examples from various fields — every profession has its growing arsenal of jargon to fire at the layman and hurl him back from its walls. But the list would be depressing and the lesson tedious. The point of raising it now is to serve notice that clutter is the enemy, whatever form it takes. It slows the reader and robs the writer of his personality, making him seem pretentious.

Discussion: Content

1. Where does Zinsser give his succinct definition of clutter?
2. What do circumlocutions like "this point in time" or "at the present time" mean?
3. Why, according to Zinsser, do people use clutter?
4. According to the examples in the essay, where is clutter most likely to be found?

Discussion: Form

1. In paragraphs 3–6 Zinsser provides examples of clutter, associating them with places or occupations. What is remarkable about each paragraph's topic sentence?
2. What device does Zinsser use in paragraph 6 to support his observation about clutter?
3. What two functions does the concluding paragraph serve?

Alchemy
Lewis Thomas

Lewis Thomas (1913–   ) is an American physician and medical researcher who has held various important administrative posts at medical schools and medical research centers. A frequent contributor to medical journals and science periodicals, Dr. Thomas has published four books of essays; the one which appears below is taken from his most recent work, *Late Night Thoughts on Listening to Mahler's Ninth Symphony* (1983). His other books are *Lives of a Cell* (1974), winner of the National Book Award; *The Medusa and the Snail* (1979); and *The Youngest Science* (1983).

Alchemy began long ago as an expression of the deepest and oldest of human wishes: to discover that the world makes sense. The working assumption — that everything on earth must be made up from a single, primal sort of matter — led to centuries of hard work aimed at isolating the original stuff and rearranging it to the alchemist's liking. If it could be found, nothing would lie beyond human grasp. The transmutation of base metals to gold was only a modest part of the prospect. If you knew about the fundamental substance, you could do much more than make simple money: you could boil up a cure-all for every disease affecting humankind, you could rid the world of evil, and, while doing this, you could make a universal solvent capable of dissolving anything you might want to dissolve. These were heady ideas, and generations of alchemists worked all their lives trying to reduce matter to its ultimate origin. 1

To be an alchemist was to be a serious professional, requiring long periods of apprenticeship and a great deal of late-night study. From the earliest years of the profession, there was a lot to read. The

Section 7: Definition

documents can be traced back to Arabic, Latin, and Greek scholars of the ancient world, and beyond them to Indian Vedic texts as far back as the tenth century B.C. All the old papers contain a formidable array of information, mostly expressed in incantations, which were required learning for every young alchemist and, by design, incomprehensible to everyone else. The word "gibberish" is thought by some to refer back to Jabir ibn Hayyan, an eighth-century alchemist, who lived in fear of being executed for black magic and worded his doctrines so obscurely that almost no one knew what he was talking about.

Indeed, black magic was what most people thought the alchemists were up to in their laboratories, filled with the fumes of arsenic, mercury, and sulphur and the bubbling infusions of all sorts of obscure plants. We tend to look back at them from today's pinnacle of science as figures of fun, eccentric solitary men wearing comical conical hats, engaged in meaningless explorations down one blind alley after another. It was not necessarily so: the work they were doing was hard and frustrating, but it was the start-up of experimental chemistry and physics. The central idea they were obsessed with — that there is a fundamental, elementary particle out of which everything in the universe is made — continues to obsess today's physicists.

They never succeeded in making gold from base metals, nor did they find a universal elixir in their plant extracts; they certainly didn't rid the world of evil. What they did accomplish, however, was no small thing: they got the work going. They fiddled around in their laboratories, talked at one another incessantly, set up one crazy experiment after another, wrote endless reams of notes, which were then translated from Arabic to Greek to Latin and back again, and the work got under way. More workers became interested and then involved in the work, and, as has been happening ever since in science, one thing led to another. As time went on and the work progressed, error after error, new and accurate things began to turn up. Hard facts were learned about the behavior of metals and their alloys, the properties of acids, bases, and salts were recognized, the mathematics of thermodynamics were worked out, and, with just a few jumps through the centuries, the helical molecule of DNA was revealed in all its mystery.

The current anxieties over what science may be doing to human society, including the worries about technology, are no new thing. The third-century Roman emperor Diocletian decreed that all manuscripts dealing with alchemy were to be destroyed, on grounds that such enterprises were against nature. The work went on in secrecy, and, although some of the material was lost, a great deal was translated into other languages, passed around, and preserved.

The association of alchemy with black magic has persisted in the public mind throughout the long history of the endeavor, partly because the objective — the transmutation of one sort of substance to another — seemed magical by definition. Partly also because of the hybrid term: *al* was simply the Arabic article, but *chemy* came from a word meaning "the black land," *Khemia,* the Greek name for Egypt. Another, similar-sounding word, *khumeia,* meant an infusion or elixir, and this was incorporated as part of the meaning. The Egyptian origin is very old, extending back to Thoth, the god of magic (who later reappeared as Hermes Trismegistus, master of the hermetic seal required by alchemists for the vacuums they believed were needed in their work). The notion of alchemy may be as old as language, and the idea that language and magic are somehow related is also old. "Grammar," after all, was a word used in the Middle Ages to denote high learning, but it also implied a practicing familiarity with alchemy. *Gramarye,* an older term for grammar, signified occult learning and necromancy. "Glamour," of all words, was the Scottish word for grammar, and it meant, precisely, a spell, casting enchantment.

Medicine, from its dark origins in old shamanism millennia ago, became closely linked in the Middle Ages with alchemy. The preoccupation of alchemists with metals and their properties led to experiments — mostly feckless ones, looking back — with the therapeutic use of all sorts of metals. Paracelsus, a prominent physician of the sixteenth century, achieved fame from his enthusiastic use of mercury and arsenic, based on what now seems a wholly mystical commitment to alchemical philosophy as the key to understanding the universe and the human body simultaneously. Under his influence, three centuries of patients with all varieties of illness were treated with strong potions of metals, chiefly mercury, and vigorous purgation became standard medical practice.

Physics and chemistry have grown to scientific maturity, medicine is on its way to growing up, and it is hard to find traces anywhere of the earlier fumblings toward a genuine scientific method. Alchemy exists only as a museum piece, an intellectual fossil, so antique that we no longer need be embarrassed by the memory, but the memory is there. Science began by fumbling. It works because the people involved in it work, and *work together.* They become excited and exasperated, they exchange their bits of information at a full shout, and, the most wonderful thing of all, they keep *at* one another.

Something rather like this may be going on now, without realizing it, in the latest and grandest of all fields of science. People in my field, and some of my colleagues in the real "hard" sciences such as physics and chemistry, have a tendency to take lightly and often disparagingly the efforts of workers in the so-called social sciences. We like to refer to their data as soft. We do not acknowledge as we should the differences between the various disciplines within behavioral research — we speak of analytical psychiatry, sociology, linguistics, economics, and computer intelligence as though these inquiries were all of a piece, with all parties wearing the same old comical conical hats. It is of course not so. The principal feature that the social sciences share these days is the attraction they exert on considerable numbers of students, who see the prospect of exploring human behavior as irresistible and hope fervently that a powerful scientific method for doing the exploring can be worked out. All of the matters on the social-science agenda seem more urgent to these young people than they did at any other time in human memory. It may turn out, years hence, that a solid discipline of human science will have come into existence, hard as quantum physics, filled with deep insights, plagued as physics still is by ambiguities but with new rules and new ways of getting things done. Like, for instance, getting rid of thermonuclear weapons, patriotic rhetoric, and nationalism all at once. If anything like this does turn up we will be looking back at today's social scientists, and their close colleagues the humanists, as having launched the new science in a way not all that different from the accomplishment of the old alchemists, by simply working on the problem — this time, the fundamental, primal universality of the human mind.

9

Discussion: Content

1. Where does the word *gibberish* come from?
2. How did the majority of people in the Middle Ages view alchemists?
3. What projects come to mind today when alchemy is mentioned?
4. What are some of the actual scientific advances that may be attributed to the studies of alchemists?
5. What is the etymology of *alchemy*? What other word with an entirely different meaning today was once applied to the practice of alchemy?
6. What sciences of today does Thomas liken to ancient alchemy? Why?

Discussion: Form

1. Thomas's first sentence is actually a definition of alchemy, but it is a rather startling one because it conflicts with the modern-day notion that alchemists were frauds. Try qualifying this definition in some way so that it is not quite so startling. What is the result of adding such a qualification?
2. As Thomas defines alchemy, what other methods of development does he use to any significant extent?
3. One ultimate purpose in this essay is to plead for some progress in dealing with such pressing matters as nuclear disarmament. To do this he toys with definitions of alchemy and draws an analogy for the reader. Study the concluding paragraph and explain how the analogy works.

Superstitions
Margaret Mead
Rhoda Metraux

Margaret Mead (1901–1978) was one of America's foremost anthropologists. Her first book, *Coming of Age in Samoa* (1928), gained her immediate fame because it helped to explode many myths about teenagers. For most of her career she served as the curator for ethnology at the American Museum of Natural History in New York. She was the author of many other books, including *Growing Up in New Guinea* (1930), *Sex and Temperament* (1935), *Male and Female: A Study of Sexes in a Changing World* (1949), and *Continuities in Cultural Evolution* (1964). This essay is taken from *A Way of Seeing* (1970), which she prepared with the assistance of her colleague, Rhoda Metraux.

Once in a while there is a day when everything seems to run smoothly and even the riskiest venture comes out exactly right. You exclaim, "This is my lucky day!" Then as an afterthought you say, "Knock on wood!" Of course, you do not really believe that knocking on wood will ward off danger. Still, boasting about your own good luck gives you a slightly uneasy feeling — and you carry out the little protective ritual. If someone challenged you at that moment, you would probably say, "Oh, that's nothing. Just an old superstition."

But when you come to think about it, what is a superstition?

In the contemporary world most people treat old folk beliefs as superstitions — the belief, for instance, that there are lucky and unlucky days or numbers, that future events can be read from omens, that there are protective charms or that what happens can be influenced by casting spells. We have excluded magic from our current world view, for we know that natural events have natural causes.

In a religious context, where truths cannot be demonstrated, we accept them as a matter of faith. Superstitions, however, belong to the category of beliefs, practices and ways of thinking that have been discarded because they are inconsistent with scientific knowledge. It is easy to say that other people are superstitious because they believe what we regard to be untrue. "Superstition" used in that sense is a derogatory term for the beliefs of other people that we do not share. But there is more to it than that. For superstitions lead a kind of half life in a twilight world where, sometimes, we partly suspend our disbelief and act as if magic worked.

Actually, almost every day, even in the most sophisticated home, something is likely to happen that evokes the memory of some old folk belief. The salt spills. A knife falls to the floor. Your nose tickles. Then perhaps, with a slightly embarrassed smile, the person who spilled the salt tosses a pinch over his left shoulder. Or someone recites the old rhyme, "Knife falls, gentleman calls." Or as you rub your nose you think, That means a letter. I wonder who's writing? No one takes these small responses very seriously or gives them more than a passing thought. Sometimes people will preface one of these ritual acts — walking around instead of under a ladder or hastily closing an umbrella that has been opened inside a house — with such a remark as "I remember my great-aunt used to . . ." or "Germans used to say you ought not. . . ." And then, having placed the belief at some distance away in time or space, they carry out the ritual.

Everyone also remembers a few of the observances of childhood — wishing on the first star; looking at the new moon over the right shoulder; avoiding the cracks in the sidewalk on the way to school while chanting, "Step on a crack, break your mother's back"; wishing on white horses, on loads of hay, on covered bridges, on red cars; saying quickly, "Bread-and-butter" when a post or a tree separated you from the friend you were walking with. The adult may not actually recite the formula "Star light, star bright . . ." and may not quite turn to look at the new moon, but his mood is tempered by a little of the old thrill that came when the observance was still freighted with magic.

Superstition can also be used with another meaning. When I discuss the religious beliefs of other peoples, especially primitive peoples, I am often asked, "Do they really have a religion, or is it all just superstition?" The point of contrast here is not between a scientific and a magical view of the world but between the clear, theologically defensible religious beliefs of members of civilized societies and what we regard as the false and childish views of the heathen who "bow down to wood and stone." Within the civilized religions, however, where membership includes believers who are educated and urbane and others who are ignorant and simple, one always finds traditions and practices that the more sophisticated will dismiss offhand as "just superstition" but that guide the steps of those who live by older ways. Mostly these are very ancient beliefs, some handed on from one religion to another and carried from country to country around the world. 7

Very commonly, people associate superstition with the past, with very old ways of thinking that have been supplanted by modern knowledge. But new superstitions are continually coming into being and flourishing in our society. Listening to mothers in the park in the 1930's, one heard them say, "Now, don't you run out into the sun, or Polio will get you." In the 1940's elderly people explained to one another in tones of resignation, "It was the Virus that got him down." And every year the cosmetics industry offers us new magic — cures for baldness, lotions that will give every woman radiant skin, hair coloring that will restore to the middle-aged the charm and romance of youth — results that are promised if we will just follow the simple directions. Families and individuals also have their cherished, private superstitions. You must leave by the back door when you are going on a journey, or you must wear a green dress when you are taking an examination. It is a kind of joke, of course, but it makes you feel safe. 8

These old half-beliefs and new half-beliefs reflect the keenness of our wish to have something come true or to prevent something bad from happening. We do not always recognize new superstitions for what they are, and we still follow the old ones because someone's faith long ago matches our contemporary hopes and fears. In the past people "knew" that a black cat crossing one's path was a bad omen, and they turned back home. Today we are fearful of taking a journey and would give anything to turn back — and then we notice a black cat running across the road in front of us. 9

Child psychologists recognize the value of the toy a child holds in his hand at bedtime. It is different from his thumb, with which he can close himself in from the rest of the world, and it is different from the real world, to which he is learning to relate himself. Psychologists

Section 7: Definition

call these toys — these furry animals and old, cozy baby blankets — "transitional objects"; that is, objects that help the child move back and forth between the exactions of everyday life and the world of wish and dream.

Superstitions have some of the qualities of these transitional objects. They help people pass between the areas of life where what happens has to be accepted without proof and the areas where sequences of events are explicable in terms of cause and effect, based on knowledge. Bacteria and viruses that cause sickness have been identified; the cause of symptoms can be diagnosed and a rational course of treatment prescribed. Magical charms no longer are needed to treat the sick; modern medicine has brought the whole sequence of events into the secular world. But people often act as if this change had not taken place. Laymen still treat germs as if they were invisible, malign spirits, and physicians sometimes prescribe antibiotics as if they were magic substances.

Over time, more and more of life has become subject to the controls of knowledge. However, this is never a one-way process. Scientific investigation is continually increasing our knowledge. But if we are to make good use of this knowledge, we must not only rid our minds of old, superseded beliefs and fragments of magical practice, but also recognize new superstitions for what they are. Both are generated by our wishes, our fears and our feelings of helplessness in difficult situations.

Civilized peoples are not alone in having grasped the idea of superstitions — beliefs and practices that are superseded but that still may evoke compliance. The idea is one that is familiar to every people, however primitive, that I have ever known. Every society has a core of transcendent beliefs — beliefs about the nature of the universe, the world and man — that no one doubts or questions. Every society also has a fund of knowledge related to practical life — about the succession of day and night and of the seasons; about correct ways of planting seeds so that they will germinate and grow; about the processes involved in making dyes or the steps necessary to remove the deadly poison from manioc roots so they become edible. Island peoples know how the winds shift and they know the star toward which they must point the prow of the canoe exactly so that as the sun rises they will see the first fringing palms on the shore toward which they are sailing.

This knowledge, based on repeated observations of reliable sequences, leads to ideas and hypotheses of the kind that underlie scientific thinking. And gradually as scientific knowledge, once developed without conscious plan, has become a great self-corrective system and the foundation for rational planning and action, old magical beliefs and observances have had to be discarded. 14

But it takes time for new ways of thinking to take hold, and often the transition is only partial. Older, more direct beliefs live on in the hearts and minds of elderly people. And they are learned by children who, generation after generation, start out life as hopefully and fearfully as their forebears did. Taking their first steps away from home, children use the old rituals and invent new ones to protect themselves against the strangeness of the world into which they are venturing. 15

So whatever has been rejected as no longer true, as limited, provincial and idolatrous, still leads a half life. People may say, "It's just a superstition," but they continue to invoke the ritual's protection or potency. In this transitional, twilight state such beliefs come to resemble dreaming. In the dream world a thing can be either good or bad; a cause can be an effect and an effect can be a cause. Do warts come from touching toads, or does touching a toad cure the wart? Is sneezing a good omen or a bad omen? You can have it either way — or both ways at once. In the same sense, the half-acceptance and half-denial accorded superstitions give us the best of both worlds. 16

Superstitions are sometimes smiled at and sometimes frowned upon as observances characteristic of the old-fashioned, the unenlightened, children, peasants, servants, immigrants, foreigners or backwoods people. Nevertheless, they give all of us ways of moving back and forth among the different worlds in which we live — the sacred, the secular and the scientific. They allow us to keep a private world also, where, smiling a little, we can banish danger with a gesture and summon luck with a rhyme, make the sun shine in spite of storm clouds, force the stranger to do our bidding, keep an enemy at bay and straighten the paths of those we love. 17

Discussion: Content

1. Before stating her ultimate definition of superstition, Mead tries out three working definitions that capture part of what she believes to be the truth. What are these three partial definitions?
2. In paragraph 9 the common element in all the trial definitions is introduced. What is it?
3. Where does the ultimate definition of superstitions occur most explicitly?
4. What is a "transitional object"? How is the psychological concept it represents related to superstitions?

5. In the time since this essay was written, new superstitions, some specialized or localized, should have come into being. What ones can you name?
6. Read the description of the reasoning error called *post hoc, ergo propter hoc* on p. 443 of the Appendix section called "A Brief Introduction to Common Logical Fallacies." How does this explanation modify your attitude toward superstitions, including some you may practice?

Discussion: Form

1. What interest-arousing device does the author use to introduce the topic?
2. Why do you suppose paragraph 2 consists of a single sentence?
3. The original title of this essay was "New Superstitions for Old." Judging from the title alone, what method or methods of rhetorical development other than definition would you expect to find most used? Be ready to support your answer.
4. What is the name of the rhetorical device used in paragraphs 10 and 11 to link "transitional objects" with superstitions?
5. What rhetorical method is the basis of paragraph 14?

Argumentative Writing

Argumentative or persuasive writing differs from expository writing in a number of ways, but the foremost differences are the writer's purpose and attitude toward the audience. In exposition the writer wishes to inform or educate the reader; that is, the writer is merely providing some information that the reader presumably lacks. With persuasion the writer's intention is different. It is assumed that the reader is already informed about the subject. Hence the writer's objective is both different and more difficult. The object is no longer to inform the reader but to change the reader's mind.

Most people — unless they are hopelessly stubborn, unreasonable, or unfeeling — will yield to two forms of persuasion: logical appeals and emotional appeals. They may also need to be shown that the reasoning that led them to their original opinions was defective in some way. Accordingly, each of the next four sections deals with a persuasive strategy. The first two treat the two kinds of logical appeals: the inductive argument and the deductive argument. The third section introduces methods of refutation or rebuttal, i.e., methods for showing how the opposing opinion is faulty or wrong; and the final section introduces emotional appeals — attempts to win the sympathy of the audience.

In order to persuade audiences, there are some new skills that you will need to develop, but the ones you have already mastered will still prove very useful. You will still need to describe, to narrate, and to explain; you will need to illustrate by examples; analyze, classify, and divide; delineate processes; make comparisons and analogies; adduce probable causes and effects; and define terms. You could not realistically hope to argue satisfactorily until you had acquired these skills. Now you can put them all to work.

The Roman statesman and orator Cicero once listed the six parts of an argument:

1. Introduction
2. Background
3. Partition, or statement of propositions
4. Confirmation, or proof of propositions
5. Refutation
6. Conclusion, or appeal to sympathy.

Cicero was not prescribing that all attempts at persuasion should contain each of those steps in exactly that order; he was merely observing that most arguments that he had witnessed — and he had witnessed a lot of them — did in fact contain those elements. For that reason it is worthwhile to discuss, at least briefly, the parts of Cicero's classical argument so that you will recognize them in the arguments that you encounter and so that you will develop the special vocabulary needed to discuss arguments knowledgeably.

The *introduction* and *background* segments of the argument are altogether expository. The introduction, as its name implies, introduces the topic, either directly or obliquely, and states that there are differences of opinion about it. The background sketches the history of events leading up to the present confrontation — facts that the reader must know in order to understand the argument. Since disagreements often arise because people are poorly informed, the background component of the argument takes on a key role. Getting readers to change their minds is sometimes simply a matter of providing them with additional information upon which to base their conclusions.

The next step, the *partition,* narrows the scope of the argument to just those issues (or perhaps even a single issue) over which there is disagreement. Usually the writer will try to search out points about which the disputing parties agree. Such concessions help to establish good will and insure an open-minded response on the part of the audience. They also serve to pare away everything that is not essential in the statement of the disputed proposition or propositions.

Here it is necessary to define very carefully what is meant by the term *proposition.* According to classical rhetoric, a proposition is a statement that can be either affirmed or denied — that is, it is a statement that you as a writer wish to affirm as true and whose truth you expect your audience to deny. In its barest form a proposition will look very much like a definition: for example, *John Smith is an honest man* or *John Smith is a man who can be trusted*. In actual practice, propositions may frequently be disguised, in sentences like *You can trust John Smith* or *Who could be more trustworthy than John Smith?* In the final analysis, though, it is John Smith's honesty that is being debated — either he is honest or he is not. These expressions qualify as propositions because each is capable of being reduced to a simple statement that can be affirmed or denied. Thus *Vote for lower taxes* is not a proposition in a strict sense but is an acceptable one in a broad sense because it can be reduced to this: *The lowering of taxes is something that deserves your vote*.

To see how the first three parts of an argument work, look at the following paragraphs, taken from a 1915 argument favoring women's right to vote.

> The men of three eastern States — Massachusetts, New York and New Jersey — will have an opportunity this fall to put themselves on record for or against woman suffrage. In each State a constitutional amendment extending the suffrage to women is to be submitted to the voters at the polls. What will the men of Massachusetts, New York, and New Jersey do with the opportunity? Will they follow the enlightened example of the men of Wyoming, Colorado, Idaho, Utah, Washington, California, Arizona, Kansas, Oregon, Alaska, Illinois, Montana, and Nevada? Or will they choose to keep their States a while longer groping in the mists of reaction?
>
> Women should vote for four good and sufficient reasons:
>
> It will be good for the women.
> It will be good for the men.
> It will be good for the family.
> It will be good for the State.

The first paragraph functions as both introduction and background. Its first sentence introduces the topic of women's suffrage and announces that three states are about to vote on the constitutional amendment needed to achieve that goal. It then brings the reader up to date on the progress of ratification: thirteen legislatures have already voted favorably. The second paragraph states the propositions to be proved in a quite unmistakable way.

Not all introductions, backgrounds, and partitions will be quite so straightforward, but it is worth pointing out that your success in sifting the facts to reveal the actual areas of disagreement will go a long way toward winning your case. In the following letter, notice how clearly and succinctly Abraham Lincoln states the areas of disagreement. Although cast as a question, each could be reduced to a proposition.

Executive Mansion, Washington, February 3, 1862

Major-General McClellan:
My dear Sir: You and I have distinct and different plans for a movement of the Army of the Potomac — yours to be down the Chesapeake, up the Rappahannock to Urbana, and across land to the terminus of the railroad on the York River; mine to move directly to a point on the railroad southwest of Manassas.
If you will give satisfactory answers to the following questions, I shall gladly yield my plan to yours.
First. Does your plan involve a greatly larger expenditure of time and money than mine?
Second. Wherein is a victory more certain by your plan than mine?
Third. Wherein is a victory more valuable by your plan than mine?
Fourth. In fact, would it not be less valuable in this, that it would break no great line of the enemy's communications, while mine would?
Fifth. In case of disaster, would not a retreat be more difficult by your plan than mine?

Yours truly,
Abraham Lincoln

Lincoln did not go on to prove each of his propositions, but one assumes that he could have. This brings us to the fourth of Cicero's parts of an argument: *confirmation,* or proof of the propositions. We stated earlier that a writer may use both logical and emotional appeals in order to change the reader's mind. But in the confirmation section, only logical proofs can be admitted. We shall examine logical proofs — induction and deduction — in the next two sections of this book. After that we shall take up Cicero's fifth part of the argument, *refutation* — the disproof of competing arguments (i.e., opposing propositions). Finally we shall take up emotional appeals, which Cicero reserved for the *conclusion* section of the classic argument.

It is worth repeating that each of the six parts of the classic argument need not always be present in every piece of persuasive writing that you encounter. The writer who fashions a logical proof of a proposition may not feel obliged to refute the opposite claim — and may or may not desire to arouse the reader's sympathy. On the other hand, the author of an emotional appeal may abandon logical argumentation altogether. It is, however, always to your advantage to be able to recognize each of these devices — inductive proofs, deductive proofs, refutations, and emotional appeals — when you see them and to be able to use them in your own writing.

After all, others often try to change our minds (think of political speeches, editorials, advertisements), just as we often want or need to change the minds of others. You will have occasion — at school, at work, and as a private citizen — to employ your persuasive skills, especially when you must communicate with persons in power or when you achieve a position of power yourself. The occupational need for such skills in a lawyer or politician is obvious, but it also exists for people in other vocations: business (especially marketing and management), education, science, and technology. To convince yourself of the wide variety of situations that call for persuasive writing, you need only to glance through the selections that follow, asking yourself in each case, "What prompted this argument?"

Section 1:
Inductive Proofs

In the Examples section of "Expository Writing," we stated that development by examples is one of the most frequently used methods of exposition. Here we must add that it is also the basis for one of the most frequently used methods of argumentation, namely *induction*.

What is the difference? When is development by examples exposition, and when is it argumentation? The main difference lies in the reader's attitude. Recall that in the Examples section we suggested that the following thesis statements could be developed by offering examples:

1. Differential equations are a terrifying experience.
2. Ellen Brown is clever as well as attractive.
3. Coach Waters can expect a winning season.
4. Neanderthal man practiced a rudimentary form of democracy.

In calling these sentences thesis statements, we assumed that the readers did not know very much, if anything at all, about differential equations, Ellen Brown, Coach Waters' team, or Neanderthal life. Our purpose in each case was to explain by providing information.

But notice now that each of these sentences could be viewed differently. Each could be a *proposition* — a statement that can be either affirmed or denied. All that is needed is to adjust the reader's expected attitude. If the reader is familiar with differential equations and thinks that they are easy, or if the reader knows Ellen Brown and thinks that she is not clever, but instead a little dumb, then the writer's problem is more difficult.

In the first case, the writer would be wise to qualify the proposition by stating that differential equations are terrifying for a great many people, a step that would exclude the mathematical wizards who might object; then the forthcoming examples could paint their grim picture. In the case of Ellen Brown, the writer must hope that the examples seeking to present her favorably will outweigh or outnumber those that can be supplied by her detractors.

In inductive proofs the writer purports to have examined all available information and come to a conclusion on the basis of that examination. But since it is never realistically possible to examine all of the possible information, the writer must settle for something less than a perfect induction. In other words, the best that a writer could hope to show would be that there tend to be more people who find differential equations difficult than otherwise and that Ellen Brown has more redeeming qualities than faults. Thus it is more correct to say that, rather than proving a proposition, induction establishes a probability that the proposition is true — in much the same way that Gallup polls establish the probability that a particular candidate will win an election.

Certainly an inductive proof may be overthrown by the appearance of sufficient contradictory support, just as Truman defeated Dewey for President in 1948, despite what the polls forecast. But what is common to all inductions is the notion of accumulating evidence that outweighs or outnumbers the contradictory evidence. Since induction is based on this accumulation of evidence, one piece of evidence is never enough, and the more evidence you can supply, the better your induction.

Another type of inductive proof is based on comparison or analogy. Take the proposition that Coach Waters' team will have a winning season. The writer could argue that this year's team is very much like the championship team of 1969 in at least four ways: in speed, in depth of reserves, in returning lettermen, and in execution of the forward pass. The contention is that teams that are alike in such a large number of points will be alike in others as well, and in this case they will both prove to be winning teams. Similarly, if archaeologists can show that the accumulated artifacts of Neanderthal society closely parallel those that can be found today among the primitive tribes of the Amazon basin — who also find a democratic social structure crucial to their survival — then it is reasonable to suppose that the Neanderthals might also have practiced democracy. In neither of these cases is the conclusion a certainty, but the data point to a probability.

Finally, the inductive examination of evidence can also be used to establish probable causes. If, for example, we wished to discover why a great many sophomore math majors shifted their major to accounting during the second semester each year, we might poll them for their reasons, and this would clearly be an inductive approach. Alternatively, we might examine the math curriculum. There are ten sophomore-level math courses, ranging from modern algebra to vector analysis, but of these ten the only one that is an absolute requirement for the second-semester sophomore is differential equations. On this evidence you might claim that it is this course in differential equations that is separating the pure mathematicians from the applied ones.

Inductive proof is often likened to the scientific method of investigation. For an easy-to-understand description of the scientific method that includes clear treatments of both induction and deduction, turn to the Appendix and read Thomas Huxley's "The Method of Scientific Investigation," which begins on p. 445. Then you will better understand the uses of induction and deduction in the model paragraphs and essays in the next two sections of this book.

Section 1:
Inductive Proofs

Paragraphs:
Inductive Proof

Strike Out Little League
Robin Roberts

I still don't know what those three gentlemen in Williamsport had in mind when they organized Little League baseball. I'm sure they didn't want parents arguing with their children about kids' games. I'm sure they didn't want to have family meals disrupted for three months every year. I'm sure they didn't want young athletes hurting their arms pitching under pressure at such a young age. I'm sure they didn't want young boys who don't have much athletic ability made to feel that something is wrong with them because they can't play baseball. I'm sure they didn't want a group of coaches drafting the players each year for different teams. I'm sure they didn't want unqualified men working with the young players. I'm sure they didn't realize how normal it is for an eight-year-old boy to be scared of a thrown or batted baseball. For the life of me, I can't figure out what they had in mind.

Discussion Questions

1. How many elements are there to Roberts' induction? That is, how many pieces of evidence does he cite to support his contention that Little League baseball should be done away with?
2. What is peculiar about the way Roberts introduces each piece of evidence? Is that method of presentation effective?
3. If you do not already know who he is, look up Robin Roberts in a baseball history or reference book. How does knowledge of his great major-league career affect your reaction to what he has written here?

Violence in the Sixties
Arthur Schlesinger

The murders within five years of John F. Kennedy, Martin Luther King, Jr., and Robert F. Kennedy raise — or ought to raise — somber questions about the character of contemporary America. One such murder might be explained away as an isolated horror, unrelated to the inner life of our society. But the successive shootings, in a short time, of three men who greatly embodied the idealism of American life suggest not so much a fortuitous set of aberrations as an emerging pattern of response and action — a spreading and ominous belief in the efficacy of violence and the politics of the deed.

Discussion Questions

1. What proposition is Schlesinger arguing? Where does he state it?
2. Upon what evidence does Schlesinger base his conclusion?
3. Consult "A Brief Introduction of Common Logical Fallacies," p. 434, and determine which of the material fallacies Schlesinger's opponents might claim he has committed.

Wait?
Martin Luther King, Jr.

We have waited for more than 340 years for our constitutional and God-given rights. The nations of Asia and Africa are moving with jetlike speed toward gaining political independence, but we still creep at horse-and-buggy pace toward gaining a cup of coffee at a lunch counter. Perhaps it is easy for those who have never felt the stinging darts of segregation to say, "Wait." But when you have seen vicious mobs lynch your mothers and fathers at will and drown your sisters and brothers at whim; when you have seen hate-filled policemen curse, kick and even kill your black brothers and sisters; when you see the vast majority of your twenty million Negro brothers smothering in an airtight cage of poverty in the midst of an affluent society; when you suddenly find your tongue twisted and your speech stammering as you seek to explain to your six-year-old daughter why she can't go to the public amusement park that has just been advertised on television, and see tears welling up in her eyes when she is told that Funtown is closed to colored children, and see ominous clouds of inferiority beginning to form in her little mental sky, and see her beginning to distort her personality by developing an unconscious bitterness toward white people; when you have to concoct an answer for a five-year-old son who is asking: "Daddy, why do white people treat colored people so mean?"; when you take a cross-country drive and find it necessary to sleep night after night in the uncomfortable corners of your automobile because no motel will accept you; when you are humiliated day in and day out by nagging signs reading "white" and "colored"; when your first name becomes "nigger," your middle name becomes "boy" (however old you are) and your last names becomes "John," and your wife and mother are never given the respected title "Mrs."; when you are harried by day and haunted by night by the fact that you are a Negro, living constantly at tiptoe stance, never quite knowing what to expect next, and are plagued with inner fears and outer resentments; when you are forever fighting a degenerating sense of "nobodiness" — then you will understand why we find it difficult to wait. There comes a time when the cup of endurance runs over, and men are no longer willing to be plunged into the abyss of despair. I hope, sirs, you can understand our legitimate and unavoidable impatience.

Discussion Questions

1. Where does King present the proposition he is arguing for? How might you state it in the barest form?
2. How many pieces of evidence does King examine in the inductive proof of his proposition?
3. What rhetorical device does King use in enumerating these pieces of evidence?

The New Illiteracy
Christopher Lasch

Mass education, which began as a promising attempt to democratize the higher culture of the privileged classes, has ended by stupefying the privileged themselves. Modern society has achieved unprecedented rates of formal literacy, but at the same time it has produced new forms of illiteracy. People increasingly find themselves unable to use language with ease and precision, to recall the basic facts of their country's history, to make logical deductions, to understand any but the most rudimentary written texts, or even to grasp their constitutional rights. One study after another documents the steady decline of basic intellectual skills. In 1966, high school seniors scored an average of 467 points on the verbal section of the Scholastic Aptitude Test — hardly cause for celebration. Ten years later they scored only 429. Scores on the mathematical part of the test dropped from an average of 495 to 470. Many publishers have simplified textbooks in response to complaints that a new generation of students, raised on television, movies, and what one educator calls "the antilanguage assumptions of our culture," find existing textbooks unintelligible. The decline of intellectual competence cannot be accounted for, as some observers would have it, on the reactionary assumption that more students from minority- and low-income groups are taking tests, going to college, and thus dragging down the scores. The proportion of these students has remained unchanged over the last ten years; meanwhile the decline of academic achievement has extended to elite schools as well as to community colleges, junior colleges, and public high schools. Every year, 40 to 60 percent of the students at the University of California find themselves required to enroll in remedial English. At Stanford, only a quarter of the students in the class entering in 1975 managed to pass the university's English placement test, even though these students had achieved high scores on the Scholastic Aptitude Test. At private high schools, average test scores in math and English dropped by eight and ten points in a single year, between 1974 and 1975.

Discussion Questions

1. What is the proposition that Lasch is arguing?
2. What evidence does he present to support this proposition?
3. Why does Lasch contend that lower SAT scores are not a result of a rise in the number of minority students taking the tests?

Student Work:
Inductive Proof

A Simple Complaint

Brown and Dodson Cafeterias are alike in just about every respect. They offer plain but nutritious food three times a day to a hungry student body. They charge the same prices for breakfast, dinner, and supper. They provide efficient, if not smiling, service. And they manage to maintain a fair standard of cleanliness. Students complain, of course, but as a rule even the complaints are the same, not varying at all as to whether the speaker is a patron of Brown or Dodson. That is, all the complaints but one. If Brown and Dodson are alike in just about every respect, shouldn't they be alike in just one more respect? Shouldn't Dodson give each breakfast customer two sausage patties the same way Brown does?

Discussion Questions

This student paragraph came in response to an assignment calling for inductive support of a proposition.
1. What is the proposition that is being argued here?
2. Is this really an inductive argument? If so, how is it organized?

The Zero-Year Jinx

Will President Reagan be the first president in over a century and a half to break the zero-election-year jinx? If he completes his term this year, it will be the first time since the election of James Monroe in 1820 that a president who won the office in a year ending in zero did not die in office. Following Monroe, William Henry Harrison, elected in 1840, died a few months after he was installed in the White House. And the same fate befell the man elected in 1860, Abraham Lincoln. Garfield and McKinley, elected in 1880 and 1900, respectively, were assassinated, and Warren Harding died of food poisoning before he could complete the term he was elected to in 1920. Franklin Roosevelt and John Kennedy, the most recent presidents to be elected in zero years, both died in office. 1

Actually, Lincoln and Roosevelt did live through their zero-year terms, but each ran for another term and died during that one. Now Ronald Reagan, elected in 1980, is approaching the end of his zero-year term, but he has declared his intention of running for another. Not a young man anymore at 73, Mr. Reagan is seriously flirting with the zero-year jinx. 2

Discussion Questions

1. What precisely is the zero-year jinx?
2. How many presidents have been victims of this jinx?
3. What does the writer suggest that President Reagan shares with Lincoln and Roosevelt?
4. Is this inductive argument convincing?

Let Women Fight

I can see but one reason why women shouldn't be drafted into combat, but there are several good reasons why they should be. 1

Women are good fighters. Other countries have not shrunk from using women fighters. Russian women were valiant in the defense of Stalingrad, hiding in shell craters and pulling the pin on a hand grenade as a Nazi tank rolled over. Israeli women have fought alongside their men in their recent wars, and the women of the Viet Cong could whittle pungi sticks just as well as the men. 2

It's worth remembering also that the Russians, the Israelis, and the Viet Cong were winners. 3

It is also worth remembering that the primary thing that makes men fight isn't patriotism or discipline. It's that they're ashamed not to — afraid their comrades-in-arms would think them cowards. Can you imagine how much fiercer the average male soldier would be if his comrade-in-arms were a woman? 4

Section 1:
Inductive Proofs

Those are the reasons for letting the women fight. The only reason why they shouldn't is that they should simply refuse — until the Constitution guarantees them equal rights.

Discussion Questions

1. Would you characterize this writer as being politically moderate, right of center, or left of center?
2. The writer asserts at the outset that there are a number of reasons why women should be drafted. How many are actually stated?
3. The clearest use of induction in this essay seems to occur in the second paragraph. What exactly is the evidence that is examined, and what is the unstated generalization arising from it?
4. Would you be surprised to learn that this student writer is the same one who wrote the definition essay "Feminist" on p. 271? What do the essays have in common?
5. Look up the term *a fortiori* in a dictionary. How is this term applicable to paragraph 4?

Beer on Campus

It's time to have beer for sale in the University Center. Before your mind fills with pictures of drunken students staggering off to class, let me hasten to add that none should be on sale until the last class for the day has begun, say around 4:30, and sales should stop at 11 P.M. There are five good reasons to begin beer sales.

First, the selling of beer on college campuses is not new or even unusual anymore. One of my professors says that when he was an undergraduate at the University of Wisconsin, beer was already on sale in their student union (and before 4:30, at that). Doubtless you have heard of beer for sale on the campuses of many other colleges and universities across the nation.

Second, the revenue from the beer sales could help reduce the current $25.00 per semester University Center fee, since surely this would be a profit-making operation.

Third, the sales could be restricted to beers brewed in North Carolina (Miller's and Schlitz), thus helping our state's industrial growth.

Fourth, since most students live on campus, the fifteen-mile round trip to Sylva to buy beer would be reduced, saving much gas and time, not to speak of getting drinking drivers off the road. 5

Fifth, the social aspect of the new beer parlor would add much to the pleasure of being on campus, especially on weekends (when hours could be extended), and there would be less drinking and noise in the dormitories, leaving them more useful for studying. 6

All in all, beer sales in the University Center make a lot of sense. Don't you agree? 7

Discussion Questions

1. In citing five reasons why there should be beer on campus, is the student employing an inductive strategy?
2. How is this essay different from "Why Students Leave College," p. 220, which also consists of five reasons?
3. Besides stating the proposition to be proved, what else does the writer do in paragraph 1?
4. Which of the five reasons offered by the writer furnishes the clearest illustration of an inductive approach?

Let's Drive Fifty-five

Tom punched the accelerator, and the orange Corvette raced down the interstate. The speedometer rose steadily from 55 to 65, 75, 80, and on up to 85 miles per hour. "There is no danger," Tom thought. "It's just road for miles." Even as Tom was thinking this, a dark form darted across the road in front of him. Automatically Tom swerved, but at the great speed he was going, he lost control, and the Corvette bounded across the median, crashing into a bank as Tom lost consciousness. 1

This is an example of the accidents that can occur due to excessive speeds on the highways. The *North Carolina Blue Book of Traffic Safety* says that no one should drive a vehicle at a speed "greater than is reasonable or prudent under existing conditions." At the present time the speed limit is fifty-five miles per hour for interstate driving. Should this be the maximum speed for highways that are specifically designed for higher speeds? There are three good reasons why the speed limit should not be raised on interstate highways. 2

Section 1: Inductive Proofs

First of all, raising the speed limit on interstates would be bad economically. "Punching it" on the interstate and driving at excessive speeds waste gasoline. Raising the speed limit nationwide would eventually result in greater dependence on foreign imports of oil.

Second, personal expenses would be higher if our present speed limit were raised. The car maintenance required is greater when driving at speeds exceeding fifty-five miles per hour. Also, last year an estimated twenty-five billion dollars was spent due to drivers' exceeding the speed limit. This total includes insurance, property damage, and hospital costs due to accidents.

Lastly, speed kills. It is the number-one reason for death on our highways. Last year over 48,000 people were killed in the United States due to speeding. Over three million people were injured last year, and 290,000 of these injured were unable to work.

What are your chances of being killed in relation to speed? The North Carolina Highway Safety Division determines that speed makes accidents and death more likely. At twenty-five miles per hour your chances of being killed are estimated at twelve percent. At fifty-five miles per hour the chances of being killed are 300 percent greater as compared with twenty-five miles per hour, and 600 percent greater when traveling at sixty-five miles per hour.

When properly enforced, the fifty-five miles-per-hour speed limit on interstate highways is safer, cuts down on personal expenses, and is smart economically. But more important, it could save a life. Few people want to become another statistic, like Tom, or have that happen to a loved one.

Discussion Questions

1. Like the preceding argument, "Beer on Campus" this essay cites reasons for keeping the speed limit at fifty-five. Are these reasons, strictly speaking, an inductive proof?
2. Examine paragraphs 5 and 6. They contain a separate inductive argument. What is the proposition, and what is the evidence?
3. Look up "due to" in a reference grammar like Fowler's *Modern English Usage,* or ask your instructor about the construction. Are the uses of that phrase in paragraphs 2, 4, and 5 consistent with accepted usage?
4. What effective rhetorical devices does the writer use in the paper's conclusion?

Essays:
Inductive Proof

Send Your Children to the Libraries
Arthur Ashe

Arthur Ashe (1943–   ) is best known for his tennis prowess, as a junior player (United States indoors singles titles, 1960, 1961), a college player at UCLA (NCAA champion in singles and doubles, 1966), a top-ranking amateur (United States national singles champion, 1968), and star professional player afterward (various championships around the world). Another, more serious side appears in the essay below.

Since my sophomore year at the University of California, Los Angeles, I have become convinced that we blacks spend too much time on the playing fields and too little time in the libraries.   1

    Please don't think of this attitude as being pretentious just because I am a black, single, professional athlete.   2

    I don't have children, but I can make observations. I strongly believe the black culture expends too much time, energy, and effort raising, praising and teasing our black children as to the dubious glories of professional sport.   3

    All children need models to emulate — parents, relatives or friends. But when the child starts school, the influence of the parent is shared by teachers and classmates, by the lure of books, movies, ministers and newspapers, but most of all by television.   4

    Which televised events have the greatest number of viewers? — Sports — The Olympics, Super Bowl, Masters, World Series, pro basketball playoffs, Forest Hills. ABC-TV even has sports on Monday night prime time from April to December.   5

    So your child gets a massive dose of O. J. Simpson, Kareem Abdul-Jabbar, Muhammad Ali, Reggie Jackson, Dr. J. and Lee Elder and other pro athletes. And it is only natural that your child will dream of being a pro athlete himself.   6

305

But consider these facts: For the major professional sports of hockey, football, basketball, baseball, golf, tennis and boxing, there are roughly only 3,170 major league positions available (attributing 200 positions to golf, 200 to tennis and 100 to boxing). And the annual turnover is small.

We blacks are a subculture of about 28 million. Of the 13½ million men, 5 to 6 million are under 20 years of age, so your son has less than one chance in 1,000 of becoming a pro. Less than one in a thousand. Would you bet your son's future on something with odds of 999 to 1 against you? I wouldn't.

Unless a child is exceptionally gifted, you should know by the time he enters high school whether he has a future as an athlete. But what is more important is what happens if he doesn't graduate or doesn't land a college scholarship and doesn't have a viable alternative job career. Our high school dropout rate is several times the national average, which contributes to our unemployment rate of roughly twice the national average.

And how do you fight the figures in the newspapers every day? Ali has earned more than $30 million boxing. O. J. just signed for $2½ million, Dr. J. for almost $3 million, Reggie Jackson for $2.8 million, Nate Archibald for $400,000 a year. All that money, recognition, attention, free cars, girls, jobs in the offseason — no wonder there is Pop Warner football, Little League baseball, National Junior Tennis League tennis, hockey practice at 5 A.M. and pickup basketball games in any center city at any hour.

There must be some way to assure that the 999 who try but don't make it to pro sports don't wind up on the street corners or in the unemployment lines. Unfortunately, our most widely recognized role models are athletes and entertainers — "runnin'" and "jumpin'" and "singin'" and "dancin.'" While we are 60 percent of the National Basketball Association, we are less than 4 percent of the doctors and lawyers. While we are about 35 percent of major league baseball, we are less than 2 percent of the engineers. While we are about 40 percent of the National Football League, we are less than 11 percent of construction workers such as carpenters and bricklayers.

Our greatest heroes of the century have been athletes — Jack Johnson, Joe Louis and Muhammad Ali. Racial and economic discrimination forced us to channel our energies into athletics and entertainment. These were the ways out of the ghetto, the ways to get that Cadillac, those alligator shoes, that cashmere sport coat.

Somehow, parents must instill a desire for learning alongside the desire to be Walt Frazier. Why not start by sending black professional athletes into high schools to explain the facts of life?

I have often addressed high school audiences and my message is always the same. For every hour you spend on the athletic field, spend two in the library. Even if you make it as a pro athlete, your career will be over by the time you are 35. So you will need that diploma.

Have these pro athletes explain what happens if you break a leg, get a sore arm, have one bad year or don't make the cut for five or six tournaments. Explain to them the star system, wherein for every O. J. earning millions there are six or seven others making $15,000 or $20,000 or $30,000 a year.

But don't just have Walt Frazier or O. J. or Abdul-Jabbar address your class. Invite a benchwarmer or a guy who didn't make it. Ask him if he sleeps every night. Ask him whether he was graduated. Ask him what he would do if he became disabled tomorrow. Ask him where his old high school athletic buddies are.

We have been on the same roads — sports and entertainment — too long. We need to pull over, fill up at the library and speed away to Congress and the Supreme Court, the unions and the business world. We need more Barbara Jordans, Andrew Youngs, union cardholders, Nikki Giovannis and Earl Graveses. Don't worry: we will still be able to sing and dance and run and jump better than anybody else.

I'll never forget how proud my grandmother was when I graduated from U.C.L.A. in 1966. Never mind the Davis Cup in 1968, 1969 and 1970. Never mind the Wimbledon title, Forest Hills, etc. To this day, she still doesn't know what those names mean.

What mattered to her was that of her more than 30 children and grandchildren, I was the first to be graduated from college, and a famous college at that. Somehow, that made up for all those floors she scrubbed all those years.

Discussion: Content

1. How would you state the main idea of this essay? Where are the parts of that main idea located in the essay?
2. To what audience does Ashe mainly direct his essay? To what other groups is his message of value or interest?
3. Why is Ashe an especially effective proponent of the essay's thesis?
4. According to Ashe, what is the greatest influence on children other than their parents, and what is special about that influence?

5. Ashe says blacks have tended to seek stardom in what two fields? Which does he refer to most? What might be the reason for that emphasis?
6. Ashe barely mentions the causes of blacks' emphasis on professional sports and entertainment. When does he do so and what are the causes he names?

Discussion: Form

1. How does this argument qualify as an induction? Has Ashe used the scientific method in gathering information and coming to a conclusion?
2. This essay originally appeared in the New York *Times,* and may have been edited to fit newspaper columns comfortably, the result being that it has a number of noticeably short paragraphs. Which of the essay's early paragraphs might easily be joined to make longer, more conventional ones?
3. Why might Ashe have decided to present the sets of contrasting percentages in the last three sentences of paragraph 11?

Straight Talk about the Living-Together Arrangement
Louise Montague

Louise Montague Athearn (1931–   ) is a prolific writer on a variety of subjects, with such titles as *The Divorcée's Handbook* (1971), *The Entertaining Woman's Cookbook* (1972), and a novel, *The Sand Castles* (1975). The essay below discusses a subject of particular importance for many young people.

As the author of two books on divorce, I try to accept as many speaking engagements in high-school and college classes as I can. For it is my feeling that one answer to the soaring divorce rate is "preventive thinking" — the time to face many of the problems of divorce is *before* marriage. Lately, however, I find that at every session someone will stand up and state that marriage is outmoded and that the answer to the divorce problem is to live with a partner without the legal commitment of marriage.

Unhappily, "living together" is a modern phenomenon, a national trend today. Between 1960 and 1970, according to the U.S. Department of the Census, there was an eightfold increase in the Living-Together Arrangement (LTA). Why are so many people opting for this arrangement? And how do they get into it?

Certainly it's a very attractive idea sexually. But many young people also say it's a good way to "test" marriage. Others claim it's a terrific financial boon. And some don't even know how they ended up together. He started staying over or she began to leave clothes in his closet. These young people feel that by not making their relationship permanent they can maintain the spontaneous atmosphere of new love. By eliminating the legal commitment, they feel they have eliminated the "bad" part of marriage.

But the phenomenon is not limited to young people. Many divorced persons burned in marriage are trying it. Some have religious convictions forbidding a second marriage. Divorced men who are financially strapped feel they can't take on the responsibility of a new wife. Or the divorced woman may be reluctant to give up the alimony which would stop with her remarriage.

With all these "pluses" why do so many people engaged in an LTA write to me about the problems they have encountered? Why *is* the Living-Together Arrangement a detriment to those involved? Let's first consider the college students who decide on or slide into an LTA. You'd be surprised, once the subject comes up for discussion in a classroom, how many youngsters tell unhappy stories about themselves or their best friends.

Take the case of the young couple at Stanford. After they moved in together, the boy lost his scholarship and was not able to meet the high tuition costs from his part-time job. The girl quit school in order to work and let him finish his education. When he graduated, he applied for — and received — a scholarship to do graduate work in England. The girl was extremely hurt and angry; she felt he owed it to her to stay and help her finish *her* education. They argued bitterly for a day, and then the young man packed and left!

This situation is typical of dozens I have heard. The LTA simply can't work when it breeds the mutual dependency of marriage without the mutual responsibility.

Another example is a young couple at Georgetown University who moved into an apartment together. The girl's parents, shocked and hurt, cut off all their daughter's funds. The boy suggested they split up and go back to their dorms, but the girl, having had a terrible row with her family, insisted that it was now his responsibility to take care of her! Both got jobs, and the young man, not a strong student, fell behind and was unable to graduate.

Certainly it's difficult to think in realistic terms when a couple imagine themselves in love. But it is unfair to expect parental values to be dropped at a whim. The censure of family and friends is one of the greatest burdens the LTA carries. Young people who need the support of family are very foolish to chuck their long-term goals for short-term pleasures.

To be sure, intimate relationships are widely accepted today, but any resourceful couple can find ways of being together without moving in together. Moreover, living alone at times and developing individuality should be a prime concern of young people. For few can handle the LTA until they have learned to live with themselves.

Some of the most heartbreaking stories I hear about LTA's concern children. Whatever life-style a single male or female chooses is that individual's responsibility. But to bring a child into this atmosphere is to involve an innocent third party in an experiment that can leave all parties damaged. Although the law generally requires a father to support his children, it is often difficult to enforce these laws. Women are frequently left with the burden of support while the air of illegitimacy hangs heavy on the child.

A divorced or widowed woman who involves her children in an LTA may also be subjecting them to undue stress. Children experience great pressures to conform. What the mother and her companion view as a marvelous, free life-style, a child could see as a freaky embarrassment. The man in question, not being either father or stepfather, has no social definition as to the role he should play in the child's life. In some states, a divorced mother in an LTA stands a good chance of losing not only support payments but custody of her children.

Even a highly motivated working couple should be aware of the consequences of their actions. How you present yourself to the world is how you will be judged. A young petroleum engineer, living with a dental hygienist, applied for a much-wanted overseas job with an oil company. When the company conducted its routine investigation, and found that the young woman with whom he was living was not his wife, he was turned down; the firm felt that his LTA smacked of indecisiveness, instability, and failure on his part to accept responsibility. Who is to say if the oil company made the right decision? But, judging from a great many instances, it happens to be the way things are. What a couple may view as a sophisticated way to live, the business community may see as a career impediment.

Heartbreak and setback are also in the cards for a woman who moves in with a man in the hope of getting married. My advice is to avoid this strategy. When you demand nothing of a relationship, that's often exactly what you get. The very impermanence of the LTA suggests that that is what each partner has settled for. If marriage is what you want, marriage is what you should have. So why commit yourself to a shaky arrangement that keeps you out of the mainstream of life where you quite possibly will meet someone who shares your views?

Many divorced women with a great need for a little security, and with little faith in themselves, seek an LTA as a temporary answer to help them get on their feet. All this does is prolong their adjustment and reinforce their self-doubts. I'm reminded of one such woman who told me she had been living with a man for four years and wanted out but was afraid to leave. "Why?" I asked. Because, she said, she feared to give up the free rent and all that "security" she had with him. "Wrong," I said. "You have no security of any kind. You stand a good chance of being replaced by a younger version of yourself. And as for free rent, that's no security either. Security is owning the building."

Probably the greatest single hazard of the LTA is that it can actually spoil a good relationship between two people who should eventually marry. Because it is entered into out of weakness rather than strength, doubt rather than conviction, drift rather than decision, it offers unnecessary obstacles. Knowing this, you shouldn't casually toss aside those inherited institutions that have had a history of success.

If I were asked to give one reason only why I am opposed to the LTA, I would state quite simply that I am morally against it. As Barbara Tuchman wrote in *McCall's:* "Standards of taste, as well as morality, need continued reaffirmation to stay alive, as liberty needs eternal vigilance." There are valid standards of judgment which come from confidence in yourself and your values. To accept a living pattern that goes against your better judgment is to chip away at your personal freedom.

And what of love? You cannot hope to find love by experimenting biologically. You don't build love by creating a living situation designed to test it. You don't create love by setting up a forced proximity. Love *is*. And when you love you commit to it — for better or for worse. When we finally realize that all our experiments in alternate life-styles, communal marriage and open-ended covenants are simply a means of running *from* responsibility and love, not *to* them, we will have reached the beginning of maturity. 18

Discussion: Content

1. What does Montague say are some causes of the increase in numbers of Living-Together Arrangements (LTA's)? What others can you name?
2. From what group does Montague draw her most specific examples of LTA's? Why do you suppose she chose these?
3. Is Montague for or against LTA's? Where does she reveal her attitude most clearly?
4. Do you see a bias for or against either sex in the essay? Where?
5. According to Montague, what is the relationship between love, maturity, and LTA's? Where in the essay is that relationship stated most clearly?
6. Montague is a divorcée and an author of books and articles on divorce. How do those facts make her essay more convincing than if she were an unmarried student writing a similar essay for a college newspaper?

Discussion: Form

1. In Montague's argument what role do paragraphs 2–4 fulfill in Cicero's terms?
2. Where in paragraph 5 do you find a partition statement? How might you state it as a proposition?
3. In the remaining paragraphs, 6–18, Montague marshals support for her position. How would you classify the kinds of support that she brings forward?
4. She apparently saves her best arguments for the last. How sound do you feel that they are? How might you refute her contentions?
5. Put yourself in the place of a person in an LTA. How might you argue for your position? What kind of argument could you construct? Outline your argument.

How to Make People Smaller Than They Are
Norman Cousins

Norman Cousins (1912–   ) has distinguished himself for over fifty years as one of America's foremost journalists. As editor of the *Saturday Review*, he made that magazine a mirror of American life. His books include *Modern Man Is Obsolete* (1945), *Dr. Schweitzer of Lambarene* (1960), *Anatomy of an Illness* (1970), and *The Healing Heart* (1983). The essay that appears here was taken from Cousins' column in *Saturday Review*, December 1978.

Three months ago in this space we wrote about the costly retreat from the humanities on all the levels of American education. Since that time, we have had occasion to visit a number of campuses and have been troubled to find that the general situation is even more serious than we had thought. It has become apparent to us that one of the biggest problems confronting American education today is the increasing vocationalization of our colleges and universities. Throughout the country, schools are under pressure to become job-training centers and employment agencies. 1

The pressure comes mainly from two sources. One is the growing determination of many citizens to reduce taxes — understandable and even commendable in itself, but irrational and irresponsible when connected to the reduction or dismantling of vital public services. The second source of pressure comes from parents and students who tend to scorn courses of study that do not teach people how to become attractive to employers in a rapidly tightening job market. 2

It is absurd to believe that the development of skills does not also require the systematic development of the human mind. Education is being measured more by the size of the benefits the individual can extract from society than by the extent to which the individual can come into possession of his or her full powers. The result is that the life-giving juices are in danger of being drained out of education. 3

Emphasis on "practicalities" is being characterized by the subordination of words to numbers. History is seen not as essential experience to be transmitted to new generations, but as abstractions that carry dank odors. Art is regarded as something that calls for indulgence or patronage and that has no place among the practical realities. Political science is viewed more as a specialized subject for people who want to go into politics than as an opportunity for citizens to develop a knowledgeable relationship with the systems by which human societies are governed. Finally, literature and philosophy are assigned the role of add-ons — intellectual adornments that have nothing to do with "genuine" education.

Instead of trying to shrink the liberal arts, the American people ought to be putting pressure on colleges and universities to increase the ratio of the humanities to the sciences. Most serious studies of medical-school curricula in recent years have called attention to the stark gaps in the liberal education of medical students. The experts agree that the schools shouldn't leave it up to students to close those gaps.

The irony of the emphasis being placed on careers is that nothing is more valuable for anyone who has had a professional or vocational education than to be able to deal with abstractions or complexities, or to feel comfortable with subtleties of thought or language, or to think sequentially. The doctor who knows only disease is at a disadvantage alongside the doctor who knows at least as much about people as he does about pathological organisms. The lawyer who argues in court from a narrow legal base is no match for the lawyer who can connect legal precedents to historical experience and who employs wide-ranging intellectual resources. The business executive whose competence in general management is bolstered by an artistic ability to deal with people is of prime value to his company. For the technologist, the engineering of consent can be just as important as the engineering of moving parts. In all these respects, the liberal arts have much to offer. Just in terms of career preparation, therefore, a student is shortchanging himself by shortcutting the humanities.

But even if it could be demonstrated that the humanities contribute nothing directly to a job, they would still be an essential part of the educational equipment of any person who wants to come to terms with life. The humanities would be expendable only if human beings didn't have to make decisions that affect their lives and the lives of others; if the human past never existed or had nothing to tell us about the present; if thought processes were irrelevant to the achievement of purpose; if creativity was beyond the human mind and had nothing to do with the joy of living; if human relationships were random aspects of life; if human beings never had to cope with panic or pain, or if they never had to anticipate the connection between cause and effect; if all the mysteries of mind and nature were fully plumbed; and if no special demands arose from the accident of being born a human being instead of a hen or a hog.

Finally, there would be good reason to eliminate the humanities if a free society were not absolutely dependent on a functioning citizenry.

If the main purpose of a university is job training, then the underlying philosophy of our government has little meaning. The debates that went into the making of American society concerned not just institutions or governing principles but the capacity of humans to sustain those institutions. Whatever the disagreements were over other issues at the American Constitutional Convention, the fundamental question sensed by everyone, a question that lay over the entire assembly, was whether the people themselves would understand what it meant to hold the ultimate power of society, and whether they had enough of a sense of history and destiny to know where they had been and where they ought to be going. 8

Jefferson was prouder of having been the founder of the University of Virginia than of having been President of the United States. He knew that the educated and developed mind was the best assurance that a political system could be made to work — a system based on the informed consent of the governed. If this idea fails, then all the saved tax dollars in the world will not be enough to prevent the nation from turning on itself. 9

Discussion: Content

1. What is Cousins' proposition, and where does he state it?
2. What are the two forces encouraging increased vocationalism in American schools?
3. According to Cousins, why do people in the professions need to be educated in the liberal arts?
4. Why does the functioning of a free, democratic society depend on education in the liberal arts?

Discussion: Form

1. Examine paragraph 6 carefully. There is an inductive argument there. What is its proposition, and how is it supported?
2. There is another induction in paragraph 7. How is it supported?
3. In the first content question you were asked to locate the main proposition of this essay. How does Cousins prove this proposition?
4. Rather than reiterating the points of his argument in his concluding paragraph, Cousins uses a historical example that especially relates to ideas in paragraph 8. Why is this unexpected conclusion effective?

Section 1:
Inductive Proofs

The Case against Man
Isaac Asimov

Isaac Asimov (1920–   ) was born in Russia, but he has lived in America since childhood. Though holding a doctorate in chemistry, he is best known as a writer, especially on science topics, including science fiction. Listing his publications would result in overkill since the prolific writer has published over two hundred books, a herculean achievement which has certainly made him America's dean of science writers. The selection below is typical of much of Asimov's writing, as it converts difficult scientific concepts and theories into a form both comprehensible and interesting to nonscientists.

The first mistake is to think of mankind as a thing in itself. It isn't. It is part of an intricate web of life. And we can't think even of life as a thing in itself. It isn't. It is part of the intricate structure of a planet bathed by energy from the Sun. 1

The Earth, in the nearly 5 billion years since it assumed approximately its present form, has undergone a vast evolution. When it first came into being, it very likely lacked what we would today call an ocean and an atmosphere. These were formed by the gradual outward movement of material as the solid interior settled together. 2

Nor were ocean, atmosphere, and solid crust independent of each other after formation. There is interaction always: evaporation, condensation, solution, weathering. Far within the solid crust there are slow, continuing changes, too, of which hot springs, volcanoes, and earthquakes are the more noticeable manifestations here on the surface. 3

Between 2 billion and 3 billion years ago, portions of the surface water, bathed by the energetic radiation from the Sun, developed complicated compounds in organization sufficiently versatile to qualify as what we call "life." Life forms have become more complex and more various ever since. 4

But the life forms are as much part of the structure of the Earth as any inanimate portion is. It is all an inseparable part of a whole. If any animal is isolated totally from other forms of life, then death by starvation will surely follow. If isolated from water, death by dehydration will follow even faster. If isolated from air, whether free or dissolved in water, death by asphyxiation will follow still faster. If isolated from the Sun, animals will survive for a time, but plants would die, and if all plants died, all animals would starve. 5

It works in reverse, too, for the inanimate portion of Earth is shaped and molded by life. The nature of the atmosphere has been changed by plant activity (which adds to the air the free oxygen it could not otherwise retain). The soil is turned by earthworms, while enormous ocean reefs are formed by coral.

The entire planet, plus solar energy, is one enormous intricately interrelated system. The entire planet is a life form made up of nonliving portions and a large variety of living portions (as our own body is made up of nonliving crystals in bones and nonliving water in blood, as well as of a large variety of living portions).

In fact, we can pursue the analogy. A man is composed of 50 trillion cells of a variety of types, all interrelated and interdependent. Loss of some of those cells, such as those making up an entire leg, will seriously handicap all the rest of the organism: serious damage to a relatively few cells in an organ, such as the heart or kidneys, may end by killing all 50 trillion.

In the same way, on a planetary scale, the chopping down of an entire forest may not threaten Earth's life in general, but it will produce serious changes in the life forms of the region and even in the nature of the water runoff and, therefore, in the details of geological structure. A serious decline in the bee population will affect the numbers of those plants that depend on bees for fertilization, then the numbers of those animals that depend on those particular bee-fertilized plants, and so on.

Or consider cell growth. Cells in those organs that suffer constant wear and tear — as in the skin or in the intestinal lining — grow and multiply all life long. Other cells, not so exposed, as in nerve and muscle, do not multiply at all in the adult, under any circumstances. Still other organs, ordinarily quiescent, as liver and bone, stand ready to grow if that is necessary to replace damage. When the proper repairs are made, growth stops.

In a much looser and more flexible way, the same is true of the "planet organism" (which we study in the science called ecology). If cougars grow too numerous, the deer they live on are decimated, and some of the cougars die of starvation, so that their "proper number" is restored. If too many cougars die, then the deer multiply with particular rapidity, and cougars multiply quickly in turn, till the additional predators bring down the number of deer again. Barring interference from outside, the eaters and the eaten retain their proper numbers, and both are the better for it. (If the cougars are all killed off, deer would multiply to the point where they destroy the plants they live off, and more would then die of starvation than would have died of cougars.)

Section 1:
Inductive Proofs

The neat economy of growth within an organism such as a human being is sometimes — for what reason, we know not — disrupted, and a group of cells begins growing without limit. This is the dread disease of cancer, and unless that growing group of cells is somehow stopped, the wild growth will throw all the body structure out of true and end by killing the organism itself.

In ecology, the same would happen if, for some reason, one particular type of organism began to multiply without limit, killing its competitors and increasing its own food supply at the expense of that of others. That, too, could end only in the destruction of the larger system — most or all of life and even of certain aspects of the inanimate environment.

And this is exactly what is happening at this moment. For thousands of years, the single species Homo sapiens, to which you and I have the dubious honor of belonging, has been increasing in numbers. In the past couple of centuries, the rate of increase has itself increased explosively.

At the time of Julius Caesar, when Earth's human population is estimated to have been 150 million, that population was increasing at a rate such that it would double in 1,000 years if that rate remained steady. Today, with Earth's population estimated at about 4,000 million (26 times what it was in Caesar's time), it is increasing at a rate which, if steady, will cause it to double in 35 years.

The present rate of increase of Earth's swarming human population qualifies Homo sapiens as an ecological cancer, which will destroy the ecology just as surely as any ordinary cancer would destroy an organism.

The cure? Just what it is for any cancer. The cancerous growth must somehow be stopped.

Of course, it will be. If we do nothing at all, the growth will stop, as a cancerous growth in a man will stop if nothing is done. The man dies and the cancer dies with him. And, analogously, the ecology will die and man will die with it.

How can the human population explosion be stopped? By raising the deathrate, or by lowering the birthrate. There are no other alternatives. The deathrate will rise spontaneously and finally catastrophically, if we do nothing — and that within a few decades. To make the birthrate fall, somehow (almost *any* how, in fact), is surely preferable, and that is therefore the first order of mankind's business today.

Failing this, mankind would stand at the bar of abstract justice (for there may be no posterity to judge) as the mass murderer of life generally, his own included, and mass disrupter of the intricate planetary development that made life in its present glory possible in the first place.

Am I too pessimistic? Can we allow the present rate of population increase to continue indefinitely, or at least for a good long time? Can we count on science to develop methods for cleaning up as we pollute, for replacing wasted resources with substitutes, for finding new food, new materials, more and better life for our waxing numbers?

Impossible! If the numbers continue to wax at the present rate.

Let us begin with a few estimates (admittedly not precise, but in the rough neighborhood of the truth).

The total mass of living objects on Earth is perhaps 20 trillion tons. There is usually a balance between eaters and eaten that is about 1 to 10 in favor of the eaten. There would therefore be about 10 times as much plant life (the eaten) as animal life (the eaters) on Earth. There is, in other words, just a little under 2 trillion tons of animal life on Earth.

But this is all the animal life that can exist, given the present quantity of plant life. If more animal life is somehow produced, it will strip down the plant life, reduce the food supply, and then enough animals will starve to restore the balance. If one species of animal life increases in mass, it can only be because other species correspondingly decrease. For every additional pound of human flesh on Earth, a pound of some other form of flesh must disappear.

The total mass of humanity now on Earth may be estimated at about 200 million tons, or one ten-thousandth the mass of all animal life. If mankind increases in numbers ten thousandfold, then Homo sapiens will be, perforce, the *only* animal species alive on Earth. It will be a world without elephants or lions, without cats or dogs, without fish or lobsters, without worms or bugs. What's more, to support the mass of human life, all the plant world must be put to service. Only plants edible to man must remain, and only those plants most concentratedly edible and with minimum waste.

At the present moment, the average density of population of the Earth's land surface is about 73 people per square mile. Increase that ten thousandfold and the average density will become 730,000 people per square mile, or more than seven times the density of the workday population of Manhattan. Even if we assume that mankind will somehow spread itself into vast cities floating on the ocean surface (or resting on the ocean floor), the average density of human life at the time when the last nonhuman animal must be killed would be 310,000 people per square mile over all the world, land and sea alike, or a little better than three times the density of modern Manhattan at noon.

We have the vision, then, of high-rise apartments, higher and more thickly spaced than in Manhattan at present, spreading all over the world, across all the mountains, across the Sahara Desert, across Antarctica, across all the oceans; all with their load of humanity and with no other form of animal life beside. And on the roof of all those buildings are the algae farms, with little plant cells exposed to the Sun so that they might grow rapidly and, without waste, form protein for all the mighty population of 35 trillion human beings.

Is that tolerable? Even if science produced all the energy and materials mankind could want, kept them all fed with algae, all educated, all amused — is the planetary high-rise tolerable?

And if it were, can we double the population further in 35 more years? And then double it again in another 35 years? Where will the food come from? What will persuade the algae to multiply faster than the light energy they absorb makes possible? What will speed up the Sun to add the energy to make it possible? And if vast supplies of fusion energy are added to supplement the Sun, how will we get rid of the equally vast supplies of heat that will be produced? And after the icecaps are melted and the oceans boiled into steam, what?

Can we bleed off the mass of humanity to other worlds? Right now, the number of human beings on Earth is increasing by 80 million per year, and each year that number goes up by 1 and a fraction percent. Can we really suppose that we can send 80 million people per year to the Moon, Mars, and elsewhere, and engineer those worlds to support those people? And even so, merely remain in the same place ourselves?

No! Not the most optimistic visionary in the world could honestly convince himself that space travel is the solution to our population problem, if the present rate of increase is sustained.

But when will this planetary high-rise culture come about? How long will it take to increase Earth's population to that impossible point at the present doubling rate of once every 35 years? If it will take 1 million years or even 100,000, then, for goodness sake, let's not worry just yet.

Well, we don't have that kind of time. We will reach that dead end in no more than 460 years.

At the rate we are going, without birth control, then even if science serves us in an absolutely ideal way, we will reach the planetary high-rise with no animals but man, with no plants but algae, with no room for even one more person, by A.D. 2430.

And if science serves us in less than an ideal way (as it certainly will), the end will come sooner, much sooner, and mankind will start fading long, long before he is forced to construct that building that will cover all the Earth's surface. 36

So if birth control *must* come by A.D. 2430 at the very latest, even in an ideal world of advancing science, let it come *now,* in heaven's name, while there are still oak trees in the world and daisies and tigers and butterflies, and while there is still open land and space, and before the cancer called man proves fatal to life and the planet. 37

Discussion: Content

1. Asimov asserts that it is a mistake to believe that mankind is a thing in itself. If it is not, what is it?
2. Our whole planet, with the addition of one crucial outside element, forms an enormous, intricate, interrelated system. What is that outside element?
3. Asimov shows that damage to one part of this interrelated system can eventually cause the death of the entire system. How does he do this?
4. What point does Asimov illustrate with his example in paragraph 11 of cougars and deer?
5. What life form, according to Asimov, is outgrowing its food supply?
6. With what dread disease does Asimov compare mankind?
7. Asimov claims that there are but two ways to save mankind from extinction. What are they?
8. How long will it be before mankind, growing at its present rate, will carpet the earth completely?

Discussion: Form

1. It is not until paragraph 19 that Asimov states his argument in its barest form. What is he doing before that?
2. Asimov constructs an analogy comparing our planet with a human body. What is his purpose in doing this?
3. Of the two alternatives presented in paragraph 19, which does Asimov prefer?
4. After stating the two alternatives in paragraph 19, where does Asimov direct his argument?
5. Show how paragraphs 21–37 constitute an induction. What is the proposition, and what is the supporting evidence?

Section 1:
Inductive Proofs

321

Sexism in English: A Feminist View
Alleen Pace Nilsen

Alleen Pace Nilsen (1936–   ), who teaches English and linguistics at Arizona State University, has published a number of essays and books on the topic she treats below, the most notable being *Sexism and Language* (1977). Her most recent book is *Literature for Young Adults* (1980).

Does culture shape language? Or does language shape culture? This is as difficult a question as the old puzzler of which came first, the chicken or the egg, because there's no clear separation between language and culture.

A well-accepted linguistic principle is that as culture changes so will the language. The reverse of this — as a language changes so will the culture — is not so readily accepted. This is why some linguists smile (or even scoff) at feminist attempts to replace *Mrs.* and *Miss* with *Ms.* and to find replacements for those all-inclusive words which specify masculinity, e.g., *chairman, mankind, brotherhood, freshman,* etc.

Perhaps they are amused for the same reason that it is the doctor at a cocktail party who laughs the loudest at the joke about the man who couldn't afford an operation so he offered the doctor a little something to touch up the X-ray. A person working constantly with language is likely to be more aware of how really deep-seated sexism is in our communication system.

Last winter I took a standard desk dictionary and gave it a place of honor on my night table. Every night that I didn't have anything more interesting to do, I read myself to sleep making a card for each entry that seemed to tell something about male and female. By spring I had a rather dog-eared dictionary, but I also had a collection of note cards filling two shoe boxes. The cards tell some rather interesting things about American English.

First, in our culture it is a woman's body which is considered important while it is a man's mind or his activities which are valued. A woman is sexy. A man is successful.

I made a card for all the words which came into modern English from somebody's name. I have a two-and-one-half-inch stack of cards which are men's names now used as everyday words. The women's stack is less than a half inch high and most of them came from Greek mythology. Words coming from the names of famous American men include *lynch, sousaphone, sideburns, Pullman, rick-*

ettsia, Shick test, Winchester rifle, Franklin stove, Bartlett pear, teddy bear, and *boysenberry*. The only really common words coming from the names of American women are *bloomers* (after Amelia Jenks Bloomer) and *Mae West jacket*. Both of these words are related in some way to a woman's physical anatomy, while the male words (except for *sideburns* after General Burnsides) have nothing to do with the namesake's body.

This reminded me of an earlier observation that my husband and I made about geographical names. A few years ago we became interested in what we called "Topless Topography" when we learned that the Grand Tetons used to be simply called *The Tetons* by French explorers and *The Teats* by American frontiersmen. We wrote letters to several map makers and found the following listings: *Nippletop* and *Little Nippletop* near Mt. Marcy in the Adirondacks, *Nipple Mountain* in Archuleta County, Colorado, *Nipple Peak* in Coke County, Texas, *Nipple Butte* in Pennington, South Dakota, *Squaw Peak* in Placer County, California (and many other places), *Maiden's Peak* and *Squaw Tit* (they're the same mountain) in the Cascade Range in Oregon, *Jane Russell Peaks* near Stark, New Hampshire, and *Mary's Nipple* near Salt Lake City, Utah.

We might compare these names to Jackson Hole, Wyoming, or Pikes Peak, Colorado. I'm sure we would get all kinds of protests from the Jackson and Pike descendants if we tried to say that these topograhical features were named because they in some way resembled the bodies of Jackson and Pike, respectively.

This preoccupation with women's breasts is neither new nor strictly American. I was amused to read the derivation of the word *Amazon*. According to Greek folk etymology, the *a* means "without" as in *atypical* or *amoral* while *mazon* comes from *mazōs* meaning "breast." According to the legend, these women cut off one breast so that they could better shoot their bows. Perhaps the feeling was that the women had to trade in part of their femininity in exchange for their active masculine role.

There are certain pairs of words which illustrate the way in which sexual connotations are given to feminine words while the masculine words retain a serious, businesslike aura. For example, being a *callboy* is perfectly respectable. It simply refers to a person who calls actors when it is time for them to go on stage, but being a *call girl* is being a prostitute.

Also we might compare *sir* and *madam*. *Sir* is a term of respect while *madam* has acquired the meaning of a brothel manager. The same thing has happened to the formerly cognate terms, *master* and *mistress*. Because of its acquired sexual connotations, *mistress* is

Section 1: Inductive Proofs

now carefully avoided in certain contexts. For example, the Boy Scouts have *scoutmasters* but certainly not *scoutmistresses*. And in a dog show the female owner of a dog is never referred to as the *dog's mistress,* but rather as the *dog's master.*

Master appears in such terms as *master plan, concert master, schoolmaster, mixmaster, master charge, master craftsman,* etc. But *mistress* appears in very few compounds. This is the way it is with dozens of words which have male and female counterparts. I found two hundred such terms, e.g., *usher–usherette, heir–heiress, hero–heroine,* etc. In nearly all cases it is the masculine word which is the base with a feminine suffix being added for the alternate version. The masculine word also travels into compounds while the feminine word is a dead end; e.g., from *king–queen* comes *kingdom* but not *queendom,* from *sportsman–sportslady* comes *sportsmanship* but not *sportsladyship,* etc. There is one — and only one — semantic area in which the masculine word is not the base or more powerful word. This is in the area dealing with sex and marriage. Here it is the feminine word which is dominant. *Prostitute* is the base word with *male prostitute* being the derived term. *Bride* appears in *bridal shower, bridal gown, bridal attendant, bridesmaid,* and even in *bridegroom,* while *groom* in the sense of *bridegroom* does not appear in any compounds, not even to name the groom's attendants or his prenuptial party.

At the end of a marriage, this same emphasis is on the female. If it ends in divorce, the woman gets the title of *divorcée* while the man is usually described with a statement, such as, "He's divorced." When the marriage ends in death, the woman is a *widow* and the *-er* suffix which seems to connote masculine (probably because it is an agentive or actor type suffix) is added to make *widower. Widower* doesn't appear in any compounds (except for *grass widower,* which is another companion term), but *widow* appears in several compounds and in addition has some acquired meanings, such as the extra hand dealt to the table in certain card games and an undesirable leftover line of type in printing.

If I were an anthropological linguist making observations about a strange and primitive tribe, I would duly note on my tape recorder that I had found linguistic evidence to show that in the area of sex and marriage the female appears to be more important than the male, but in all other areas of the culture, it seems that the reverse is true.

But since I am not an anthropological linguist, I will simply go on to my second observation, which is that women are expected to play a passive role while men play an active one.

One indication of women's passive role is the fact that they are often identified as something to eat. What's more passive than a plate of food? Last spring I saw an announcement advertising the Indiana University English Department picnic. It read "Good Food! Delicious Women!" The publicity committee was probably jumped on by local feminists, but it's nothing new to look on women as "delectable morsels." Even women compliment each other with "You look good enough to eat," or "You have a peaches and cream complexion." Modern slang constantly comes up with new terms, but some of the old standbys for women are: *cute tomato, dish, peach, sharp cookie, cheese cake, honey, sugar,* and *sweetie-pie.* A man may occasionally be addressed as *honey* or described as a *hunk of meat,* but certainly men are not laid out on a buffet and labeled as women are. 16

Women's passivity is also shown in the comparisons made to plants. For example, to *deflower* a woman is to take away her virginity. A girl can be described as a *clinging vine,* a *shrinking violet,* or a *wall flower.* On the other hand, men are too active to be thought of as plants. The only time we make the comparison is when insulting a man we say he is like a woman by calling him a *pansy.* 17

We also see the active-passive contrast in the animal terms used with males and females. Men are referred to as *studs, bucks,* and *wolves,* and they go *tomcatting around.* These are all aggressive roles, but women have such pet names as *kitten, bunny, beaver, bird, chick, lamb,* and *fox.* The idea of being a pet seems much more closely related to females than to males. For instance, little girls grow up wearing *pigtails* and *ponytails* and they dress in *halters* and *dog collars.* 18

The active-passive contrast is also seen in the proper names given to boy babies and girl babies. Girls are much more likely to be given names like *Ivy, Rose, Ruby, Jewel, Pearl, Flora, Joy,* etc., while boys are given names describing active roles such as *Martin* (warlike), *Leo* (lion), *William* (protector), *Ernest* (resolute fighter), and so on. 19

Another way that women play a passive role is that they are defined in relationship to someone else. This is what feminists are protesting when they ask to be identified as *Ms.* rather than as *Mrs.* or *Miss.* It is a constant source of irritation to women's organizations that when they turn in items to newspapers under their own names, that is, Susan Glascoe, Jeanette Jones, and so forth, the editors consistently rewrite the item so that the names read Mrs. John Glascoe, Mrs. Robert E. Jones. 20

Section 1:
Inductive Proofs

In the dictionary I found what appears to be an attitude on the part of editors that it is almost indecent to let a respectable woman's name march unaccompanied across the pages of a dictionary. A woman's name must somehow be escorted by a male's name regardless of whether or not the male contributed to the woman's reason for being in the dictionary, or in his own right, was as famous as the woman. For example, Charlotte Brontë is identified as Mrs. Arthur B. Nicholls, Amelia Earhart is identified as Mrs. George Palmer Putnam, Helen Hayes is identified as Mrs. Charles MacArthur, Zona Gale is identified as Mrs. William Llewelyn Breese, and Jenny Lind is identified as Mme. Otto Goldschmidt. 21

Although most of the women are identified as Mrs. ___ or as the wife of ___, other women are listed with brothers, fathers, or lovers. Cornelia Otis Skinner is identifed as the daughter of Otis, Harriet Beecher Stowe is identified as the sister of Henry Ward Beecher, Edith Sitwell is identified as the sister of Osbert and Sacheverell, Nell Gwyn is identified as the mistress of Charles II, and Madame Pompadour is identified as the mistress of Louis XV. 22

The women who did get into the dictionary without the benefit of a masculine escort are a group sort of on the fringes of respectability. They are the rebels and the crusaders: temperance leaders Frances Elizabeth Caroline Willard and Carry Nation, women's rights leaders Carrie Chapman Catt and Elizabeth Cady Stanton, birth control educator Margaret Sanger, religious leader Mary Baker Eddy, and slaves Harriet Tubman and Phillis Wheatley. 23

I would estimate that far more than fifty percent of the women listed in the dictionary were identified as someone's wife. But of all the men — and there are are probably ten times as many men as women — only one was identified as "the husband of...." This was the unusual case of Frederic Joliot, who took the last name of Joliot-Curie and was identified as "husband of Irene." Apparently Irene, the daughter of Pierre and Marie Curie, did not want to give up her maiden name when she married and so the couple took the hyphenated last name. 24

There are several pairs of words which also illustrate the more powerful role of the male and the relational role of the female. For example a *count* is a high political officer with a *countess* being simply the wife of a count. The same is true for a *duke* and a *duchess* and a *king* and a *queen*. The fact that a king is usually more powerful than a queen might be the reason that Queen Elizabeth's husband is given the title of *prince* rather than *king*. Since *king* is a stronger word than *queen,* it is reserved for a true heir to the throne because if it were given to someone coming into the royal family by marriage, then the subjects might forget where the true power lies. With the weaker word of *queen,* this would not be a problem; so a woman marrying a ruling monarch is given the title without question.

My third observation is that there are many positive connotations connected with the concept of masculine, while there are either trivial or negative connotations connected with the corresponding feminine concept.

Conditioning toward the superiority of the masculine role starts very early in life. Child psychologists point out that the only area in which a girl has more freedom than a boy is in experimenting with an appropriate sex role. She is much freer to be a *tomboy* than is her brother to be a *sissy.* The proper names given to children reflect this same attitude. It's perfectly all right for a girl to have a boy's name, but not the other way around. As girls are given more and more of the boys' names, parents shy away from using boy names that might be mistaken for girl names, so the number of available masculine names is constantly shrinking. Fifty years ago *Hazel, Beverly, Marion, Frances* and *Shirley* were all perfectly acceptable boys' names. Today few parents give these names to baby boys and adult men who are stuck with them self-consciously go by their initials or by abbreviated forms such as *Haze* or *Shirl.* But parents of little girls keep crowding the masculine set and currently popular girls' names include *Jo, Kelly, Teri, Cris, Pat, Shawn, Toni,* and *Sam.*

When the mother of one of these little girls tells her to *be a lady,* she means for her to sit with her knees together. But when the father of a little boy tells him to *be a man,* he means for him to be noble, strong, and virtuous. The whole concept of manliness has such positive connotations that it is a compliment to call a male a *he-man, a manly man,* or a *virile man* (*virile* comes from the Indo-European *vir,* meaning "man"). In each of these three terms, we are implying that someone is doubly good because he is doubly a man.

Compare *chef* with *cook, tailor* and *seamstress,* and *poet* with *poetess.* In each case, the masculine form carries with it an added degree of excellence. In comparing the masculine *governor* with the feminine *governess* and the masculine *major* with the feminine *majorette,* the added feature is power.

The difference between positive male and negative female connotations can be seen in several pairs of words which differ denotatively only in the matter of sex. For instance compare *bachelor* with the terms *spinster* and *old maid. Bachelor* has such positive connotations that modern girls have tried to borrow the feeling in the term *bachelor-girl. Bachelor* appears in glamorous terms such as *bachelor pad, bachelor party,* and *bachelor button.* But *old maid* has such strong negative feelings that it has been adopted into other areas, taking with it the feeling of undesirability. It has the metaphorical meaning of shriveled and unwanted kernels of pop corn, and it's the name of the last unwanted card in a popular game for children.

Patron and *matron* (Middle English for *father* and *mother*) are another set where women have tried to borrow the positive masculine connotations, this time through the word *patroness,* which literally means "female father." Such a peculiar term came about because of the high prestige attached to the word *patron* in such phrases as *"a patron of the arts"* or *"a patron saint." Matron* is more apt to be used in talking about a woman who is in charge of a jail or a public rest room.

Even *lord* and *lady* have different levels of connotation. *Our Lord* is used as a title for deity, while the corresponding *Our Lady* is a relational title for Mary, the moral mother of Jesus. *Landlord* has more dignity than *landlady* probably because the landlord is more likely to be thought of as the owner while the landlady is the person who collects the rent and enforces the rules. *Lady* is used in many insignificant places where the corresponding *lord* would never be used, for example, *ladies' room, ladies' sizes, ladies' aid society, ladybug,* etc.

This overuse of *lady* might be compared to the overuse of *queen,* which is rapidly losing its prestige as compared to *king.* Hundreds of beauty queens are crowned each year and nearly every community in the United States has its *Dairy Queen* or its *Freezer Queen,* etc. Male homosexuals have adopted the terms to identify the "feminine" partner. And advertisers who are constantly on the lookout for euphemisms to make unpleasant sounding products salable have recently dealt what might be a death blow to the prestige of the word *queen.* They have begun to use it as an indication of size. For example, *queen-size* panty hose are panty hose for fat women. The meaning comes through a comparison with *king-size,* meaning big. However, there's a subtle difference in that our culture considers it desirable for males to be big because size is an indication of power, but we prefer that females be small and petite. So using *king-size* as a term to indicate bigness partially enhances the prestige of *king,* but using *queen-size* to indicate bigness brings unpleasant associations to the word *queen.*

Another set that might be compared are *brave* and *squaw.* The word *brave* carries with it the connotations of youth, vigor, and courage, while *squaw* implies almost opposite characteristics. With the set *wizard* and *witch,* the main difference is that *wizard* implies skill and wisdom combined with magic, while *witch* implies evil intentions combined with magic. Part of the unattractiveness of both *squaw* and *witch* is that they suggest old age, which in women is particularly undesirable. When I lived in Afghanistan (1967–1969), I was horrified to hear a proverb stating that when you see an old man you should sit down and take a lesson, but when you see an old woman you should throw a stone. I was equally startled when I went to compare the connotations of our two phrases *grandfatherly advice* and *old wives' tales*. Certainly it isn't expressed with the same force as in the Afghan proverb, but the implication is similar. 34

In some of the animal terms used for women the extreme undesirability of female old age is also seen. For instance consider the unattractiveness of *old nag* as compared to *filly,* of *old crow* or *old bat* as compared to *bird,* and of being *catty* as compared to being *kittenish.* The chicken metaphor tells the whole story of a girl's life. In her youth she is a *chick,* then she marries and begins feeling *cooped up,* so she goes to *hen parties* where she *cackles* with her friends. Then she has her *brood* and begins to *henpeck* her husband. Finally she turns into *an old biddy.* 35

Discussion: Content

1. How did Nilsen secure the evidence that she presents in this essay to prove that there is sexism in our language?
2. According to Nilsen, the English language reveals that men and women are not valued for the same reasons. What are women valued for? And men?
3. What does she mean by "Topless Topography"?
4. Nilsen claims that in English masculine words form more compounds than do feminine words — except in what area?
5. Passivity of women in American society is illustrated by what facts of language, according to Nilsen?
6. List five examples of masculine words which have more positive connotations than their female counterparts.

Discussion: Form

1. An inductive argument follows the scientific method of investigation, gathering evidence and then making generalizations based on the evidence accumulated. Explain how Nilsen's argument follows this pattern.

Section 1:
Inductive Proofs

2. In what paragraph does Nilsen state the proposition to be proved in its most general terms? After that initial statement she organizes her evidence into three parts to support three distinct and more concrete propositions, each subordinate to the general one. In what paragraphs does she introduce these three concrete propositions? What are they?
3. The evidence that Nilsen presents to support each of these propositions is very clearly examples — and a great many of them. What differentiates this presentation of examples in support of a thesis from those that appear in the exposition section of this text?

Section 2: Deductive Proofs

Suppose you were to be stopped for speeding and were to tell the highway patrolman, "You shouldn't give me a ticket. The speed limit is not clearly marked." You would not be arguing inductively. Admittedly you would have to produce some evidence, namely, the speed limit sign — to show that, for instance, it was missing, knocked down, obscured, or defaced. But there is more to the argument than that.

In effect, what you are doing is appealing to a much more basic assumption, about which you hope that you and the patrolman agree: you should not be held accountable for things you were not told. The case in point is this sign, which did not adequately inform you of the legal speed limit. The conclusion is quite obvious: you shouldn't be held accountable in this situation.

The patrolman, of course, has an argument of his own, and it is structured very much like yours. "State Law 76352-81," he says, "prescribes that persons who exceed the posted speed limit shall be fined fifty dollars. You have exceeded the posted limit; therefore, you shall be fined fifty dollars."

What you and the patrolman have been doing is engaging in deductive argumentation. Each of you has used a *syllogism* — a statement consisting of three propositions. The propositions are so interrelated that if your audience will admit that the first two are true, then they *must* admit that the last is true! To show how the relationship works, let's begin with the argument you used on the patrolman. You began with a very broad and comprehensive statement: "I shouldn't be held accountable for things I'm not informed of." Let's convert that to a proposition. *People who have not been informed about certain things are people who should not be held accountable for those things.* You might draw a diagram to illustrate the proposition.

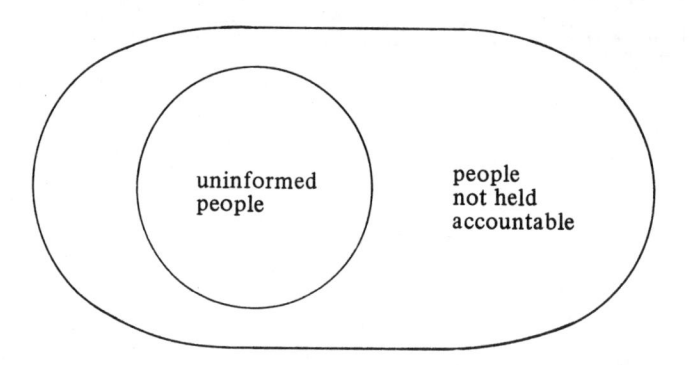

The diagram shows that the uninformed people are part of a larger group of persons who are not held accountable. We could assume that the remainder of those not held accountable would consist of mentally incompetent people and relatives of the sheriff — i.e., people who would not be held accountable even though they had been informed. The second proposition in your syllogism states: "I was not informed about this thing." A diagram of this proposition will place you inside the inner circle in the first diagram, specifying you as a member of the group of uninformed people.

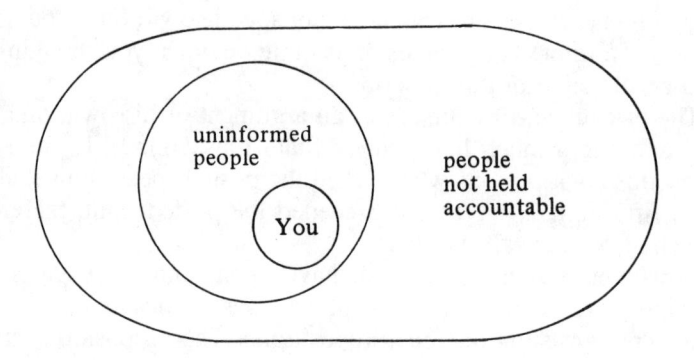

If you are inside the inner circle, you must be inside the larger circle, which you remember represented the group of people who were not to be held accountable. Your conclusion is unchallengeable: "I should not be held accountable."

Of course, we could also diagram the patrolman's argument this way:

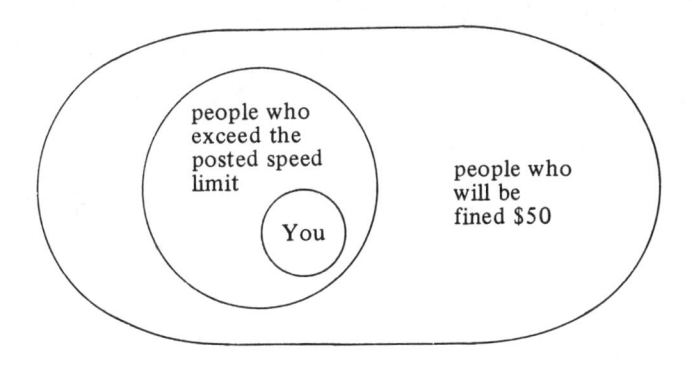

[Diagram: A large oval containing "people who will be fined $50"; inside it a smaller oval labeled "people who exceed the posted speed limit"; inside that, a small circle labeled "You".]

And this argument too is unchallengeable; according to it, you now owe fifty dollars.

Remember, however, that deductive arguments work only if the opponent admits the truth of the first two propositions. You might question the patrolman's propositions. The first one, that speeders forfeit fifty dollars, is a law; the patrolman has quoted a competent authority and you'll have to admit that he's right. The officer will prove his second proposition by offering inductive proof — a freshly calibrated radar set, which clocked you at 53 miles per hour — clearly in excess of the posted limit of 45. Thus, he says, you owe the fine.

You can't challenge the first proposition, and you can't challenge the conclusion, but you can challenge the second proposition — and that is what you have done with your argument. You've argued that the limit you exceeded was not posted. As you said in your second proposition, you were not informed. In order to prove your case, you would have to go back along the road you traveled and point out the absence or illegibility of the speed limit signs — again an inductive proof. If our officer accepts this demonstration and agrees with your first proposition that people should not be held accountable for things they don't know about (which seems reasonable enough even though you have offered no proof), then he will accept your conclusion and tear up your ticket.

To sum up deductive arguments, we might say the following things:

1. Deductive proofs consist of statements called syllogisms; these syllogisms are made up of propositions so related that if the first and second are true, the third must logically be true.

Section 2:
Deductive Proofs

2. The first two propositions of a syllogism must be acceptable to your opponent because:
   a. they are intuitively true (People should not be held accountable for things they don't know about.)
   b. they are supported by authority (Speeders will be fined $50.00: State Law 76352-81.)
   c. they are proved inductively (I was not informed; the signs were torn down. You were speeding; I clocked you at 53 m.p.h.).
3. To challenge a deductive proof, you may not attack the conclusion, but you can attack one or both of the first two propositions. If either of them is unsound, the argument collapses.
4. Very few syllogisms are ever stated as nakedly as those we have examined here. More often they look like your initial statement: "You shouldn't give me this ticket; the speed limit isn't clearly marked." This statement contains only your second proposition and the conclusion, leaving unsaid your first proposition (I shouldn't be held accountable for things I don't know about). Syllogisms with missing but understood propositions are called *enthymemes,* and you should become familiar with them.

Here are some additional examples of enthymemes. Remember that most deductive proofs appear in the form of enthymemes.

1. I wouldn't trust her; she's a politician.
   (Politicians aren't to be trusted.)
   She's a politician.
   Therefore, she's not to be trusted.
2. As long as he gossips that way, he won't be a friend of mine.
   (None of my friends are gossips.)
   He is a gossip.
   Therefore, he is not one of my friends.
3. I wouldn't be surprised if he flunks; he cuts classes at least once a week.
   (People who cut class frequently will flunk out.)
   He cuts class frequently.
   Therefore, he will flunk out.
4. If cutting classes causes people to flunk out, he's a goner for sure.
   People who cut class frequently will flunk out.
   (He cuts class frequently.)
   Therefore, he will flunk out.

At this point you are ready to examine the following deductive paragraphs and essays. You should be able to locate enthymemes and convert them into formal, complete syllogisms. And you should be able to determine how the propositions within syllogisms are supported.

For additional background information concerning deductive proofs, turn to the Appendix and study "A Brief Introduction to Common Logical Fallacies," which begins on p. 434.

Section 2:
Deductive Proofs

Paragraphs:
Deductive Proof

If the Slave Is a Man
Abraham Lincoln

But if the Negro is a man, is it not to that extent a total destruction of self-government to say that he shall not govern himself? When the white man governs himself, that is self-government; but when he governs himself and also governs another man, that is more than self-government — that is despotism. If the Negro is a man, why then my ancient faith teaches me that "all men are created equal," and that there can be no moral right in connection with one man's making a slave of another.

Discussion Questions

1. Lincoln is clearly arguing in a logical or deductive way in this passage. One proposition that he asks his audience to consider is whether or not a Negro is a man. If the audience accepts the affirmative of this proposition and couples it with Lincoln's major premise, then it must accept Lincoln's conclusions. What is Lincoln's major premise, and what is his conclusion?
2. What does Lincoln gain by his reference to his "ancient faith [that] teaches . . . that 'all men are created equal' "?

Balance of Power
Walter Lippmann

The democratic system cannot be operated without effective opposition. For, in making the great experiment of governing people by consent rather than by coercion, it is not sufficient that the party in power should never outrage the minority. That means that it must listen to the minority and be moved by the criticisms of the minority. That means that its measures must take account of the minority's objections, and that in administering measures it must remember that the minority may become the majority. The opposition is indispensable. A good statesman, like any other sensible human being, always learns more from his opponents than from his fervent supporters. For his supporters will push him to disaster unless his opponents show him where the dangers are. So if he is wise he will often pray to be delivered from his friends, because they will ruin him. But, though it hurts, he ought also to pray never to be left without opponents; for they keep him on the path of reason and good sense. The national unity of a free people depends upon a sufficiently even balance of political power to make it impracticable for the administration to be arbitrary and for the opposition to be revolutionary and irreconcilable. Where that balance no longer exists, democracy perishes. For unless all the citizens of a state are forced by circumstances to compromise, unless they feel that they can affect policy but that no one can wholly dominate it, unless by habit and necessity they have to give and take, freedom cannot be maintained.

Discussion Questions

1. What proposition is Lippmann arguing and where does he state it?
2. Is rule by the majority the same thing as never outraging the minority? How is this point crucial to Lippmann's argument?
3. Why does Lippmann argue that opposition is indispensable? How does he prove this proposition?

The Tramp-Monster Myth
George Orwell

As a matter of fact, very little of the tramp-monster will survive inquiry. Take the generally accepted idea that tramps are dangerous characters. Quite apart from experience, one can say *a priori* that very few tramps are dangerous, because if they were dangerous they would be treated accordingly. A casual ward will often admit a hundred tramps in one night, and these are handled by a staff of at most three porters. A hundred ruffians could not be controlled by three unarmed men. Indeed, when one sees how tramps let themselves be bullied by the workhouse officials, it is obvious that they are the most docile, broken-spirited creatures imaginable. Or take the idea that all tramps are drunkards — an idea ridiculous on the face of it. No doubt many tramps would drink if they got the chance, but in the nature of things they cannot get the chance. At this moment a pale watery stuff called beer is sevenpence a pint in England. To be drunk on it would cost at least half a crown, and a man who can command half a crown at all often is not a tramp. The idea that tramps are impudent social parasites ("sturdy beggars") is not absolutely unfounded, but it is only true in a few percent of the cases. Deliberate, cynical parasitism, such as one reads of in Jack London's books on American tramping, is not in the English character. The English are a conscience-ridden race, with a strong sense of the sinfulness of poverty. One cannot imagine the average Englishman deliberately turning parasite, and this national character does not necessarily change because a man is thrown out of work. Indeed, if one remembers that a tramp is only an Englishman out of work, forced by law to live as a vagabond, then the tramp-monster vanishes.

Discussion Questions

1. Look up *a priori* in a dictionary. What purpose does this term serve in Orwell's argument?
2. Two of the syllogisms to be found in this paragraph may be skeletally stated as follows. Supply the missing propositions.

   All dangerous people are hard to control.
   _____
   Therefore, tramps are not dangerous people.

Tramps have no money.
Therefore, tramps are not drunkards.

3. The conclusion of the last syllogism in this paragraph may be stated this way. "No tramp is a social parasite." Can you construct the first two premises of the syllogism?

Laws We Need Not Obey
Martin Luther King, Jr.

You express a great deal of anxiety over our willingness to break laws. This is certainly a legitimate concern. Since we so diligently urge people to obey the Supreme Court's decision of 1954 outlawing segregation in public schools, at first glance it may seem rather paradoxical for us consciously to break laws. One may well ask: "How can you advocate breaking some laws and obeying others?" The answer lies in the fact that there are two types of laws: just and unjust. I would be the first to advocate obeying just laws. Conversely, one has a moral responsibility to disobey unjust laws. I would agree with St. Augustine that "An unjust law is no law at all."

Now, what is the difference between the two? How does one determine whether a law is just or unjust? A just law is a manmade code that squares with the moral law or the law of God. An unjust law is a code that is out of harmony with the moral law. To put it in the terms of St. Thomas Aquinas: An unjust law is a human law that is not rooted in eternal law and natural law. Any law that uplifts human personality is just. Any law that degrades human personality is unjust. All segregation statutes are unjust because segregation distorts the soul and damages the personality. It gives the segregator a false sense of superiority and the segregated a false sense of inferiority. Segregation, to use the terminology of the Jewish philosopher Martin Buber, substitutes an "I-it" relationship for an "I-thou" relationship and ends up relegating persons to the status of things. Hence segregation is not only politically, economically, and sociologically unsound, it is morally wrong and sinful. Paul Tillich has said that sin is separation. Is not segregation an existential expression of man's tragic separation, his awful estrangement, his terrible sinfulness? Thus it is that I can urge men to obey the 1954 decision of the Supreme Court, for it is morally right; and I can urge them to disobey segregation ordinances, for they are morally wrong.

Discussion Questions

1. We might state the first proposition of King's syllogism this way: All laws that degrade human personality are laws that we have no moral responsibility to obey. Supply his next proposition and the conclusion.
2. Does King support the first two propositions in his syllogism? If so, how?
3. The argument is taken from King's 1963 "Letter from Birmingham Jail," addressed to the clergy who had suggested he be more patient in his quest for civil rights. What is there about King's argument that has a special appeal for this audience?

Student Work:
Deductive Proof

Let's Eat at Home Instead

Every red-blooded American is well acquainted with the classic fast-food meal: burger, fries, and a Coke. It's a quick, tasty, and not too expensive. But nutritionists tell us that too much fat, too much salt, too many carbohydrates in our diets can lead to weight, heart, and other health problems. The classic fast-food meal is overloaded in all three areas, so it can be harmful to our health. We're better off eating a well-balanced meal at home instead.

Discussion Questions

1. Can you complete the syllogism in the following paragraph?

    Foods containing excess fat, salt, and carbohydrates are not healthful.
    A classic fast-food meal contains excess fat, salt, and carbohydrates.

2. How does the writer support the first two propositions of this logical argument?

The Right to Pray in School

Ever since the days of William Penn, Roger Williams, and the Toleration Act of 1649, religious freedom has been one of the uppermost concerns of the citizens of this country. Religious freedom is one of the things guaranteed to each citizen of the United

States by our Constitution and its Bill of Rights. The right to worship as one pleases certainly includes the right to pray as one pleases — either privately or publicly. And yet this precious right is being challenged today by those who would limit the places where citizens may pray, denying children the right to pray in school. This blatant obstruction of guaranteed citizen rights has got to end.

Discussion Questions

1. Who were William Penn and Roger Williams, and why are their names useful in this argument? How about the Toleration Act?
2. How might you state the syllogism that is embedded in this paragraph? Its conclusion is clearly this: "Public prayer is a right guaranteed by the Constitution."
3. The syllogism is valid. Is it materially sound?

The Plight of the Railroads

Unless there is a sudden and radical change in the government's attitude toward railroads, they are simply not going to prosper in this country. Let's face it; government has become so involved with business these days that unless a business can count on federal favors, it can't expect to do well. You don't have to look very far to see the truth of this proposition. The textile industry in this state benefits tremendously from the heavy tariffs that government places on imported cloth. Farmers and dairymen can expect government to keep prices high by buying the surplus in good years and by loan help in lean years. The auto industry has benefited from government expenditures. Not only has Chrysler been bailed out, but the federal money sunk in interstate highways promotes automobiles for public conveyance and the trucking industry for moving goods. The railroads in comparison receive nowhere near the kind of financial support that has been lavished on the thriving industries just mentioned. Amtrak gets a handout each time it threatens to go broke, but what it gets is small potatoes compared with what Chrysler gets. Without real financial assistance the railroad industry is necessarily doomed.

Discussion Questions

1. The writer in this paragraph makes the claim that "unless a business can count on federal favors, it can't expect to do well." This is the major premise of the syllogism contained in the argument. How is this proposition supported?
2. What is the remainder of the syllogism?
3. Is the argument valid?

CIA Immunity

Emmet John Hughes wrote in the February 21, 1966, issue of *Newsweek* that: "A government of checks and balances cannot act with integrity if the executive branch is free to determine the gravest matters of war and peace with no operative brake on its power other than the President's own prudence or restraint." If the Central Intelligence Agency, which is an integral part of the executive branch, is structurally immune to congressional checks on its powers, constituting a dangerous concentration of power, then its autonomy violates our system of checks and balances, endangering our democratic system.

The CIA was initially instituted for the purpose of compiling and coordinating the intelligence input of the numerous military agencies. However, the statute which created the CIA, the National Security Act of 1947, gave the agency broad, arbitrary powers through the words "additional services" and "other functions," over and above coordination, that the CIA might have to perform. History has shown that these additional services and other functions may include U-2 spying missions, the Bay of Pigs invasion, the Pueblo affair, the raid on the empty prisoner of war compound in North Vietnam, and now domestic surveillance of "revolutionaries," senators, and congressmen. In addition to being dangerously counterproductive, these missions were ordered and executed at the discretion of a single branch of government.

Furthermore, the Central Intelligence Agency, skirting Congress's power of the purse, has unchecked financial power. Burns and Peltason reported in their book, *Government by the People,* that: "The CIA has over 10,000 employees, although the exact number is secret, and spends from 500 million to one billion dollars annually. The work of the agency is so secret that its appropriations are concealed even from Congress by being distributed throughout the federal budget." Thus direct appropriation to the CIA must be justified to the budget scrutinizers of Congress; instead, small sums are tacked onto the appropriations of the many other departments and agencies receiving federal funds. To further insure that Congress and the public are kept in the dark regarding CIA finances, as the *New Republic* pointed out in June 1961, "The CIA is the only agency whose books are not open to review by the General Accounting Office," the official government auditors.

It is difficult to deny the validity of the assertion that the Central Intelligence Agency is immune from checks on its power. Consequently, such extreme autonomy can be seen as a threat not only to peace but to the democratic principle of checks and balances among the three branches of government. The question remains: Can effective controls be instituted?

Discussion Questions

1. "CIA Immunity" was submitted as a deductive argument. Does it succeed in meeting the requirements?
2. What is the syllogism upon which it is based? Write the syllogism out. Is it valid?
3. How are the initial propositions supported?
4. Cite more recent CIA abuses.

No Finals for A-Students

The Student Government Association is debating a plan that would allow students with an average of A in a course to skip the final exam. I think the plan should be adopted, not only by the Student Government but also by the Faculty Senate.

It would be nice if I could cite examples from colleges where such plans have been adopted and proved successful. But the fact that I don't know of any shouldn't be used as an argument against my position. Surely the students and faculty will not discard a proposal simply because it's original.

Just imagine how it would be if this plan were put into effect. Cramming would not be nearly as widespread during exam week as it is now. Students who wanted to make A's would study consistently throughout the semester, because that would be the surest way of getting an A. Poor students would still have to cram, but it would no longer be the kind of thing good students would feel they had to do.   3

Not only would the plan serve to promote good study habits; it would provide a very real reward for them. A-students would have the luxury of going home during finals, and, beyond that, they could get the jump on their classmates in securing those scarce summer jobs.   4

Perhaps best of all, this plan would give the faculty and university administration a way of rewarding excellence in scholarship. All that the good students see nowadays are awards going to actors, band members, debaters, fraternity fund raisers, and athletes. This plan would be an outstanding way to give an overlooked but deserving group of students (perhaps even the most deserving group) a well-earned tribute.   5

Discussion Questions

1. The last three paragraphs of this essay can be reduced to syllogisms. The one in paragraph 3 might be stated this way:

   Anything that reduces cramming is a good idea.
   This plan reduces cramming.
   Therefore, this plan is a good idea.

   Here is a partial formulation for the remaining syllogisms. Fill in the missing premises.

   Anything that rewards good study habits is a good idea.
   _____
   Therefore, this plan is a good idea.

   _____
   This plan rewards deserving students.
   Therefore, this plan is a good plan.

2. How are the missing premises in the above syllogisms supported?
3. At one point the writer appears to have toyed with the idea of arguing inductively but dismissed the notion. Where do you get this impression?

Essays:
Deductive Proof

What Employees Need Most
Peter Drucker

Peter Drucker (1909–   ) was born in Vienna, but he has lived in the United States since 1937. A management consultant, educator, and writer, he has been a professor at New York University and currently holds an endowed chair at the Claremont Graduate Schools, California. Among his many influential books are *Concept of the Corporation* (1944), *Practice of Management* (1954), *Managing for Results* (1962), *The Effective Executive* (1967), *Technology, Management and Society* (1970), and *Management: Tasks, Responsibilities, Practices* (1973).

Most of you . . . will be employees all your working life, working for somebody else and for a pay check. And so will most, if not all, of the thousands of other young Americans . . . in all the other schools and colleges across the country. 1

Ours has become a society of employees. A hundred years or so ago only one out of every five Americans at work was employed, i.e., worked for somebody else. Today only one out of five is not employed but working for himself. And where fifty years ago "being employed" meant working as a factory laborer or as a farmhand, the employee of today is increasingly a middle-class person with a substantial formal education, holding a professional or management job requiring intellectual and technical skills. Indeed, two things have characterized American society during these last fifty years: the middle and upper classes have become employees; and middle-class and upper-class employees have been the fastest-growing groups in our working population — growing so fast that the industrial worker, that oldest child of the Industrial Revolution, has been losing in numerical importance despite the expansion of industrial production. 2

This is one of the most profound social changes any country has ever undergone. It is, however, a perhaps even greater change for the individual young person about to start. Whatever he does, in all likelihood he will do it as an employee; wherever he aims, he will have to try to reach it through being an employee.

Yet you will find little if anything written on what it is to be an employee. You can find a great deal of very dubious advice on how to get a job or how to get a promotion. You can also find a good deal on work in a chosen field, whether it be metallurgy or salesmanship, the machinist's trade or bookkeeping. Every one of these trades requires different skills, sets different standards, and requires a different preparation. Yet they all have employeeship in common. And increasingly, especially in the large business or in government, employeeship is more important to success than the special professional knowledge or skill. Certainly more people fail because they do not know the requirements of being an employee than because they do not adequately possess the skills of their trade; the higher you climb the ladder, the more you get into administrative or executive work, the greater the emphasis on ability to work within the organization rather than on technical competence or professional knowledge.

Being an employee is thus the one common characteristic of most careers today. The special profession or skill is visible and clearly defined; and a well-laid-out sequence of courses, degrees, and jobs leads into it. But being an employee is the foundation. And it is much more difficult to prepare for it. Yet there is no recorded information on the art of being an employee.

The first question we might ask is: what can you learn in college that will help you in being an employee? The schools teach a great many things of value to the future accountant, the future doctor, or the future electrician. Do they also teach anything of value to the future employee? The answer is: "Yes — they teach the one thing that it is perhaps most valuable for the future employee to know. But very few students bother to learn it."

This one basic skill is the ability to organize and express ideas in writing and in speaking.

As an employee you work with and through other people. This means that your success as an employee — and I am talking of much more here than getting promoted — will depend on your ability to communicate with people and to present your own thoughts and ideas to them so they will both understand what you are driving at and be persuaded. The letter, the report or memorandum, the ten-minute spoken "presentation" to a committee are basic tools of the employee.

Section 2: Deductive Proofs

Of course . . . if you work on a machine your ability to express yourself will be of little importance. But as soon as you move one step up from the bottom, your effectiveness depends on your ability to reach others through the spoken or the written word. And the further away your job is from manual work, the larger the organization of which you are an employee, the more important it will be that you know how to convey your thoughts in writing or speaking. In the very large organization, whether it is the government, the large business corporation, or the military, this ability to express oneself is perhaps the most important of all the skills a [person] can possess. 9

Of course, skill in expression is not enough by itself. You must have something to say in the first place. The popular picture of the engineer, for instance, is that of a man who works with a slide rule, T square, and compass. And engineering students reflect this picture in their attitude toward the written word as something quite irrelevant to their jobs. But the effectiveness of the engineer — and with it his usefulness — depends as much on his ability to make other people understand his work as it does on the quality of the work itself. 10

Expressing one's thoughts is one skill that the school can really teach, especially to people born without natural writing or speaking talent. Many other skills can be learned later — in this country there are literally thousands of places that offer training to adult people at work. But the foundations for skill in expression have to be laid early: an interest in and an ear for language; experience in organizing ideas and data, in brushing aside the irrelevant, in wedding outward form and inner content into one structure; and above all, the habit of verbal expression. If you do not lay these foundations during your school years, you may never have an opportunity again. 11

If you were to ask me what strictly vocational courses there are in the typical college curriculum, my answer — now that the good old habit of the "theme a day" has virtually disappeared — would be: the writing of poetry and the writing of short stories. Not that I expect many of you to become poets or short-story writers — far from it. But these two courses offer the easiest way to obtain some skill in expression. They force one to be economical with language. They force one to organize thought. They demand of one that he give meaning to every word. They train the ear for language, its meaning, its precision, its overtones — and its pitfalls. Above all they force one to write. 12

I know very well that the typical employer does not understand this as yet, and that he may look with suspicion on a young college graduate who has majored, let us say, in short-story writing. But the same employer will complain — and with good reason — that the young [people] whom he hires when they get out of college do not know how to write a simple report, do not know how to tell a simple story, and are in fact virtually illiterate. And he will conclude — rightly — that the young [people] are not really effective, and certainly not employees who are likely to go very far. 13

Discussion: Content

1. What does Drucker say is the ratio of employees to employers in America? How does this differ from the situation a hundred years ago? Does Drucker assign any reasons for the change?
2. What one characteristic, according to Drucker, do all the professions taught in universities have in common?
3. What is the one basic skill in which Drucker claims all employees should strive to achieve proficiency?
4. List three vocations in which "ability to organize and express ideas in writing and speaking" is important. Is your chosen vocation among them, or could it be?
5. What particular courses does Drucker recommend for students to make them more proficient in written and spoken communication? Why?

Discussion: Form

1. Drucker's argument rests upon a syllogism. The initial proposition could be stated: An employee's most-needed skill is the ability to speak and write. How might you complete this syllogism, providing the second, more specific proposition and the conclusion?
2. How does Drucker support his first proposition?
3. What is Drucker trying to accomplish in paragraphs 1–3?
4. Why is paragraph 7 so brief?
5. Who is probably Drucker's audience for this argument?

Bad Grammar Seen as Unsafe
Virginia Hall

Virginia Hall (1943–   ), a native of Texas, was educated at the University of Kansas, Lawrence, where she taught Freshman English for two years while completing her master's degree. After two more years of teaching English, at a private school in Kansas City, Hall joined the editorial staff of The Kansas City *Star* and *Times* in 1969. Also a published poet, Hall in 1972 began writing a weekly column, "Random Views," for the *Star* and, in 1976, for the *Times*. The essay below, which reflects her experiences and concerns as a teacher, citizen, and writer, appeared November 3, 1979, in the *Times*.

One of the most literally radical explanations of the frightful turn of events at Three Mile Island last spring was understandably not acknowledged by the presidential commission investigating that episode. A quite longer probe than six months would be required to come up with a root cause consisting of split infinitives, poor spelling, faulty punctuation and meandering tenses. 1

Richard Mitchell, instructor of English at Glassboro State College, New Jersey, and publisher of *The Underground Grammarian*, apparently has been long at the tap waiting for just such an occurrence as the nuclear power plant dysfunction at Harrisburg, Pa. Immediate causes of the near disaster are generally thought to have been a combination of human and mechanical failures pyramiding to the point of huge confusion, but, as Governor Bruce Babbit of Arizona, a member of the commission, put it recently, "The Three Mile Island accident was *pre-eminently* a case of operator error." 2

It is clear, according to the governor, that "the operators erred because they had not been adequately trained. . . . The manufacturer of the nuclear system blames the utility for exercising improper control over its employees. The utility points its finger at the manufacturer for failing to provide adequate technical guidance. Nearly everyone blames the Nuclear Regulatory Commission for failing to ride herd on the industry." 3

Mr. Mitchell, in turn, sees the whole thing as the consequence of deliberate meltdown in the American educational system in general and blames the National Council of Teachers of English in particular. 4

A linguistic stickler who crusades against language abuse, especially abuse by educators, Mitchell believes the Three Mile Island incident and subsequent panic might have been avoided if the mechanics of writing, spelling and punctuation were not so blithely passed over by permissive pedagogues favoring "holistic" composition. Students who are permitted — indeed, encouraged — to skip the fundamentals of English usage, he asserts, "learn that the mastery of skills is of little importance. . . . They learn to be shoddy workers in any endeavor, comforting themselves, as their teachers did, by fantasies of holistic excellence unfettered by precision in small details, or 'emphasis on trivia.' Then they take jobs with power companies . . . where machines and toxic substances, unmindful of 'holistic ratings,' take heed only — and always, always — of the little things, the valves and the switches, the trivia."

If language does, as many linguists contend, shape as well as reflect the user's worldview, Mitchell could be striking at the core of ideological matters as troublesome as Three Mile Island. Critics of public school spending like to point out that the more money local, state and federal governments commit to education the lower students score on standard tests, costly "frills" apparently diverting educators from their primary purpose of communicating basic skills. (Pennsylvania is among the top ten states in the nation in per-pupil spending.) Cadres of functional illiterates are loosed on the job market or sent off to college where standards must be lowered to accommodate them — lowered not slightly, but in some instances to the sixth- or seventh-grade level.

Ask instructors of freshman English at state universities. Those teachers confront classes in which half or more of the students can't spell, are barely able to read and haven't an inkling of how to put a sentence together other than as a string of hip phrases loosely related and connected by the surrogate conjunctive "you-know."

Attempting to teach an eithteen-year-old what should have been absorbed ten or more years earlier is very nearly impossible. Where does the instructor start with a young adult who believes the planet is populated by human "beans"? It is more than a spelling problem; it's a mindset. It makes no difference to the student. Being. Bean. What's the big deal about a few lousy letters, anyway? *Or a few lousy valves and switches and stuff. . . .*

Coming around to Mitchell's viewpoint is scary. Malfunctioning machinery can be fixed or shut down, but what is to be done with sloppy mentalities in the work force — on auto assembly lines, at air terminals, behind desks, in board rooms, at hospitals; teaching, operating computers, handling insurance claims, policing the streets, or serving hot soup in your lap?

Might this language deficiency notion about Three Mile Island be right? Could it be that lack of discipline and precision in language use

Section 2:
Deductive Proofs

is back of very many current problems? Government is bogged up in oceans of turbid memos and regulatory doublespeak. Business communications often are just as bad. Advertising, education, and journalism perpetrate "deliberately deformed jargons," linguist L. E. Sissman has charged. "Writers in these fields," he observes, "shroud themselves in such opaque English that they lose their ability to distinguish right from wrong." There are, of course, no longer any such creatures as "right" and "wrong" in the opinion of psychologists, whose seductive babblegab has infiltrated every area of work and play.

I recently attended a PTA meeting at which a specialist in child psychology spoke of "information processing" when he meant (I think) "talking" to a child and referred to "cognitive-level behavior" for "seeing." Worse, though, was the frequent and obviously calculated use of four-letter words to prove that despite such erudition he was just an ordinary guy. He called to mind a former student whose, uh, *delayed entry* into *the controlled learning environment of higher education* apparently was due to several years devoted to memorization of bureaucratic directives, Roget's *Thesaurus* and gutter comics. Words flowed from him endlessly in elaborate combination as he strove throughout the semester to say something, one thing, meaningful. He never did, and I hope not to have to try to listen to him again in the here and now or ever after. And I don't want him working on my car or carrying soup in my direction either. Heaven help us if he's into energy.

Discussion: Content

1. What, according to Hall, were generally thought to be the "immediate causes" of the Three Mile Island nuclear plant near-disaster in Spring 1979? What do Hall and Richard Mitchell, publisher of *The Underground Grammarian,* believe the real or remote or "root" cause was?
2. Hall believes the "root cause" problem is not confined to the Three Mile Island incident, but affects what other parts of American society?
3. Hall uses *grammar* as a catch-all term for spelling, punctuation, and grammatical usage; in the last two paragraphs she discusses another English language problem. What is it, and why is it as much a problem as bad grammar?

Discussion: Form

1. Part of Hall's argument rests on deduction. Her key syllogism, minus its major premise, would look something like this:

   Bad grammar is an example of inattention to detail.
   Therefore, bad grammar is dangerous.

   What is her first or major premise? How does she support it?
2. Hall also argues inductively, using an analogy she gets from Mitchell's writings. Mitchell, himself an English teacher, says that students who learn that details of grammar are unimportant then "learn to be shoddy workers in any endeavor." Does this analogy necessarily hold true? Why, or why not?
3. Hall's essay is not clearly organized into a unified whole; this can be seen by removing some of its paragraphs. Which ones can be extracted without really damaging her basic argument?

The Declaration of Independence
Thomas Jefferson

Thomas Jefferson (1743–1826), lawyer, scientist, inventor, and statesman, served his state, Virginia, and his country in numerous capacities, most notably as the author of *The Declaration of Independence* and as the third President of the United States.

When in the course of human events, it becomes necessary for one people to dissolve the political bands which have connected them with another, and to assume among the Powers of the earth, the separate and equal station to which the Laws of Nature and of Nature's God entitle them, a decent respect to the opinions of mankind requires that they should declare the causes which impel them to the separation.

We hold these truths to be self-evident, that all men are created equal, that they are endowed by their Creator with certain unalienable Rights, that among these are Life, Liberty and the pursuit of Happiness. That to secure these rights, Governments are instituted among

Men, deriving their just powers from the consent of the governed. That whenever any Form of Government becomes destructive of these ends, it is the Right of the People to alter or to abolish it and to institute new Government, laying its foundation on such principles and organizing its powers in such form, as to them shall seem most likely to effect their Safety and Happiness. Prudence, indeed, will dictate that Governments long established should not be changed for light and transient causes; and accordingly all experience hath shown, that mankind are more disposed to suffer, while evils are sufferable, than to right themselves by abolishing the forms to which they are accustomed. But when a long train of abuses and usurpations pursuing invariably the same Object evinces a design to reduce them under absolute Despotism, it is their right, it is their duty, to throw off such government, and to provide new Guards for their future security. Such has been the patient sufferance of these Colonies; and such is now the necessity which constrains them to alter their former Systems of Government. The history of the present King of Great Britain is a history of repeated injuries and usurpations, all having in direct object the establishment of an absolute Tyranny over these States. To prove this, let Facts be submitted to a candid world.

He has refused his Assent to Laws, the most wholesome and necessary for the public good.

He has forbidden his Governors to pass Laws of immediate and pressing importance, unless suspended in their operation till his Assent should be obtained; and when so suspended, he has utterly neglected to attend to them.

He has refused to pass other Laws for the accommodations of large districts of people, unless those people would relinquish the right of Representation in the Legislature, a right inestimable to them and formidable to tyrants only.

He has called together legislative bodies at places unusual, uncomfortable, and distant from the depository of their Public Records, for the sole purpose of fatiguing them into compliance with his measures.

He has dissolved Representative Houses repeatedly, for opposing with manly firmness his invasions on the rights of the people.

He has refused for a long time, after such dissolutions, to cause others to be elected; whereby the Legislative Powers, incapable of Annihilation, have returned to the People at large for their exercise, the State remaining in the mean time exposed to all the dangers of invasion from without, and convulsions within.

He has endeavoured to prevent the population of these States; for that purpose obstructing the Laws for Naturalization of Foreigners, refusing to pass others to encourage their migrations hither, and raising the conditions of new Appropriations of Lands. 9

He has obstructed the Administration of Justice, by refusing his Assent to Laws for establishing Judiciary Powers. 10

He has made Judges dependent on his Will alone, for the tenure of their offices, and the amount and payment of their salaries. 11

He has erected a multitude of New Offices, and sent hither swarms of Officers to harass our People, and eat out their substance. 12

He has kept among us, in times of peace, Standing Armies without the Consent of our Legislature. 13

He has affected to render the Military independent of and superior to the Civil Power. 14

He has combined with others to subject us to jurisdiction foreign to our constitution, and unacknowledged by our laws; giving his Assent to their acts of pretended Legislation: 15

For quartering large bodies of armed troops among us: 16

For protecting them, by a mock Trial, from Punishment for any murders which they should commit on the Inhabitants of these States: 17

For cutting off our Trade with all parts of the world: 18

For imposing Taxes on us without our Consent: 19

For depriving us in many cases, of the benefits of Trial by Jury: 20

For transporting us beyond Seas to be tried for pretended offences: 21

For abolishing the free System of English Laws in a Neighbouring Province, establishing therein an Arbitrary government, and enlarging its boundaries so as to render it at once an example and fit instrument for introducing the same absolute rule into these Colonies: 22

For taking away our Charters, abolishing our most valuable Laws, and altering fundamentally the Forms of our Governments: 23

For suspending our own Legislatures, and declaring themselves invested with Power to legislate for us in all cases whatsoever. 24

He has abdicated Government here, by declaring us out of his Protection and waging War against us. 25

He has plundered our seas, ravaged our Coasts, burnt our towns, and destroyed the Lives of our people. 26

He is at this time transporting large Armies of foreign Mercenaries to compleat the works of death, desolation and tyranny, already begun with circumstances of Cruelty and perfidy scarcely paralleled in the most barbarous ages, and totally unworthy the Head of a civilized nation. 27

He has constrained our fellow Citizens taken Captive on the high Seas to bear Arms against their Country, to become the executioners

Section 2:
Deductive Proofs

of their friends and Brethren, or to fall themselves by their Hands.

He has excited domestic insurrections amongst us, and has endeavoured to bring on the inhabitants of our frontiers, the merciless Indian Savages, whose known rule of warfare is an undistinguished destruction of all ages, sexes and conditions.

In every stage of these Oppressions we have Petitioned for Redress in the most humble terms: Our repeated petitions have been answered only by repeated injury. A Prince, whose character is thus marked by every act which may define a Tyrant, is unfit to be the ruler of a free People.

Nor have we been wanting in attention to our British brethren. We have warned them from time to time of attempts by their legislature to extend an unwarrantable jurisdiction over us. We have reminded them of the circumstances of our emigration and settlement here. We have appealed to their native justice and magnanimity and we have conjured them by the ties of our common kindred to disavow these usurpations, which would inevitably interrupt our connections and correspondence. They too have been deaf to the voice of justice and of consanguinity. We must, therefore acquiesce in the necessity, which denounces our Separation, and hold them, as we hold the rest of mankind, Enemies in War, in Peace, Friends.

We, therefore, the Representatives of the United States of America, in General Congress, Assembled, appealing to the Supreme Judge of the world for the rectitude of our intentions, do, in the Name, and by Authority of the good People of these Colonies, solemnly publish and declare, That these United Colonies, are, and of Right ought to be Free and Independent States; that they are Absolved from all Allegiance to the British Crown, and that all political connection between them and the State of Great Britain, is and ought to be totally dissolved; and that as Free and Independent States, they have full power to levy War, conclude Peace, contract Alliances, establish Commerce, and to do all other Acts and Things which Independent States may of right do. And for the support of this Declaration, with a firm reliance on the protection of Divine Providence, we mutually pledge to each other our lives, our fortunes and our sacred Honor.

Discussion: Content

1. Most readers of the Declaration of Independence pass rapidly over paragraph 1, but Jefferson, a brilliant lawyer and statesman, included it. What is its subject? Does it seem necessary to you? Why, or why not?

2. According to paragraph 2, why are oppressed people naturally reluctant to overthrow long-established governments?
3. Can you group the "injuries and usurpations" listed in paragraphs 3–29 into a limited number of classes? What problems do you encounter? What overlap or repetition do you notice?
4. Look at the U.S. Constitution and the original Bill of Rights. Which injuries and usurpations are corrected by them?
5. Condense the long first sentence of paragraph 32 into a shorter sentence of your own composition while retaining the basic thought of the original.

Discussion: Form

1. What is Jefferson's syllogism in the Declaration of Independence? State it in its barest terms.
2. What support does he offer for his major premise?
3. What support does he offer for his minor premise?
4. Why do you suppose that Jefferson puts each piece of support for his minor premise in a separate paragraph?
5. Which of his examples could be more specific?
6. Comment on the emotional appeal of the final sentence.

Declaration of Sentiments
Elizabeth Cady Stanton

Elizabeth Cady Stanton (1815–1902) was one of the most gifted and versatile leaders of the American feminist movement. The daughter of a judge, she became a feminist as a child after hearing her father tell abused women that they had no legal recourse but must endure mistreatment from fathers and husbands. Although well educated for the time, she was not allowed to attend college or to participate actively in the legal profession, despite her experience and training. She married the abolitionist leader Henry B. Stanton in 1840, with the word "obey" omitted from the wedding vows, and in 1848 she helped organize the first women's rights convention in America at Seneca Falls, New York, where the Stantons lived with their five children. There, under Mrs. Stanton's leadership, the convention issued the declaration reprinted below, modeled after *The Declaration of Independence*. She continued her active role, joining with Susan B. Anthony during the Civil War to create the National Women's Suffrage Group, which she later served as president. Mrs. Stanton also helped write the *History of Woman Suffrage* (1881–1886) and edit *The Woman's Bible,* and she wrote articles on a variety of subjects for contemporary magazines.

When, in the course of human events, it becomes necessary for one portion of the family of man to assume among the people of the earth a position different from that which they have hitherto occupied, but one to which the laws of nature and of nature's God entitle them, a decent respect to the opinions of mankind requires that they should declare the causes that impel them to such a course. 1

We hold these truths to be self-evident: that all men and women are created equal; that they are endowed by their Creator with certain inalienable rights; that among these are life, liberty, and the pursuit of happiness; that to secure these rights governments are instituted, deriving their just powers from the consent of the governed. Whenever any form of government becomes destructive of these ends, it is the right of those who suffer from it to refuse allegiance to it, and to insist upon the institution of a new government, laying its foundation on such principles, and organizing its powers in such form, as to them shall seem most likely to effect their safety and happiness. Prudence, indeed, will dictate that governments long established should not be changed for light and transient causes; and accordingly all experience hath shown that mankind are more disposed to suffer, while evils are sufferable, than to right themselves by abolishing the forms to which they were accustomed. But when a long train of abuses and usurpations, pursuing invariably the same object evinces a design to reduce them under absolute despotism, it is their duty to throw off such government, and to provide new guards for their future security. Such has been the patient sufferance of the women under this government, and such is now the necessity which constrains them to demand the equal station to which they are entitled. 2

The history of mankind is a history of repeated injuries and usurpations on the part of man toward woman, having in direct object the establishment of an absolute tyranny over her. To prove this, let facts be submitted to a candid world. 3

He has never permitted her to exercise her inalienable right to the elective franchise. 4

He has compelled her to submit to laws, in the formation of which she had no voice. 5

He has withheld from her rights which are given to the most ignorant and degraded men — both natives and foreigners. 6

Having deprived her of this first right of a citizen, the elective franchise, thereby leaving her without representation in the halls of legislation, he has oppressed her on all sides.

He has made her, if married, in the eye of the law, civilly dead.

He has taken from her all right in property, even to the wages she earns.

He has made her, morally, an irresponsible being, as she can commit many crimes with impunity, provided they be done in the presence of her husband. In the covenant of marriage, she is compelled to promise obedience to her husband, he becoming, to all intents and purposes, her master — the law giving him power to deprive her of her liberty, and to administer chastisement.

He has so framed the laws of divorce, as to what shall be the proper causes, and in case of separation, to whom the guardianship of the children shall be given, as to be wholly regardless of the happiness of women — the law, in all cases, going upon a false supposition of the supremacy of man, and giving all power into his hands.

After depriving her of all rights as a married woman, if single, and the owner of property, he has taxed her to support a government which recognizes her only when her property can be made profitable to it.

He has monopolized nearly all the profitable employments, and from those she is permitted to follow, she receives but a scanty remuneration. He closes against her all the avenues to wealth and distinction which he considers most honorable to himself. As a teacher of theology, medicine, or law, she is not known.

He has denied her the facilities for obtaining a thorough education, all colleges being closed against her.

He allows her in Church, as well as State, but a subordinate position, claiming Apostolic authority for her exclusion from the ministry, and, with some exceptions, from any public participation in the affairs of the Church.

He has created a false public sentiment by giving to the world a different code of morals for men and women, by which moral delinquencies which exclude women from society are not only tolerated, but deemed of little account in man.

He has usurped the prerogative of Jehovah himself, claiming it as his right to assign for her a sphere of action, when that belongs to her conscience and to her God.

He has endeavored, in every way that he could, to destroy her confidence in her own powers, to lessen her self-respect, and to make her willing to lead a dependent and abject life.

Now, in view of this entire disenfranchisement of one-half the people of this country, their social and religious degradation — in view of the unjust laws above mentioned, and because women do feel themselves aggrieved, oppressed, and fraudulently deprived of their most sacred rights, we insist that they have immediate admission to all the rights and privileges which belong to them as citizens of the United States.

In entering upon the great work before us, we anticipate no small amount of misconception, misrepresentation, and ridicule; but we shall use every instrumentality within our power to effect our object. We shall employ agents, circulate tracts, petition the State and National legislatures, and endeavor to enlist the pulpit and the press in our behalf. We hope this Convention will be followed by a series of Conventions embracing every part of the country.

Discussion: Content

1. What do you suppose Mrs. Stanton and the other women at the Seneca Falls Convention hoped to gain by making their Declaration public?
2. King George III was Jefferson's villain; who or what is Mrs. Stanton's?
3. How many "injuries and usurpations" are listed? Which ones still exist?

Discussion: Form

1. The "Declaration of Sentiments" obviously parallels the Declaration of Independence. Is its syllogism as valid? State the syllogism in simple terms. Be careful here — this is not as simple as it seems.
2. Examine this declaration for examples of language with emotional appeal; name three of the best, in your opinion.
3. The conclusion of this declaration seems to lack the emotional impact of the ending of the Declaration of Independence. Is that because of the style, the content, or both?

The Duty of a Citizen
Plato

A student of Socrates and the sole reporter of that philosopher's teachings, Plato (429–347 B.C.) was a citizen of Athens, where he founded his academy in 386 B.C. He was the teacher of Aristotle. All of Plato's works are cast in the form of dialogues in which Socrates discusses with his disciples the points of his philosophy. They include *The Republic,* which contains Socrates' thoughts on the ideal state, and the *Apology,* the *Crito,* and the *Phaedo,* which deal with the trial and death of Socrates. This excerpt comes from the *Crito,* in which Socrates' follower Crito beseeches his master, who has been unjustly condemned to death by the Athenian jury, to flee to Thessaly.

soc. Let us consider the matter together, and do you either refute me if you can, and I will be convinced; or else cease, my dear friend, from repeating to me that I ought to escape against the wishes of the Athenians: for I highly value your attempts to persuade me to do so, but I may not be persuaded against my own better judgment. And now please to consider my first position, and try how you can best answer me.

CR. I will.

soc. Are we to say that we are never intentionally to do wrong, or that in one way we ought and in another we ought not to do wrong, or is doing wrong always evil and dishonourable, as I was just now saying, and as has been already acknowledged by us? Are all our former admissions which were made within a few days to be thrown away? And have we, at our age, been earnestly discoursing with one another all our life long only to discover that we are no better than children? Or, in spite of the opinion of the many, and in spite of consequences whether better or worse, shall we insist on the truth of what was then said, that injustice is always an evil and dishonour to him who acts unjustly? Shall we say so or not?

CR. Yes.

soc. Then we must do no wrong?

CR. Certainly not.

soc. Nor when injured injure in return, as the many imagine; for we must injure no one at all?

CR. Clearly not.

soc. Again, Crito, may we do evil?

CR. Surely not, Socrates.

soc. And what of doing evil in return for evil, which is the morality of the many — is that just or not?

cr. Not just.

soc. For doing evil to another is the same as injuring him?

cr. Very true.

soc. Then we ought not to retaliate or render evil for evil to any one, whatever evil we may have suffered from him. But I would have you consider, Crito, whether you really mean what you are saying. For this opinion has never been held, and never will be held, by any considerable number of persons; and those who are agreed and those who are not agreed upon this point have no common ground, and can only despise one another when they see how widely they differ. Tell me, then, whether you agree with and assent to my first principle, that neither injury nor retaliation nor warding off evil by evil is ever right. And shall that be the premise of our argument? Or do you decline and dissent from this? For so I have ever thought, and continue to think; but, if you are of another opinion, let me hear what you have to say. If, however, you remain of the same mind as formerly, I will proceed to the next step.

cr. You may proceed, for I have not changed my mind.

soc. Then I will go on to the next point, which may be put in the form of a question: — Ought a man to do what he admits to be right, or ought he to betray the right?

cr. He ought to do what he thinks right.

soc. But if this is true, what is the application? In leaving the prison against the will of the Athenians, do I wrong any? Or rather do I not wrong those whom I ought least to wrong? Do I not desert the principles which were acknowledged by us to be just — what do you say?

cr. I cannot tell, Socrates; for I do not know.

soc. Then consider the matter in this way: — Imagine that I am about to play truant (you may call the proceeding by any name which you like), and the laws and the government come and interrogate me: 'Tell us, Socrates,' they say, 'what are you about? are you not going by an act of yours to overturn us — the laws, and the whole state, as far as in you lies? Do you imagine that a state can subsist and not be overthrown, in which the decisions of law have no power, but are set aside and trampled upon by individuals?' What will be our answer, Crito, to these and the like words? Any one, and especially a rhetorician, will have a good deal to say on behalf of the law which requires a sentence to be carried out. He will argue that this law should not be set aside; and shall we reply, 'Yes; but the state has injured us and given an unjust sentence.' Suppose I say that?

cr. Very good, Socrates.

SOC. 'And was that our agreement with you?' the law would answer; 'or were you to abide by the sentence of the state?' And if I were to express my astonishment at their words, the law would probably add: 'Answer, Socrates, instead of opening your eyes — you are in the habit of asking and answering questions. Tell us, — What complaint have you to make against us which justifies you in attempting to destroy us and the state? In the first place did we not bring you into existence? Your father married your mother by our aid and begat you. Say whether you have any objection to urge against those of use who regulate marriage?' None, I should reply. 'Or against those of us who after birth regulate the nurture and education of children, in which you also were trained? Were not the laws, which have the charge of education, right in commanding your father to train you in music and gymnastic?' Right, I should reply. 'Well then, since you were brought into the world and nurtured and educated by us, can you deny in the first place that you are our child and slave, as your fathers were before you? And if this is true you are not on equal terms with us; nor can you think that you have a right to do to us what we are doing to you. Would you have any right to strike or revile or do any other evil to your father or your master, if you had one, because you have been struck or reviled by him, or received some other evil at his hands? — you would not say this? And because we think right to destroy you, do you think that you have any right to destroy us in return, and your country as far as in you lies? Will you, O professor of true virtue, pretend that you are justified in this? Has a philosopher like you failed to discover that our country is more to be valued and higher and holier far than mother or father or any ancestor, and more to be regarded in the eyes of the gods and of men of understanding? also to be soothed, and gently and reverently entreated when angry, even more than a father, and either to be persuaded, or if not persuaded, to be obeyed? And when we are punished by her, whether with imprisonment or stripes, the punishment is to be endured in silence; and if she leads us to wounds or death in battle, thither we follow as is right; neither may any one yield or retreat or leave his rank, but whether in battle or in a court of law, or in any other place, he must do what his city and his country order him; or he must change their view of what is just: and if he may do no violence to his father or mother, much less may he do violence to his country.' What answer shall we make to this, Crito? Do the laws speak truly, or do they not?

CR. I think that they do.

SOC. Then the laws will say, 'Consider, Socrates, if we are speaking truly that in your present attempt you are going to do us an injury. For, having brought you into the world, and nurtured and educated you, and given you and every other citizen a share in every good which we had to give, we further proclaim to any Athenian by the liberty which we allow him, that if he does not like us when he has become of age and has seen the ways of the city, and made our acquaintance, he may go where he pleases and take his goods with him. None of us laws will forbid him or interfere with him. Any one who does not like us and the city, and who wants to emigrate to a colony or to any other city, may go where he likes, retaining his property. But he who has experience of the manner in which we order justice and administer the state, and still remains, has entered into an implied contract that he will do as we command him. And he who disobeys us is, as we maintain, thrice wrong; first, because in disobeying us he is disobeying his parents; secondly, because we are the authors of his education; thirdly, because he has made an agreement with us that he will duly obey our commands; and he neither obeys them nor convinces us that our commands are unjust; and we do not rudely impose them, but give him the alternative of obeying or convincing us; — that is what we offer, and he does neither. 25

'These are the sort of accusations to which, as we were saying, you, Socrates, will be exposed if you accomplish your intentions; you, above all other Athenians.' Suppose now I ask, why I rather than anybody else? They will justly retort upon me that I above all other men have acknowledged the agreement. 'There is clear proof,' they will say, 'Socrates, that we and the city were not displeasing to you. Of all Athenians you have been the most constant resident in the city, which, as you never leave, you may be supposed to love. For you never went out of the city either to see the games, except once when you went to the Isthmus, or to any other place unless when you were on military service; nor did you travel as other men do. Nor had you any curiosity to know other states or their laws: your affections did not go beyond us and our state; we were your special favourites, and you acquiesced in our government of you; and here in this city you begat your children, which is a proof of your satisfaction. Moreover, you might in the course of the trial, if you had liked, have fixed the penalty at banishment; the state which refuses to let you go now would have let you go then. But you pretended that you preferred death to exile, and that you were not unwilling to die. And now you have forgotten these fine sentiments, and pay no respect to us the laws, of whom you are the destroyer; and are doing what only a miserable slave would do, running away and turning your back upon the compacts and agreements which you made as a citizen. And first of all answer this very question: Are we right in saying that you agreed to be governed according to us in deed, and not in word only? Is that true or not?' How shall we answer. Crito? Must we not assent?

CR. We cannot help it, Socrates.

SOC. Then will they not say: 'You, Socrates, are breaking the covenants and agreements which you made with us at your leisure, not in any haste or under any compulsion or deception, but after you have had seventy years to think of them, during which time you were at liberty to leave the city, if we were not to your mind, or if our covenants appeared to you to be unfair. You had your choice, and might have gone either to Lacedaemon or Crete, both which states are often praised by you for their good government, or to some other Hellenic or foreign state. Whereas you, above all other Athenians, seemed to be so fond of the state, or, in other words, of us her laws (and who would care about a state which has no laws?), that you never stirred out of her; the halt, the blind, the maimed were not more stationary in her than you were. And now you run away and forsake your agreements. Not so, Socrates, if you will take our advice; do not make yourself ridiculous by escaping out of the city.

'For just consider, if you transgress and err in this sort of way, what good will you do either to yourself or to your friends? That your friends will be driven into exile and deprived of citizenship, or will lose their property, is tolerably certain; and you yourself, if you fly to one of the neighboring cities, as, for example, Thebes or Megara, both of which are well governed, will come to them as an enemy, Socrates, and their government will be against you, and all patriotic citizens will cast an evil eye upon you as a subverter of the laws, and you will confirm in the minds of the judges the justice of their own condemnation of you. For he who is a corrupter of the laws is more than likely to be a corrupter of the young and foolish portion of mankind. Will you then flee from well-ordered cities and virtuous men? And is existence worth having on these terms? Or will you go to them without shame, and talk to them, Socrates? And what will you say to them? What you say here about virtue and justice and institutions and laws being the best things among men? Would that be decent of you? Surely not. But if you go away from well-governed states to Crito's friends in Thessaly, where there is great disorder and licence, they will be charmed to hear the tale of your escape from prison, set off with ludicrous particulars of the manner in which you were wrapped in a goatskin or some other disguise, and metamorphosed as the manner is of runaways; but will there be no one to remind you that in your old age you were not ashamed to violate the most sacred laws from a miserable desire of a little more life? Perhaps

26
27

28

Section 2:
Deductive Proofs

not, if you keep them in a good temper; but if they are out of temper you will hear many degrading things; you will live, but how? — as the flatterer of all men, and the servant of all men; and doing what? — eating and drinking in Thessaly, having gone abroad in order that you may get a dinner. And where will be your fine sentiments about justice and virtue? Say that you wish to live for the sake of your children — you want to bring them up and educate them — will you take them into Thessaly and deprive them of Athenian citizenship? Is this the benefit which you will confer upon them? Or are you under the impression that they will be better cared for and educated here if you are still alive, although absent from them; for your friends will take care of them? Do you fancy that if you are an inhabitant of Thessaly they will take care of them, and if you are an inhabitant of the other world that they will not take care of them? Nay; but if they who call themselves friends are good for anything, they will — to be sure they will.

'Listen, then, Socrates, to us who have brought you up. Think not of life and children first, and of justice afterwards, but of justice first, that you may be justified before the princes of the world below. For neither will you nor any that belong to you be happier or holier or juster in this life, or happier in another, if you do as Crito bids. Now you depart in innocence, a sufferer and not a doer of evil; a victim, not of the laws but of men. But if you go forth, returning evil for evil, and injury for injury, breaking the covenants and agreements which you have made with us, and wronging those whom you ought least of all to wrong, that is to say, yourself, your friends, your country, and us, we shall be angry with you while you live, and our brethren, the laws of the world below, will receive you as an enemy; for they will know that you have done your best to destroy us. Listen, then, to us and not to Crito.'

This, dear Crito, is the voice which I seem to hear murmuring in my ears, like the sound of the flute in the ears of the mystic; that voice, I say, is humming in my ears, and prevents me from hearing any other. And I know that anything more which you may say will be vain. Yet speak, if you have anything to say.

CR. I have nothing to say, Socrates.

SOC. Leave me then, Crito, to fulfil the will of God, and to follow whither he leads.

Discussion: Content

1. What is Crito suggesting that Socrates do?
2. Why does Socrates resist Crito's suggestion?

3. Why is Socrates so loyal to the laws of Athens despite the fact that they have been administered unjustly in his case?
4. Do you feel the same way about the responsibilities of a person who accepts citizenship as Socrates does in paragraph 25?
5. Crito has suggested that Socrates might flee to Thessaly and that his children would thus be spared the loss of their father. Why does Socrates reject this idea?

Discussion: Form

1. What is the basic syllogism behind Socrates' argument?
2. In paragraphs 17–19, Socrates sets up another syllogism which might be stated this way:

> To betray the right is something that we must not do.
> To disobey the law is to betray the right.
> Therefore, to disobey the law is something we must not do.

He then suggests that Crito might try to refute such a syllogism. How might this be done?
3. What technique does Socrates use in his conclusion, which begins with paragraph 30?
4. What is gained by casting an argument in the form of a dialogue or conversation, rather than as a conventional essay divided into paragraphs?

Section 3: Refutation

Sports commentators tell us that the best defense is a strong offense, and the same thing is true in persuasive writing. If you fashion your own arguments soundly and forcefully, then you needn't always be concerned about refuting your opponent's arguments. Nevertheless, knowing how to go about preparing a refutation is still a good idea, since you can't always be on the offensive; sometimes you have to counterattack.

First, it is necessary to study your opponent's argument to determine whether the approach is an inductive or deductive one. Your strategies will vary accordingly. If, for example, your opponent argues inductively, offering examples to illustrate that a certain proposition is true — or at least is likely to be true — you may counter the argument by claiming that your opponent's conclusion was made too hastily, that it was based on too little evidence. You would support your claim by supplying examples that tend to weaken the opponent's claim or perhaps even prove the opposite claim.

To cite a specific example, suppose your opponent argues that high schools are doing a worse job each year in preparing students for college. The evidence produced is the steadily declining college board scores over the past fifteen years. These figures seem to be fairly convincing. Nevertheless, you might point out that with more and more students wanting to attend college, the number taking the tests during each of the past fifteen years has also grown. Now the declining scores — representing the work of a large portion of each senior class, not just the top third — do not seem quite so devastating, and you have correctly pointed out that your opponent has not examined all the evidence.

Similarly, your opponent might argue from analogy, claiming that this year's football team is likely to win the conference title because it has at least six things in common with the last conference champion, the team of '69. Your response might well be that the analogy is a faulty one since there are some significant differences between this team and the 1969 champions which your opponent has overlooked. And suppose your opponent argues from cause, claiming that many majors abandon math for accounting at the end of the sophomore year because of their terrifying experiences in the required course in differential equations. You might respond that your opponent has not discovered the correct cause at all but has assumed that since many students drop out of math *after* taking differential equations, they have done so *because of* differential equations. The more convincing reason for the shift in majors is that it is among sophomore math majors that the accounting department does its most strenuous recruiting, luring them away from the pursuit of pure mathematics by tantalizing them with promises of financial rewards in the business world.

When you refute arguments by showing that your opponent has made a *hasty generalization, a faulty analogy,* or has proposed a *false cause,* you are pointing out some logical fallacies which entrap a great many writers. Other logical fallacies exist besides these three, and the most common are defined for you in "A Brief Introduction to Common Logical Fallacies," which appears in the Appendix, pp.433–444.

Deductive arguments, like inductive ones, may also prove to be faulty and subject to refutation. You have already seen one way to refute a deductive argument — i.e., to attack one or the other of the first two propositions, showing it to be untrue, unsupported, fallacious, or otherwise indefensible. If one of the first two propositions fails, the conclusion is unacceptable. Recall the example of the contested speeding ticket:

> Those who exceed the posted speed limit will pay $50.
> You exceeded the posted speed limit.
> Therefore, you will pay $50.

Your chance of avoiding the fine depended on your success at refuting the second proposition by showing that the speed limit had not been properly posted — proving, in other words, that the proposition was not completely true.

Besides showing that one of the propositions of a syllogism is untrue, you may perhaps wish to claim that the reasoning itself is

Section 3: Refutation

faulty and that the conclusion is therefore invalid. For example, a person might argue that since those who spare the rod spoil their children and since Mr. Smith's children are all spoiled rotten, then he is certainly not a believer in corporal punishment. This syllogism is not valid, as the diagram below will show.

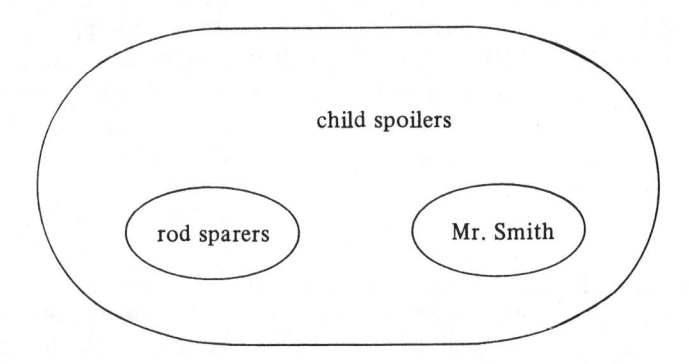

```
         ╭─────────────────────────────────╮
        ╱                                   ╲
       │          child spoilers             │
       │    ╭──────────╮      ╭──────────╮   │
       │    │rod sparers│     │ Mr. Smith│   │
       │    ╰──────────╯      ╰──────────╯   │
        ╲                                   ╱
         ╰─────────────────────────────────╯
```

The diagram shows that although we have asserted that rod sparers are child spoilers and that Mr. Smith is a child spoiler, we do not necessarily have to agree that Mr. Smith is a rod sparer. The person who argues in this way is guilty of a formal fallacy, that is, one that violates the proper form of a syllogism. Formal fallacies are discussed in detail on pp. 434–439 of "A Brief Introduction to Common Logical Fallacies."

There is still another way to refute an argument, and that is to agree with it — or at least to pretend to agree. For instance, you might pretend to agree with your opponent who has proposed the dropping of freshman composition from the curriculum. Your purpose, you say, is merely to point out some additional reasons that had been overlooked. Then you state your reasons for abolishing freshman composition: (1) it robs students of valuable time they could otherwise use to drink beer and to attend various campus activities, such as concerts and ball games, (2) it discriminates against students who are illiterate, and (3) it demands that students spend precious hours in grim places like libraries. The purpose of this type of ironic approach is to induce the audience to laugh at the opponent's argument by reducing it to an absurdity.

Even some apparently sound arguments are vulnerable to this kind of treatment, so it is very wise to examine your arguments carefully. Recall once again the seemingly airtight argument that you used on the highway patrolman:

People should not be held accountable for laws they don't know about.
I was not informed about this law (the speed limit).
Therefore, I should not be held accountable for it.

You fully expected the officer to accept your first proposition as being intuitively sound. But suppose he or she had responded with a smirk, "And I guess the next thing you'll tell me will be that babies who don't know about the law of gravity will never fall out of their cribs." It's clear that to prevent this kind of reduction to absurdity, you'll need to tighten the language of your first proposition.*

The paragraphs and essays which follow offer abundant illustrations of the variety of approaches to refutation.

---

*If you have been guilty of *dicto simpliciter* (see p. 441) in the construction of your proposition, the officer is also guilty of *equivocation* (see p. 441) in deliberately confusing physical laws with traffic laws, but the remark does hint at the way your proposition should be amended; that is, your argument gains force, rather than loses it, if you tighten the first proposition to read, "People should not be held accountable for traffic laws that they haven't been informed of."

Paragraphs:
Refutation

For the Death Penalty
William F. Buckley, Jr.

The business about the poor and the black suffering excessively from capital punishment is no argument against capital punishment. It is an argument against the *administration* of justice, not against the penalty. Any punishment can be unfairly or unjustly applied. Go ahead and reform the process by which capital punishment is inflicted, if you wish; but don't confuse maladministration with the merits of capital punishment.

Discussion Questions

1. What is the specific argument against capital punishment that Buckley is refuting?
2. Under Material Fallacies on p. 442, look up the definition of *irrelevance (red herring)*. How does this fallacy apply to Buckley's refutation?

The Right to Die
Norman Cousins

The general reaction to suicide is bound to change as people come to understand that it may be a denial, not an assertion, of moral or religious ethics to allow life to be extended without regard to decency or pride. What moral or religious purpose is celebrated by the annihilation of the human spirit in the triumphant act of keeping the body alive? Why are so many people more readily appalled by an unnatural form of dying than by an unnatural form of living?

Discussion Questions

1. What proposition is Cousins refuting?
2. Look up *dicto simpliciter* in the list of material fallacies on p. 441. How does it apply to Cousins' refutation?
3. Look up *rhetorical question* in the Glossary. How often does Cousins employ this device?

On Not Prosecuting Civil Disobedience
Ronald Dworkin

The argument that, because the government believes a man has committed a crime, it must prosecute him is much weaker than it seems. Society "cannot endure" if it tolerates all disobedience; it does not follow, however, nor is there evidence, that it will collapse if it tolerates some. In the United States prosecutors have discretion whether to enforce criminal laws in particular cases. A prosecutor may properly decide not to press charges if the lawbreaker is young, or inexperienced, or the sole support of a family, or is repentant, or turns state's evidence, or if the law is unpopular or unworkable or generally disobeyed, or if the courts are clogged with more important cases, or for dozens of other reasons. This discretion is not license — we expect prosecutors to have good reasons for exercising it — but there are, at least *prima facie,* some good reasons for not prosecuting those who disobey the draft laws out of conscience. One is the obvious reason that they act out of better motives than those who break the law out of greed or a desire to subvert government. If motive can count in distinguishing between thieves, then why not in distinguishing between draft offenders? Another is the practical reason that our society suffers a loss if it punishes a group that includes — as the group of draft dissenters does — some of its most loyal and law-respecting citizens. Jailing such men solidifies their alienation from society, and alienates many like them who are deterred by the threat. If practical consequences like these argued for not enforcing prohibition, why do they not argue for tolerating offenses of conscience?

Discussion Questions

1. What proposition is Dworkin refuting? Does he state it specifically?
2. How does Dworkin proceed in his refutation of the proposition? Does he appeal to formal or material fallacies? Or does he reduce the proposition to an absurdity?
3. Dworkin offers more than one type of support for his claim that some criminals need not be prosecuted. What are they?

Are Democracies Obstructive?
Charles W. Eliot

An argument against democracy, which evidently had great weight with Sir Henry Maine, because he supposed it to rest upon the experience of mankind, is stated as follows: Progress and reformation have always been the work of the few, and have been opposed by the many; therefore, democracies will be obstructive. This argument is completely refuted by the first century of the American democracy, alike in the field of morals and jurisprudence, and the field of manufactures and trade. Nowhere, for instance, has the great principle of religious toleration been so thoroughly put in practice as in the United States; nowhere have such well-meant and persistent efforts been made to improve the legal status of women; nowhere has the conduct of hospitals, asylums, reformatories, and prisons been more carefully studied; nowhere have legislative remedies for acknowledged abuses and evils been more promptly and perseveringly sought. There was a certain plausibility in the idea that the multitude, who live by labor in established modes, would be opposed to inventions which would inevitably cause industrial revolutions; but American experience completely upsets this notion. For promptness in making physical forces and machinery do the work of men, the people of the United States surpass incontestably all other peoples. The people that invented and introduced with perfect commercial success the river steamboat, the cotton-gin, the parlor-car and the sleeping-car, the grain-elevator, the street railway — both surface and elevated — the telegraph, the telephone, the rapid printing-press, the cheap book and newspaper, the sewing-machine, the steam fire-engine, agricultural machinery, the pipe-lines for natural oil and gas, and machine-made clothing, boots, furniture, tools, screws, wagons, fire-arms, and watches — this is not a people to vote down or hinder labor-saving invention or beneficent industrial revolution. The fact is that in a democracy the interests of the greater number will ultimately prevail, as they should. It was the stage-drivers and innkeepers, not the multitude, who wished to suppress the locomotive; it is some publishers and typographical unions, not the mass of the people, who wrongly imagine that they have an interest in making books dearer than they need be. Furthermore, a just liberty of combination and perfect equality before the law, such as prevail in a democracy, enable men or companies to engage freely in new undertakings at their own risk and bring them to triumphant success, if success be in them, whether the multitude approve them or not. The consent of the multitude is not necessary to the success of a printing-press which prints twenty thousand copies of a newspaper in an hour, or of a machine cutter which cuts out twenty overcoats at one chop. In short, the notion that democracy will hinder religious, political, and social reformation and progress, or restrain commercial and industrial improvement, is a chimera.

Discussion Questions

1. Is Eliot's paragraph based on deductive or inductive reasoning? How can you tell?
2. The list of inventions is dated. What would you substitute to convince modern readers that democracy does not stand in the way of progress?

Student Work:
Ced
Refutation

Death and Logic

Although the argument for capital punishment is logical enough, it just won't wash. We are expected to believe that the death penalty will act as a deterrent to potential criminals because death threats are always effective deterrents. The logic is beautiful: death threats are effective deterrents; capital punishment is a death threat; therefore, capital punishment is an effective deterrent. This is beautiful, but wrong. The first premise is not true. When did the threat of death ever prevent people from smoking? When did the threat of death turn people off to drugs? When did the threat of death keep speeders at 55? When did the threat of death ever stop a war? The premise (and the argument) would be sound if people were logical — but they aren't.

Discussion Questions

1. What proposition is the student writer attacking?
2. Does the refutation involve an appeal to a formal or material fallacy or the reduction to absurdity? Explain.

The Pleasures of Dormitory Life

Four years from now, having graduated and joined the real world, with an apartment of my own, I'm sure I will look back fondly on the pleasures of dormitory life. But I will not forget my homey room, with its spacious closets and clever built-in chests and desks. What memories I will have of the venetian blinds, such fun to raise and lower, and the tastefully coordinated colors of walls, floor, and ceiling, and the perfectly comfortable chairs and beds. Can I ever forget gourmet meals creatively cooked in a popcorn popper and a percolator? And there will also remain the pleasant aromas of roommate's overflowing laundry bag and the sweet little kittens next door, plus the sophisticated blend of smoke from cigarettes, pot, and incense. These will be joined by the gentle late-night echoes of favorite rock records and the sweetly voiced profanity of the preacher's daughter next door. And which will be the strongest memory, the comradely joy of sharing a bathroom with all the girls on the hall (and an occasional guy), or the thrill of returning to the room to find my roommate all snug in bed with still another new friend? Ah, bliss — the pleasures of dormitory life, how they will linger!

Discussion Questions

1. This student uses one logical method and one nonlogical method to create refutation. What are the two methods?
2. For what sort of audience does this writer seem to have written? How can you tell?
3. What do you suppose has bothered this student most about dormitory life? What about the paragraph's organization suggests her pet dislikes?

Guns Aren't for Everyone

People who argue for unlimited ownership of firearms seem to have it all going their way. Their case is hardly open to rebuttal. The Constitution insures all citizens the right to bear arms. They are citizens of this country; therefore, they have the right to bear arms. What could be simpler? 1

Their logic is unassailable. Their citizenship cannot be challenged, nor can the Constitution unless we choose to amend it. But wait a moment. Does the Constitution really guarantee to all the right to own firearms? Is that part of their argument as solid as they would have us believe? 12

Let's look at what the Constitution actually says: "A well regulated Militia, being necessary to the security of a free State, the right of the people to keep and bear Arms, shall not be infringed."

Now to me that statement seems to stop short of insuring every citizen the right to keep and bear arms. It insures citizens that right just as long as they are willing to take up the responsibility to protect the security of this free state by serving in the militia or national guard. I think we have been misreading the Constitution for a long time in allowing anyone with enough money to buy a gun. The fathers of our country clearly intended that the right to bear arms should carry with it the responsibility to use that weapon to defend the country.

Well, those who favor free access to guns usually make all kinds of claims about protecting their homes from all sorts of enemies, ranging from burglars to invading Russians. You would think they wouldn't mind my interpretation of the Constitution. But just mention registration of firearms and they go berserk. Nevertheless, it seems quite clear that the fathers of our country intended that too. For here is another argument as sound and as logical as theirs. A governor must know how to locate all the members of his militia. And all gun owners are constitutionally obligated to be members of the militia. Therefore, the governor must know how to locate all gun owners.

Let them argue their way out of that one.

Discussion Questions

1. The syllogism to be refuted is stated in the opening paragraph. What is it?
2. How does the writer refute this argument?
3. The rebuttal turns into an argument in favor of gun registration, one that is also based on a syllogism. How can that syllogism be stated?

Against Public Prayer in the Schools

Those who favor prayer in the public schools usually do so because of deeply felt religious convictions. They say that it is not enough for students to pray silently but that they should be allowed to express openly and publicly the feelings they hold in the privacy of their hearts. They feel that in denying students this right the government is overstepping itself and denying them a promised freedom, one insured by our Constitution, namely, freedom of religion. 1

Since the overwhelming majority of those who protest this denial of religious freedom are Christians, I am quite sure that they would be surprised to learn that in finding a right to public prayer in the Constitution they are appealing to a false authority, for Jesus Himself denied His followers such a privilege when He said in the Sermon on the Mount: "And when thou prayest, thou shalt not be as the hypocrites are: for they love to pray standing in the synagogues and in the corners of the streets, that they may be seen of men. Verily I say unto you, they have their reward. But when thou prayest enter into thy closet, and when thou hast shut thy door, pray to thy Father which is in secret; and thy Father which is in secret shall reward thee openly." 2

Regardless of how we might interpret our Constitution, Jesus — it seems — has come down on the side of those who oppose public prayer in the schools. 3

Discussion Questions

1. How can the argument in favor of public prayer in the schools be stated?
2. In what way does the writer attack the argument?

Why We Should Study Abbreviations in English Classes

Abbreviations are as old as man. They have been found on the earliest tombs, monuments, and coins. Roman soldiers discovered it was easier to scratch SPQR on their shields than to write out *Senatus Populusque Romanus*. Monks saved hundreds of strokes of their quills, not to speak of pages of parchment, by using such abbreviations as A.D. for *Anno Domini,* and they certainly needed every shortcut available in those years before the invention of the printing press. Many such abbreviations are still used, along with countless others created in the centuries since then.

In fact, abbreviations, acronyms, contractions, initials, nicknames, slang shortcuts, and the like make up an important portion of our vocabularies. It is estimated that these short forms comprise more

Section 3: Refutation

than 25 percent of the words we hear and use. Yet this facet of our language is all but ignored by today's educators — when not flatly prohibited! The time spent in English classes is too often wasted on spelling, grammar, and punctuation — three areas that are fast becoming obsolete. It is clear that eventually all unabbreviated nouns will disappear and that only standard, abbreviated adverbs and adjectives, plus a few essential verbs, will survive.

Of course, some die-hard scholars will continue to follow the conventional rules of spelling, grammar, and punctuation, so that the standard dictionary and a few grammar handbooks will remain. But as more and more efficient verbal shortcuts are used, it will be more and more essential to know how to implement them effectively. Those shortcuts are what we should really be studying in our English classes.

For instance, acronyms are already in widespread use, for many inventions, organizations, governmental agencies, and industries whose names consist of more than one word. In fact, many acronyms are more familiar to us than the words they represent: LASER, RADAR, AFL-CIO, NASA, HUD, GM, IBM. It is sometimes necessary to pause for a moment to recall how these acronyms were formed; nevertheless, these groups of letters are perfectly meaningful to us. Should we not be concentrating on such new words as SALT instead of bothering to learn to spell Strategic Arms Limitation Talks? Consider, if you will, how much more efficient, logical, and clear it is to use ZIP instead of Zone Improvement Plan. With proper study and attention, all such cumbersome phrases can be eliminated entirely in favor of much shorter terms.

Similarly, ideograms were used thirty-three centuries ago by the Egyptians to express objects or ideas. Chinese characters are forms of ideograms, and so are $, %, @, & #. Although few of these symbols are now acceptable in formal writing, they are used extensively in every other form of written communication from newspaper articles to package labels. Shouldn't we be working to develop more of these symbols? Surely typewriter keyboards could accommodate many more. And think of the time we would save by writing ∿ instead of water, or ☺ instead of one of the myriad of words that expresses happiness. There would be no need to check the spelling of *congenial* or *ecstasy* or *felicity*. Would this not save time?

Of course, traffic signs already use abbreviations and symbols extensively, and, furthermore, international pictorial signs are eliminating words completely. But the figure shown wearing a skirt on the doors of women's rest rooms still causes me to hesitate at times, especially when I and most of the other women entering are wearing pants. This needs investigation! Is *that* the best symbol? However, the people most equipped to do this research, college professors, are not doing it. Instead, they are going over old ground — grammar, punctuation, and spelling. We need these people to develop new and better abbreviations and symbolic signs. Brevity is beautiful! 6

In fact, to demonstrate how conciseness can be implemented, I have the condensed the words of "The Star Spangled Banner" thus:

> Look, it's A.M. & last noct. emb. still vis.
> The R W & B still A-OK o'er Ft. McHenry.
> M-16's flash illum. Old Glory at int.
> √ if Stars & //// curr. displ. r. of USA.

Now isn't that an improvement? 7

Discussion Questions

1. This student uses *irony* (see Glossary) as a means of refutation. Disregarding the title, where do you first notice an ironic contrast in the essay?
2. What is the purpose of paragraph 3?
3. This student is particularly skillful at the use of specific examples. Which paragraphs best illustrate that skill?
4. Some students whose writing skills are weak would likely agree with this student's argument that study of abbreviations should replace the standard English curriculum; but how does this student's writing ability suggest that weak skills were not her reason for choosing this topic?

Section 3:
Refutation

381

Essays:
Refutation

Gun Control: Shifting the Blame
Sydney J. Harris

Sydney J. Harris (1917–   ) was born in London and came to the United States in 1922. He was educated at the University of Chicago and worked for various newspapers in the Chicago area before joining the Chicago *Daily News* as a reporter in 1941. Harris developed the column "Strictly Personal," which is now syndicated by Field Newspaper Syndicate and appears in hundreds of newspapers throughout the United States, Canada, and South America. This essay first appeared in his column. Many of Harris's essays have been anthologized: *Strictly Personal* (1953), *A Majority of One* (1957), *The Best of Harris* (1975).

I wonder if the pro-handgun people in America realize what they are saying about our citizens when they repeat their familiar slogan, "Guns don't kill — people do."

If guns don't kill, but people do, this makes Americans the most murderous population on the face of the earth. In 1980, for instance (the last year for which we have accurate international statistics), handguns killed 77 people in Japan, eight in Great Britain, 24 in Switzerland, eight in Canada, 18 in Sweden, four in Australia — and 11,522 in the United States.

What can this mean? If it is not the availability of guns here that is responsible for such a massacre, it can only mean that our citizens are by far the most vicious, violent, homicidal people in the world.

Do you believe this? Do you believe that Americans are so much worse than other people — so contemptuous of human life — that our death rate from guns is thousands of times larger than those countries that have enacted civilized and sensible gun laws?

This is a terrible indictment to make about a nation that prides itself upon its decency and humanity, that likes to hold itself up as a model of democratic friendliness.   5

But this is what the pro-gun partisans would have us believe. That it is not the mere possession of firearms, but the people behind them, who are responsible for our appalling mortality, year after year.   6

It is by their own tortured logic that we must condemn, then, not the instrument, but the agent. And condemning the agent means that we condemn the American public, individually and collectively, for being brutally indifferent to the taking of human life.   7

Shifting the burden of guilt from the gun to the gunslinger inexorably marks our people as the outlaws of the Western world, who willfully or carelessly kill off one another in quantities that other countries find shockingly inexcusable.   8

I firmly believe that it is guns in the hands of people that kill, and not that we Americans are so much more murderous, by nature or training, than people elsewhere. It is the easy availability of guns that accounts for our infamous death toll, not our vile dispositions.   9

You can take your choice — blame the gun or blame the person. And if you blame the person, as the gun lobby prefers to do, you are indicting the nation itself for being the most bloodthirsty on earth.   10

I cannot believe this of our people, which is why I must blame the false conception of "freedom" which puts this weapon in their hands.   11

Discussion: Content

1. Why does Harris suggest that Americans are the most murderous people on the face of the earth?
2. The title of this essay refers to a shifting of blame. With what shifting of blame is Harris dealing?
3. What alternative does Harris offer?

Discussion: Form

1. How does Harris go about refuting the slogan, "Guns don't kill — people do"?
2. Look up the term *Either/or (false dilemma)* in the "Brief Introduction to Common Logical Fallacies," p. 441. How does this fallacy apply to Harris's refutation?

Section 3: Refutation

3. Like some earlier essays in this book, this one was written for a newspaper, to be printed in columns. Consequently, Harris has written short paragraphs, none over two sentences. As an editor for a magazine or one of his books, you might prefer to create longer paragraphs. Do you see any that might be logically combined?

Life after Death
Carl Sagan

Carl Sagan (1934–   ), a native of New York City, received his Ph.D. from the University of Chicago in 1960 and is now on the faculty at Cornell University. An adviser to NASA and the National Academy of Sciences, Sagan is probably the best known scientist in America, largely because of his popular public television series *Cosmos,* which he converted into a best-seller in 1980. *Dragons of Eden* won him the Pulitzer Prize in 1978. The following essay is taken from *Broca's Brain* (1979).

William Wolcott died and went to heaven. Or so it seemed. Before being wheeled to the operating table, he had been reminded that the surgical procedure would entail a certain risk. The operation was a success, but just as the anaesthesia was wearing off his heart went into fibrillation and he died. It seemed to him that he had somehow left his body and was able to look down upon it, withered and pathetic, covered only by a sheet, lying on a hard and unforgiving surface. He was only a little sad, regarded his body one last time — from a great height, it seemed — and continued a kind of upward journey. While his surroundings had been suffused by a strange permeating darkness, he realized that things were now getting brighter — looking up, you might say. And then he was being illuminated from a distance, flooded with light. He entered a kind of radiant kingdom and there, just ahead of him, he could make out in silhouette, magnificently lit from behind, a great godlike figure whom he was now effortlessly approaching. Wolcott strained to make out His face.... 1

And then awoke. In the hospital operating room where the defibrillation machine had been rushed to him, he had been resuscitated at the last possible moment. Actually, his heart had stopped, and by some definitions of this poorly understood process, he had died. Wolcott was certain that he *had* died, that he had been vouchsafed a glimpse of life after death and a confirmation of Judaeo-Christian theology.

Similar experiences, now widely documented by physicians and others, have occurred all over the world. These perithanatic, or near-death, epiphanies have been experienced not only by people of conventional Western religiosity but also by Hindus and Buddhists and skeptics. It seems plausible that many of our conventional ideas about heaven are derived from such near-death experiences, which must have been related regularly over the millennia. No news could have been more interesting or more hopeful than that of the traveler returned, the report that there is a voyage and a life after death, that there is a God who awaits us, and that upon death we feel grateful and uplifted, awed and overwhelmed.

For all I know, these experiences may be just what they seem and a vindication of the pious faith that has taken such a pummeling from science in the past few centuries. Personally, I would be delighted if there were a life after death — especially if it permitted me to continue to learn about this world and others, if it gave me a chance to discover how history turns out. But I am also a scientist, so I think about what other explanations are possible. How could it be that people of all ages, cultures and eschatological predispositions have the *same sort* of near-death experience?

We know that similar experiences can be induced with fair regularity, cross-culturally, by psychedelic drugs. Out-of-body experiences are induced by dissociative anaesthetics such as the ketamines (2-[*o*-chlorophenyl]-2-[methylamino] cyclohexanones.) The illusion of flying is induced by atropine and other belladonna alkaloids, and these molecules, obtained, for example, from mandrake or jimson weed, have been used regularly by European witches and North American *curanderos* ("healers") to experience, in the midst of religious ecstasy, soaring and glorious flight. MDA (2,4-methylenedioxyamphetamine) tends to induce age regression, an accessing of experiences from youth and infancy which we had thought entirely forgotten. DMT (*N,N*-dimethyltryptamine) induces micropsia and macropsia, the sense of the world shrinking or expanding, respectively — a little like what happens to Alice after she obeys instructions on small containers reading "Eat me" or "Drink me." LSD (lysergic acid diethylamide) induces a sense of union with the universe, as in the identification of Brahman with Atman in Hindu religious belief.

Can it really be that the Hindu mystical experience is pre-wired into us, requiring only 200 micrograms of LSD to be made manifest? If something like ketamine is released in times of mortal danger or near-death, and people returning from such an experience always provide the same account of heaven and God, then must there not be a sense in which Western as well as Eastern religions are hard-wired in the neuronal architecture of our brains?

It is difficult to see why evolution should have selected brains that are predisposed to such experiences, since no one seems to die or fail to reproduce from a want of mystic fervor. Might these drug-inducible experiences as well as the near-death epiphany be due merely to some evolutionarily neutral wiring defect in the brain which, by accident, occasionally brings forth altered perceptions of the world? That possibility, it seems to me, is extremely implausible, and perhaps no more than a desperate rationalist attempt to avoid a serious encounter with the mystical.

The only alternative, so far as I can see, is that every human being, without exception, has already shared an experience like that of those travelers who return from the land of death: the sensation of flight; the emergence from darkness into light; an experience in which, at least sometimes, a heroic figure can be dimly perceived, bathed in radiance and glory. There is only one common experience that matches this description. It is called birth.

Discussion: Content

1. What two unusual experiences or sensations accompanied William Wolcott's brush with death?
2. Near-death experiences like Wolcott's are frequently cited as evidence for what common belief?
3. What is especially peculiar and intriguing about such experiences, according to Sagan?
4. What does Sagan propose as an alternative explanation for the occurrence of these near-death sensations?
5. Why is it important to Sagan's argument that many of the near-death sensations can be duplicated by taking drugs?

Discussion: Form

1. Sagan's refutation begins with a brief narrative. What purpose does it serve?
2. Paragraph 4 is a crucial one for this essay. What purpose does it serve?

3. The technique that Sagan uses in his refutation is to point out the material fallacy of labored hypothesis (see p. 442 of "A Brief Introduction to Common Logical Fallacies"). How does this fallacy apply here?

Why I Want a Wife
Judy Syfers

Judy Syfers (1937–   ) is a California native who graduated from the University of Iowa. She is now a free-lance writer and, as the essay below makes abundantly clear, a housewife and mother. Syfer's essay has become a classic, chosen to conclude the Tenth Anniversary Edition of *Ms.* (where it first appeared) as well as to appear in many other anthologies.

I belong to that classification of people known as wives. I am A Wife. And, not altogether incidentally, I am a mother.

Not too long ago a male friend of mine appeared on the scene fresh from a recent divorce. He had one child, who is, of course, with his ex-wife. He is looking for another wife. As I thought about him while I was ironing one evening, it suddenly occurred to me that I, too, would like to have a wife. Why do I want a wife?

I would like to go back to school so that I can become economically independent, support myself, and, if need be, support those dependent upon me. I want a wife who will work and send me to school. And while I am going to school I want a wife to take care of my children. I want a wife to keep track of the children's doctor and dentist appointments. And to keep track of mine, too. I want a wife to make sure my children eat properly and are kept clean. I want a wife who will wash the children's clothes and keep them mended. I want a wife who is a good nurturant attendant to my children, who arranges for their schooling, makes sure that they have an adequate social life with their peers, takes them to the park, the zoo, etc. I want a wife who takes care of the children when they are sick, a wife who arranges to be around when the children need special care, because, of course, I cannot miss classes at school. My wife must arrange to lose time at work and not lose the job. It may mean a small cut in my wife's income from time to time, but I guess I can tolerate that. Needless to say, my wife will arrange and pay for the care of the children while my wife is working.

I want a wife who will take care of *my* physical needs. I want a wife who will keep my house clean. A wife who will pick up after my

Section 3: Refutation

children, a wife who will pick up after me. I want a wife who will keep my clothes clean, ironed, mended, replaced when need be, and who will see to it that my personal things are kept in their proper place so that I can find what I need the minute I need it. I want a wife who cooks the meals, a wife who is a *good* cook. I want a wife who will plan the menus, do the necessary grocery shopping, prepare the meals, serve them pleasantly, and then do the cleaning up while I do my studying. I want a wife who will care for me when I am sick and sympathize with my pain and loss of time from school. I want a wife to go along when our family takes a vacation so that someone can continue to care for me and my children when I need a rest and change of scene.

I want a wife who will not bother me with rambling complaints about a wife's duties. But I want a wife who will listen to me when I feel the need to explain a rather difficult point I have come across in my course of studies. And I want a wife who will type my papers for me when I have written them.

I want a wife who will take care of the details of my social life. When my wife and I are invited out by friends, I want a wife who will take care of the babysitting arrangements. When I meet people at school that I like and want to entertain, I want a wife who will have the house clean, will prepare a special meal, serve it to me and my friends, and not interrupt when I talk about things that interest me and my friends. I want a wife who will have arranged that the children are fed and ready for bed before my guests arrive so that the children do not bother us. I want a wife who takes care of the needs of my guests so that they feel comfortable, who makes sure that they have an ashtray, that they are passed the hors d'oeuvres, that they are offered a second helping of the food, that their wine glasses are replenished when necessary, that their coffee is served to them as they like it. And I want a wife who knows that sometimes I need a night out by myself.

I want a wife who is sensitive to my sexual needs, a wife who makes love passionately and eagerly when I feel like it, a wife who makes sure that I am satisfied. And, of course, I want a wife who will not demand sexual attention when I am not in the mood for it. I want a wife who assumes the complete responsibility for birth control, because I do not want more children. I want a wife who will remain sexually faithful to me so that I do not have to clutter up my intellectual life with jealousies. And I want a wife who understands that *my* sexual needs entail more than strict adherence to monogamy. I must, after all, be able to relate to people as fully as possible.

If, by chance, I find another person more suitable as a wife than the wife I already have, I want the liberty to replace my present wife with another one. Naturally, I will expect a fresh, new life; my wife will take the children and be solely responsible for them so that I am left free. 8

When I am through with school and have a job, I want my wife to quit working and remain at home so that my wife can more fully and completely take care of a wife's duties. 9

My God, who *wouldn't* want a wife? 10

Discussion: Content

1. The reasons that Syfers cites for wanting a wife constitute a serious indictment of the institution of marriage as it exists today. Do you agree or disagree with her? State your reasons.
2. Draw up a list of Syfers's grievances against the behavior of husbands. How many items does the list contain?
3. Which of Syfers' grievances seems to bother her most? Why do you suppose that is so?
4. What does Syfers mean when she says in paragraph 7, "And I want a wife who understands that *my* sexual needs entail more than strict adherence to monogamy"?

Discussion: Form

1. Clearly Judy Syfers doesn't want a wife; the title is meant ironically. State the thesis in a straightforward way.
2. What purpose is served by paragraph 1? By paragraph 2? What effect would be created if the essay began with the last sentence of paragraph 2?
3. Practically every supporting sentence in this essay begins with the expression, "I want a wife." Do you find this repetition to be an effective device? Why or why not?
4. Notice the last sentence of the essay. What is gained by making it short? Repetitive? A rhetorical question?
5. Try your hand at writing a counterargument in a similar fashion: "Why I Want a Husband."

Section 3:
Refutation

Let's Keep Christmas Commercial
Grace April Oursler Armstrong

Grace April Oursler Armstrong is an American writer of over ten books, mostly on religion, such as *The Book of God* (1957), *The Tales Christ Told* (1959), and *What's Happening to the Catholic Church* (1966). She comes by that interest naturally, for her father, Fulton Oursler, wrote *The Greatest Story Ever Told* (1949), a continuing best-seller in the religious field, and after his death she completed *The Greatest Faith Ever Known* for him. Mrs. Armstrong's essay below demonstrates her skill at discussing religious subjects.

Every year right after Halloween, the world becomes Christmas-conscious — and people begin deploring. If only we could have a *real* Christmas, they say. The good old kind. Quiet, inexpensive, simple, devout. If only we could retrieve the holy day from the hands of vulgar moneygrubbers, they say. They say, with earnest horror, that the price tag has become the liturgical symbol of the season. 1

As a Christian, I do find facets of the Christmas season ridiculous, offensive or disturbing, but I believe most complaints about the commercialization of Christmas are unconsciously hypocritical nonsense. I'm afraid that often the complainers are kidding themselves, striking spiritual poses. I'm not ashamed to admit that if I had to spend Christmas somewhere far from the crowd and the vulgar trappings, I'd hate it. I love the lights, the exquisite ones in *boutiques,* the joyful ones in village centers, even the awkward ones strung on drugstores and filling stations. I love the Santa Clauses, including those on street corners, the intricately animated windows, the hot bewilderment of the bargain basement, the sequins of the dime store. Cut off from the whole wild confusion, I'd not be holier. I'd be forlorn. So, I suspect, would most of us. 2

What's supposed to be wrong with a commercialized Christmas? 3

For one thing, it's usually said that Christmas has become the time of parties where people drink and eat too much. ("Turning Yuletide into fooltide" — that exact phrase was used to describe the holiday in Merrie Olde England, so those who yearn for the "good old Christmas" should carefully define their terms.) Oddly enough, it seems to me that often the people who most loudly criticize this holiday partying are those folks who acquire Christmas hangovers and indigestion. And they deplore it as if no one ever had to avoid hangovers, indigestion or exhaustion at any other time of the year. 4

They say that commercialization has made the buying of Christmas presents a rat race. God knows, most of the gifts we peddle to each other have nothing to do with the infant of Bethlehem. For my part, I enjoy gawking in the catalogues at the new luxuries for people who have everything. My imagination romps over items for my private Ostentatious Wastefulness list: silver-plated golf clubs, hundred-dollar dresses for little girls to spill ice cream on. Dime and department stores are crammed with gifts no wise man would bring anyone. Things like stuffed dinosaurs twelve feet high and replicas of the *Pietà* that glow in the dark. 5

With rare exceptions it is foolishly pompous to get scandalized and accuse manufacturers, advertisers and vendors of desecrating Christmas by trying to sell what you or I may think is silly junk. Obviously some people like it and buy it, and that's their business. It's said to be the fault of the commercializers that parents buy overpriced, unnecessary toys for children. And that's a fancy alibi. If you don't like what's being hawked this Christmas, you don't have to buy it. And if you're a sucker, your problem isn't seasonal. 6

Christians began giving presents to each other to celebrate Jesus' birthday in imitation of the Wise Men who came to Bethlehem. The basic idea was and is to bring joy, to honor God in others, and to give in His name with love for all. But in our social structure, with or without the blessings of the Internal Revenue Service, Christmas presents serve many purposes. Gift givers are, in practice, often diplomats, almoners, egoists, or investors. A shiny box with gold ribbon may be a guilt assuager, a bribe, a bid for attention, or merely payment for services past or future. And what is in the box must look rightly lavish, conveying subliminal impact while not costing too much. That kind of petty ugliness we all know about. And we know that often, too, gift givers play Santa Claus against their will, badgered by cozy reminders in the parking lot about how the boys wish you Season's Greetings, or by collections taken up in offices, clubs, Sunday schools, Scouts and third grades. 7

But are extortion, begging, status seeking and advantage taking so unusual among us that they occur only once a year? Isn't it more realistic to admit that whatever is sleazy about Christmas isn't seasonal? 8

After all, the instinct and art of commercialization are neither good nor bad. People normally, naturally, make a living from every kind of want, aspiration and occasion. We exploit births, weddings, deaths, first communions, bar mitzvahs, the wish to smell nice, the craving for amusement, and the basic desires for housing, clothes, love and

Section 3: Refutation

food. Is anything more commercialized than food? But no one complains when millions cash in on our need to eat.

Do we assume that eating is so earthy and undignified that commercialization upgrades it, while celebrating Christmas should be so totally ethereal a process that it shouldn't be treated in a human way? If so, we are both pretentious and mistaken. We are creatures who both eat and worship, and God doesn't want us as split personalities. When Christ once raised a little girl from death, the next thing He did was to tell her mother to feed her.

Simony is a sin, the sin of trying to buy or sell what is sacred. But this is not simony or sin, this peddling of manger sets, this pitchman heralding the season. No one can buy or sell Christmas. No one can steal it from us, or ruin it for us, except ourselves. If we become self-seeking, materialistic, harried and ill-willed in this Christmas melee, that's our problem, not the fault of the world in which we live.

Some people are dismayed today in a different way, because they honestly fear Christmas is being de-Christianized, made nonsectarian. They are upset when someone who does not share their faith sets up a tree and exchanges gifts and wishes them "Season's Greetings" instead of naming the holy day. They resent the spelling "Xmas." Others fret over the way Santa Claus and snowmen crowd out the shepherds. Put Christ back into Christmas, these offended people cry.

As far as I know, Christ never left it. He could never be cut out of Christmas, except in the privacy of individual hearts. I don't care if some people designate Xmas as the Time for Eggnog, or Toys. Let them call it the Time to Buy New Appliances, the Time to Use the Phone, or the Time for New Loans. The antics of the rest of the world can't change Christmas. Why on earth should we expect everyone to share our special joy our way?

Actually, what bothers most people who decry the vulgar American Christmas is a matter of taste, not of morals or of religious commitment. Taste is a very personal matter, relative, changing and worldly; we're all a rather tacky lot anyway, religious or not. Some Christians like those new stark liturgical Christmas cards, and some dote on luminous plastic crèches, and I hate both, and the Lord doesn't care a bit. Maybe you can't stand Rudolf, are bored with the same old carols, and cringe at Santa in a helicopter. But don't blame your discomfort on commercialization and become righteous and indignant. After all, if your taste is better than that of most other people, you're probably proud of it, and you should be willing to suffer the consequences in kindly forbearance.

I believe the root of complaints about commercialized Christmas is that we're falling into the dangerous habit of thinking that religion is somehow coarsened by contact with real people. I suspect that unconsciously we're embarrassed at the prospect of trying to live with God here and now. At times we modern Christians seem to have a neurotic refusal to embrace reality in the name of the Lord who was the supreme realist, and maker of the real. 15

It's always easier, if you're not doing very well religiously, to insist that the secularizing world prevents you from devotion. Christmas is meant to be lived in the noisy arena of the shopping day countdown, amid aluminum trees, neckties and counterfeit French perfume. If all the meditation I get around to is listening to Scrooge and Tiny Tim, or begging heaven for patience to applaud a school pageant, I'm a fool to blame anyone but myself. Census time in Bethlehem was distracting too. 16

I know a man who confides that he learns more about patience and love of his neighbor in post-office lines than anywhere else. More than one mother has learned that Christmas shopping on a tight budget can be a lesson in mortification, humility, willpower and joy. There's grist for meditation in the reflection of tree lights in a sloshy puddle. Families have their own customs, their private windows on glory. And families that are honest and relaxed find that the commercially generated atmosphere of goodwill hinders them not at all in their celebration. God works in wondrous ways still, even among assemble-it-yourself toys. 17

Christmas is a parable of the whole Christian venture. The Christian's attitude toward it, his willingness to make it relevant repeatedly in his own time and space, is a symptom of his whole encounter with God. The first Christmas happened, so Christians believe, because God lovingly plunged Himself into human nature to transform it. He is not honored by men and women who want to disown other people's human nature in His name. 18

Let's not make the mealy-mouthed error of complaining that paganism threatens Christmas today. Christmas has already absorbed and recharged the vestiges of Druid feasts, Norse gods and sun worship. Christmas took the world as it was and built on it, and it's still doing just that. 19

To those who fear that Christmas is prostituted by the almighty dollar, I suggest that it's remarkable and beautiful that Christmas is publicly touted at all. Nor do I make that suggestion, as some might suspect, in a tone of meek appeasement to groups that object to Christmas celebrations in public schools, or crèches in town squares.

Section 3: Refutation

Realistically, I know that in our society what is important to people and concerns them deeply, whether it's cancer or get-rich-quick schemes, patriotism or religion, is talked about and exploited. 20

If Christmas becomes for some people primarily a subject for commercials, at least God is getting equal time with toothpaste. If people didn't care about Him, He wouldn't even get that. 21

In good taste or bad, by your standards or mine, the fact of Christ, the good news of the meeting of heaven and earth, the tidings of love and peace for human nature, are announced everywhere. It is still true that he who has ears to hear will hear. 22

Discussion: Content

1. In paragraphs 4–8 Armstrong notes that people who deplore the commercialism of Christmas do so because they feel that the real meaning of Christmas has been lost as a result of three kinds of human activity. What are they?
2. In the remainder of the essay Armstrong examines another common objection. What is it?
3. To make her argument succeed, Armstrong must demonstrate not only her knowledge of the development of Christian traditions, but also her religious background. Where in the essay does she demonstrate these?
4. What does Armstrong mean when she says that Christmas is a parable of the whole Christian venture?
5. Why does Armstrong take it as a hopeful sign that Christmas has become commercialized?

Discussion: Form

1. In refuting the notion that the commercialization of Christmas tempts people to purchase overpriced, unnecessary junk, Armstrong responds that such an argument is a fancy alibi, that if a person is a sucker, the problem isn't seasonal. What fallacy is she pointing out?
2. What about the suggestion that Christmas gifts are a form of extortion, begging, status seeking, or advantage taking? How does Armstrong refute this one?
3. By pointing out that commercialism is found objectionable only during Christmas season, while the commercialism attendant on

other occasions — such as births, deaths, and weddings — is judged acceptable, Armstrong is pointing up what fallacy?
4. How is the claim that the commercialization of Christmas is in bad taste an example of the bandwagon fallacy?
5. In paragraph 9, Armstrong begins to construct her final argument. What proposition is she refuting, and how does she go about it?

A Modest Proposal
Jonathan Swift

Jonathan Swift (1667–1745) is the author of numerous poems, essays, and political tracts. He is best known for *Gulliver's Travels* (1726), one of the foremost satirical works in the English language. Swift's penchant for satire is also readily evident in "A Modest Proposal," which first appeared in 1729. Also evident is his genuine concern for the suffering poor of Ireland, where he labored as an Anglican priest, eventually attaining the deanship of St. Patrick's in Dublin.

It is a melancholy object to those who walk through this great town [Dublin], or travel in the country, when they see the streets, the roads, and cabin-doors, crowded with beggars of the female sex, followed by three, four, or six children, all in rags, and importuning every passenger for an alms. These mothers, instead of being able to work for their honest livelihood, are forced to employ all their time in strolling to beg sustenance for their helpless infants; who, as they grow up, either turn thieves for want of work, or leave their dear native country to fight for the Pretender in Spain, or sell themselves to the Barbadoes. 1

I think it is agreed by all parties, that this prodigious number of children in the arms, or on the backs, or at the heels of their mothers, and frequently of their fathers, is, in the present deplorable state of the kingdom, a very great additional grievance; and, therefore, whoever could find out a fair, cheap, and easy method of making these children sound, useful members of the commonwealth, would deserve so well of the public, as to have his statue set up for a preserver of the nation. 2

But my intention is very far from being confined to provide only for the children of professed beggars; it is of a much greater extent, and shall take in the whole number of infants at a certain age, who are

Section 3: Refutation

born of parents in effect as little able to support them, as those who demand our charity in the streets.

As to my own part, having turned my thoughts for many years upon this important subject, and maturely weighed the several schemes of our projectors, I have always found them grossly mistaken in their computation. It is true, a child, just dropped from its dam, may be supported by her milk for a solar year, with little other nourishment; at most, not above the value of two shillings, which the mother may certainly get, or the value in scraps, by her lawful occupation of begging; and it is exactly at one year old that I proposed to provide for them in such a manner, as, instead of being a charge upon their parents, or the parish, or wanting food and raiment for the rest of their lives, they shall, on the contrary, contribute to the feeding and partly to the clothing, of many thousands.

There is likewise another great advantage in my scheme, that it will prevent those voluntary abortions, and that horrid practice of women murdering their bastard children, alas, too frequent among us! sacrificing the poor innocent babes, I doubt more to avoid the expense than the shame, which would move tears and pity in the most savage and inhuman breast.

The number of souls in this kingdom being usually reckoned one million and a half, of these I calculate there may be about two hundred thousand couple whose wives are breeders; from which number I subtract thirty thousand couple, who are able to maintain their own children (although I apprehend there cannot be so many, under the present distresses of the kingdom); but this being granted, there will remain a hundred and seventy thousand breeders. I again subtract fifty thousand, for those women who miscarry, or whose children die by accident or disease within the year. There only remain a hundred and twenty thousand children of poor parents annually born. The question therefore is, How this number shall be reared and provided for? which, as I have already said, under the present situation of affairs, is utterly impossible by all the methods hitherto proposed. For we can neither employ them in handicraft, or agriculture; we neither build houses (I mean in the country,) nor cultivate land: they can very seldom pick up a livelihood by stealing, till they arrive at six years old, except where they are of towardly parts; although I confess they learn the rudiments much earlier; during which time they can, however, be properly looked upon only as probationers; as I have been informed by a principal gentleman in the county of Cavan, who protested to me, that he never knew above one or two instances under the age of six, even in a part of the kingdom so renowned for the quickest proficiency in that art.

I am assured by our merchants, that a boy or a girl before twelve years old is no saleable commodity; and even when they come to this age they will not yield above three pounds, or three pounds and a half-a-crown at most, on the exchange; which cannot turn to account either to the parents or kingdom, the charge of nutriment and rags having been at least four times that value.

I shall now, therefore, humbly propose my own thoughts, which I hope will not be liable to the least objection.

I have been assured by a very knowing American of my acquaintance in London, that a young healthy child, well nursed, is, at a year old, a most delicious, nourishing, and wholesome food, whether stewed, roasted, baked, or boiled; and I make no doubt that it will equally serve in a fricassee or a ragout.

I do therefore humbly offer it to public consideration, that of the hundred and twenty thousand children already computed, twenty thousand may be reserved for breed, whereof only one-fourth part to be males; which is more than we allow to sheep, black-cattle, or swine; and my reason is, that these children are seldom the fruits of marriage, a circumstance not much regarded by our savages, therefore one male will be sufficient to serve four females. That the remaining hundred thousand may, at a year old, be offered in sale to the persons of quality and fortune through the kingdom; always advising the mother to let them suck plentifully in the last month, so as to render them plump and fat for a good table. A child will make two dishes at an entertainment for friends; and when the family dines alone, the fore or hind quarter will make a reasonable dish, and, seasoned with a little pepper or salt, will be very good boiled on the fourth day, especially in winter.

I have reckoned, upon a medium, that a child just born will weigh twelve pounds, and in a solar year, if tolerably nursed, will increase to twenty-eight pounds.

I grant this food will be somewhat dear, and therefore very proper for landlords, who, as they have already devoured most of the parents, seem to have the best title to the children.

Infants' flesh will be in season throughout the year, but more plentifully in March, and a little before and after: for we are told by a grave author, an eminent French physician, that fish being a prolific diet, there are more children born in Roman Catholic countries about nine months after Lent, than at any other season; therefore, reckoning a year after Lent, the markets will be more glutted than usual, because the number of Popish infants is at least three to one in this kingdom; and therefore it will have one other collateral advantage, by lessening the number of Papists among us.

Section 3: Refutation

I have already computed the charge of nursing a beggar's child (in which list I reckon all cottagers, labourers, and four-fifths of the farmers) to be about two shillings per annum, rags included; and I believe no gentleman would repine to give ten shillings for the carcass of a good fat child, which, as I have said, will make four dishes of excellent nutritive meat, when he has only some particular friend, or his own family, to dine with him. Thus the squire will learn to be a good landlord, and grow popular among his tenants; the mother will have eight shillings net profit, and be fit for work till she produces another child. 14

Those who are more thrifty (as I must confess the times require) may flay the carcass; the skin of which, artificially dressed, will make admirable gloves for ladies, and summer-boots for fine gentlemen. 15

As to our city of Dublin, shambles [slaughter houses] may be appointed for this purpose in the most convenient parts of it, and butchers, we may be assured, will not be wanting; although I rather recommend buying the children alive, then dressing them hot from the knife, as we do roasting pigs. 16

A very worthy person, a true lover of his country, and whose virtues I highly esteem, was lately pleased, in discoursing on this matter, to offer a refinement upon my scheme. He said, that many gentlemen of this kingdom, having of late destroyed their deer, he conceived that the want of venison might be well supplied by the bodies of young lads and maidens, not exceeding fourteen years of age, nor under twelve; so great a number of both sexes in every country being now ready to starve for want of work and service; and these to be disposed of by their parents, if alive, or otherwise by their nearest relations. But, with due deference to so excellent a friend, and so deserving a patriot, I cannot be altogether in his sentiments; for as to the males, my American acquaintance assured me, from frequent experience, that their flesh was generally tough and lean, like that of our schoolboys, by continual exercise, and their taste disagreeable; and to fatten them would not answer the charge. Then as to the females, it would, I think, with humble submission, be a loss to the public, because they soon would become breeders themselves: and besides, it is not improbable that some scrupulous people might be apt to censure such a practice (although indeed very unjustly), as a little bordering upon cruelty; which, I confess, has always been with me the strongest objection against any project, how well soever intended. 17

But in order to justify my friend, he confessed that this expedient was put into his head by the famous Psalmanazar, a native of the island Formosa, who came from thence to London above twenty years ago; and in conversation told my friend, that in his country, when any young person happened to be put to death, the executioner sold the carcass to persons of quality as a prime dainty; and that in his time the body of a plump girl of fifteen, who was crucified for an attempt to poison the emperor, was sold to his imperial majesty's prime minister of state, and other great mandarins of the court, in joints from the gibbet, at four hundred crowns. Neither indeed can I deny, that, if the same use were made of several plump young girls in this town, who, without one single groat to their fortunes, cannot stir abroad without a chair, and appear at playhouse and assemblies in foreign fineries which they never will pay for, the kingdom would not be the worse.

Some persons of a desponding spirit are in great concern about that vast number of poor people, who are aged, diseased, or maimed; and I have been desired to employ my thoughts, what course may be taken to ease the nation of so grievous an encumbrance. But I am not in the least pain upon that matter, because it is very well known, that they are every day dying, and rotting, by cold and famine, and filth and vermin, as fast as can be reasonably expected. And as to the young labourers, they are now in almost as hopeful a condition: they cannot get work, and consequently pine away for want of nourishment, to a degree, that if at any time they are accidentally hired to common labour, they have not strength to perform it; and thus the country and themselves are happily delivered from the evils to come.

I have too long digressed, and therefore shall return to my subject. I think the advantages by the proposal which I have made are obvious and many, as well as of the highest importance.

For first, as I have already observed, it would greatly lessen the number of Papists, with whom we are yearly over-run, being the principal breeders of the nation, as well as our most dangerous enemies; and who stay at home on purpose to deliver the kingdom to the Pretender, hoping to take their advantage by the absence of so many good Protestants, who have chosen rather to leave their country than stay at home and pay tithes against their conscience to an Episcopal curate.

Secondly, The poorer tenants will have something valuable of their own, which by law may be made liable to distress, and help to pay their landlord's rent; their corn and cattle being already seized, and money a thing unknown.

Thirdly, Whereas the maintenance of a hundred thousand children, from two years old and upward, cannot be computed at less than ten shillings a piece per annum, the nation's stock will be thereby increased fifty thousand pounds per annum, beside the profit of a new

Section 3: Refutation

dish introduced to the tables of all gentlemen of fortune in the kingdom, who have any refinement in taste. And the money will circulate among ourselves, the goods being entirely of our own growth and manufacture.

Fourthly, The constant breeders, beside the gain of eight shillings sterling per annum by the sale of their children, will be rid of the charge of maintaining them after the first year.

Fifthly, This food would likewise bring great custom to taverns; where the vintners will certainly be so prudent as to procure the best receipts for dressing it to perfection, and, consequently, have their houses frequented by all the fine gentlemen, who justly value themselves upon their knowledge in good eating; and a skilful cook, who understands how to oblige his guests, will contrive to make it as expensive as they please.

Sixthly, This would be a great inducement to marriage, which all wise nations have either encouraged by rewards, or enforced by laws and penalties. It would increase the care and tenderness of mothers toward their children, when they were sure of a settlement for life to the poor babes, provided in some sort by the public, to their annual profit or expense. We should see an honest emulation among the married women, which of them could bring the fattest child to the market. Men would become as fond of their wives during the time of their pregnancy as they are now of their mares in foal, their cows in calf, their sows when they are ready to farrow; nor offer to beat or kick them (as is too frequent a practice) for fear of a miscarriage.

Many other advantages might be enumerated. For instance, the addition of some thousand carcasses in our exportation of barrelled beef; the propagation of swine's flesh, and improvement in the art of making good bacon, so much wanted among us by the great destruction of pigs, too frequent at our table; which are no way comparable in taste or magnificence to a well-grown, fat, yearling child, which, roasted whole, will make a considerable figure at a lord mayor's feast, or any other public entertainment. But this, and many others, I omit, being studious of brevity.

Supposing that one thousand families in this city would be constant customers for infants' flesh, beside others who might have it at merry-meetings, particularly at weddings and christenings, I compute that Dublin would take off annually about twenty thousand carcasses; and the rest of the kingdom (where probably they will be sold somewhat cheaper) the remaining eighty thousand.

I can think of no one objection, that will possibly be raised against this proposal, unless it should be urged, that the number of people will be thereby much lessened in the kingdom. This I freely own, and it was indeed one principal design in offering it to the world. I desire the reader will observe, that I calculate my remedy for this one individual kingdom of Ireland, and for no other that ever was, is, or I think ever can be, upon earth. Therefore let no man talk to me of other expedients: of taxing our absentees at five shillings a pound: of using neither clothes, nor household furniture, except what is our own growth and manufacture: of utterly rejecting the materials and instruments that promote foreign luxury: of curing the expensiveness of pride, vanity, idleness, and gaming in our women: of introducing a vein of parsimony, prudence, and temperance: of learning to love our country, in the want of which we differ even from Laplanders, and the inhabitants of Topinamboo: of quitting our animosities and factions, nor acting any longer like the Jews, who were murdering one another at the very moment their city was taken: of being a little cautious not to sell our country and conscience for nothing: of teaching landlords to have at least one degree of mercy toward their tenants: lastly, of putting a spirit of honesty, industry, and skill into our shopkeepers; who, if a resolution could now be taken to buy only our native goods, would immediately unite to cheat and exact upon us in the price, the measure, and the goodness, nor could ever yet be brought to make one fair proposal of just dealing, though often and earnestly invited to it.

Therefore I repeat, let no man talk to me of these and the like expedients, till he has at least some glimpse of hope, that there will be ever some hearty and sincere attempt to put them in practice.

But, as to myself, having been wearied out for many years with offering vain, idle, visionary thoughts, and at length utterly despairing of success, I fortunately fell upon this proposal; which, as it is wholly new, so it has something solid and real, of no expense and little trouble, full in our own power, and whereby we can incur no danger in disobliging England. For this kind of commodity will not bear exportation, the flesh being of too tender a consistence to admit a long continuance in salt, although perhaps I could name a country, which would be glad to eat up our whole nation without it.

After all, I am not so violently bent upon my own opinions as to reject any offer proposed by wise men, which shall be found equally innocent, cheap, easy, and effectual. But before something of that kind shall be advanced in contradiction to my scheme, and offering a better, I desire the author, or authors, will be pleased maturely to consider two points. First as things now stand, how they will be able to find food and raiment for a hundred thousand useless mouths and backs. And, secondly, there being a round million of creatures in human figure throughout this kingdom, whose whole subsistence put into a common stock would leave them in debt two millions of pounds sterling, adding those who are beggars by profession, to the bulk of farmers, cottagers, and labourers, with the wives and children who are beggars in effect; I desire those politicians who dislike my overture, and may perhaps be so bold as to attempt an answer, that they will first ask the parents of these mortals, whether they would not at this day think it a great happiness to have been sold for food at a year old, in the manner I prescribe, and thereby have avoided such a perpetual scene of misfortunes, as they have since gone through, by the oppression of landlords, the impossibility of paying rent without money or trade, the want of common sustenance, with neither house nor clothes to cover them from the inclemencies of the weather, and the most inevitable prospect of entailing the like, or greater miseries, upon their breed for ever. 32

I profess, in the sincerity of my heart, that I have not the least personal interest in endeavouring to promote this necessary work, having no other motive than the public good of my country, by advancing our trade, providing for infants, relieving the poor, and giving some pleasure to the rich. I have no children by which I can propose to get a single penny; the youngest being nine years old, and my wife past child-bearing. 33

Discussion: Content

1. What problem does Swift intend to remedy by his proposal?
2. How does Swift reckon the number of children who will be available yearly to supply his plan?
3. What are some of the advantages that Swift asserts will arise from his proposal?
4. What additional proposal, similar to his first, does Swift put forward tentatively and then reject?
5. How does Swift propose to cure the suffering of the older Irishmen?
6. With what disclaimer does Swift conclude his proposal?

Discussion: Form

1. Swift's modest proposal is so absolutely outrageous as not to be taken seriously. It is obviously a kind of reduction-to-absurdity attack on some commonly held position of his time or an alternative to some less ridiculous plan that has been ignored or rejected. Do you find evidence of either case in the essay?

2. How does Swift slant or color his language to make the slaughter of children seem somehow less than brutal?
3. Swift accuses himself of digression in paragraph 20. What actually constituted the digression, and what purpose, if any, did it serve?
4. *Tone* (see p. 460 in the Glossary) is crucial to the success of "A Modest Proposal," starting with the words chosen for the title and following through to the essay's conclusion. How would you describe the tone, and what are some specific ways Swift's tone contributes to the success of his essay?

Section 4: Emotional Appeals

By now you will probably have read "A Brief Introduction to Common Logical Fallacies," which begins on p. 434 in the Appendix. If you have not, now is an excellent time to do so. The discussions of such fallacies as *appeal to pity* and *appeal to the people* are likely to convince you that there is an inherent weakness in arguments that play on people's sympathies and prejudices. After all, we have pointed out these fallacies, and in the preceding section we showed how some of them could be used in refuting arguments. That was the purpose of discussing fallacies, wasn't it?

The answer to that question is a guarded "yes." We do like to believe that arguments that are free from both formal and informal fallacies and appeal to our reason rather than to our emotions are the best kind. This is true because we are logical, reasoning beings. But we also cry at movies. We also like to be flattered; we want to feel good. And these very natural, very human tendencies are in many cases very likely to overrule our reason.

It is because of this likelihood that emotional appeals prove to be so effective. We are bored by television commercials that seek to prove through tedious induction that one pain reliever is more effective than another — that it contains more "active ingredients" or that it provides more "hours of long-lasting relief." We may silently resolve that the next time acid indigestion strikes, we will get the remedy that goes "plop, plop, fizz, fizz" instead of the one that shows us in sickening color how much stomach acid it can absorb. We also suspect that pretty girls in seductive apparel and employing the fallacy of *transfer* (see p.444) have sold more automobiles than serious gentlemen in business suits, convincingly armed with fuel-consumption statistics.

The paragraphs and essays in the following pages offer some examples of unabashed emotional appeals. We make no apology for that since we feel that for purposes of instruction you should see some purely emotional arguments, ones that have not been much contaminated by logic or evidence. We strongly suggest, however, that the best approach to persuasion is one that appeals both to reason and to emotions. And that is not just our recommendation but Cicero's too. Remember that in his model argument, Cicero demanded that the propositions were to be proved rationally, but he reserved the concluding, and hence the most climactic, portion, for emotional appeals.

Paragraphs:
Emotional Appeals

Dunkirk
Winston Churchill

I have, myself, full confidence that if all do their duty, if nothing is neglected, and if the best arrangements are made, as they are being made, we shall prove ourselves once again able to defend our Island home, to ride out the storm of war, and to outlive the menace of tyranny, if necessary for years, if necessary alone. At any rate, that is what we are going to try to do. That is the resolve of His Majesty's Government — every man of them. That is the will of Parliament and the nation. The British Empire and the French Republic, linked together in their cause and in their need, will defend to the death their native soil, aiding each other like good comrades to the utmost of their strength. Even though large tracts of Europe and many old and famous States have fallen or may fall into the grip of the Gestapo and all the odious apparatus of Nazi rule, we shall not flag or fail. We shall go on to the end, we shall fight in France, we shall fight on the seas and oceans, we shall fight with growing confidence and growing strength in the air, we shall defend our Island, whatever the cost may be, we shall fight on the beaches, we shall fight on the landing grounds, we shall fight in the fields and in the streets, we shall fight in the hills; we shall never surrender, and even if, which I do not for a moment believe, this Island or a large part of it were subjugated and starving, then our Empire beyond the seas, armed and guarded by the British Fleet, would carry on the struggle, until, in God's good time, the New World, with all its power and might, steps forth to the rescue and the liberation of the old.

Discussion Questions

1. What is Dunkirk? What does it have to do with Churchill's statements here?

2. What is the effect of the long succession of clauses, each beginning "we shall fight . . ."?
3. Underline those words and expressions which you find to be especially emotion-charged.
4. What is Churchill's ultimate objective? Where does he state it?

Liberty or Death
Patrick Henry

It is vain, sir, to extenuate the matter. Gentlemen may cry, peace, peace — but there is no peace. The war is actually begun! The next gale that sweeps from the north will bring to our ears the clash of resounding arms! Our brethren are already in the field! Why stand we here idle? What is it that gentlemen wish? What would they have? Is life so dear, or peace so sweet, as to be purchased at the price of chains and slavery? Forbid it, Almighty God! I know not what course others may take; but as for me, give me liberty or give me death!

Discussion Questions

1. Patrick Henry, the governor of Virginia during the American Revolution, made his famous speech, of which this is the concluding paragraph, on March 23, 1775, before the convention which was to decide whether the colony of Virginia would participate in the planned rebellion against Great Britain. What reasons does Henry give in this paragraph for joining the rebellion?
2. Examine the list of material fallacies in the "Brief Introduction to Common Logical Fallacies," pp. 439–444. How many of them does Henry appear to be guilty of here? Nevertheless, this speech, known to every schoolchild, is one of the foremost examples of effective oratory. How do you account for that?
3. Less than a month after Henry delivered this address to the Virginia Revolutionary Convention, the battles of Concord and Lexington in New England marked the outbreak of hostilities that led to war, thus making one portion of this paragraph especially prophetic — which portion?
4. Does Henry expect answers to the three questions he asks? What is the effect of these questions? (Hint: Look up *rhetorical question* in the Glossary.)

Section 4:
Emotional Appeals

Henry V's Speech at Agincourt
William Shakespeare

For his history play, *The Life of Henry the Fifth,* William Shakespeare wrote the speech below, to be spoken by the great English warrior-king, Henry V, before the battle at Agincourt, France, in October 1415, where the English were outnumbered five to one. The speech, familiarly called "The St. Crispin's Day Speech," is in Early Modern English of about 1600, and also in the poetic form called blank verse, but the strength of its emotional appeal still comes through despite these constraints. (You will want to compare this speech to the famous one that begins this section, also by a great English leader, Sir Winston Churchill, speaking during World War II about the English forces at Dunkirk, France.) As the English forces are about to enter the battle (and win decisively), King Henry speaks:

> . . . he which hath no stomach to* this fight,
> Let him depart. His passport shall be made
> And crowns for convoy* put into his purse.
> We would not die in that man's company
> That fears his fellowship to die with us.*   5
> This day is called the feast of Crispian:*
> He that outlives this day, and comes safe home,
> Will stand a-tiptoe* when this day is named,
> And rouse him at the name of Crispian.
> He that shall live* this day and see old age   10
> Will yearly on the vigil feast his neighbors*
> And say, "Tomorrow is Saint Crispian."
> Then will he strip* his sleeve and show his scars,
> And say, "These wounds I had on Crispin's Day."
> Old men forget; yet all shall be forgot,   15
> But he'll remember with advantages*
> What feats he did that day. Then shall our names,
> Familiar in his mouth as household words,
> Harry the King, Bedford and Exeter,

Notes: 1. *stomach to:* courage ("guts") for; 3. *crowns . . . convoy:* money for transportation; 5. *fears . . . us:* is afraid to share death with us; 6. *Crispian:* St. Crispin's Day is October 25. Crispin and Crispian were early Christian martyrs; 8. *a-tiptoe:* straight, tall; 10. *live:* survive; 11. *yearly . . . neighbors:* host an annual public dinner the evening before St. Crispin's Day; 13. *strip:*

Argumentative Writing

Warwick and Talbot, Salisbury and Gloucester, 20
Be in their flowing cups* freshly remembered.
This story shall the good man teach his son,
And Crispin Crispian shall ne'er go by,
From this day to the ending of the world,
But we in it shall be remembered — 25
We few, we happy few, we band of brothers;
For he today that sheds his blood with me
Shall be my brother; be he ne'er so vile,*
This day shall gentle his condition.*
And gentlemen in England now abed* 30
Shall think themselves accursed they were not here,
And hold their manhoods cheap whiles* any speaks
That fought with us upon Saint Crispin's Day.

(Act IV, Scene iii)

Discussion Questions

1. To what emotion is King Henry appealing in lines 1–5?
2. How might you characterize other basic human emotions that the king exploits?
3. What emotion is triggered by the last four lines?

Shame
Malcolm X

As long as the white man sent you to Korea, you bled. He sent you to Germany, you bled. He sent you to the South Pacific to fight the Japanese, you bled. You bleed for white people, but when it comes to seeing your own church being bombed and little black girls murdered, you haven't got any blood. You bleed when the white man says bleed; you bite when the white man says bite; and you bark when the white man says bark.

roll up, raise; 16. *advantages:* embellishments; 21. *in . . . cups:* as toasts are drunk; 28. *vile:* lower class; 29. *gentle . . . condition:* raise him to a gentleman's rank; 30. *abed:* asleep; 32. *hold . . . whiles:* think themselves less than men while.

Discussion Questions

1. Malcolm X mentions a church being bombed and little girls murdered. What event is he probably referring to?
2. What is the effect of the repetitions Malcolm uses in his delivery?
3. What device does Malcolm use in the last sentence to heighten the feeling of shame that he wishes to instill in his audience?

Student Work:
Emotional Appeals

Guns for Self-Defense

Of all the reasons why an American's right to own guns should never be challenged, there is a very personal one that for me outweighs all the rest. I want to protect my home. My home, my family, and our possessions mean more to me than all the constitutional and humanitarian claims of the gun controllers put together. Their arguments look good on paper, and they sound good when you hear them. But you can bet your next paycheck that they would each like to have a .38 in a drawer by their bed the next time they hear the tinkle of breaking glass and know that somewhere in their home there is a thief, a rapist, or a murderer.

Discussion Questions

1. A contrast is the basis of the argument in "Guns for Self-Defense." What is the contrast between?
2. What specific factors of the writer's stance or tone, word choice, and organization make the last sentence of this paragraph so emotionally appealing?
3. Does this paragraph's argument have any basis in logic, or is it totally emotional? How might this argument be refuted, if at all?

All Reasons but One

I agree that rape victims should have the right to abortions on demand. And I also agree that victims of incest should have the same right. I am even sympathetic with the mother who cannot afford to raise another unplanned child. And I do not think that the high school or college girl should have to be the victim of a tragic sexual accident, one that the male partner can walk away from uninjured. I can find abortion acceptable in a good many situations which do not endanger the mother's life. All but one. I'm glad my mother didn't have one.

Discussion Questions

1. What is the purpose of the first five sentences in this paragraph? Do they establish any emotional rapport with the audience?
2. Are there any additional reasons for supporting abortion that the writer has neglected to mention?
3. What is grammatically wrong with the next to last sentence? How would you correct that flaw? Or if you were the student writer, what might you say in defense of your original choice?
4. Why is the last sentence so effective?

Preserve Joyner Hall

The Joyner Building should not be torn down; instead it should be restored and preserved. After all, it is the oldest building on the campus, and that makes it even more important. You cannot walk through its cool hallways without being reminded of all the traditions that through the years have come to be such a large part of student life. The creak of your foot on the wooden stairway is a gentle reminder that we have allowed this symbol of our campus to deteriorate. Joyner houses memories for my parents, who were members of the class of '53. They attended classes in it, studied in it when its upper floors were the library, and were graduated in the grove in front of it. They pay it a visit when they return each year for homecoming. And I hope it will still be around when this member of the class of '82 comes back to pay his respects.

Discussion Questions

1. Underscore the words or expressions in "Preserve Joyner Hall" that are specifically intended to arouse the reader's emotions.
2. Who is the intended audience for this paragraph?
3. As an argument, "Preserve Joyner Hall" is not very successful, but it does arouse the reader's emotions and as such would prove to be an excellent conclusion for a longer argument. What kinds of reasoned arguments might precede this emotional appeal?

Cafeteria Food

Enough is enough! It's time to do something about the food in the school cafeterias. I and my friends are tired of paying for slop disguised as food, and we think if they can't serve food fit for humans to eat, something should be done. 1

For one thing, serving hot dogs for lunch three times a week is overdoing it. Also, the chili on the hot dogs is so blah that you need hot pepper sauce just to wake it up. Why can't we have hamburgers more often instead? 2

For another thing, I think a person should have unlimited refills of iced tea. It's very inexpensive to make (my mother makes a pot from one tea bag, which costs about a cent and a half), and that rule change would probably lead people to choose it instead of soda or milk, both costing more. 3

Another major complaint is dessert. How come two cookies count the same as a piece of pie or of cake? Is that fair? I do not think so. 4

The meat choices have improved some since the September food fight, the time the choices were liver, fried bologna, and meatloaf that was half soymeal powder and half grease and people started flipping bits of their "choice" at other people with their forks and spoons. But the portion size sure isn't anything to brag about. 5

Also, the vegetables, which are cooked pretty well, are often served in weird combinations. Can you believe pizza with baked beans and sauerkraut? How about turnip greens or spinach (they look the same to me) and mashed potatoes (not french fries or Tater Tots) with hot dogs? I think the dietitian must have had an accident with her food choice wheels. 6

Before I forget, let me say something about breakfast. It's hopeless. Serving stops at 8:30, and since my first class is not until 10, I

Section 4:
Emotional Appeals

skip it on Tuesday and Thursday, even if it's already paid for. I mean, why get up for the same old things, eggs and bacon or cereal and toast? Never any omelets or waffles, except on the weekends, when I usually go home, and only rarely some ham or sweet rolls.

I could list plenty of other problems, but why go into more detail? It's probably a fact of life that cafeteria food is not going to be good, but they say the squealing wheel gets the grease. Maybe the complaining mouth will get some food for a change.

Discussion Questions

1. What seems to be the proposition in "Cafeteria Food" that its writer intends to prove?
2. How does the student go about proving that proposition? What is wrong or inconsistent in the practice of the chosen approach?
3. Despite the fact that the essay is not logically sound, it might still sway some readers. Why? What persons on the campus are likely not to be persuaded?

Rock Music and Me

My father is always criticizing me about my love of rock music. He says that it's meaningless, uncouth, and too loud to be enjoyable. On most other things we see eye to eye, but I doubt there will ever be much agreement on this score.

It very well may be that there is very little meaning attached to rock songs, but it's the music that moves me. When I can't make out the words of a new video that I've heard and enjoyed on Music Television, it's an added pleasure to go and buy the record so that I can read the lyrics on the record jacket. That's what my father does too when he listens to his grand opera records in Italian and German. So what's the big difference? He says it's the music that moves him too.

Rock music may be uncouth when compared with opera or symphony, but I don't think so. It's just different. My parents get enjoyment from listening to their records, and I get pleasure from mine. They like to dress up and go to operas and concerts, and so do I. But I really think that I get more out of it than they do. Last month when I got to go downstate to hear the Police in concert, I was the envy of all my friends. I got to see the group I most admire, and I actually got to touch one of them. And I got to be with thousands of other people who were just as excited as I was. When we screamed together, we were really adding to the performance, making it something more than the ones on TV.   3

Besides that, the fun didn't end there; I still get to rub it in with my friends who weren't there when they see the Police decal on the rear window of my car or when I wear my Synchronicity tee shirt that I got at the concert.   4

Finally, rock music is more than loudness. It's sparkle and dazzle, everything coming together and falling into place. It's reaching out and touching with a sound, words that don't appeal just to the ears but to the whole body. Rock doesn't make you want to tap your foot; it makes your whole body want to move; it makes you want to jump and twitch and scream, especially when you're there in person with thousands of people around you. Something electric begins to charge through the whole group, and it moves together.   5

You know sometimes how when somebody says something sentimental or you see a good poster with special words on it, the hairs on your arms start to prickle. Well, when the Police have just about reached the end of "Roxanne," and you think that the lead singer, Sting, has done about all that he can to hype you up and that it's going to be over and you'll feel a relief from the tension and you can scream and stamp and applaud — and instead of doing that he whirls around and ducks and goes into the theme again, this time *really* loud, and the other voices and instruments come in with even more volume — that's when it's prickles and not just your arm hairs, and you absolutely die.   6

And that's something my father will never understand.   7

Discussion Questions

1. Are all the writer's arguments based on an emotional appeal? Which ones are not?
2. How does the writer generate emotional appeal in the concluding paragraphs?
3. How effective is the concluding sentence?

Essays:
Emotional Appeals

Let My Son Play
Val Wilson

The essay below appeared in the March 14, 1983, issue of *Sports Illustrated,* bearing the following subtitle: "A Mother Whose Son Shines Only in Sports Laments His Clouded Future."

I've heard a lot of discussion lately about putting new restrictions on the eligibility requirements for participation in high school and college athletics. It has been suggested that kids who can't carry a C average should not be allowed to play high school sports or qualify for an athletic scholarship to college. It's a national disgrace, I've read, that high school boys and girls who can't even pass English are allowed to be on teams, just because they are good in sports. Some critics complain that colleges make it easier for sports stars to maintain their grades by allowing them to take only "easy" classes, like phys ed. My feeling is, why not?

I should admit right from the start that I'm not an impartial observer in this argument, but the mother of a son who has been labeled a "dumb jock." This is written, with pain, in his defense and in the defense of others like him.

Randy has never been good in school. I'm not exactly sure why. He was diagnosed by a school psychometrist as severely dyslexic, but I'm not completely comfortable with an explanation that seems to be a catchall for a whole collection of learning problems. Whatever the reason, despite his higher than average IQ, each of Randy's nine years in school — he repeated third grade and is now in eighth — has been a struggle.

Randy can tear a racing bike completely apart and put it back together; he can draw a good likeness of the human form; he can carry on an intelligent conversation on almost any subject; he conscientiously does his homework every night and studies hours for each test, but to no avail. He's still one of those kids who can't pass English. Randy is a standout in football, baseball, wrestling and track, but to his school the only thing that really matters is his grade-point average.

Randy played football this year, as a running back on offense and a linebacker on defense, and was first in yards per carry and second in tackles. His football statistics give him some pride in himself. If he feels small and anxious in the classroom, the gridiron is a place where he can shine. I don't know if he will get to play again. He was just pulled from the wrestling team because of his English grade. I know that participating in sports is supposed to be a carrot — an incentive for kids to measure up scholastically. But for some, like Randy, no matter how much they want the carrot, they simply aren't capable of making the grade.

Larry Bird was not a noted scholar in high school or in college — but he almost single-handedly took Indiana State to the NCAA finals in 1979. He went to the Boston Celtics after graduation and is acknowledged by many to be one of the all-time great basketball players. Basketball was his best subject. So what if he wasn't a genius in the classroom; he *is* a genius on the basketball court. Isn't that reason enough to let him play?

Americans like to think of athletics as endowed with the innocence of freckle-faced boys playing casual games of sandlot baseball. But in this we fool ourselves. Sports today mean multimillion-dollar TV contracts for colleges and universities with superior teams because fans enjoy watching outstanding young athletes perform. High school and college sports are virtually the only means by which a young person may enter professional athletics. Only a few especially talented boys and girls will ultimately succeed, but they deserve the opportunity to compete in their area of excellence, the same as aspiring engineers and economists do.

All kids don't excel in all areas. Is it fair to tell some that because they can't live up to the standards in the area that we have deemed most important, they don't deserve to participate in any other? What if the situation were reversed? Would it be just to tell a child he couldn't qualify for computer classes because he couldn't punt a football? Why must we classify our young people so rigidly? Why can't we let each boy and girl go in the direction that their natural talents take them? If it happens to be jumping a hurdle or dunking a basketball, so be it. Are we to reserve all the rewards for the lucky few who are able to master everything and deny for the others, like Randy, any pride in themselves? Do we tell kids like Randy — "If you can't do this one thing, you can't do anything?" Isn't it possible to give all of our children the feeling that they can belong, whether it be in scholastics or sports?

8

Discussion: Content

1. Why does Wilson argue for lowering or removing scholastic requirements for participation in high school and college sports?
2. Wilson's son Randy is *dyslexic*. What is his problem?
3. Why does Wilson fear that Randy's sports career will be blighted?
4. Why does Wilson single out Larry Bird to use as an example?
5. In addition to giving young athletes a chance to shine, why does Wilson feel that high school and college sports are so important?

Discussion: Form

1. Wilson may safely be accused of committing at least a couple of material fallacies in this essay — *appeal to pity* and *hypothesis contrary to fact*. Where do these fallacies occur?
2. How well does Wilson's argument survive these fallacies?
3. How does the illustration involving Larry Bird serve as a crucial transition on this piece?
4. How might you refute Wilson's claim that high school and college sports are virtually the only means of entry into the pro ranks?

Unnatural Metamorphosis
Ron Harley

Ron Harley is a journalist who has also worked for an advertising agency in St. Louis. His essay, given a title by the editors of this book, was originally printed in Harley's column, "Over Easy," in *Farm Quarterly*.

I would start with a valley — a green valley made of orchards and vineyards and fields of barley and oats. Sheep and cattle would graze on tall spring grass in the rolling hills and low mountains along the sides of the valley. And in the late afternoons, after the setting sun had softened the shadows and the subtle differences in hue, the greens would run together at the edges like watercolors.

The people who owned the animals and cultivated the crops would live in white houses at the ends of tree-lined lanes. And on the whole, they, like their fathers and grandfathers before them, would be happy in the valley.

I would bring in only a few bulldozers at first. But later, after the people in the white houses had become more accustomed to them, I would bring in more. A bulldozer is a versatile piece of machinery. You can push over a tree with a bulldozer, or level the ground for parking lots and freeways.

I would use some of the bulldozers to build a freeway through the valley. I would take my time — there would be no hurry — and I would use thick concrete reinforced with steel where necessary. A freeway, if it is built right, may last forever.

It is true that some of the farms and orchards would be cut into two pieces by the freeway, and that a few might be replaced by cloverleaf interchanges. But then there are other valleys where the soil is just as fertile. And with the freeway, a man would be able to drive all the way through the valley without stopping. I would plant some red oleander, which blooms all summer long, along the center strip. And with some ice plant along the sides and some three-year-old evergreens around the interchanges, the freeway would not look bad at all.

And when the freeway was finished, I would build some factories — low, sprawling concrete buildings with a contemporary look. And on the fronts of the buildings I would print some magic words like "aerospace" and "electronics" and "data processing."

On Sunday afternoons, the people who lived in the white houses would go for drives and they would see the places where the bulldozers had been working and they would see the new factories with the magic words. They would make smalltalk about progress and prosperity and perhaps, secretly, they would be a little proud.

The people who lived in the small valley towns would be proud too. And they would erect signs near the city limits that said "Industry Welcome" and "Watch Us Grow." The people in the chambers of commerce would talk about a "dynamic, growing, expanding marketplace."

Perhaps some of the people on the farms and in the towns would complain about the smog, but many would consider it a small price to pay.

I would bring in more bulldozers and I would clear more farmland for subdivisions and high-rise condominiums and shopping centers

Section 4:
Emotional Appeals

for the people who would be moving into the valley. And I would build a larger airport — with runways long enough for the biggest jets. If there were complaints about the noise, I would call in the slogan people and the new airport would become a place where "the roar of progress meets with the excitement of people." 10

It would be important to keep the people in the valley happy and so I would build golf courses and a football stadium that would seat thousands and a zoo that would contain "rare and exotic animals unblemished by captivity." Maybe I would even build a park where some of the fruit trees would be maintained. 11

And so that all of the people could get to all of the places they wanted to go, I would build more freeways and more expressways. And at each interchange, I would build motels, service stations, and franchised fried chicken restaurants. 12

And when all of the valley had been covered with concrete and asphalt and smog, and when the last motel had been erected at the last interchange, I would give the valley a new name. I would call it Hell. 13

Discussion: Content

1. Who or what does Harley oppose? Why? How accurate is his view of the effect of "progress"?
2. How is Harley's purpose, and the probable futility of it, related to Black Hawk's, pp. 423–425.
3. Why does Harley call certain terms in paragraph 6 "magic words"?
4. What is your reaction to the slogans mentioned in paragraphs 8, 10, and 11? Do you see any inconsistency in them?
5. Harley's essay was originally printed in a farm magazine. What in it would make it especially appealing to that reading audience? What persons or groups might react negatively to Harley's essay, and why?

Discussion: Form

1. Compare Harley's "Unnatural Metamorphosis" with the other examples of emotional argumentation. What difference do you notice in *tone?* Harley is very calm, and he never raises his voice, as we might imagine some of the other speakers would. Yet there is one word that he must emphasize, in speaking or writing. What is the word, and how has he given it emphasis in this essay?

Argumentative Writing

2. What part do description, narration, and comparison play in this essay?
3. If you have read the examples of ironic refutation, consider whether Harley's essay *might* have been placed there, and why it was not.

Wasteland
Marya Mannes

Marya Mannes (1904–   ) has long been active as a reviewer, editor, poet, and essayist, with her work often demonstrating her gift for satire. She has published several books, the most important being *More in Anger* (1958), a collection of essays from her years as a staff writer for the American liberal magazine *Reporter*. The essay below clearly belongs in a book with such a title.

Cans. Beer cans. Glinting on the verges of a million miles of roadways, lying in scrub, grass, dirt, leaves, sand, mud, but never hidden. Piels, Rheingold, Ballantine, Schaefer, Schlitz, shining in the sun or picked up by moonlight or the beams of headlights at night; washed by rain or flattened by wheels, but never dulled, never buried, never destroyed. Here is the mark of savages, the testament of wasters, the stain of prosperity.   1

Who are these men who defile the grassy borders of our roads and lanes, who pollute our ponds, who spoil the purity of our ocean beaches with the empty vessels of their thirst? Who are the men who make these vessels in millions and then say, "Drink — and discard"? What society is this that can afford to cast away a million tons of metal and to make of wild and fruitful land a garbage heap?   2

What manner of men and women need thirty feet of steel and two hundred horsepower to take them, singly, to their small destinations? Who demand that what they eat is wrapped so that forests are cut down to make the paper that is thrown away, and what they smoke and chew is sealed so that the sealers can be tossed in gutters and caught in twigs and grass?   3

What kind of men can afford to make the streets of their towns and cities hideous with neon at night, and their roadways hideous with signs by day, wasting beauty; who leave the carcasses of cars to rot in heaps; who spill their trash into ravines and make smoking mountains of refuse for the town's rats? What manner of men choke off the life in rivers, streams and lakes with the waste of their produce, making poison of water?

Who is as rich as that? Slowly the wasters and despoilers are impoverishing our land, our nature, and our beauty, so that there will not be one beach, one hill, one lane, one meadow, one forest free from the debris of man and the stigma of his improvidence.

Who is so rich that he can squander forever the wealth of earth and water for the trivial needs of vanity or the compulsive demands of greed; or so prosperous in land that he can sacrifice nature for unnatural desires? The earth we abuse and the living things we kill will, in the end, take their revenge; for in exploiting their presence we are diminishing our future.

And what will we leave behind us when we are long dead? Temples? Amphorae? Sunken treasure?

Or mountains of twisted, rusted steel, canyons of plastic containers, and a million miles of shores garlanded, not with the lovely wrack of the sea, but with the cans and bottles and light bulbs and boxes of a people who conserved their convenience at the expense of their heritage; and whose ephemeral prosperity was built on waste.

Discussion: Content

1. What is the subject of the first two paragraphs? Why do you suppose Mannes began with that?
2. What is the essay's thesis? Do you notice more than one meaning in the title? How is the title related to the thesis?
3. Who are the villains of Mannes' essay? List as many as you can.
4. Name three items not mentioned in the essay but available in a grocery store that Mannes would condemn as contributing to wastefulness.
5. How fair is Mannes' condemnation of American habits? What criticism, if any, is unjustified? What habits, if any, have changed?

Discussion: Form

1. Does this essay move from the abstract to the concrete or vice versa? Does it matter which it does?
2. Look up *rhetorical question* in the Glossary. How important are such questions to Mannes' approach to her subject? What effect

do they have on her essay's tone? What word would you use to describe that tone?
3. What is your reaction to the sentence fragments that Mannes uses to begin and end her argument? Would the force of her argument be lessened if the fragments were turned into sentences?
4. What words or phrases in particular seem more likely to create an emotional reaction in readers? Why?

Black Hawk's Farewell
Black Hawk

Ma-ka-tai-me-she-kia-kiah (Black Sparrow Hawk, 1767–1838) was an American Indian, a chief of the Sauk tribe in the upper Midwest. Always a valiant foe, he led his first war party against the Americans at age seventeen, and he fought on the British side under Tecumseh against them during the War of 1812. In 1831 and 1832 he led the Sauk in an attempt to recover their traditional village at Rock River, Illinois, but he was driven back both times by United States troops. In 1832 the Black Hawk War began after Illinois militiamen killed two Sauk who were advancing under a flag of truce to parley. The Sauk fled north, finally surrendering in Wisconsin, where Black Hawk delivered the speech below.

You have taken me prisoner with all my warriors. I am much grieved, for I expected, if I did not defeat you, to hold out much longer, and give you more trouble before I surrendered. I tried hard to bring you into ambush, but your last general understands Indian fighting. The first one was not so wise. When I saw that I could not beat you by Indian fighting, I determined to rush on you, and fight you face to face. I fought hard. But your guns were well aimed. The bullets flew like birds in the air, and whizzed by our ears like the wind through the trees in the winter. My warriors fell around me; it began to look dismal. I saw my evil day at hand. The sun rose dim on us in the morning, and at night it sunk in a dark cloud, and looked like a ball of fire. That was the last sun that shone on Black Hawk. His heart is dead, and no longer beats quick in his bosom. He is now a prisoner to the white men; they will do with him as they wish. But he can stand torture, and is not afraid of death. He is no coward. Black Hawk is an Indian.

Section 4:
Emotional Appeals

He has done nothing for which an Indian ought to be ashamed. He has fought for his countrymen, the squaws and papooses, against white men, who came, year after year, to cheat them and take away their lands. You know the cause of our making war. It is known to all white men. They ought to be ashamed of it. The white men despise the Indians, and drive them from their homes. But the Indians are not deceitful. The white men speak bad of the Indian, and look at him spitefully. But the Indian does not tell lies; Indians do not steal.   2

An Indian who is as bad as the white men could not live in our nation; he would be put to death, and eaten up by the wolves. The white men are bad schoolmasters; they carry false looks, and deal in false actions; they smile in the face of the poor Indian to cheat him; they shake them by the hand to gain their confidence, to make them drunk, to deceive them, and to ruin our wives. We told them to let us alone, and keep away from us; but they followed on, and beset our paths, and they coiled themselves among us, like the snake. They poisoned us by their touch. We were not safe. We lived in danger. We were becoming like them, hypocrites and liars, adulterers, lazy drones, all talkers, and no workers.   3

We looked up to the Great Spirit. We went to our great father. We were encouraged. His great council gave us fair words and big promises; but we got no satisfaction. Things were growing worse. There were no deer in the forest. The opossum and beaver were fled; the springs were drying up, and our squaws and papooses without victuals to keep them from starving; we called a great council, and built a large fire. The spirit of our fathers arose and spoke to us to avenge our wrongs or die. We all spoke before the council fire. It was warm and pleasant. We sent up the war-whoop, and dug up the tomahawk; our knives were ready, and the heart of Black Hawk swelled high in his bosom when he led his warriors to battle. He is satisfied. He will go to the world of spirits contented. He has done his duty. His father will meet him there, and commend him.   4

Black Hawk is a true Indian, and disdains to cry like a woman. He feels for his wife, his children, and his friends. But he does not care for himself. He cares for his nation and the Indians. They will suffer. He laments their fate. The white men do not scalp the head; but they do worse — they poison the heart; it is not pure with them. His countrymen will not be scalped, but they will, in a few years, become like the white men, so that you can't trust them, and there must be, as in the white settlements, nearly as many officers as men, to take care of them and keep them in order.   5

Farewell, my nation! Black Hawk tried to save you, and avenge your wrongs. He drank the blood of some of the whites. He has been taken prisoner, and his plans are stopped. He can do no more. He is near his end. His sun is setting, and he will rise no more. Farewell to Black Hawk. 6

Discussion: Content

1. What does Black Hawk apparently hope to accomplish with this speech — what is his purpose? Do you think he achieves his purpose?
2. Late in the nineteenth century, another American Indian said, "The white man broke every promise he made to us but one; he said he would take our land, and he took it." How does Black Hawk's speech confirm or refute this statement?
3. Assume you are a white U.S. military officer accepting Black Hawk's surrender and listening to his speech. What is your reaction to each of the speech's parts?

Discussion: Form

1. How is comparison basic to Black Hawk's approach? What does he compare? Is the comparison probably accurate and fair, or not?
2. Look for examples of figurative language. In your estimation, where is the most effective use?
3. Black Hawk's speech is by no means a formal argument, yet his opening paragraph does correspond to what Ciceronian element?
4. This speech shows in particular the emotional impact of short sentences; cite instances.

There Is No News from Auschwitz
A. M. Rosenthal

A(braham) M(ichael) Rosenthal (1922–   ) was born in Ontario and became an American citizen in 1951. In 1944 he became a writer for the New York *Times,* where this selection first appeared, and today is executive editor. He received the Pulitzer Prize for international reporting in 1960 and is the author of many articles for the *New York Times Magazine, Saturday Evening Post, Collier's,* and *Foreign Affairs.*

Section 4:
Emotional Appeals

Rosenthal's books include *Thirty-eight Witnesses* (1964), *The Night the Lights Went Out* (1965), *The Pope's Journey* (1965), and *One More Victim* (1967).

The most terrible thing of all, somehow, was that at Brzezinka the sun was bright and warm, the rows of graceful poplars were lovely to look upon and on the grass near the gates children played.

It all seemed frighteningly wrong, as in a nightmare, that at Brzezinka the sun should ever shine or that there should be light and greenness and the sound of young laughter. It would be fitting if at Brzezinka the sun never shone and the grass withered, because this is a place of unutterable terror.

And yet, every day, from all over the world, people come to Brzezinka, quite possibly the most grisly tourist center on earth. They come for a variety of reasons — to see if it could really have been true, to remind themselves not to forget, to pay homage to the dead by the simple act of looking upon their place of suffering.

Brzezinka is a couple of miles from the better-known southern Polish town of Oswiecim. Oswiecim has about 12,000 inhabitants, is situated about 171 miles from Warsaw and lies in a damp, marshy area at the eastern end of the pass called the Moravian Gate. Brzezinka and Oswiecim together formed part of that minutely organized factory of torture and death that the Nazis called Konzentrationslager Auschwitz.

By now, fourteen years after the last batch of prisoners was herded naked into the gas chambers by dogs and guards, the story of Auschwitz has been told a great many times. Some of the inmates have written of those memories of which sane men cannot conceive. Rudolf Franz Ferdinand Hoess, the superintendent of the camp, before he was executed wrote his detailed memoirs of mass exterminations and the experiments on living bodies. Four million people died here, the Poles say.

And so there is no news to report about Auschwitz. There is merely the compulsion to write something about it, a compulsion that grows out of a restless feeling that to have visited Auschwitz and then turned away without having said or written anything would somehow be a most grievous act of discourtesy to those who died here.

Brzezinka and Oswiecim are very quiet places now; the screams can no longer be heard. The tourist walks silently, quickly, at first to get it over with and then, as his mind peoples the barracks and the chambers and the dungeons and flogging posts, he walks draggingly. The guide does not say much either, because there is nothing much for him to say after he has pointed.

For every visitor, there is one particular bit of horror that he knows he will never forget. For some it is seeing the rebuilt gas chamber at Oswiecim and being told that this is the "small one." For others it is the fact that at Brzezinka, in the ruins of the gas chambers and the crematoria the Germans blew up when they retreated, there are daisies growing.

There are visitors who gaze blankly at the gas chambers and the furnaces because their minds simply cannot encompass them, but stand shivering before the great mounds of human hair behind the plate glass window or the piles of babies' shoes or the brick cells where men sentenced to death by suffocation were walled up.

One visitor opened his mouth in a silent scream simply at the sight of boxes — great stretches of three-tiered wooden boxes in the women's barracks. They were about six feet wide, about three feet high, and into them from five to ten prisoners were shoved for the night. The guide walks quickly through the barracks. Nothing more to see here.

A brick building where sterilization experiments were carried out on women prisoners. The guide tries the door — it's locked. The visitor is grateful that he does not have to go in, and then flushes with shame.

A long corridor where rows of faces stare from the walls. Thousands of pictures, the photographs of prisoners. They are all dead now, the men and women who stood before the cameras, and they all knew they were to die.

They all stare blank-faced, but one picture, in the middle of a row, seizes the eye and wrenches the mind. A girl twenty-two years old, plumply pretty, blonde. She is smiling gently, as at a sweet, treasured thought. What was the thought that passed through her young mind and is now her memorial on the wall of the dead at Auschwitz?

Into the suffocation dungeons the visitor is taken for a moment and feels himself strangling. Another visitor goes in, stumbles out and crosses herself. There is no place to pray at Auschwitz.

The visitors look pleadingly at each other and say to the guide, "Enough."

There is nothing new to report about Auschwitz. It was a sunny day and the trees were green and at the gates the children played.

Discussion: Content

1. What are Brzezinka and Oswiecim?
2. Why does Rosenthal say that he feels compelled to write about his visit to Auschwitz?

3. According to the Poles, how many people died at Auschwitz? Why?
4. Which exhibit is Rosenthal's tour prevented from seeing?
5. The author presents several examples of unforgettable "bits of horror." List them.
6. What photograph especially captures his attention?

Discussion: Form

1. Is Rosenthal guilty of the fallacy of *appeal to pity* in this essay?
2. How does he excite sympathy or pity for the dead at Auschwitz?
3. What is the effect of Rosenthal's repeated claim that there is no news from Auschwitz?
4. Rosenthal begins and ends his essay with some descriptions that strike him as incongruous. What are they, and how do they serve to reinforce another experience he describes which for him was clearly the most poignant part of his visit?

Appendix

How to Mark a Book
Mortimer J. Adler

Mortimer J. Adler (1902–   ) is a native of New York City whose professional life since 1930 has been centered in Chicago, first as a philosophy professor at the University of Chicago (1930–1952) and then with *Encyclopaedia Britannica,* especially with its "Great Books of the Western World" and related series. Adler is the author, editor, or coauthor of over thirty books, the most influential of which is probably *How to Read a Book: The Art of Getting a Liberal Education* (1940, revised 1972). The essay below, which first appeared in *Saturday Review of Literature,* is an important component of that book.

You know you have to read "between the lines" to get the most out of anything. I want to persuade you to do something equally important in the course of your reading. I want to persuade you to "write between the lines." Unless you do, you are not likely to do the most efficient kind of reading. 1

I contend, quite bluntly, that marking up a book is not an act of mutilation but of love. 2

You shouldn't mark up a book which isn't yours. Librarians (or your friends) who lend you books expect you to keep them clean, and you should. If you decide that I am right about the usefulness of marking books, you will have to buy them. Most of the world's great books are available today, in reprint editions, at less than a dollar.

There are two ways in which one can own a book. The first is the property right you establish by paying for it, just as you pay for clothes and furniture. But this act of purchase is only the prelude to possession. Full ownership comes only when you have made it a part of yourself, and the best way to make yourself a part of it is by writing in it. An illustration may make the point clear. You buy a beefsteak and transfer it from the butcher's ice-box to your own. But you do not own the beefsteak in the most important sense until you consume it and get it into your bloodstream. I am arguing that books, too, must be absorbed in your bloodstream to do you any good.

Confusion about what it means to *own* a book leads people to a false reverence for paper, binding, and type — a respect for the physical thing — the craft of the printer rather than the genius of the author. They forget that it is possible for a man to acquire the idea, to possess the beauty, which a great book contains, without staking his claim by pasting his bookplate inside the cover. Having a fine library doesn't prove that its owner has a mind enriched by books; it proves nothing more than that he, his father, or his wife, was rich enough to buy them.

There are three kinds of book owners. The first has all the standard sets and best-sellers — unread, untouched. (This deluded individual owns woodpulp and ink, not books.) The second has a great many books — a few of them read through, most of them dipped into, but all of them as clean and shiny as the day they were bought. (This person would probably like to make books his own, but is restrained by a false respect for their physical appearance.) The third has a few books or many — every one of them dog-eared and dilapidated, shaken and loosened by continual use, marked and scribbled in from front to back. (This man owns books.)

Is it false respect, you may ask, to preserve intact and unblemished a beautifully printed book, an elegantly bound edition? Of course not. I'd no more scribble all over the first edition of *Paradise Lost* than I'd give my baby a set of crayons and an original Rembrandt! I wouldn't mark up a painting or a statue. Its soul, so to speak, is inseparable from its body. And the beauty of a rare edition or of a richly manufactured volume is like that of a painting or a statue.

But the soul of a book *can* be separated from its body. A book is more like the score of a piece of music than it is like a painting. No great musician confuses a symphony with the printed sheets of music. Arturo Toscanini reveres Brahms, but Toscanini's score of the C-minor Symphony is so thoroughly marked up that no one but the maestro himself can read it. The reason why a great conductor makes notations on his musical scores — marks them up again and again each time he returns to study them — is the reason why you should mark up your books. If your respect for magnificent binding or typography gets in the way, buy yourself a cheap edition and pay your respects to the author.

Why is marking up a book indispensable to reading it? First, it keeps you awake. (And I don't mean merely conscious; I mean wide awake.) In the second place, reading, if it is active, is thinking, and thinking tends to express itself in words, spoken or written. The marked book is usually the thought-through book. Finally, writing helps you remember the thoughts you had, or the thoughts the author expressed. Let me develop these three points.

If reading is to accomplish anything more than passing time, it must be active. You can't let your eyes glide across the lines of a book and come up with an understanding of what you have read. Now an ordinary piece of light fiction, like say, *Gone with the Wind,* doesn't require the most active kind of reading. The books you read for pleasure can be read in a state of relaxation, and nothing is lost. But a great book, rich in ideas and beauty, a book that raises and tries to answer great fundamental questions, demands the most active reading of which you are capable. You don't absorb the ideas of John Dewey the way you absorb the crooning of Mr. Vallee. You have to reach for them. That you cannot do while you're asleep.

If, when you've finished reading a book, the pages are filled with your notes, you know that you read actively. The most famous *active* reader of great books I know is President Hutchins, of the University of Chicago. He also has the hardest schedule of business activities of any man I know. He invariably reads with a pencil, and sometimes, when he picks up a book and pencil in the evening, he finds himself, instead of making intelligent notes, drawing what he calls "caviar factories" on the margins. When that happens, he puts the book down. He knows he's too tired to read, and he's just wasting time.

But, you may ask, why is writing necessary? Well, the physical act of writing, with your own hand, brings words and sentences more sharply before your mind and preserves them better in your memory. To set down your reaction to important words and sentences you have read, and the questions they have raised in your mind, is to preserve those reactions and sharpen those questions.

Even if you wrote on a scratch pad, and threw the paper away when you had finished writing, your grasp of the book would be surer. But you don't have to throw the paper away. The margins (top and bottom, as well as side), the end-papers, the very space between the lines, are all available. They aren't sacred. And, best of all, your marks and notes become an integral part of the book and stay there forever. You can pick up the book the following week or year, and there are all your points of agreement, disagreement, doubt, and inquiry. It's like resuming an interrupted conversation with the advantage of being able to pick up where you left off.

And that is exactly what reading a book should be: a conversation between you and the author. Presumably he knows more about the subject than you do; naturally, you'll have the proper humility as you approach him. But don't let anybody tell you that a reader is supposed to be solely on the receiving end. Understanding is a two-way operation; learning doesn't consist in being an empty receptacle. The learner has to question himself and question the teacher. He even has to argue with the teacher, once he understands what the teacher is saying. And marking a book is literally an expression of your differences, or agreements of opinion, with the author.

There are all kinds of devices for marking a book intelligently and fruitfully. Here's the way I do it:

1. *Underlining:* Of major points, of important or forceful statements.
2. *Vertical lines at the margin:* To emphasize a statement already underlined.
3. *Star, asterisk, or other doo-dad at the margin:* To be used sparingly, to emphasize the ten or twenty most important statements in the book. (You may want to fold the bottom corner of each page on which you use such marks. It won't hurt the sturdy paper on which most modern books are printed, and you will be able to take the book off the shelf at any time and, by opening it at the folded-corner page, refresh your recollection of the book.)
4. *Numbers in the margin:* To indicate the sequence of points the author makes in developing a single argument.
5. *Numbers of other pages in the margin:* To indicate where else in the book the author made points relevant to the point marked; to tie up the ideas in a book, which, though they may be separated by many pages, belong together.
6. *Circling of key words or phrases:*
7. *Writing in the margin, or at the top or bottom of the page, for the sake of:* Recording questions (and perhaps answers) which a passage raised in your mind; reducing a complicated discussion to a simple statement; recording the sequence of major points right through the book. I use the end-papers at the back of the book to

make a personal index of the author's points in the order of their appearance.

The front end-papers are, to me, the most important. Some people reserve them for a fancy bookplate. I reserve them for fancy thinking. After I have finished reading the book and making my personal index on the back endpapers, I turn to the front and try to outline the book, not page by page, or point by point (I've already done that at the back), but as an integrated structure, with a basic unity and an order of parts. This outline is, to me, the measure of my understanding of the work.

If you're a die-hard anti-book-marker, you may object that the margins, the space between the lines, and the end-papers don't give you room enough. All right. How about using a scratch-pad slightly smaller than the page-size of the book — so that the edges of the sheets won't protrude? Make your index, outlines, and even your notes on the pad, and then insert these sheets permanently inside the front and back covers of the book.

Or, you may say that this business of marking books is going to slow up your reading. It probably will. That's one of the reasons for doing it. Most of us have been taken in by the notion that speed of reading is a measure of our intelligence. There is no such thing as the right speed for intelligent reading. Some things should be read quickly and effortlessly, and some should be read slowly and even laboriously. The sign of intelligence in reading is the ability to read different things differently according to their worth. In the case of good books, the point is not to see how many of them you can get through, but rather how many can get through you — how many you can make your own. A few friends are better than a thousand acquaintances. If this be your aim, as it should be, you will not be impatient if it takes more time and effort to read a great book than it does a newspaper.

You may have one final objection to marking books. You can't lend them to your friends because nobody else can read them without being distracted by your notes. Furthermore, you won't want to lend them because a marked copy is a kind of intellectual diary, and lending it is almost like giving your mind away.

If your friend wishes to read your *Plutarch's Lives*, "Shakespeare," or *The Federalist Papers*, tell him gently but firmly, to buy a copy. You will lend him your car or your coat — but your books are as much a part of you as your head or your heart.

A Brief Introduction to Common Logical Fallacies

A fallacy is any of various types of deceptive, erroneous, or false reasoning that causes an argument to be logically flawed, even though the argument may be psychologically persuasive and may seem to be true.

After you read the following brief descriptions of common logical fallacies, it should be clear why it is advantageous for all people, whether students or not, to recognize these fallacies. As consumers, we are constantly greeted with media advertisements and salespersons' rhetoric full of fallacies; as citizens, we are frequently offered political speeches, government announcements, and official explanations that contain fallacies; as employees and employers, we may expect to find fallacies that damage the logical foundations of the private and public communications which are central to business and professional activities. Consequently, whether at home, at work, or at play, we should guard against and refuse to tolerate conscious or unconscious fallacies, because they either hinder or prevent honest, reasonable discussions and correct, logical decisions.

For convenience and as an aid to understanding, fallacies may be divided into three categories (although there is some overlapping among them): structural fallacies, language fallacies, and emotional fallacies. Structural fallacies (sometimes called *formal* fallacies) are the result of errors in the structure or form of deductive and inductive arguments; language and emotional fallacies (sometimes grouped together as *material* fallacies) are a result of errors in the content or matter of arguments. You will also notice that some fallacies have more than one name or have commonly used Latin names, for example, *dicto simpliciter*. Learn these names for use in class discussions of various samples of argumentation.

Formal Fallacies

Formal fallacies arise from the improper construction of syllogisms, i.e., fallacies of *form*. In order to understand them, you will have to take a closer look at syllogisms. A syllogism is a series of three statements arranged according to the following formula:

All A's are B. (First premise)
C is an A. (Second premise)

Therefore, C is a B. (Conclusion)

The syllogism must meet certain standards to be logically consistent, or *valid*.

First, it must contain exactly three two-term statements: two propositions *(premises)* and a conclusion. Second, it must contain exactly three different *terms* (A, B, and C in the above example), with one term appearing in both premises but not in the conclusion, and each of the other terms appearing in one premise and in the conclusion. The term that appears in both premises but not in the conclusion (A) is called the *middle term;* the other terms (B and C) are called *end terms*. Third, the syllogism must not violate three simple rules, the most important being that the middle term must be *distributed* only once. To be distributed, a term, whether middle or end, must appear as the subject of a universal statement (one that by means of words such as "all" or "no" totally includes or excludes all of a class or group) or as the predicate term of a negative statement. A term is *undistributed* if it is the subject of a particular statement or the predicate term of a positive statement. (A predicate term is one that completes either the verb "to be" or some other linking verb.) In this syllogism,

All Frenchmen are lovers of wine. (First premise)
Ralph is not a lover of wine. (Second premise)

Ralph is not a Frenchman. (Conclusion)

the middle term, "lover(s) of wine," is undistributed in the first premise, since it is the predicate term of a positive statement, and distributed in the second premise as the predicate term of a negative statement. The end term "Ralph" is undistributed in both of its positions, being the subject of a particular statement, while "Frenchmen" is distributed twice, once as the subject of a universal statement ("*All* Frenchmen . . .") and once as the predicate term of a negative statement (". . . is *not* a Frenchman"). The case of the end term "Frenchmen" also illustrates the second rule: No end term may be distributed only once. The final rule, as we shall see later, is that no syllogism can have two negative premises.

Either to understand why this last rule is necessary or to check on the validity of any syllogism, you may find it useful to draw circles to represent the various classes or groups and individuals named. For

Common Logical Fallacies

instance, draw a large circle to represent the class of lovers of wine, and since all Frenchmen are lovers of wine, draw a small circle within the large circle to represent all Frenchmen (you must leave room for the rest of the world's lovers of wine, of course). Now, where does Ralph's small individual circle go? Outside both circles, of course:

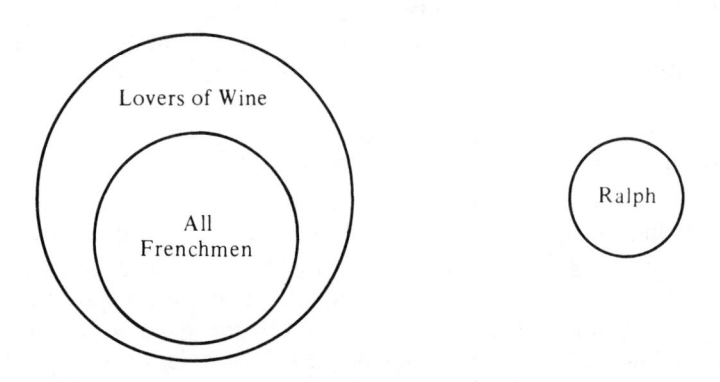

If you then give the syllogism two negative premises, for example,

No Frenchmen are lovers of wine.
Ralph is not a lover of wine.

what can you conclude? By drawing the circles you will see that you cannot really say anything exclusively and positively about Ralph's nationality, for you do not know exactly where to place Ralph's circle:

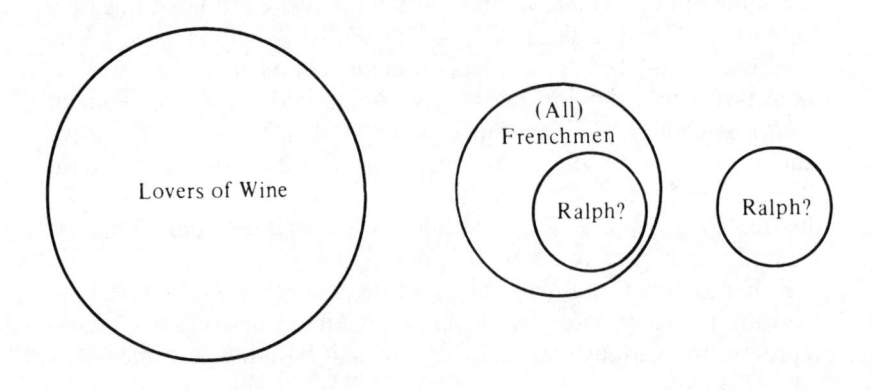

Ralph may or may not be a Frenchman, which is hardly a useful conclusion. Now you should understand why rule three is important. By using the circles you should also be able to determine why the rest of the standards and rules for validity are important.

So far you have concentrated on the question of the *validity* of the deductive syllogism. A quick glance at the sample syllogisms and circles, however, will suggest that the question of *truth* in a deductive syllogism is a separate one, for while it is commonly known that many Frenchmen are winelovers, you can also be reasonably confident that at least some Frenchmen prefer beer, absinthe, Coca-Cola, coffee, milk, etc. However, and this is a point you must understand, *if* a syllogism meets the standards of *validity*, and *if* the premises are accepted as true propositions, whether intuitively, inductively, or even deductively as conclusions of other syllogisms, then the conclusion of the syllogism in question is logically and undeniably true. Of course, few of us consciously use deductive syllogisms in the formal sense, although we do use deductive logic daily, often in an abbreviated form called the *enthymeme*.

An enthymeme is a syllogism with one of its three statements missing or unstated, and perhaps with its conclusion preceding its premise(s), such as: "Ralph's no Frenchman. He doesn't like wine." Clearly the first premise, "All Frenchmen are lovers of wine," is absent, perhaps because the speaker thinks it is so obvious that it need not be mentioned. Yet the speaker's audience, if they are critical thinkers, might realize the problem with the *truth* of the unstated first premise and reject the speaker's conclusion about Ralph's nationality. (They could also reject the conclusion without really knowing exactly why, perhaps on the basis of "common sense.") Similarly, another speaker might state, "Professor Smith is probably a liberal, since he teaches political science." But this conclusion might also be false, perhaps because the syllogism is invalid:

Most political science professors are liberals.
Professor Smith is a political science professor.

Professor Smith is a liberal. X

Here the middle term ("political science professor(s)") is not distributed, for "most" is not a word that includes or excludes all of a class or group. Or even if in valid form, with "all" substituted for "most," the first premise or proposition would be rejected as inductively false by a person who knows of one or more conservative political science professors.

This is not to suggest, though, that all enthymemes are either invalid or false. Instead, you should be aware when they are being used and examine the total syllogism for validity and for true, acceptable propositions before you agree with or reject deductive conclusions.

The most commonly cited formal fallacies are discussed below.

The four-term argument.

All persons who drink to excess are alcoholics.
Roscoe drinks beer.
_____
Therefore, Roscoe is an alcoholic.

The four terms here are "persons who drink to excess," "Roscoe," "drinkers of beer," and "alcoholics." To make the argument a valid one, it must be shown that Roscoe drinks to excess, thus eliminating the fourth term and providing a properly distributed middle term, "persons who drink to excess."

Improperly distributed middle term. This fallacy results when the middle term of a deductive syllogism is distributed more or less than once. For instance, in this invalid syllogism the middle term, "lovers of wine," is not distributed at all:

All Frenchmen are lovers of wine.
Luigi loves wine.
_____
Luigi is a Frenchman. X

Nothing prevents people of other nationalities from joining the class of winelovers, since the middle term is not distributed. So Luigi may well be of some nationality other than French. If the middle term is distributed more than once, this invalid syllogism results:

All Frenchmen are lovers of wine.
All Frenchmen are sociable.
_____
?

When the middle term drops out, as it always does in a valid syllogism, we are left with no conclusion at all, for some lovers of wine are not Frenchmen and some sociable people are not Frenchmen; we can assert nothing validly or positively about the sociability of non-French winelovers.

Unequal distribution. In this fallacy, an end term is distributed only once, as in this example:

All Frenchmen are lovers of wine.
No Italians are Frenchmen.
___
No Italians are lovers of wine. X

Here, since the end term "lovers of wine" is distributed in the conclusion (as the predicate of a negative statement) yet not distributed in the premise (as the predicate of a universal statement), it violates the basic rule of deduction that no end term may be distributed only once.

Two particular premises. No valid conclusion may be drawn from two particular premises; for example,

Some bald-headed men are extremely sexy.
George is bald-headed.
___
Therefore, George is extremely sexy.

Maybe he is, and maybe he isn't.

Two negative premises. This fallacy results because no valid syllogism may have two negative premises, for then no exclusive and no positive conclusion can be drawn; for example,

No Italians are lovers of wine.
Ralph is not a lover of wine.
___
?

Ralph may be an Italian — or not; we can't say for sure either way.

Material Fallacies

The material fallacies, you will recall, arise from either improper or inexact use of language or from appeals to emotion instead of reason. Those most commonly cited are discussed below.

Appeal to force. In this case, force or the threat of force is used to cause the acceptance of a conclusion. The fallacy may be somewhat veiled, as in a threat to deliver or withhold votes for a politician in response to certain governmental actions that he may control, or it may be open, as in the case of bombings, beatings, or war.

Appeal to the people. This fallacy is the "friends and fellow

Americans" (or North Carolinians or Bostonians or whatever) approach favored by some politicians who hope to obscure the weakness of an idea or argument with a cloud of friendliness.

Appeal to pity (ad misericordiam). Here an attempt is made to arouse the sympathy or pity of a person or group in order to influence a decision. Thus, a lawyer for a criminal suspect may have the suspect's family in the courtroom in order to get the judge or jury to believe that the family's future welfare depends entirely on lenient treatment of the suspect. A similar approach is used by the student who, having cut class — or desiring to do so — fabricates a story to tell the instructor, usually of the illness, accident, death, or funeral of a close friend or relative, in order to get an excused absence.

Argument ad hominem (at the person). This fallacy results when a person attacks the personal character of an adversary in the course of an argument. Such a fallacy often appears openly as "name calling," when a person's ideas are condemned because he or she is divorced, or has served a prison sentence, or did not graduate from high school or college, etc. Sometimes, though, the fallacy may be veiled, particularly through the use of popular psychological labels for neuroses, such as Oedipus complex, inferiority complex, and the like. However, such criticisms are not relevant factors. The *genetic fallacy* is very similar. Here, a person's idea is condemned because of the person's race, sex, creed, national origin, and the like. But a Texan's idea about the oil depletion allowance or a Catholic's about abortion might be perfectly sound, even if suspect because of possible self-interest. Still, the background of the person should be kept separate from the idea presented. A subvariety of these two fallacies is called *poisoning the well*. Here, the attack on the person's character or background or on the person or group that originated the idea is made before the argument really even begins.

Bandwagon. This common fallacy has great emotional appeal because of our desire to be in the parade, so to speak; thus, we "jump on the bandwagon" as it goes by because we are anxious to be part of a group. Consequently, we buy products because they are the most popular (or so the advertisements say) or we hasten to support a political candidate who is obviously going to win. Yet we should have logical reasons for the choices we make. "Everybody else is doing it" is not a logical reason; "everybody else" may well be wrong again, just as they sometimes have been before.

Begging the question (circular reasoning). In this fallacy the conclusion of a deductive argument is contained among the deductive argument's premises: "Naturally drug addicts lack willpower. That's why they're drug addicts." This fallacy is especially difficult to find when it is concealed in a lengthy argument or when it is expressed in difficult language, such as this: "To allow every man unbounded freedom of speech must always be, on the whole, advantageous to the state; for it is highly conducive to the interests of the community that each individual should enjoy a liberty, perfectly unlimited, of expressing his sentiments." In other words, "Free speech is good for the state because it's good for the state when there is free speech." We have made a full circle without proving anything.

Dicto simpliciter (unqualified generalization). This fallacy results when an argument is based upon a generalization that is totally inclusive and is accepted unequivocally as true for all circumstances. "Milk is good for you" is simply not true for everybody; neither is "alcohol is bad for you," since some doctors prescribe beer for nursing mothers and a moderate amount of alcohol for some aged patients.

Either/or (false dilemma). This fallacy denies that there is any intermediate possibility between two extremes. Examples of this fallacy include: "Mr. Bender must be a communist; he refused to join the Downtown Merchants' Association with the rest of the businessmen." "Mary is an atheist; she never goes to church." "John wants to become a killer; he's accepted an appointment to the Air Force Academy." Unfortunately, since such assertions may appeal to our prejudices, we may accept them as true without considering any probable alternatives.

Equivocation. This fallacy results from deliberate or accidental misuse of two or more meanings of the same word in a statement. The result may sometimes be amusing, as in these sample newspaper headlines: "Beauty Unveils Bust at Ceremony," "Mother of 18 in Trouble Again," "Snowplow Clears Way for Street Walkers," "Southern Railroad to Drop Passengers from Two Trains." Unfortunately, equivocation can occur in serious contexts, causing crucial disagreement. This is especially true when abstract words such as "equality," "freedom," or the like are used. It is best in such cases to define equivocal words so that there will be no possibility of misunderstandings.

Faulty analogy. In this fallacy two subjects are compared. Although the two subjects share certain similarities, their differences may be important enough to destroy the value of the comparison. Thus, comparison of the current economic situation to one several decades ago may be interesting and even useful, but numerous factors have changed in the intervening time span, so that the conclusions based on such an analogy are likely to be imperfect. A related fallacy is faulty metaphor, in which a comparison based on a few (or on just one) resemblances is made, usually to criticize. Though colorful, such metaphor-laden assertions as "Knee-jerk, milktoast-eating liberals always want to take away our guns, leaving us red-blooded men nothing but tooth and nail as protection for the living treasures of our homes against a host of fiends," offer little basis for rational understanding or logical choice.

Faulty (hasty) generalization. This fallacy results when an inductive conclusion is proposed but is based on a too limited number of examples or on unrepresentative examples. For instance, you and most of the people in your dormitory or in your neighborhood may prefer a certain candidate for president of the United States, but that sample of voter preferences is so small and localized that it is of questionable value.

Hypostatization. This fallacy results from the failure to differentiate between abstract and concrete words, speaking of abstractions such as *nature, justice, science,* and the like as though they were concrete. Although such abstract words can convey and create emotion, they are not specific enough to convey useful, precise information that will help in reaching a rational decision, "Have you thanked nature today?" is an example of this fallacy, as are "Love conquers all" and "Science puts industry to work."

Hypothesis contrary to fact. In this fallacy a hypothesis (proposition offered as an explanation for the occurrence of some event or phenomenon) that is not true is used as the starting place for a deductive argument. "If Albert Einstein had stayed in Germany, the Nazis would have had an atomic bomb before the United States did" is such a fallacious argument, for Albert Einstein did not stay in Germany, and even if he had, various other factors might well have prevented the Nazis from producing an atomic bomb before the United States did.

Irrelevance (red herring). In this fallacy the argument or discussion strays off the subject and begins to deal with another, even unrelated, subject, just as dragging smoked (red) herring across a trail will divert hunting dogs and lead them off in another direction. Thus, opponents of gun registration may display bumper stickers reading: "If guns are outlawed, only outlaws will have guns." This slogan has emotional appeal, but it has fallaciously changed the point of contention from *registering* guns to *outlawing* them, thus misrepresenting the gun registration supporters' position.

Labored hypothesis. This fallacy results when a hypothesis drawn from one body of evidence is more complex or unusual than an alternative hypothesis; for example, "Ten of the buses used to transport children across the city to achieve racial balance were turned over and burned last night; there were no witnesses, but the people who support busing must have done it in order to make the antibusing organization look bad."

Non sequitur. The Latin term for this fallacy means "It does not follow"; the conclusion in such an argument lacks a connection to the premises: "My grandparents came to this country during the nineteenth century; therefore, I always prefer Ford cars." This example is obviously silly, but sometimes the argument may go astray in a less noticeable way: "Free enterprise is being undermined by the federal government, which tells all businesses how to operate, has taken over railroads and created electric utility companies, and continues to support the spread of agricultural cooperatives. Democracy is now on the verge of extinction." If your bias is "right," then this argument has considerable emotional appeal for you. But since free enterprise is an economic system and democracy is a political system, the argument has shifted, and there is no connection between premises and conclusion.

Post hoc, ergo propter hoc (false cause). This fallacy is identified by the Latin term meaning "after this, therefore because of this." The problem results when a person assumes that a cause and effect relationship exists just because one event follows another. But there must be a demonstrable causal link between the two events before such reasoning can be considered sound. Perhaps the most famous literary example occurs when Huck Finn thinks to himself, ". . . I've always reckoned that looking at the new moon over your left shoulder is one of the carelessest and foolishest things a body can do. Old Hank Bunker done it once, and bragged about it, and in less than two years he got drunk and fell off of the shot-tower and spread himself out so that he was just a kind of a layer . . . and they slid him edgeways between two barn doors for a coffin and buried him so. . . ." It's clear that Huck is being led astray by his superstitious nature, but most of us too often resort to similar fallacious reasoning, attributing our good and bad experiences to some questionably related causes.

Special pleading (card stacking). This inductive fallacy results when certain evidence, generally numerical or statistical, is brought to the fore, while other evidence, equally or even more pertinent, is suppressed or minimized. Mark Twain made oblique reference to this fallacy when he said, "There are three kinds of lies: lies, damn lies, and statistics." News media are sometimes guilty of this fallacy when they feature the activities of certain political figures or government programs that they favor and ignore or give abbreviated coverage to those they do not.

Syntactic ambiguity. This fallacy results from faulty sentence structure, either with parts misplaced ("Lawyers to Offer Poor Free Advice"; "The students could not understand why Shakespeare was so well liked in high school"; "The instructor explained why plagiarism is wrong on Thursday") or with so-called multiple or complex questions that are self-incriminating if answered either yes or no ("Are you still cheating on tests?" or "Have you stopped spending all of your money on beer?"). Similarly, because pause and emphasis can create different meanings, they can result in deliberate or accidental misunderstandings. If you repeat the short sentence, "You knew this," three times and emphasize a different word each time, the potential for ambiguity will become clear.

Transfer. This fallacy depends on the principle of favorable association, even though there may be little or no logical connection. In one variety, the subject is identified with some idea or entity that is inherently pleasing or attractive. Any viewer of television or reader of popular magazines is constantly bombarded with advertisements or commercials that use transfer. The association may be with a good time (see soft drink, liquor, and cigarette ads) or with pleasant memories (telephone and food) or with looking better (clothing and cosmetics, always with attractive models). During 1976 the most popular association was with America, past or present, as advertisers capitalized on the bicentennial celebration. Another variety of transfer, also much loved by advertisers, is similar to the use of authority in an argument, except here the prestige or reputation of a respected person or institution is used to support an idea. The fallacy occurs when the person becomes removed from his area of expertise; a star football player is not necessarily an expert on popcorn poppers or pantyhose, but Joe Namath was featured in advertising for both products. Similarly, biblical references may be used to support political or other ideas. In any case, the association or identification must be examined for a logical connection; if there is none, the result is a fallacy of transfer.

Tu quoque. This fallacy is identified by the Latin term for "you also" or "you're another"; it avoids the subject or deflects questions and accusations by making similar accusations against the opponent. For instance, a person being criticized for eating a second dessert might say to the critic, "Well, you're already too fat or you'd take a second one!" or "If you weren't on a diet, you'd be reaching for a *third* dessert!" Neither of these responses gives logical reasons for eating a second dessert, but instead attempts to divert attention elsewhere.

The Method of Scientific Investigation
Thomas Henry Huxley

Thomas Henry Huxley (1825–1895), a British surgeon and scientist, was especially active in nineteenth-century research centered on the theory of evolution proposed by his contemporary, Charles Darwin. The essay below is excerpted from a lecture Huxley gave in 1863 at The Museum of Practical Geology, London.

The method of scientific investigation is nothing but the expression of the necessary mode of working of the human mind. It is simply the mode at which all phenomena are reasoned about, rendered precise and exact. There is no more difference, but there is just the same kind of difference, between the mental operations of a man of science and those of an ordinary person as there is between the operations and methods of a baker or of a butcher weighing out his goods in common scales and the operations of a chemist in performing a difficult and complex analysis by means of his balance and finely graduated weights. It is not that the action of the scales in the one case and the balance in the other differ in the principles of their construction or manner of working; but the beam of one is set on an infinitely finer axis than the other and of course turns by the addition of a much smaller weight.

You will understand this better, perhaps, if I give you some familiar example. You have all heard it repeated, I dare say, that men of science work by means of induction and deduction, and that by the help of these operations they, in a sort of sense, wring from nature certain other things which are called natural laws and causes, and that out of these, by some cunning skill of their own, they build up hypotheses and theories. And it is imagined by many that the operations of the common mind can be by no means compared with these processes, and that they have to be acquired by a sort of special apprenticeship to the craft. To hear all these large words you would think that the mind of a man of science must be constituted differently from that of his fellow men; but if you will not be frightened by terms, you will discover that you are quite wrong and that all these terrible apparatus are being used by yourselves every day and every hour of your lives.

There is a well-known incident in one of Molière's plays where the author makes the hero express unbounded delight on being told that he had been talking prose during the whole of his life. In the same way I trust that you will take comfort and be delighted with yourselves on the discovery that you have been acting on the principles of inductive and deductive philosophy during the same period. Probably there is not one here who has not in the course of the day had occasion to set in motion a complex train of reasoning of the very same kind, though differing of course in degree, as that which a scientific man goes through in tracing the causes of natural phenomena.

A very trivial circumstance will serve to exemplify this. Suppose you go into a fruiterer's shop, wanting an apple. You take up one, and on biting it you find it is sour; you look at it and see that it is hard and green. You take up another one, and that too is hard, green, and sour. The shopman offers you a third; but before biting it you examine it and find that it is hard and green, and you immediately say that you will not have it, as it must be sour like those that you have already tried.

Nothing can be more simple than that, you think; but if you will take the trouble to analyze and trace out into its logical elements what has been done by the mind, you will be greatly surprised. In the first place you have performed the operation of induction. You found that in two experiences hardness and greenness in apples go together with sourness. It was so in the first case, and it was confirmed by the second. True, it is a very small basis, but still it is enough to make an induction from; you generalize the facts, and you expect to find sourness in apples where you get hardness and greenness. You found upon that a general law that all hard and green apples are sour; and that, so far as it goes, is a perfect induction. Well, having got your natural law in this way, when you are offered another apple which you find is hard and green, you say, "All hard and green apples are sour; this apple is hard and green; therefore this apple is sour." That train of reasoning is what logicians call a syllogism and has all its various parts and terms — its major premise, its minor premise, and its conclusion. And by the help of further reasoning, which if drawn out would have to be exhibited in two or three other syllogisms, you arrive at your final determination, "I will not have that apple." So that, you see, you have, in the first place, established a law by induction, and upon that you have founded a deduction and reasoned out the special conclusion of the particular case. Well now, suppose, having got your law, that at some time afterwards you are discussing the qualities of apples with a friend. You will say to him, "It is a very curious thing, but I find that all hard and green apples are sour!" Your friend says to you, "But how do you know that?" You at once reply, "Oh, because I have tried them over and over again and have always found them to be so." Well, if we were talking science instead of common sense, we should call that an experimental verification. And if still opposed you go further and say, "I have heard from the people in Somersetshire and Devonshire, where a large number of apples are grown, that they have observed the same thing. It is also found to be the case in Normandy and in North America. In short, I find it to be the universal experience of mankind wherever attention has been directed to the subject." Whereupon, your friend, unless he is a very unreasonable man, agrees with you and is convinced that you are quite right in the conclusion you have drawn. He believes, although perhaps he does not know he believes it, that the more extensive verifications are that the more frequently experiments have been made and results of the same kind arrived at, that the more varied the conditions under which the same results have been attained the more certain is the ultimate conclusion, and he disputes the question no further. He sees that the experiment has been tried under all sorts of conditions as to time, place, and people with the same result; and he says with you, therefore, that the law you have laid down must be a good one and he must believe it.

In science we do the same thing; the philosopher exercises precisely the same faculties, though in a much more delicate manner. In scientific inquiry it becomes a matter of duty to expose a supposed law to every possible kind of verification, and to take care, moreover, that this is done intentionally and not left to mere accident as in the case of the apples. And in science, as in common life, our confidence in a law is in exact proportion to the absence of variation in the result of our experimental verifications. For instance, if you let go your grasp of an article you may have in your hand, it will immediately fall to the ground. That is a very common verification of one of the best established laws of nature, that of gravitation. The method by which men of science established the existence of that law is exactly the same as that by which we have established the trivial proposition about the sourness of hard and green apples. But we believe it in such an extensive, thorough, and unhesitating manner because the universal experience of mankind verifies it, and we can verify it ourselves at any time; and that is the strongest possible foundation on which any natural law can rest.

So much by way of proof that the method of establishing laws in science is exactly the same as that pursued in common life. Let us now turn to another matter (though really it is but another phase of the same question), and that is the method by which from the relations of certain phenomena we prove that some stand in the position of causes towards the others.

I want to put the case clearly before you, and I will therefore show you what I mean by another familiar example. I will suppose that one of you, on coming down in the morning to the parlor of your house, finds that a teapot and some spoons which had been left in the room on the previous evening are gone; the window is open, and you observe the mark of a dirty hand on the window-frame; and perhaps, in addition to that, you notice the impress of a hobnailed shoe on the gravel outside. All these phenomena have struck your attention instantly, and before two seconds have passed you say, "Oh, somebody has broken open the window, entered the room, and run off with the spoons and the teapot!" That speech is out of your mouth in a moment. And you will probably add, "I know there has; I am quite sure of it." You mean to say exactly what you know; but in reality what you have said has been the expression of what is, in all essential particulars, an hypothesis. You do not *know* it at all; it is nothing but an hypothesis rapidly framed in your own mind! And it is an hypothesis founded on a long train of inductions and deductions.

What are those inductions and deductions, and how have you got at this hypothesis? You have observed, in the first place, that the window is open; but by a train of reasoning involving many inductions and deductions, you have probably arrived long before at the general law — and a very good one it is — that windows do not open of themselves; and you therefore conclude that something has opened the window. A second general law that you have arrived at in the same way is that teapots and spoons do not go out of a window spontaneously, and you are satisfied that, as they are not now where you left them, they have been removed. In the third place, you look at the marks on the window and the shoe marks outside, and you say that in all previous experience the former kind of mark has never been produced by anything else but the hand of a human being; and the same experience shows that no other animal but man at present wears shoes with hobnails on them such as would produce the marks in the gravel. I do not know, even if we could discover any of those "missing links" that are talked about, that they would help us to any other conclusion! At any rate the law which states our present experience is strong enough for my present purpose. You next reach the conclusion that as these kinds of marks have not been left by any other animal than man, or are liable to be formed in any other way than by a man's hand and shoe, the marks in question have been formed by a man in that way. You have, further, a general law founded on observation and experience, and that too is, I am sorry to say, a very universal and unimpeachable one — that some men are thieves; and you assume at once from all these premises — and that is what constitutes your hypothesis — that the man who made the marks outside and on the window sill opened the window, got into the room, and stole your teapot and spoons. You have now arrived at a *vera causa;* you have assumed a cause which it is plain is competent to produce all the phenomena you have observed. You can explain all these phenomena only by the hypothesis of a thief. But that is an hypothetical conclusion, of the justice of which you have no absolute proof at all; it is only rendered highly probable by a series of inductive and deductive reasonings.

I suppose your first action, assuming that you are a man of ordinary common sense and that you have established this hypothesis to your own satisfaction, will very likely be to go off for the police and set them on the track of the burglar with the view to the recovery of your property. But just as you are starting with this object, some person comes in and on learning what you are about says, "My good friend, you are going on a great deal too fast. How do you know that the man who really made the marks took the spoons? It might have been a monkey that took them, and the man may have merely looked in afterwards." You would probably reply, "Well, that is all very well, but you see it is contrary to all experience of the way teapots and spoons are abstracted; so that, at any rate, your hypothesis is less probable than mine." While you are talking the thing over in this way, another friend arrives, one of that good kind of people that I was talking of a little while ago.

And he might say, "Oh, my dear sir, you are certainly going on a great deal too fast. You are most presumptuous. You admit that all these occurrences took place when you were fast asleep, at a time when you could not possibly have known anything about what was taking place. How do you know that the laws of nature are not suspended during the night? It may be that there has been some kind of supernatural interference in this case." In point of fact, he declares that your hypothesis is one of which you cannot at all demonstrate the truth and that you are by no means sure that the laws of nature are the same when you are asleep as when you are awake.

Well, now, you cannot at the moment answer that kind of reasoning. You feel that your worthy friend has you somewhat at a disadvantage. You will feel perfectly convinced in your own mind, however, that you are quite right, and you will say to him, "My good friend, I can only be guided by the natural probabilities of the case, and if you will be kind enough to stand aside and permit me to pass, I will go and fetch the police." Well, we will suppose that your journey is successful and that by good luck you meet with a policeman; that eventually the burglar is found with your property on his person and the marks correspond to his hand and to his boots. Probably any jury would consider those facts a very good experimental verification of your hypothesis touching the cause of the abnormal phenomena observed in your parlor, and would act accordingly.

Now, in this suppositious case I have taken phenomena of a very common kind in order that you might see what are the different steps in an ordinary process of reasoning, if you will only take the trouble to analyze it carefully. All the operations I have described, you will see, are involved in the mind of any man of sense in leading him to a conclusion as to the course he should take in order to make good a robbery and punish the offender. I say that you are led, in that case, to your conclusion by exactly the same train of reasoning as that which a man of science pursues when he is endeavoring to discover the origin and laws of the most occult phenomena. The process is, and always must be, the same; and precisely the same mode of reasoning was employed by Newton and Laplace in their endeavors to discover and define the causes of the movements of the heavenly bodies as you, with your own common sense, would employ to detect a burglar. The only difference is that, the nature of the inquiry being more abstruse, every step has to be most carefully watched so that there may not be a single crack or flaw in your hypothesis. A flaw or crack in many of the hypotheses of daily life may be of little or no moment as affecting the general correctness of the conclusions at which we may arrive; but in a scientific inquiry a fallacy, great or small, is always of importance and is sure to be in the long run constantly productive of mischievous if not fatal results.

Do not allow yourselves to be misled by the common notion that an hypothesis is untrustworthy simply because it is an hypothesis. It is often urged in respect to some scientific conclusion that, after all, it is only an hypothesis. But what more have we to guide us in nine-tenths of the most important affairs of daily life than hypotheses, and often very ill-based ones? So that in science, where the evidence of an hypothesis is subjected to the most rigid examination, we may rightly pursue the same course. You may have hypotheses and hypotheses. A man may say, if he likes, that the moon is made of green cheese; that is an hypothesis. But another man, who has devoted a great deal of time and attention to the subject and availed himself of the most powerful telescopes and the results of the observations of others, declares that in his opinion it is probably composed of materials very similar to those of which our own earth is made up; and that is also only an hypothesis. But I need not tell you that there is an enormous difference in the value of the two hypotheses. That one which is based on sound scientific knowledge is sure to have a corresponding value; and that which is a mere hasty random guess is likely to have but little value. Every great step in our progress in discovering causes has been made in exactly the same way as that which I have detailed to you. A person observing the occurrence of certain facts and phenomena asks, naturally enough, what kind of operation known to occur in nature, applied to the particular case, will unravel and explain the mystery. Hence you have the scientific hypothesis; and its value will be proportionate to the care and completeness with which its basis has been tested and verified. It is in these matters as in the commonest affairs of practical life: the guess of the fool will be folly, while the guess of the wise man will contain wisdom. In all cases you see that the value of the result depends on the patience and faithfulness with which the investigator applies to his hypothesis every possible kind of verification. 14

Glossary

This list contains useful rhetorical, logical, and stylistic terms, alphabetically arranged and briefly defined; italics indicate that a word or term used in a definition also has its own definition elsewhere in this glossary.

abstract words   Words representing ideas, feelings, or generalities (peace, hate, food) as opposed to *concrete words,* which represent specific and particular objects or things. Since their meanings are sometimes ambiguous and their subjects cannot be readily visualized or otherwise imagined, abstract words are usually less effective than concrete words. However, only abstract words will serve in certain contexts and must be used; in such cases the writer should not assume the *audience* agrees with or even understands the use of abstract words and should make some effort to define such words.

allegory   A kind of *narration* based on an extended *metaphor* or pattern of *symbol*s in which persons, places, and things are associated with meanings in the basic story, but also with another, correlated set of meanings (and perhaps persons, places, or things) which lie outside the original narrative. The characters in an allegory are often *personification*s of abstract qualities such as virtues or vices; in some allegories, the names of characters make clear the association with the abstract qualities. Familiar varieties of allegory include some parables of Christ and those nursery tales or fables which have animal or machine characters who talk and act like representative human types.

allusion   A kind of *figurative language* which makes brief reference to a person, place, or event, or to another literary work or passage.

453

Allusions are sometimes classified as historical, literary, or topical (referring to current events).

analogy   A comparison of two things that are alike in some but not in all respects. Analogy can be an effective aid in communicating in speech or in writing because it helps one's *audience* understand a strange or difficult concept or thing by reference to one that is familiar and similar. Thus, African wedding customs might be compared to American ones, or the flow of electricity in a wire to the flow of water in a pipe.

anecdote   A brief story that illustrates a concept or idea.

argumentation   One of the three basic forms of *prose* (sometimes called modes of discourse). Because it often uses one or more of the other forms *(exposition, narration, description)*, it may be confused with them, particularly exposition. The key difference is in *purpose:* the writer of argumentative prose assumes there is more than one side to the subject being discussed, but intends to resolve the conflict by influencing the reader to favor one side. A distinction may be made between *logical argument* and *persuasion* (the former appeals to reason, while the latter appeals to emotions), but their aims are the same and they are often blended.

assertion   An unsupported statement of belief or opinion that the writer must support with *evidence* in order to gain audience acceptance.

audience   The reader(s) for whom a piece of writing is composed. Most often a student's audience will be the instructor or classmates, though sometimes the writing may be for a more general audience or for some specific group outside the classroom. In any case, the writer should consider the possible prejudices or opinions of the supposed audience, as well as its knowledge or ignorance of the subject, when determining *purpose* in writing the essay, selecting and arranging the essay materials, and choosing a *tone*.

cause and effect   An important *method of development* that focuses on results (effects) and the reasons for (causes of) those results.

classification   An important *method of development,* based on the technique of grouping together types or classes of persons, things, or ideas on the basis of shared characteristics.

cliché   An overused or trite expression whose freshness and originality have long been lost, so that its use in current writing indicates either lack of creativity or excess of laziness — if not both. Examples: "quick as a wink," "sharp as a tack," "All that glitters is not gold."

coherence The integrated whole formed when the various parts of a sample of prose, such as a paragraph or an essay, fit together logically and clearly. Thus, the sentences that compose a given paragraph and the paragraphs that compose an essay should be arranged in logical order and their relationship(s) with one another should be clear. (See also *unity, transition.*)

comparison/contrast An important *method of development* which uses the similarities and/or differences of two or more members of the same class of things or ideas as the foundation for orderly, logical, and informative analysis.

conclusion The closing sentence, paragraph, or summary section of a piece of writing. The conclusion should add a sense of unity and finality to the entire composition while directing attention to the main point(s). Practices to avoid include apologizing, rambling, repetition, and stopping in the middle of things.

concrete words Words representing specific and particular objects and things which can be perceived by the human senses; because of their sensory appeal, concrete words (as opposed to *abstract words*) help one's *audience* to visualize or otherwise specifically imagine the object or thing named, thus adding clarity of expression while reducing ambiguity.

connotation Secondary or associated meanings that many words have, either because of the contexts in which they are used or because of the emotional associations they have for the reader. (See *denotation.*)

deduction A method of *logical argument* in which conclusions (specific statements) are derived from premises (general or inclusive statements). (See *induction.*)

definition Most frequently, simply a statement of the exact meaning(s) of a word. As a *method of development,* definition uses various means (including other methods of development) to demonstrate the meaning of a word, concept, or entity.

denotation The literal dictionary meaning of a word, as opposed to the word's *connotation.*

description A form of writing that relies heavily on *concrete words* to convey sensory impressions of persons, places, and things. It is used most often in conjunction with *narration.*

diction The selection of words in speaking or writing, with emphasis on accuracy, *level of usage,* and appropriateness.

essay A brief *prose* composition which attempts to explain something, discuss a topic, express an attitude, or persuade an *audience* to accept some proposition.

exemplification Perhaps the most common and most important *method of development*, it is based on the use of examples to clarify a subject or support a *thesis*.

exposition One of three basic forms of *prose* (sometimes called modes of discourse). The key difference is in *purpose;* the writer of expository prose is attempting to explain or illustrate a subject, or to inform his or her *audience* about it. One or both of the other two forms of prose may be used to achieve the writer's goal(s).

evidence Facts, statistics, or other data used to support an *assertion* or *thesis*.

fact A truth known because of experience or observation, and which all sensible persons will accept as true (an elephant weighs more than a mouse; water consists of hydrogen and oxygen atoms; there are more people living in North Carolina today than there were in 1776). Contrary to fact is opinion (lemon pie tastes better than chocolate; roses are more beautiful than orchids; waterskiing is more fun than snowskiing).

fallacy Any of various types of deceptive, erroneous, or false reasoning that cause an argument to be logically flawed, even though the fallacy may be psychologically persuasive and seem to be true. (For a more complete discussion, see the essay, "A Brief Introduction to Common Logical Fallacies," in the Appendix, p. 434.

figurative language Writing that includes one or more figures of speech, among which are *allusion, metaphor, simile,* and *personification*. Figures of speech are brief comparisons based on the intentional departure from the ordinary or literal meanings of words in order to achieve such desired results as clarity, freshness, or additional special meanings.

free modifier A modifier that is set off from the main clause by punctuation. Usually such modifiers are nonrestrictive, describing some part of the main clause or the main clause itself. They may be placed before the main clause, after it, or between the subject and predicate: *His hands in his pockets,* the hobo stood beside the lamppost. The hobo stood beside the lamppost, *his hands in his pockets.* The hobo, *his hands in his pockets,* stood beside the lamppost.

induction A method of *logical argument* in which a generalization (general statement or conclusion) is reached based on observation of representative things, actions, or other phenomena which serve as evidence. The best and most representative evidence must be sought before a generalization is offered, and even then it can only be tentative: the conclusion that a new neighbor is a physician because he leaves home at irregular hours, carries a black bag, and drives a new Cadillac may be true — or he could be a safecracker.

introduction The beginning of a prose composition, it may vary in length from one sentence to several pages, depending on the complexity of the subject and the length of the entire composition. An effective introduction will identify the subject, put limits on the subject, interest the *audience,* and possibly indicate the organizational pattern to come.

invalid Violating the rules of *logical argument*. An invalid argument does not follow the correct form, and thus its conclusion does not necessarily follow from its premises.

irony Saying or presenting one thing on the surface while meaning one or more contrasting or opposing things. Irony may make use of exaggeration, understatement, or sarcasm, and it can sometimes be used effectively for argumentation.

level of generality Any of the points existing between the extremes of abstract and concrete. For example, if we place *abstract words* at one end of a scale and *concrete words* at the other end, we might have a scale that looks like this:

abstract word: vehicle
                      automobile
                      Chevrolet
concrete word: Corvette

Level of generality refers to any point on this scale; *Chevrolet* is at a higher level of generality than *Corvette; vehicle* is at the highest level of generality; and *Corvette* is at the lowest level of generality. With modification we can achieve an even lower level of generality: *used Corvette convertible*.

level of usage The kind of English, especially in terms of word choice and *syntax,* appropriate to one's *audience.* Frequently the levels are separated into four categories: general (consisting of words or phrases listed in dictionaries without special usage labels and suitable for both formal and informal writing); informal (based on words or phrases labeled "informal" or "colloquial" in dictionaries and though widely used by everyone, not always suitable in formal contexts); formal (basically a written form, ordinarily composed for a restricted audience consisting of specially educated or trained readers); nonstandard (words or expressions not part of the preceding categories; primarily spoken, these are labeled in dictionaries as "illiterate," "slang," "vulgar," and so on). It should be obvious that the level of usage in a letter to an ex-roommate might be primarily informal or even nonstandard, while general or even formal would be the choice for a letter to a prospective employer.

logical argument   A kind of *argumentation* which relies on an appeal to reason (in contrast to *persuasion,* which appeals primarily to emotions). The *tone* is often reserved and detached, while *deduction* and *induction* are relied upon to carry the rational force of the argument.

metaphor   A figure of speech that suggests an unstated comparison between one object and another, basically unlike object. Unless a *cliché,* the metaphor can make prose more lively and interesting, as well as increase the clarity of the writing. Example: The farmer's brick red hands rested on the snowy hospital sheet.

method of development   Organizational techniques used in *paragraphs* or larger units of *prose,* especially *exposition,* with the intent of achieving best rhetorical effect. The most common methods of development are *cause and effect, classification, comparison/contrast, definition,* and *exemplification.* It should be remembered that several or even all of these methods of development may be used concurrently in writing.

narration   Combined with description, this constitutes one of the three basic forms of *prose* (sometimes called modes of discourse). Narration is the process of telling about events; we generally call the product of that process a story. Narration often is used for the purposes of *exposition* or *argumentation,* but it also may exist independently of either purpose.

objective   Expressing opinions or ideas based on detached observation, undistorted by personal feelings. (See *subjective.*)

paradox   A statement that seems self-contradictory or in conflict with general belief, but in fact may contain some truth. "There are none so believing as infidels" is an example.

paragraph   A distinct division of a composition, usually set off by indentation, which most often defines or indicates the limits of a subtopic of the overall subject. Paragraphs may serve as *introduction, transition,* and *conclusion* elements of an *essay,* while the main body of the essay will be composed of paragraphs used for development or presentation of the subject.

personification A figure of speech in which nonhuman creatures, objects, or ideas are given human characteristics.

persuasion A kind of *argumentation* which relies on an appeal to emotions (in contrast to *logical argument,* which appeals primarily to reason). The *tone* is usually more personal and friendly while little reliance is placed upon *fact* or logical argument.

plagiarism Offering someone else's words and/or ideas as one's own, especially in the case of term papers or similar documented research.

proposition A statement that is to be affirmed or denied, offered near the beginning of an example of *argumentation.* Example: "all men are created equal" in the opening sentences of the Declaration of Independence.

prose Spoken or written language without metrical structure (as opposed to poetry or verse). Its three basic forms (sometimes called modes of discourse) are *argumentation, description-narration,* and *exposition.*

purpose The writer's intended goal. The purpose may be to describe *(description),* to tell a story *(narration),* to explain *(exposition),* to change the *audience*'s opinion *(argumentation),* or some combination of the four. In any case, the most effective writing is usually done when the writer clearly determines the purpose before beginning to write.

refutation The process of examining statements, theories, arguments, and the like, and of showing logical reasons for rejecting them.

rhetoric Written or spoken language intended to influence the thought and conduct of the *audience.*

rhetorical question A question posed merely for effect, with either no answer expected or else an obvious answer implied. Most often a rhetorical question is used to elicit agreement by the *audience* with what the writer assumes is obvious.

simile A figure of speech in which a similarity between two things is directly expressed, most often by using *like, as,* or *than* to link the pair. Example: Among the unpainted, tumbledown houses, the neatly kept white house stood, like a sound tooth in a rotting mouth.

style The distinctive features of a writer's work, especially as found in *diction, syntax,* and arrangement of material. (See also *tone.*)

subjective Expressing opinions or ideas based on personal feelings or interests rather than detached, disinterested observation. (See *objective*.)

syllogism An orderly process of *deduction,* consisting of a major premise (general or inclusive proposition), a minor premise (a specific factual proposition), and a conclusion drawn from terms or parts of each premise. The most famous syllogism is this one:

"All men are mortal." (major premise)
"Socrates is a man." (minor premise)
"Socrates is mortal." (conclusion)

The so-called "middle" term (in this case "men/man") is common to and links both premises; the "major" term becomes the predicate ("is mortal") of the conclusion; the minor term becomes the subject ("Socrates") of the conclusion. While syllogisms in their pure, orderly forms seldom appear in writing, they are used by us in our reasoning, and the student should have some knowledge of the basic process.

symbol something which has a separate existence yet also represents or suggests something else. A familiar example is the cross, standing for Christianity.

syntax The relationship and arrangement of words and phrases and sentences.

thesis An assumption or a specific statement made by a writer, usually in the *introduction,* which the writer then attempts to validate. A thesis statement or sentence (in a paragraph, called a topic sentence) often reveals the writer's *purpose*.

tone The writer's attitude toward both subject and *audience*. Tone is determined by and revealed by *diction,* selection of details, and inferences made. (See also *style*.)

transition Any means of linking one topic (or aspect of a topic) to another. Logical organization is the most basic way to achieve effective transitions, but a writer must also depend upon transitional words and phrases (*first*, *second*, *finally*, *in conclusion*, *but*, *however*, and the like), repetition of key words and phrases, repetition of sentence structure, and similar means.

unity The quality found in a piece of writing that is limited to a single idea or topic. In an essay that single idea is usually stated in the introductory paragraph and is called the *thesis*.

valid Following the rules of *logical argument*. A valid argument follows the correct form, and thus its conclusion necessarily follows from its premises.

Index
of Authors

Adler, Mortimer J.   118, 429
Agee, James   46
Armstrong, Grace April
  Oursler   390
Ashe, Arthur   305
Asimov, Isaac   316
Auden, W. H.   185

Barnett, Lincoln   89
Becker, Marion
  Rombauer   148
Bede   193
Berne, Eric   140
Bierce, Ambrose   261
Black Hawk   423
Buckley, William F., Jr.   372
Burke, Edmund   231

Carroll, Lewis   208
Carson, Rachel   120, 147, 180
Cather, Willa   27
Chase, Stuart   87
Churchill, Winston   406
Cousins, Norman   313, 372

Darrow, Clarence   245
Drucker, Peter   346
Durrell, Gerald   128
Dworkin, Ronald   373

Eddington, Sir Arthur   195
Eiseley, Loren   236
Eliot, Charles W.   374
Ellis, William D.   104
Emerson, Ralph Waldo   88

Fixx, James A.   98
Fortune   164
Fowler, H. W.   265
Francis, W. Nelson   266
Fulbright, J. William   171

Gallico, Paul   171
Gray, Alice   157

Hall, Virginia   350
Harley, Ron   418
Harris, Sydney J.   382
Henry, Patrick   407
Highet, Gilbert   29
Holmes, Oliver Wendell   173
Holt, John   133
Hughes, Langston   69
Humphrey, William   205
Huxley, Thomas Henry   445

Jacobs, Jane   55
James, William   216
Jefferson, Thomas   353

461

Kadesch, Robert   159
Kahan, Stanley   87
Keller, Helen   215
Kemelman, Harry   187
King, Martin Luther, Jr.   297, 339
Kuralt, Charles   147

Lasch, Christopher   298
Leopold, Aldo   228
Lichtenstein, Grace   149
Lincoln, Abraham   336
Lippmann, Walter   337
Lipset, Seymour Martin   118
Lukas, J. Anthony   202

McCarthy, Mary   42
Malcolm X   409
Mannes, Marya   421
Mead, Margaret   281
Mebane, Mary E.   67
Melville, Herman   162
Metraux, Rhoda   281
Momaday, N. Scott   56
Montague, Louise   308

Nichols, Anne   264
Nilsen, Alleen Pace   322

Orwell, George   338

Parker, Robert B.   35
Paulk, William   28
Plato   361
Postman, Neil   203

Roberts, Robin   296
Rombauer, Irma S.   148
Rosenthal, A. M.   425

Safire, William   110
Sagan, Carl   384
Schell, Jonathan   217
Schlesinger, Arthur   297
Scudder, Samuel H.   75
Shakespeare, William   408
Shaw, Irwin   57
Stanton, Elizabeth Cady   357
Steinbeck, John   26
Sturtevant, Edgar H.   273
Swift, Jonathan   395
Syfers, Judy   387

Teale, Edwin Way   108
Thomas, Lewis   101, 277
Toffler, Alvin   137
Truman, Margaret   86
Twain, Mark   38, 194

Ward, Andrew   216
Weingartner, Charles   203
Welty, Eudora   25
White, E. B.   119, 267
Willis, Ellen   172
Wilson, Val   416
Wilson, Woodrow   194
Wolfe, Tom   182
Woolf, Virginia   72
Wright, Richard   54

Zinsser, William   275

To the Student:

Part of our job as educational publishers is to try to improve the textbooks we publish. Thus, when revising, we take into account the experience of both instructors and students with the previous edition. At some time your instructor will be asked to comment extensively on *Rhetorical Models for Effective Writing,* third edition, but right now we want to hear from you. After all, though your instructor assigned this book, you are the one who paid for it.

Please help us by completing this questionnaire and returning it to College English, Little, Brown and Company, 34 Beacon Street, Boston, Massachusetts 02106.

School _____ Course title _____

Instructor's name _____

Other books assigned _____

	Liked Best			Liked Least		Didn't Read
Welty, Phoenix Jackson	5	4	3	2	1	_____
Steinbeck, The Bunk House	5	4	3	2	1	_____
Cather, Hanover, Nebraska	5	4	3	2	1	_____
Paulk, The White Glove	5	4	3	2	1	_____
Highet, Subway Station	5	4	3	2	1	_____
Parker, Private Eye Calling	5	4	3	2	1	_____
Twain, Boyhood Memories	5	4	3	2	1	_____
McCarthy, Miss Gowrie	5	4	3	2	1	_____
Agee, Shady Grove, Alabama, July, 1936	5	4	3	2	1	_____
Wright, Granny's Fall	5	4	3	2	1	_____
Jacobs, Morning Ballet	5	4	3	2	1	_____
Momaday, Mating Flight	5	4	3	2	1	_____
Shaw, Eighty-Yard Run	5	4	3	2	1	_____
Mebane, Nonnie's Day	5	4	3	2	1	_____
Hughes, Saved from Sin	5	4	3	2	1	_____
Woolf, The Death of the Moth	5	4	3	2	1	_____
Scudder, Look at Your Fish	5	4	3	2	1	_____
Truman, American Women in Wartime	5	4	3	2	1	_____
Kahan, The Actor's Voice	5	4	3	2	1	_____
Chase, Form and Design in Mexico	5	4	3	2	1	_____
Emerson, Beauty	5	4	3	2	1	_____
Barnett, Relativity	5	4	3	2	1	_____
Fixx, Asking the Wrong Questions	5	4	3	2	1	_____
Thomas, Clever Animals	5	4	3	2	1	_____
Ellis, Solve That Problem — With Humor	5	4	3	2	1	_____
Teale, The Legs of Insects	5	4	3	2	1	_____
Safire, I Led the Pigeons to the Flag	5	4	3	2	1	_____

Adler, Three Kinds of Book Owners	5	4	3	2	1	_____
Lipset, Intellectuals	5	4	3	2	1	_____
White, The Three New Yorks	5	4	3	2	1	_____
Carson, Types of Whales	5	4	3	2	1	_____
Durrell, The Naturalist's What's What	5	4	3	2	1	_____
Holt, Three Kinds of Discipline	5	4	3	2	1	_____
Toffler, The Duration of Human Relationships	5	4	3	2	1	_____
Berne, Can People Be Judged by Their Appearances?	5	4	3	2	1	_____
Kuralt, Maine Clambake	5	4	3	2	1	_____
Carson, Formation of the Earth	5	4	3	2	1	_____
Rombauer and Becker, Carving a Fowl	5	4	3	2	1	_____
Lichtenstein, Brewing Coors	5	4	3	2	1	_____
Gray, Mosquito Bite	5	4	3	2	1	_____
Kadesch, Centrifugal Force	5	4	3	2	1	_____
Melville, Making Tappa	5	4	3	2	1	_____
Fortune, Riveting a Skyscraper	5	4	3	2	1	_____
Gallico, Boxing and Fencing	5	4	3	2	1	_____
Fulbright, Two Americas	5	4	3	2	1	_____
Willis, Women and Blacks	5	4	3	2	1	_____
Holmes, The Old Practitioner and the Young	5	4	3	2	1	_____
Carson, Fable for Tomorrow	5	4	3	2	1	_____
Wolfe, Columbus and the Moon	5	4	3	2	1	_____
Auden, The Almighty Dollar	5	4	3	2	1	_____
Kemelman, Education and Training	5	4	3	2	1	_____
Bede, The Flight of a Sparrow	5	4	3	2	1	_____
Wilson, Renewal from the Roots	5	4	3	2	1	_____
Twain, A River Pilot's Knowledge	5	4	3	2	1	_____
Eddington, Daedalus and Icarus	5	4	3	2	1	_____
Lukas, Pinball	5	4	3	2	1	_____
Postman and Weingartner, The Change Revolution	5	4	3	2	1	_____
Humphrey, The Salmon Instinct	5	4	3	2	1	_____
Carroll, Feeding the Mind	5	4	3	2	1	_____
Keller, W-a-t-e-r	5	4	3	2	1	_____
Ward, Little Lost Appetite	5	4	3	2	1	_____
James, Habit	5	4	3	2	1	_____
Schell, The Destructive Power of a One-Megaton Bomb on New York City	5	4	3	2	1	_____
Leopold, Thinking Like a Mountain	5	4	3	2	1	_____
Burke, Causes of the American Spirit of Liberty	5	4	3	2	1	_____
Eiseley, How Flowers Changed the World	5	4	3	2	1	_____
Darrow, Crime and Criminals	5	4	3	2	1	_____
Some Campus Definitions	5	4	3	2	1	_____
Eight Definitions of Religion	5	4	3	2	1	_____
Bierce, Some Definitions from *The Devil's Dictionary*	5	4	3	2	1	_____
Nichols, Slang	5	4	3	2	1	_____
Fowler, Abstractitis	5	4	3	2	1	_____
Francis, Good	5	4	3	2	1	_____
White, Democracy	5	4	3	2	1	_____
Sturtevant, Language	5	4	3	2	1	_____
Zinsser, Clutter	5	4	3	2	1	_____
Thomas, Alchemy	5	4	3	2	1	_____

Mead and Metraux, Superstitions	5	4	3	2	1	_____
Roberts, Strike Out Little League	5	4	3	2	1	_____
Schlesinger, Violence in the Sixties	5	4	3	2	1	_____
King, Wait?	5	4	3	2	1	_____
Lasch, The New Illiteracy	5	4	3	2	1	_____
Ashe, Send Your Children to the Libraries	5	4	3	2	1	_____
Montague, Straight Talk about the Living-Together Arrangement	5	4	3	2	1	_____
Cousins, How to Make People Smaller Than They Are	5	4	3	2	1	_____
Asimov, The Case against Man	5	4	3	2	1	_____
Nilsen, Sexism in English: A Feminist View	5	4	3	2	1	_____
Lincoln, If the Slave Is a Man	5	4	3	2	1	_____
Lippmann, Balance of Power	5	4	3	2	1	_____
Orwell, The Tramp-Monster Myth	5	4	3	2	1	_____
King, Laws We Need Not Obey	5	4	3	2	1	_____
Drucker, What Employees Need Most	5	4	3	2	1	_____
Hall, Bad Grammar Seen as Unsafe	5	4	3	2	1	_____
Jefferson, The Declaration of Independence	5	4	3	2	1	_____
Stanton, A Declaration of Sentiments	5	4	3	2	1	_____
Plato, The Duty of a Citizen	5	4	3	2	1	_____
Buckley, For the Death Penalty	5	4	3	2	1	_____
Cousins, The Right to Die	5	4	3	2	1	_____
Dworkin, On Not Prosecuting Civil Disobedience	5	4	3	2	1	_____
Eliot, Are Democracies Obstructive?	5	4	3	2	1	_____
Harris, Gun Control: Shifting the Blame	5	4	3	2	1	_____
Sagan, Life after Death	5	4	3	2	1	_____
Syfers, Why I Want a Wife	5	4	3	2	1	_____
Armstrong, Let's Keep Christmas Commercial	5	4	3	2	1	_____
Swift, A Modest Proposal	5	4	3	2	1	_____
Churchill, Dunkirk	5	4	3	2	1	_____
Henry, Liberty or Death	5	4	3	2	1	_____
Shakespeare, Henry V's Speech at Agincourt	5	4	3	2	1	_____
Malcolm X, Shame	5	4	3	2	1	_____
Wilson, Let My Son Play	5	4	3	2	1	_____
Harley, Unnatural Metamorphosis	5	4	3	2	1	_____
Mannes, Wasteland	5	4	3	2	1	_____
Black Hawk, Black Hawk's Farewell	5	4	3	2	1	_____
Rosenthal, There Is No News from Auschwitz	5	4	3	2	1	_____
Adler, How to Mark a Book	5	4	3	2	1	_____
A Brief Introduction to Common Logical Fallacies	5	4	3	2	1	_____
Huxley, The Method of Scientific Investigation	5	4	3	2	1	_____

1. Are there any authors not included whom you would like to see represented? _____

2. Were the Student Work sections in each chapter useful? _____ How might they be improved? _____

3. Were the Discussion Questions following each selection useful? _____

   How might they be improved? _____

4. Will you keep this book for your library? _____

5. Please add any comments or suggestions. _____
   _____
   _____

6. May we quote you in our promotional efforts for this book?

   _____ yes _____ no

date _____ signature _____

mailing address _____
_____